André Previn

André Previn
A BIOGRAPHY

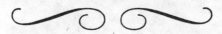

Martin Bookspan
&
Ross Yockey

DOUBLEDAY & COMPANY, INC.
GARDEN CITY, NEW YORK
1981

ISBN: 0-385-15157-8
Library of Congress Catalog Card Number 80-2746
Copyright © 1981 by Martin Bookspan and Ross Yockey
ALL RIGHTS RESERVED
PRINTED IN THE UNITED STATES OF AMERICA
FIRST EDITION

Prologue

Mary Pickford's liveried doorman looks down his nose at an unimposing young man, sixteen or younger. His ears seem to tilt forward slightly from his round face. His nose is too thin and long. His arched eyebrows and heavy circles beneath the eyes give him an owlish expression. His rented tuxedo does not fit very well.

"I'm André Previn," the young man says. "I'm here to play the piano."

The butler tells him to go around to the back door. The front door slams shut in his face. If it weren't for the money and the thought of having to face his father, mission unperformed, he would turn and walk away. Instead André walks around to the rear entrance, the servants' entrance of Pickfair.

Everyone in Hollywood knows that this walled, ominous estate at the summit of Summit Drive was a wedding present from Douglas Fairbanks to his bride, Mary Pickford. Little Mary of the golden curls. From the Zeus of filmdom to his Hera. And no matter the setting-on of age and the proliferation of a thousand lesser deities, this is still Hollywood's Mount Olympus. The spare young man with his music is a bit in awe, even at the servants' entrance.

Pickfair from the inside is a different-feeling place, going seamy like a flash-forward to *Sunset Boulevard*, cluttered with sofas and chairs, tables piled with framed photographs, like a properties warehouse. America's Sweetheart is clinging to

Buddy Rogers, just within the entrance way, reminding each guest to sign her visitors' book.

The boy has looked over this scene before, from other piano benches in homes just slightly less pretentious. Like transsexual peafowl in perpetual season, the men are drab in black-and-white, the women overdressed in Technicolor. A covey of brown and gray press photographers cluck and bob at the perimeter, foraging for food and drink. There are the slick-backed Don Juans sniffing for the mating scent, glaring impatiently at the lingering photographers. Liveried waiters pass the piano, exchanging glances as they pass going to and from the kitchen; those on the return trip discreetly drain glasses.

He begins to play, on a piano that sounds tuned but feels unused, a grand. Rodgers and Hart he has brought along, Porter and Kern, Gershwin and Schwartz. His lissome fingers drift over the keyboard, filling in of their own volition the spaces between the notes of the melody. Occasionally he glances at the music spread out bandleader-style on the piano.

He assumes that no one is paying attention, but then he notices a man standing to one side, alone, sipping a drink and pulping the paper napkin that nestles his glass. Their eyes meet and the boy knows he has a rapt audience of one. A few moments later the man moves to the crook of the piano and leans over to watch his fingers work. As the piece ends with an impromptu key change into a cadence, the man nods and speaks a word of admiration.

The man wants to know his name and he replies that his name is André Previn. The man gives a knowing nod and says that he has heard of the new kid over at Metro in Culver City. He reaches out to shake André's hand and introduces himself as Eddie Duchin. André lets his eyes widen slightly, suspecting that mild astonishment is what the occasion calls for. The famous society bandleader, of course. He represents a kind of music for which André has no affection and little respect. André cannot think what to say, so he simply smiles and gives a savvy nod. The man has a rather honest look about him, the boy concludes.

He says he feels it is only right that he should warn André

about the likely course of the party. Before long, Duchin says, someone is going to ask him to play a couple of pieces on the piano and—he being who he is and the other guests being who they are—he will have to agree. When he is finished, says Duchin, the whole place will break into an uproar. He will be applauded, he says, by this same crowd which now is paying not the slightest attention to what André is playing, simply because Eddie Duchin is a Name and André Previn is not.

Duchin finishes his drink and signals to a waiter. There is just one thing he wants the boy to know: Eddie Duchin is a good-enough piano player to know that André Previn is a *better* piano player. He wants him to know that, he says. Duchin wanders off and André returns to the keyboard, lost in thought and not concentrating on "How High the Moon."

Twenty minutes later the scenario is staged just as Duchin predicted it would be. Mary Pickford herself gets the crowd's attention after first signaling the young man to stop his playing. She tells everyone that Eddie Duchin has consented to play a few numbers for them, as only he can. André moves quietly away from the piano to find a Coke and a finger sandwich. From near the kitchen doorway he listens to the older man's playing, clean but unremarkable, dispirited. Between pieces, during the clapping and whistling, Duchin turns to seek out the young pianist and gives him a knowing wink. Duchin has read the script. It all happens just as he said it would, including the part about André's being the superior pianist. After three "numbers," Duchin leaves the piano, Mary Pickford on his arm. André notices that all the glasses which were placed on tables or chair arms to free hands for applauding now are returned to the hands and the drinking resumes. He retreats into his music.

When the guests begin to drift out, the boy asks the time of a waiter and he realizes he will have to hurry to catch the last bus home. In the kitchen the dour butler slips him a watermarked envelope and shows him out, the back way. Outside, he opens the envelope and finds six crisp ten-dollar bills, one of which is a tip.

Stepping from the lawn onto the circular drive, André is

nearly run down by a limousine, which skids to a halt. Out a window of the big car pokes the unmistakable head of Louis B. Mayer, in a remote way André's employer. They have never met, but each knows who the other is. Mayer offers the boy a lift and he climbs into the plush walnut-and-leather limousine.

As the big car coasts down Summit Drive, Mayer points out the homes of the stars. Charlie Chaplin. Ronald Colman. Harold Lloyd. Near the bottom of the hill is a rambling un-fenced house which belongs to Mayer's daughter and her hus-band, David O. Selznick. "The schnook," Mayer calls his son-in-law.

The car picks up speed as it leaves Summit Drive and turns onto the canyon road. There are no streetlights, only the faint glow of stars above the trees and the sweep of the headlamps. André clutches his music to him as though it is his only de-fense against being swallowed up by the leathery wealth about him. Louis B. Mayer lights a cigar and puffs a long time before speaking again.

"I heard what's-his-name at the Bowl the other night. Hei-fetz."

A familiar name at last. Jascha Heifetz is a friend of the boy's mother and father. He considers saying so, but Mayer speaks first.

"The guy's pretty good."

"Yes, sir."

"Pret-ty good." Mayer chips out the words as though he is chiseling them in stone. "Tell you what, though, the guy'll never make it with the kind of stuff he plays."

"You mean the concerto he played the other night? The Sibelius?" André was there for the concert, with the rest of his family.

"Whatever. I never heard it before. A *lot* of people never heard it before. A guy like that's gotta play the things people love to get ahead."

André remains silent, trying to comprehend the profound philosophy he has just heard.

"Yeah, the man could be a success. A big success."

"But Heifetz *is* . . . I mean, don't you think he is sort of a success, Mr. Mayer? I mean, he played at the Hollywood Bowl."

"Sure, sure, he played the Bowl. Lots of people play the Bowl. But you don't see him in the movies, do you? If the guy was big, he'd be in the movies."

André Previn was sixteen then and, in some ways, young for his years. So it was only later that he understood how thunderstruck he should have been by that remark, that he should have felt the way St. Paul felt when God smote him from his horse. He should have understood right then and there that the forces of the film world had no respect and little tolerance for art. Had Louis B. Mayer been any less than a step removed from God, perhaps André would have fallen from the limousine and the ground might have made a firmer impression than the leather seat. Then, perhaps, he might have realized he belonged not in Hollywood, but in serious pursuit of a career in classical music. That fact was plainly apparent to many people around him.

On the day following the party a messenger arrived at the studio with a gift for André. It was an album of three 78-rpm records, a recent import from England, of music he had never heard before: the Passacaglia and Sea Interludes from Benjamin Britten's opera *Peter Grimes*. The card taped to the album was signed Eddie Duchin.

André Previn was sixteen then and for nearly sixteen years more he would not understand, would not take Eddie Duchin's hint, would not realize why the gift had been necessary.

PART ONE

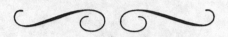

The Hollywood Life

I

André Ludwig Prewin was born on the sixth of April, 1929, in the city of Berlin. He was the third and last child of Jack Prewin and Charlotte Epstein, who maintained a spacious and elegantly furnished apartment in a fashionable district of the capital city. His brother was named Stefan and his sister Leonore, though everyone knew her as "Lolo."

His first name is evidence of the family's ties to France; Charlotte was born in Alsace. But the Prewins considered themselves German, even though both branches stemmed from small villages in Russia. In any event, both Charlotte and Jack were cultivated to a degree that obscured their humble origins.

Charlotte received a finishing-school education in Switzerland, where her armor of etiquette and propriety was polished to a blinding luster. The baser necessities—grocery shopping, preparing meals, doing laundry—were left to servants.

Her husband was a hardworking and extremely successful criminal lawyer whose cases frequently carried him into the arena of government and politics. His name was prominent among attorneys and within those circles of society they dominate, and his friends were influential: members of the Reichstag (Parliament), intellectuals, and musicians.

It was music, not the law, that Jack Prewin loved most of life's pursuits. As a child he had received thorough training in the discipline of music and he expected to apply that same discipline to his children. Indeed, Stefan and Lolo had begun their piano lessons, as he had begun them, at the age of five, and each of them demonstrated the aptitude one could only expect in a child whose life was filled with music.

There was always music-making of one kind or another at the Prewin home in Innsbruckerstrasse. Jack loved to bang away at sonatas and to join one of the children in a four-hand piano piece, buoyant with enthusiasm despite the fistfuls of wrong notes. Often the apartment would be transformed into a music hall, filled with Jack's amateur friends, reveling in the chamber music of Mozart or Brahms or Haydn. Stefan and Lolo, and even baby André who sat under the piano were required to listen attentively. Charlotte served the tea.

Fortunately for her sanity, Charlotte did enjoy music, even to the point of joining in Jack's musical guessing games. "Aha!" he would say upon tuning the radio to a symphony already begun, "I'll bet you can't tell me who wrote that." She would answer, "Mozart," and he would declare, "Wrong, Haydn." But she would catch him smiling and know that she hadn't been *too* far off.

She shared his pleasure in all the arts and together they cultivated art in a way that has become rare among the middle classes. They were forever befriending artists: painters, musicians, actors, writers, and adding them to their collection. Sometimes the addition would be a nobody, or it could be a Thomas Mann or a Jascha Heifetz, both of whom shared the hospitality of 19 Innsbruckerstrasse in those years.

It was, in many ways, the urban version of an idyllic existence: a prominent, respected husband, a cultured wife, a shared love for beauty, sufficient income to indulge their tastes, talented children, a comfortable home, even devoted servants. That was the life into which André was born in the spring of 1929 and it might have been perfect.

It might have been perfect but for two things absolutely beyond their control. One was the fact that Nazism was on the rapid rise; the other was the fact that the Prewins were Jewish.

Their social status in Berlin gives testimony to the prominence of Jews in the Germany of the twenties. When the Em-

pire collapsed at the end of the World War there was a vacuum of power into which tumbled bourgeoisie and working
class, Jew and Christian. The German Jews rose quickly in the
professions, the arts, the sciences, education, and the civil service. By decade's end the Fatherland seemed ready to acknowledge the legitimacy of its Jewish children. But the post-War
prosperity was built on shaky foundations and as the economy
sagged, Germany looked for new answers. The elections of
1930 brought Adolf Hitler's Nazi Party to political power in
the Reichstag and the die was cast.

Jack Prewin was politically astute and so must have known
something about what was going on. He chose not to discuss it
within earshot of the children, preferring family life to go on
as always. So it is that André would grow up remembering
virtually nothing of the monstrous presence that shadowed his
childhood.

He remembers instead the border of the Oriental rug that
covered the shiny boards of their living room floor, and the
fine width it was for the coursing of toy automobiles: around
and around, past flowers and fanciful birds and paisley trees,
under chairs and tea table tunnels. He remembers instead
walks with his British-born governess through the Zoological
Gardens and, with his Mama, feeding the Tiergarten ducks on
the hard ends of bread and turning excitedly at the sound of
"the family whistle" (the opening phrase of the Beethoven
Eighth) to see his father striding down the path to meet them.
Those are the sights and the sounds and the feelings he finds
when he reaches back into the chaos of 1930s Germany.

His father's world was crumbling. Jack Prewin felt suddenly
disoriented in the halls of justice and of government; they were
being torn apart and reconstructed by order of Adolf Hitler.
New laws made a mockery of the Law. Constitutional amend-
ments were rubber-stamped by the Reichstag when they should
have been subjected to a vote of the people. Almost without
warning, the carefully constructed system of German juris-
prudence reverted to a primitive code based on the Volksrecht,
the common law; that was supposed to bring justice into closer
touch with "the German consciousness."

Lawyers were suddenly placed under a "National Civil Service," membership in which was restricted almost exclusively to "Aryans." Non-Aryans, or Jews, could have their legal licenses peremptorily revoked. Moreover, the Deutsch-Israelitischer Gemeinde-Bund sprang into existence to take over any and all corporate affairs in the hands of Jews. It was, said the government, "in their best interest."

Even so, Jack Prewin felt that the best interests of his family lay in the uninterrupted pursuit of life as it had been led before Hitler. Music went on as usual at 19 Innsbruckerstrasse, although less and less of it was supplied by the propagandizing radio. As Stefan and Lolo had done before him, André celebrated his fifth birthday, in 1934, by taking his first piano lesson.

It proved to be something of a revelation to the Prewin household. The chubby-cheeked child took to the keyboard as though it were an exciting new toy. His short, almost stubby legs, dangling over the edge of the piano bench, swung in perfect time with the music, and his long and narrow fingers seemed never to miss an appointed key. When, after a few lessons, André mastered exercises that had taken Stefan and Lolo years of practice, the older chidren vowed angrily that they would never play again. Jack didn't seem to mind; he simply turned their lesson times over to André. One of his secret dreams had been to sire a musical genius and now André was made to play Wolfgang Amadeus to his Leopold.

One day Jack came home with a present for André, a windup phonograph and a set of 78-rpm recordings. "I remember those records to this day," says Previn. "They were of Stokowski and the Philadelphia Orchestra playing Debussy's *Nocturnes*. The moment in 'Fêtes' where the faraway trumpets enter triggered some kind of emotional response in me. I remember I blunted several packages of needles listening to those trumpets over and over again."

Something in music was quite obviously calling him and it wasn't long before he learned the direction of the call. In the autumn of '34 André went to his first symphony concert, a very small boy with short trousers and high socks, his little hand planted deep in his father's large hand, his long eyelashes almost glued to his forehead as he stared up in astonishment at the press of formal attire all around him and the glitter of crystal high above. He could not sit but had to stand on the floor in order to peer past the larger heads in front of his, to where the musicians were assembled onstage.

He had never seen so many of them at once, had never known that so many different people could be expected to make music together. They were adjusting stands and seats, pulling out and pushing in and turning and adjusting, each one to himself. Then a tall man strode out carrying a violin. Is he the conductor? He must be, for he mounts the podium and waves his bow and the sound of a single note rises above the hushed assemblage. The note is an "A" the boy thinks, seeing in his mind the precise piano key he would press to hit that note. And then the man with the violin is drawing his bow across the string, playing the same note, on precisely the same pitch. And all at once, as though the "A" were a seed planted, the stage sprouts a hundred different "A's," of a hundred different hues, that suddenly give rise to other notes, and others, blowing and bowing and banging one upon the other, as though the instruments of the orchestra were shouting to the audience: *Listen to us! Hear what we can do!*

Just as well he does not sit now, for he is tense with excitement, feeling that each instrument has cried particularly to him and he has made a secret bond with every one. As the man with the violin steps down and takes a seat with the other violinists, the cacophony gives a final gasp, faints, and dies away. In the hushed, awesome moment, André grips the seat in front of him. A ripple of applause begins, cascades into a cataract as a thin, imperious man enters the light.

"Furtwängler," his father whispers behind him, but he does not have to be told. Here at last is the man who will tame the wild, unruly instruments and set them to his bidding, here is the conductor. A stiff acknowledgment of the audience, a step up to the platform, an upward sweep of his arms and the applause is instantly stilled. André tenses, riveting his gaze to the small pointed stick in the conductor's right hand; it quivers, jerks upward suddenly, then plunges down and forward like a sword cutting the bonds of music . . .

We know that what André heard that night was an all-Brahms program, by Wilhelm Furtwängler and the Berlin Philharmonic. *How* he heard it, we can never be sure, except that it must have been with an inner ear sensitive and tuned far beyond the capacities of most five-year-olds. We have his assurance that "all it took was one beat and I knew I was going to spend the rest of my life chasing after music," but that is the studied assurance of a man at fifty, nicely phrased with just the right touch of humility. To the boy of five, it must have been gut-wrenching and cataclysmic, with no need or calling for that sort of pretty intellectualizing: that is what we can imagine. What we know is that he went home from the concert and threw up.

With archetypical German methodism, Jack Prewin decided that André's next musical exposure should be to the opera. It so happened that what was playing on the evening of Jack's choice was an opera which certain critics (American ones) had labeled "gruesome," "repulsive," and "unmusical," Richard Strauss's *Salome*. It was rather heady fare for one so young, but Jack's strategy was to plunge André in up to the neck, and the boy seemed to revel in the lush music. Curiously, the Berlin Opera patrons considered *Salome*'s length several veils too short to make a complete evening. Even more curiously, the company chose to pair it with *Coppélia,* that pleasant little ballet about a toymaker and his wares. It would be many years before André discovered that John the Baptist did *not* lose his head in a toy shop.

Though his father had more or less proclaimed him a prodigy, still André was a little boy, fond of all the usual little-boy recreations. When winter brought snow, he received ice skates and a sled of his own and went chasing after his big brother over the white hills of the Tiergarten. On a frozen pond, his feet began to skim across the ice as fast as his fingers moved across the keyboard, but the brief skating career came to a crashing halt at the base of a stone wall: one leg was broken in three places. His father could only say, "At least the *hands* are not damaged."

For several months he was confined to the apartment, left alone with his records, the piano, and his toys. It was a home with high ceilings and wide rooms, with windows that became doors, opening onto narrow balconies that afforded a good view of the street below. On sunny days André would sit on the balconies, spying through the grillwork at the people below, people whose colorful clothing gradually shifted to brown as more and more of Berlin's young men were inducted into the armed services. Sometimes, from the balconies, he would see planes in formation, screaming overhead, and once a huge zeppelin floated by, so close he thought he could touch it.

Inside the house, the room he loved most was his father's library. It was a room to which admission had to be won; it could be a prize for a piano piece well played. "Very good, André. You may go in and look at my books for a while." Then, through doors of frosted glass that yielded grudgingly over a thick-piled rug, he could enter the cool brown cave. The great wooden desk was like an altar, the walls around it studded with gold, emerald, and ruby, all the colors of rich leather bindings. But mostly there were law books, packed against the walls in dark clusters, like bats piled layer on layer, some so high that even his father needed a ladder to reach them. André would choose a volume from a lower shelf, on art or music, a lexicon or an encyclopedia, something filled with illustrations and smelling deliciously of starch and adventure. He would sit there until someone called him to supper or to bed.

He had learned to read words even before he read music, again thanks to his father's methodology. As with music, André was the fastest learner among the three children and Jack never missed an opportunity to show off his prodigious son. "Watch this," he would say to the unsuspecting visitor. Then he would hand the boy some weighty tome, the likes of Gibbon's *Decline and Fall of the Roman Empire*, through which André would plod until his father took the book away beaming, "There. What did I tell you?"

Jack Prewin clearly enjoyed the dual role of father-teacher, though he seems to have placed more emphasis on the teaching half in André's case. He urged the boy on to more and more difficult exercises on the piano, demanding that his child's fingers stretch far beyond their natural limits, refusing, in the son's words, "to let me become just a pianist. He wanted me to get more out of music than that. He instilled in me a love for music and, along with that love, a passion for sight-reading."

Sight-reading, the ability to transform "on sight" a sheet of *written* music into *played* music, is a basic tool in the trade of many professional musicians—accompanists, orchestra players, and conductors among others—but it is a tool used with widely varying degrees of skill and of success. In the simplest context it means being able to pick up a strange piece of music and play through it for the first time, making it sound more or less the way the composer intended it.

Jack Prewin's system of teaching sight-reading was the sink-or-swim method. Almost every night he would pull out one of his volumes of familiar symphonies, reduced to four-hand piano arrangements. Seated side-by-side on the piano bench, Jack would take the secondo part and André the primo, "flogging our way through a couple of symphonies every night. He would insist we go all the way at the correct speed and to hell with the mistakes. It taught me a lot about the music, to be sure, but even more about sight-reading, how to read several measures ahead. Now I can sight-read like a demon."

It also taught him that his memory works photographically, for even today when he opens a full orchestra score of one of those symphonies by Mozart, Haydn, Beethoven, Schubert, or Brahms, he sees the color of the binding of the old four-hand reduction. "I still see in my mind the green cover with the gold lettering. I remember where the tricky page turns were. I even remember that the primo part of the second movement of the 'Pastoral' had four bars torn off and I'd have to fake them."

It was the beginning of a long musical forced march. At first Jack was content to call the cadence himself, but after more than a year he began to feel inadequate to the task. Though André was, by regulation, too young, Jack decided to make application for his membership in the famed Berlin conservatory, the Hochschule. At first André was assigned to a young Polish professor, Alfred Meisel, but before long he was taken under the wing of the head of the piano department, Professor Breithaupt. A venerable old pedagogue of eighty years, Breithaupt had taught virtually anyone who had made music in Berlin during the previous half century. He was so impressed by André's audition performance of the Beethoven E-major sonata that he awarded him a full scholarship. André was thus indentured into the service of music.

Age was no consideration in the Hochschule, so André was forced into the same rigid mold cast for boys several years his senior. Besides piano he had to study theory, harmony, counterpoint, and music history. At the same time he had to work at his nonmusical education at a private school, the Sickelschule, located near the Prewin home. It was just as well not to travel too far from home in those days: signs reading "Juden verboten" (Jews Keep Out) were beginning to spring up in shops and restaurants around Berlin.

Hitler was head of state now and Goebbels, his propaganda minister, was Hitler's voice: "We have been very lenient to the Jews. But if they think that therefore they can still be allowed on German stages, offering art to the German people . . . if they think they can still strut across the Kurfürstendamm as though nothing had happened, they might take these words as final warning . . . If the Jews do not listen to this warning, they will have only themselves to blame for whatever happens."

The Prewins had never been "conscious" Jews. They did not go to temple and their attempts at home religious observations were generally halfhearted. The Passover Seder would be barely begun when Jack would remove his yarmulka and say, "All right, all right. Enough of this. Let's eat." Now the tightening vise of Nazism was forcing them together with other Jewish families, making them seek their "own kind." Unable to deny or any longer ignore their heritage, Jack and Charlotte tried to wrap it around the family as a cloak, hoping it would give them the same strength it gave others.

Jack rarely spoke of his fears in front of the children, but he realized there was no future for him, for his gifted son, for any of their family in Nazi Germany. His standing in the community had been taken away; his only status under the Third Reich was "Jew." Regretfully and with more than a little envy for those who'd had the foresight to apply earlier, Jack applied for travel visas to the United States, receiving numbers he doubted would ever be called under the strict American immigration quotas.

Jack Prewin had a dream. He saw himself and his family settled comfortably in the United States, with little André growing in skill and stature as a professional musician, providing them with all the income they would need to feast on strawberries under the warm California sun. The vision had come to him in a darkened cinema house as he sat transfixed by the first color motion picture he'd ever seen. The film was *Ramona* and the wide-eyed, dark-eyed beauty eating the luscious scarlet berries was Loretta Young; her lover, Don Ameche. Ironic that it should be the movies that first drew Jack's mind to California.

The Sunshine State had yet another attraction to Jack, for it was there that his cousin Charles lived, working in the film industry. Jack had met and corresponded with Charles and knew that he was somehow employed as a professional musician. That could open doors for André when they got there. Still, if they were ever to be allowed into the United States, they must have a sponsor who was not related by blood or marriage.

That is where Rudolph Polk came in. Polk was also involved in the music business, as an artists' representative. Charlotte had befriended him when he came to Berlin with Jascha Heifetz and she had maintained a regular correspondence with him over the years. At Jack's instruction, she wrote Polk to ask if he would "sponsor" the family's immigration to the United States. From his home in New York City, Rudolph Polk wrote that he would be delighted, even suggesting a way to bend the rules so that one member of the family could come ahead of the others and find a place for them to settle, provided a job could be found.

The family decided that the first to cross the ocean should be Stefan. Perhaps Charles—"Uncle Charlie" as they began to call him—could find work for him. Charles wrote that he could secure Stefan a job as a messenger boy at Universal Studios where, Jack and Charlotte were surprised to learn, Uncle Charlie was head of the music department. Stefan (whose name Uncle Charlie spelled "Steve") would be paid eighteen dollars a week and could soon be apprenticed into some more lucrative studio trade. The matter was decided and within a few weeks "Steve" was bound for America. In the mid 1930s Berlin was no place for a young man who was Jewish.

In New York, Rudolph Polk picked up his *Herald Tribune* on September 17, 1935, to read a story from Nuremberg: "Stringent new laws depriving German Jews of all the rights of German citizens and prohibiting marriages between Jews and 'Aryans' were decreed by a subservient, cheering Reichstag here tonight after an address by Chancellor Adolf Hitler . . . Jews in Germany will be put back abruptly to their position in Europe during the Middle Ages and the Renaissance." Polk set down the paper and said to his wife, "Soon we will be seeing the Prewins."

He was wrong. Jack Prewin's education in the law, his preaching and practice of due process would not let him see that Justice's scales were weighted. The law protected him. The law said he could not leave Germany until his immigration number was called up. The forces of anarchy would not swerve him from the path of righteousness. And so he waited, the tensions increasing with the passing months at the house in Innsbruckerstrasse.

On a warm summer day, when he was eight years old, André and a friend (who, of course, was also Jewish) packed a lunch in their knapsacks and caught a tram to the edge of the city, where they went on a woodland hike. They found a field full of wildflowers, odd-looking insects fretting along the grass, even a pond thick with polliwogs. They disturbed a rabbit and

André threw a rock after his disappearing tail, but they had to be content with their sandwiches for a meal. Being boys, they quite naturally ignored their parents' stern and repeated warnings to "be home before dark."

By six o'clock the friend's parents were huddled in the parlor at Innsbruckerstrasse, worrying with Jack and Charlotte over the fate of their sons. What had befallen them? How had they been so stupid as to let them go out alone, in times like these? Remember the man in, where was it? Straslund? who was thrown in jail for failing to salute the Horst Wessel song? What about that judge—he *calls* himself a judge—who took away the children of a Waldenberger couple because they had instructed the little ones not to return the Nazi salute? It is said the family isn't even Jewish.

"My God, listen to that!" Outside the window, an approaching military band and a swelling, chilling roar of crowds. "The parade! There is a parade this evening!" The street below fills with people, running to the corner. From the balcony, they can see torchlights approaching along the boulevard. They wonder if they will ever see their children again. Leonore is sobbing and soon she is joined by the two mothers. The fathers can only glare at each other in mute frustration.

Meanwhile, André and his friend, having missed the last inward-bound tram of the afternoon, are running toward the boulevard from the other direction. "I told you I heard drums. It's a *parade!*" The sky is lit with passing torches by the time they arrive and they realize immediatey they will never be able to see over all the heads in front of them. "Let's climb that tree," André suggests, and soon they are straddling a limb, directly over a platoon of goose-stepping, helmeted infantrymen, their fixed bayonets shining gold in the torchlight and pointing menacingly in their direction. Because they wore brown, André knew the soldiers were somehow the enemy, but that did not make the moment any less thrilling. "They were the bad guys," he recalls, "just like in the movies."

When summer vacation ended, it became impossible to pretend the family could remain in Berlin and be untouched by the erupting prejudice. André reported as usual to Professor

Breithaupt at the Hochschule, but he was sent home, with a message that the professor would like a consultation with the boy's father. Jack went alone to the conservatory the next day to hear the words for himself:

"Under the circumstances," the old man sighed, "I cannot afford to have a Jewish pupil." He paused, waiting for a reply from Jack, but none came. "I simply cannot afford it, particularly a talented pupil. He will be noticed, you understand."

Jack Prewin did understand. He took the steps that he had delayed taking months, perhaps years, earlier, and on an evening early in 1938 he arrived home wearing a particularly solemn face. "Tomorrow," he told the assembled family, "we leave for Paris."

II

In the first half century of his life André Previn has been involved in the making of more than two hundred phonograph records and the jackets of many of these records contain thumbnail biographies of the pianist, or the arranger, or the composer, or the conductor, depending on which of his musical hats he was wearing for the occasion. Pick up one of these record jackets and look for information on the man's country of origin and you are likely to find something like:

"Born in Germany but educated in the United States . . ."

"A native of Berlin, André Previn spent his formative years in America . . ."

"Fleeing from wartime Germany, his parents settled in California . . ."

All the clichés are there, if you look. Previn himself is quite likely responsible for most of them. He tends to dismiss the first nine years of his life, in conversation and in interviews, with such verbal shrugs as: "I think that I had a very nice childhood," or "I knew I was Jewish because they threw rocks at me." He has pretty well ignored that identity and, as the years pass, it seems to matter little to him. His first wife did not even realize he was Jewish until a few days before their wedding. "I had the vague impression he was an Englishman," she says.

The matter of being Jewish aside, it is clear that Germany left an indelible impression on André. For his first nine years he played, or listened to others play, German music in his German home; for the last four of those years he attended German concerts and operas; for most of the last three years he was enrolled in the Berlin Hochschule, a twig bent under the strict German discipline of music. He left the country at the age of nine and would not return until he was nearly forty, but never would he shake the grip of Germany and its music.

Twenty-four years later, in 1962, André would conduct for the first time the First Symphony of Brahms, one of the works he had heard on that memorable first concert by the Berlin Philharmonic. The orchestra may have been less prestigious—it was the symphony of St. Louis, Missouri—but there is testimony that at least subconsciously André felt himself back in Berlin that evening. The testimony comes from Schuyler Chapin, then head of Columbia Records' Masterworks Division and later general manager of the Metropolitan Opera:

"It was not at all what I'd expected. I was absolutely amused by the—well, how shall I put it?—by the *Furtwängler* tempi. It was all so stately, so slow; yet it held together. I suddenly realized that his German heritage was a lot stronger than he chose to acknowledge, that the enormous impression of all those childhood concerts had not worn off. They had made some sort of psychic imprint."

Several years after that, André would finally accept an invitation to conduct in Berlin and would return to the city of his birth to conduct the first orchestra he'd ever heard. Accompanied by Steve, he went slogging through snow-filled streets on a search for his roots. Many things about the old neighborhood were just as they remembered them, but 19 Innsbruckerstrasse was gone. Evidently it had been bombed out during the war and eventually torn down.

Turning to leave, one of the brothers spotted a kiosk near the far corner. They remembered it as a signpost of their youth, where the weekly expectations and births of the city's cultural life could be read, all the attractions of the concert halls and the theaters and the cinema houses, and where seasons long dead could be glimpsed in bright-colored scraps of paper somehow left unburied by the younger past. They made their way to it, through the weather, on a whim, and began scraping the snow away to see what they might find.

"André, take a look," Steve called from the other side.

On the kiosk the man of forty looked at a blue-and-white advertisement that the boy of five, in the thrill of his first concert, never could have imagined. It was a poster for that week's concert of the Berlin Philharmonic and just below the orchestra's name were the words "*Dirigent: André Previn.*"

In the light of the present, the past has never seemed of enormous import to André, and so the search for his German heritage ended; his memories of the first nine years remained forever muddled, as our own earliest memories remain for most of us. Today, the clearest pictures he paints are those of his father, the single greatest influence in his young life:

"I remember most of all his taking me to places *he* would enjoy, to the opera, to concerts, or to the botanical gardens. I have no memories at all of playing games with him. Of course I really didn't get to visit with him all that much. He was very busy in those days."

In the child's imagination, the father went each day to "some Grand Guignol courtroom," where skulls leered like gargoyles from smoke-blackened benches, where lawyers scowled and growled from deep within the folds of scarlet-hooded robes, where criminals' screams penetrated from the torture chambers below. His first trip to court was a thudding disappointment, dull as gray suits, scripted by some fourth-rate, clerk-bench Schiller. André never again accepted his father's offer of a visit to the halls of justice. He preferred to see his father in the role of teacher.

"My father taught me that a day without music is a day wasted, a day irretrievably gone. He played more wrong notes than I've ever heard in my life, but those wrong notes were conquered by his enthusiasm, by his absolute adoration of music, and that enthusiasm, that adoration, he instilled in me. My father instilled that in me."

Jack Prewin's plan for escaping Germany in 1938 was a simple one.

His law office had an associate firm in Paris, so it would not be thought unnatural for him to travel there. Weekend pleasure trips by Jewish families were still allowed, provided the travelers took no money and only such possessions as would be needed in their time spent out of Germany. The ruse was effective, provided the members of the family were willing to leave forever their friends and business associates, their books and records, their china and crystal and clothes. Of course, there was no time for discussion or even for good-byes. One evening they were citizens of Germany; the next morning they were people without a country, aboard a plane bound for Paris.

The flight was filled with Jewish families just like theirs, dispossessed, disenfranchised, and terrified. For reasons unexplained by the pilot or attendant, the airplane made several sudden and unscheduled stops. At each descent a new wave of sobbing and shushing would grip the cabin. Would there be soldiers waiting on the ground to carry them off? And each time the plane lifted off again, no soldiers having been seen, there would be fitful laughter and applause. Finally, when Jack knew they must be near the border, the plane touched down again. This time men with guns came aboard, but their uniforms were blue and their faces wore smiles as they said, "Bienvenue à la France."

In Paris they were aided by the Alsatian side of the family. Charlotte's brother, George Epstein, was a professor at the Sorbonne and he found them a cheap hotel in which to live for the time being. The stay was to be brief, only until Jack's associates in Berlin could cut through the red tape and secure for them passage to America. But weeks became months and they found themselves confined to Paris for nearly a year.

Confinement, though, it could hardly be called, coming from the end of winter in grim Berlin to the start of springtime in Paris. There were sunny walks in the Bois de Boulogne and soccer games on Sunday for André, and tagging along with Lolo as she explored the Tuilleries and the art galleries of the West Bank. When September came, George Epstein suggested that the children be sent to school; embarkation seemed no nearer than it had on the day of their arrival.

Through George's connections, André gained admittance to

the Conservatoire, where he studied for a while under some of the finest musicians in France, including the world renowned organist Marcel Dupré, whose improvisational abilities were legend. So dedicated was he to improvisation that the story is told of Dupré's invitation to the American jazz pianist Fats Waller to play on the hallowed organ of Notre Dame Cathedral, so that Dupré might observe another form of improvisation. It is said that Waller made the cathedral ring with "Honeysuckle Rose," but that Dupré never developed a taste for "le jazz."

For the rest of 1938 and the early part of 1939, André steeped himself in French music. Then, at last, the final snarl of bureaucracy was unraveled and the Prewins traveled by train to Le Havre, where they boarded the S.S. *Manhattan* for New York.

They were leaving Europe none too soon. André's first theory teacher, Alfred Meisel, soon would die defending his native Poland from Hitler's advancing troops. Less than a year later George Epstein would be dead in a concentration camp.

Incredibly, life for the Prewins was outwardly untouched by the gathering war. In an effort to leave as little as possible of Jack's belongings to the Third Reich, his associates in Berlin—his "Aryan" associates—converted whatever they could to cash. That, along with Jack's bank accounts, came to a rather large amount of money. Since they could not spirit the money out of the country, the lawyers contrived to spend it in the only way they could that would be of value to their friends. At steamship offices in Berlin, they booked the most lavish first-class passages for Jack, Charlotte, Leonore, and André, first to New York and then through the Panama Canal to California. The dates and names of the ships could be filled in when the information became available.

So it was that this wandering family, with hardly more than the clothes on their backs and the five dollars in American currency that George Epstein had procured for them, traveled across the Atlantic in the lap of luxury. The staterooms were Sybaritic, the meals sumptuous, the days on deck filled with shuffleboard and indolence: all prepaid in Deutschmarks that otherwise would have been poured into the Nazi war machine.

Ten-year-old André played the piano in the ship's lounge and became a great favorite of passengers and crew alike. But when Jack and Charlotte heard him referred to as "young maestro Proo-win," they realized the time had come to take Uncle Charlie's advice. "Change the name to 'Previn,' with a V," he had written, "or everybody in this country is going to make it a W, and before you know it they'll be calling the boy 'André Prune.' Take my word for it, he'll never get rich and famous as André Prune. The family on this side of the ocean has been using 'Previn' as far back as anybody can remember." By the time they arrived in New York each member of the family had learned to sign the family name the new way.

The night before the voyage ended, Charlotte realized that they had no money with which to tip the waiters and the other crew members who had looked after them so well. They had only the American five-dollar bill which George had pressed into her hand at Le Havre. Over Jack's loud protestations, Charlotte took the five dollars and used it to gamble, betting in a ship-wide pool on the precise time land would be sighted.

She won a hundred dollars.

After carefully determining who should get how much, Charlotte placed the hundred one-dollar bills in individual envelopes and distributed them to the crew.

"Before, we had at least five dollars," grumbled Jack as they left their stateroom for the last time.

"That is true," answered Charlotte. "We were five dollars richer. But now I don't mind being poor."

It was in the summer of 1939 that the Previns arrived in New York. They were greeted at the 42nd Street Terminal by Uncle Charlie's sister and her rather large family, with whom they had arranged to stay until they could secure ship passage to California. They had to travel by ship rather than by rail or air because that had been the only way to pay for the entire trip in Berlin.

The sudden exposure to America must have been another of

those culture-shock experiences for André, for his system reacted to it as violently as it had to that first concert in Berlin: upon arriving at his relatives' home, André immediately threw up. It should be noted, however, that on this occasion the culture-shock was abetted by his first ice cream soda, a large and bubbly one, at a Times Square drugstore.

Their New York hostel was a brownstone apartment on the Upper West Side of Manhattan, an apartment filled to overflowing by the addition of four Previns. Never one for crowds, André quickly discovered a movie house on Broadway to which he could escape for hours at a stretch. After borrowing a dime for his ticket and a nickel for a hot dog, he would dash off to sit through showing after showing of the same film program, with its newsreel, cartoons, and short subjects. He began to study the ways in which music was employed in the movies, telling him just what was happening at all times, even though he couldn't understand the language.

He was *beginning* to understand it, though, just by the force of repetition, sitting through the same movies over and over again, and he was beginning to love the sound of it. There were fascinating similarities between English and German, he noticed, and at the same time other similarities between English and French, which he had studied at the Sickelschule and spoken in Paris. He was a long way from speaking English, he knew, but so was his father, who spent *his* days buried in a German-English dictionary. At least the movies were entertaining.

The amazing thing to André was that one could manage well enough in New York without speaking English at all. The Upper West Side was a polyglot neighborhood where minorities were in the majority. In the open-air shops and marketplaces along Broadway, one could hear German, French, Polish, Russian, Italian, plus a number of languages whose identity André could not even guess. All in all, he found the city fascinating and he wondered what California could hold that might compare.

During their protracted stay in New York, the Previns spent a good deal of time with their sponsors, the Rudolph Polks, and through them came to breathe the rarefied atmosphere of New York's musical Olympus. At concerts and parties, Jack, Charlotte, and the two children were guests of the Polks and were introduced to the likes of Toscanini, Rubinstein, and Piatigorsky.

It was at the Polks' home, at an after-concert party, that André first met the famous Jascha Heifetz, about whom his parents had spoken so highly. André was standing in the dining room at the time, astonished by an enormous buffet, spread out over several tables. At a side table he noticed a man piling cold cuts onto slices of rye bread, ignoring the more exotic opportunities. A maid offered him a cup of bisque homard, but he refused it with a shake of his hand, settling down to the business of getting the sandwich into his mouth. Suddenly he stopped, realizing he had forgotten something important. Not seeing what he wanted, he turned belligerently on the maid.

"Wait a minute. Don't tell me there aren't any pickles around here?" He said it in German, so André understood. A few minutes later André heard the man introduced as Jascha Heifetz.

In the fall the Previns left New York aboard the *City of Newport News*, steaming down the Atlantic seaboard, across the Gulf of Mexico, and through the Panama Canal to the Pacific Ocean. Again, the most expensive staterooms in firstclass had been reserved for them and once more the Previns settled into that leisurely limbo which Jack and Charlotte knew must soon come crashing to a halt. The fact was that they were strangers in a strange land, had no idea what was waiting for them and no real clue as to how they would earn a living. Steve's salary as a messenger boy at Universal Studios could hardly support a family of five. There was no hope, at least not for the present, of Jack's return to the practice of law. Perhaps he might supplement their income by giving private piano lessons, but they couldn't know that for sure until they got to their destination.

It was all of no concern to André. He polished his skill at shuffleboard, wore a souvenir straw hat, and entertained in the ship's lounge. He also made friends with the other children on board and did his best to communicate with them in English. A few weeks, though, and it was all over. The *City of Newport News* was easing into a berth in the Los Angeles harbor and there was Uncle Charlie, waving and shouting from the dock.

III

"If our distant American relative had been a fruit dealer in
Ohio, we might've wound up in Akron. Thank God Uncle
Charlie happened to live in California. All that sunshine, all
those oranges . . . for us, coming from Germany, it was Para-
dise."

Charles Previn, the man André Previn credits with saving
him from Akron, is a rather interesting character in his own
right. Uncle Charlie was born in Brooklyn, New York, in the
year 1888, and from his earliest days it was decreed that he
should be a musician.

After studying at the New York College of Music, Cornell
University, and Ithaca Conservatory, all by virtue of scholar-
ships, Charlie seemed destined for a serious career in serious
music. It was probably a disappointment to his family that he
fell prey to the lure of vaudeville and went on the road as a
piano player. But if Uncle Charlie had an ear for music, he
also had an eye for a buck, and when vaudeville houses began
turning into movie houses, Charlie very quickly established
himself as one of New York's top accompanists of silent films,
improvising on the organ or piano through the twenties. For
when Lillian Gish breathed her last gasp as Mimi in *La
Bohème* or when John Gilbert waltzed Mae Murray off her
feet in *The Merry Widow*, each theater had to provide its own
Puccini or Lehár.

As word filtered through the young industry that the talkies were on their way, Charles packed up and moved to Hollywood, billing himself as a composer and conductor. He was hired by Universal Studios and eventually became head of that company's Music Department, his position secured when the very first film on which he worked as music director, *100 Men and a Girl*, won him an Academy Award. Although he seems to have done very little actual composing, Charles Previn's name is still highly visible on the credits of late night television movies and festivals of old classics. W. C. Fields's *The Bank Dick*, the original *Frankenstein*, *It Started with Eve*, and *Buck Privates* are all his films.

With Uncle Charlie's help Jack and his family were quickly settled in what was to be the first in a series of rather unpleasant Los Angeles dwellings. This one was a two-bedroom walk-up on Camel Road, off Hollywood Boulevard, in a development called Palacio Apartments. Palatial it wasn't, with Murphy beds and a pullman kitchen, a far cry from the shipboard elegance.

André was close to eleven then but he was still the baby of the family, still protected as much as possible from the harshness of their new reality. "I find it very sad," he says, "that I was so unaware of my parents' trauma, even of the trauma going on in Europe. My mother had left everything she knew; the quiet heroism of my father did not hit me until much, much later. I simply had no perception of the tragedy of their situation: it was all a great adventure."

For Charlotte Previn, there was also a sense of adventure, but not a pleasant one. Her upbringing had been virtually aristocratic and had led to a dependency upon servants; suddenly she was thrust into the role of homemaker. A kitchen was foreign territory for her, but she had to equip their kitchen and learn how to cook. She seems not to have minded being the butt of the family's evening humor when the meal was served and the others would take turns guessing what it was supposed to be. Her task was made doubly hard by the fact that for a long time there was very little income.

It was out of the question that Jack should attempt to go on with his law career. Learning English and studying American law would require time and money, neither of which he could afford. His only recourse was to establish himself as a neighborhood piano teacher.

For a man who had reached the inner circles of Berlin's politics and law, for a man who had entertained great scholars and musicians in his home, this must have been a bitter time: walking door-to-door, tipping his hat, passing out cheaply printed business cards. Perhaps it was, as André puts it, a kind of "quiet heroism." As it turned out, Jack's greatest advantage as a piano teacher lay not in his grasp of music theory but in his dubious command of the language. His thick and growling accent coupled with his German stiffness soon made him the talk of Hollywood motherhood: Beethoven had come to teach their little darlings to play the piano. Before many weeks went by, Jack's calendar was so filled with beginning pupils that he hadn't the time to bemoan his fate.

André had been out of school now since his studies at the Conservatoire in Paris, nearly a year before, and Charlotte was eager to have him enrolled immediately. Since there was no such thing as a decent music conservatory in Los Angeles, it would have to be public school. Even though it was the middle of the school year, he was admitted and the next morning found himself aboard a school bus, brown bag in hand, off to some new adventure.

A smiling teacher showed him to a seat near the front of the room. He took his place there, setting his bag on the desk top, and looked around at his companions. They were more or less the same size as he was, though a few were considerably larger, yet they seemed younger in their banter and their play. The letters on the door had told him that this was Grade Four, but he had no idea what that meant.

"No, no, no," the teacher was saying, tapping lightly on her desk with a pencil. "We do *not* keep our lunch bags at our desks, young man. We put them in the cloakroom."

André hadn't the faintest idea what she was talking about, but it seemed to him that she must be welcoming him to the class. Not wanting to appear impolite, he stood up and bowed stiffly. There was a titter of laughter around him. He sat down again.

"Did you hear me, young man?" There was an edge on the teacher's voice now and she had her arms folded, looking over the tops of her glasses at him. He thought he'd better say something.

"Yes?"

"Well, then, please get up this instant and take that lunch bag to the cloakroom." The students' laughter was by now uproarious. Every one of them had discovered, well before the class bell rang, that André was a foreigner, but apparently the principal had neglected to inform the teacher of that fact.

André was smiling, rather sheepishly now, and the teacher was scowling, pointing toward the back of the room with her pencil. André looked in that direction and saw the other children laughing, which made him laugh too. "Young man, I am going to tell you one more time. If you . . ."

"Teacher, teacher." A little girl's hand was waving frantically. The teacher acknowledged her.

"Yes, what is it?"

"I think the new boy doesn't understand English so good," the little girl said.

But his understanding of English grew by leaps and bounds, so that within a few weeks André was able to communicate with the teacher and his classmates. By the time the school year ended in June, his command of the language had progressed remarkably, so that his advanced degree of learning in other subjects could be appreciated. His European education, since the age of five, had given him a significant head start on his ten- and eleven-year-old peers. The principal and teachers thought it unwise to advance him into too high an age bracket, but they did set him ahead one year, so that when September came André found himself reporting not to fifth grade but to sixth.

He was still the most advanced pupil in his class and now also the smallest. With all of that and his German accent too, he must have been something of an oddball, although he says he made friends easily and quickly. Still, he began to develop a reputation for shyness and reticence which would remain for many years as dominant personality traits.

André was developing into a teenager now, his features beginning to lose their little-boy look. His nose had lengthened, a rather Gallic nose, the image of his mother's. His eyes were deep-set, with circles below and high-arched eyebrows that lightened as they went out from the bridge of his nose. His lashes were long and so were the fingers of his thin hands. His hair remained as dark, as fine, and as straight as it had been when he was a baby and he parted it now on the left.

He was too small for football, not at all interested in baseball, but he liked basketball, even though he was too short to make the school team. He concentrated on handball and tennis, where his lack of size and strength could be more than compensated for by quickness and agility, both of which he had in abundance. His favorite pastime, the one he'd so studiously cultivated in New York, was the movies. He spent as much time as he could in the dark theaters, watching the mysteries of life unreel in double features. Previn looks back on these days as "rather uninspiring stuff."

An absence of music conservatories in southern California by no means implied a dearth of music teachers, even for pupils as advanced as André was. At the suggestion of Jascha Heifetz, Jack placed André under the tutelage of pianist Max Rabinowitsch.

Rabinowitsch had been born and educated in Tsarist Russia and achieved fame there as accompanist to the great basso Feodor Chaliapin. He was attempting to make a concert career of his own when the Revolution came. He would up in southern California, teaching and playing piano sound tracks for the movies. The experience turned Rabinowitsch into "the most cynical man I ever met," according to André, and it was from the Russian that André first tasted the bitterness and disillusionment of serious musicians trapped in the film industry.

Max Rabinowitsch's hands were world-famous, having been filmed dozens of times as "stand-ins" for the hands of actors who were supposed to play the piano, and there were an awful lot of movies about musicians in those days. Yet as familiar as his hands might have been to movie audiences, his face was unknown. Rabinowitsch was anonymous, yet his name was known to every producer in Hollywood. Rabinowitsch was invisible from the wrists up, yet he was far more wealthy than most of the bit-part actors who appeared in ten films a year. Rabinowitsch was extraordinarily gifted, but the only orchestras that wanted him were the struggling, small-time ensembles that played semiprofessionally in California. Rabinowitsch wanted nothing more than to play the great concertos; his pride, however, would not let him accept the paltry concert fees he was offered.

At one of André's first lessons, Rabinowitsch's telephone rang. André could hear only one side of the conversation, but he knew there must be an orchestra manager on the other end. "Do I play the Tchaikovsky? Of course I play the Tchaikovsky. Fine . . . What's my fee? . . . Oh, no. No, no, no, no. For that, my friend, Rabinowitsch does not even practice." And he hung up.

The reason Rabinowitsch made so much money pretending to be someone else was that he could sight-read, in André's words, "better than anyone else of my experience." He continued André in that discipline which Jack Previn had so assiduously begun. Rabinowitsch's two original contributions to the boy's musical arsenal were respect and love for the craft of accompanying, while a vocalist or other instrumentalist took the principal melody line, and an exposure to music which André had never before seen. Sometimes the teacher could give all three lessons—sight-reading, accompanying, and new music—in one exercise:

"He would hand me Brahms or Schumann Lieder (art songs) and tell me to croak along at the melody while I played the accompaniment. It was simple, but highly effective." André's respect for the old man's musicianship grew with each such lesson and enabled him to break through the barrier of cynicism which Rabinowitsch had built around himself. André came to view that cynicism as "mostly self-protective" and the Russian teacher as "a terrific fellow. I loved him."

No more, perhaps, than a child's adulation of a worldly wise professional, but that may have been the only sort of love of which André was capable then, for anyone outside his family circle. The life of a young artist, particularly a young musician, is single-purposed once his identity is clear, once he roots all his needs and desires in music, and André had done that at the age of five.

> I think we musicians have always had rather selfish childhoods. The luxury of having a unilateral talent, which makes one's future life inevitable, is wonderful, but it also makes you selfish. It makes you insular and your perspective tends to be quite narrow. I myself was always so concerned with being a musician, with becoming a good musician, with becoming a better musician, with learning this and with learning that, that even my areas of amusement and leisure time, even my play time seemed to be connected inevitably with music. As a result, I never really bothered to look around me to see what else was going on in the world, as someone else might have done, someone whose interests were more divergent.

There was certainly no looking to his father for divergence. That single-minded gentleman had by now turned his full attention to music pedagogy. Nor could André look to his mother; she was entrenched in homemaking battles. Steve was greatly admired but was already in his twenties, too old and too preoccupied with his work and his other interests to spend much time with a kid brother. Within the family, only Leonore took a hand in broadening André's interests. Only three years his senior, Lolo loved literature and paintings, a passion inherited from both parents, and she shared her discoveries with André, taking him to galleries and museums, leading him deep into American and English literature, becoming "very close" to her brother.

Yet there seems to have been something missing in Lolo's own life, for she soon rebelled against the family's religious apathy and became a zealot. In Los Angeles she joined a militant

Zionist youth organization, Hashomer Hatzair, and soon after
the creation of the state of Israel she emigrated there to work
on a kibbutz. Two years of oranges and hard labor proved
enough and Leonore returned to California, where she put her
idealism to use as a social worker in Watts. Eventually she got
married and gave birth to a daughter. Then in 1957 she died
from cancer at the age of thirty-one. Her husband and daughter moved away from Los Angeles and severed all ties with the
Previns.

There was no forewarning of unhappiness during André's
sunny school days. At the age of thirteen in 1942 he was
enrolled in high school, which, by a rather jocular turn of fate,
happened to be Beverly Hills High. The still-impoverished
Previns had just moved again to another in the series of low-in-
come dwellings when André went to register for high school. It
turned out that the new home was a few feet inside the
Beverly Hills district, so André went to school with the rich
kids.

> I was amazed to find that my new school was popu-
> lated almost exclusively by kids who were rich almost
> to the point of decadence. And you must remember
> that not too far back in my mind were the memories
> of Europe, gearing up for the war. I was fascinated to
> see something called a "Student Parking Lot," which
> accommodated something in the neighborhood of a
> thousand cars. I just couldn't believe it. It was a little
> bit like my mental picture of a country club, like
> something I had read in *The Great Gatsby*.

For all its snobbish exterior, Beverly Hills High School
turned out to have fairly high academic standards and André
was soon plunged into the rigors of new subjects for which he
showed very little aptitude. "Biology was beyond me. I was
simply no good at cutting up a frog that'd been soaking two
years in formaldehyde. As far as the more sophisticated forms
of mathematics, whenever I hear the words 'geometry' or 'trig-
onometry' a great iron door clangs shut somewhere in my
head." But he muddled through those classes, and there were

subjects he was good at: history, literature, geography, and, of course, foreign languages.

His school companions at Beverly Hills High may have been rich but they certainly weren't famous. "It would be wonderful for the sake of an anecdote," he jokes, "if I could say I hung around a lot with Zubin Mehta and Seiji Ozawa. But the kids I hung around with were just kids."

The time was the early forties with the war a long way off from California, where the high-stepping economy mocked the grim devastation of Europe and the far Pacific and where the footfalls of campus unrest and drug cultivation were still years away, too distant to be heard. It was a time of sunshine hedonism, of convertible rides to nearby beaches, of palmtree indolence and back-seat romance, a time when the school roué kept his glove compartment filled with show-off parking tickets and condoms and went on maybe one serious drunk a year to preserve his image.

> It all sounds so much like ancient history today, much more than stories of the eighteenth century would. That kind of life is so gone into a scene of dope-pushing and vague cultism. The madness that gripped California's adolescents in the sixties was nowhere to be found. It was all Henry Aldrich and we had a magnificent time.

It was in high school that André discovered, under the careful stewardship of his older and wiser male friends, the opposite sex. "If you took a girl on a date," he remembers, "you probably went dancing. And dancing in those days meant that you got to put your arm around her. You actually *touched*." He refuses to go into any more detail but, in the words of an old Spanish proverb, "To use a woman and a guitar, one must know how to tune them." Hindsight suggests that André learned well and probably quickly which frets to use when tuning a woman.

In school he encountered that peculiar condescension of the American education system called Music Appreciation. As taught at Beverly Hills by a Mrs. Moore, Music Appreciation meant finding some sort of programmatic intent behind every piece of classical music.

> It didn't matter whether it was a late Beethoven quartet or *Till Eulenspiegel*, by Christ there had to be a *story* to it. Even then I resented that and I would sit in class just listening to the music, completely shutting out Mrs. Moore's storytelling. I would deliberately hand in papers outlining the wildest stories for the tamest works and when the question appeared on the test about which theme represented the death of Beethoven's pet dog, I'd never have the faintest idea. Still, it was the only class where one got to listen to good music on the phonograph for a few hours a week and Mrs. Moore had the good grace to give me passing grades. She knew, of course, that as stupid as I appeared to be, I was already working more or less as a professional musician.

Becoming a professional musician, in one way or another, had always been a given for André. He never considered being anything else, so that choosing a career path was simply a matter of finding which door opened onto a marketplace for his talents. There were several of those doors, and one of them led to the dance floor, where 1940s America was flailing its arms and wriggling its bottoms as dissolutely as it had in the twenties, where Arthur Murray was the guru nonpareil and where a music machine in every room had replaced a chicken in every pot as the slogan of the epoch.

During his first year at Beverly Hills High, André organized a band to play at the school dances. The fact that making the music kept him usually off the dance floor and "out of touch" with the girls seemed unimportant. Romance in his life would always play second fiddle to music. Besides, unless he earned his own pocket money, he'd never be able to afford the dating game.

So he played for the dances on weekends. After school he got a job at Barker Brothers Department Store demonstrating electric organs for seventy-five cents an hour, from 4 to 6 P.M.

Occasionally he would pick up a few extra dollars by appearing as a pianist on a local radio program called "California Melodies," and on Saturdays he could earn five dollars for an afternoon at a local dancing academy.

He broadened his horizons by leading a pit orchestra for the annual Beverly Hills High School Variety Show. The show had always been done with two pianos, but André talked the drama teacher into letting him form a band, which he conducted and for which he wrote all the arrangements, his first ventures into those realms of music.

All the while he was earning a living with popular music, his studies in the classics continued. At age eleven, André began theory studies with Joseph Achron, a fifty-four-year-old Lithuanian violinist who came highly recommended by Jascha Heifetz. Like the piano teacher Max Rabinowitsch, Achron was educated in Russia and, like Rabinowitsch, he'd made more than a respectable career as a soloist before joining the Hollywood gold rush. Achron had also established his credentials as an educator at the Kharkov Conservatory and later at the Westchester Conservatory in New York. Furthermore, he had translated Nikolai Rimsky-Korsakov's *Manual of Harmony* into English. It was abundantly clear to Jack Previn that his son could learn a lot from Achron.

The Rimsky book was Achron's bible. It contained a seemingly endless continuum of exercises in counterpoint, ranging from its simplest to its most complex forms, studded with devious problems to be solved by the hapless pupil. André recalls that it took him a year or better to complete the series and that after his winning bout with the final exercise, Achron closed the book reverently and said, "There, we've finished it. And now you'll see that when we start again with Exercise One, it will go much, much easier." Joseph Achron proved to be a stern taskmaster, providing André's youthful exuberance for music with a firm bed for his long pupation.

It sounds boringly like the sort of when-I-was-your-age remark young people so hate to read, but it's true. I remember once, after we'd finally graduated to fugues, Achron asked me to write a fugue for a quartet. I worked like a dog on it before I brought it to him. Then he took my fugue over to this small table he had with a bright light on it and he pored over it.

Finally, he looked up and said, absolutely amazed, "There are no mistakes." I was about to shout, "Oh, boy!" when he glared at me and said, "Just a minute." And he went through it again with a fine-toothed comb before saying, "Well, it does seem to be in order. Let me examine it just once more." So again I held my breath. Suddenly his face seemed to light up and he slapped the page almost gleefully. "Aha! I knew it. Hidden parallel fifths!"

He picked up a red pencil and slashed through my entire fugue, handed it over to me and said, "Now go and write me another one, with no mistakes this time."

The arduousness of studying with Achron was compounded by the difficulty of reaching his home and studio. André had to travel nearly an hour and a half on three buses to get from school to Achron's tiny home high up in the Hollywood hills. He would work there for two hours, not reaching his own home until nearly 8 P.M. Once he made the mistake of bringing along his tennis racquet to a lesson, thereby incurring Achron's outrage. "Don't you know you could damage your hands with that game?" he bellowed. "Either play music or play tennis." André continued to play both, but thereafter found room in his school locker for the racquet.

Achron was a splendid teacher, but André's studies with him lasted less than three years. An illness forced him to curtail his activities and he died a few weeks before André's fourteenth birthday, leaving behind the Rimsky *Harmony* along with a handful of compositions for violin, piano, orchestra, and chorus. Before he died he arranged for André to continue his theory studies under composer Ernst Toch, but the teacher and pupil did not get along well and the relationship ended after a few lessons. In fact, many years later, the two men met and Toch could not remember ever having taught André.

Rabinowitsch, Achron, and Toch were among that remarkable crowd of music notables who were driven from Europe by the world-shaking events of the first half of the century to settle in southern California, almost as far from the music capitals of the Old World as one could get. One result of this singular migration was the formation of an incredibly rich musical soil into which another generation of musical expatriates would be planted and from which they would bloom lush and luxuriant. Thus it was not only possible but likely that André would come into contact with Toch and Achron, with Miklós Rózsa and Gregor Piatigorsky, with Joseph Szigeti and Jascha Heifetz, even with Stravinsky and Schoenberg; they all lived near Los Angeles in those days.

> It has become fashionable, I suppose, for any musician who ever stopped at Los Angeles Airport in the forties and fifties to say, "I studied with Arnold Schoenberg." Let me say quite plainly that I did *not* study with Schoenberg. However, I was taken to his house on two occasions and I remember them both vividly.

No wonder. On his first visit to the composer's villa, André was walking up the drive when he was attacked and bowled over by an enormous St. Bernard. Once inside, he was shown to a piano and asked to improvise on a theme Schoenberg gave him. On hearing him play, Schoenberg was "noncommittally complimentary."

The second time around the dog was chained up, but so was Schoenberg's willingness to discuss music. Instead, he said a great many uncomplimentary things about his native Austria and poured tea. When the pot ran dry he challenged André to a match of table tennis, considering himself a past master at the game. Alas, "there was no trick in a fifteen-year-old boy beating an aging serial composer," and André was not invited back.

He had worse luck at piano competitions than at Ping-Pong.

> I found piano competitions a particularly disgusting experience. I entered two and both times I finished

second. Now, if you come in fiftieth you can always
blame it on the judges' idiosyncracies or the effects of
that day's weather on the fingers or *something*. And
of course if you come in first you can take all the
credit. But to come in second, and do it *twice*, that's
completely inexcusable. The names of the kids who
won are forever emblazoned on my brain and it helps
not a whit to know that neither has been heard from
since in the music world. The whole thing left me
very distrustful of competitions. Oh, there may be a
few good ones, like the Queen Elizabeth and the
Tchaikovsky, but even in those the most interesting
people can quite easily finish tenth.

The judges notwithstanding, André was making remarkable
strides as a pianist. His technical skills, coupled with his ever-
enlarging capacity for sight-reading, made it inevitable that he
should be noticed by the professional music community. He
was noticed early on by Feri Roth, head of the string department at the University of Southern California and founder of
the Roth String Quartet. Possibly at Joseph Achron's suggestion, Roth approached André to join his string players for a
series of budget recordings which, although they were not the
best ("I don't think we want to count those"), do constitute
André's first foray into professional recording.

These years of the early 1940s, these early teenage years,
were for André a season of expanding awareness. The cocoon
of Mozart, Beethoven, and Brahms, so carefully spun by his father, was beginning to crack. These were the glory years of the
78-rpm record, when some recording companies were beginning
to strive for an expansion of the recorded repertory. André
took advantage of that, gorging himself on a gourmand's feast
of everything from Bach to Benny Goodman.

They were years, too, of musical Los Angeles brimming over
with yet a new flood of immigrants and a California willingness to try anything exotic in the way of music. André went
"completely crazy" over his first hearings of *Elektra* and *Der
Rosenkavalier*. He talked his way into rehearsals at every op-

portunity and once he heard Alfred Wallenstein preparing the Los Angeles Philharmonic for the West Coast premiere of Béla Bartók's *Concerto for Orchestra*. The music seemed to him something new and wonderful and it was not long before he got his hands on a score to see for himself what the composer had done to make an orchestra sound like that. He got his father to take him to the performance, but after it was over Jack could only shrug and say, "Well, it's not the *Eroica*."

Had Jack ever been able to understand that all composers were not Beethoven, could not and should not be Beethoven, he might have grown musically closer to his son, who was trying hard to come to grips with too many musical forces that were pulling him in too many directions at once. André clung steadfastly to his childhood blanket of Mozart and Brahms, but his head danced to Bartók and Strauss, Debussy and Ravel, and all the while he was buying up each new jazz record that appeared. He was growing, but into what?

> My growth was only technical in those days, not growth in terms of a clearer perception of music. I never bothered to figure out *why*. And I tended to be overfond of things that sounded wonderful.

What sounded most wonderful of all to his ears was the siren song of Hollywood, the call of the film industry that had lured Max Rabinowitsch, Joseph Achron, Uncle Charlie, his own father in a way, so many serious musicians who were, if not wiser, certainly older than fifteen-year-old André. The song of Hollywood may have been vulgar; it was certainly not the *Eroica*. But it was hard not to heed, being shrilly seductive and with a raucous jingling of coin in the percussion.

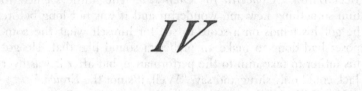

IV

Hollywood loved nothing better in those days than to hype itself in its own films as the pinnacle of artistic success, so it seems a shame no one thought to call in a screenwriter that afternoon in early 1945 when André Previn first set foot on an MGM recording stage. *The Boy with the Magic Fingers* could have been a box office smash. Especially with someone like Mickey Rooney playing young André.

The Boy with the Magic Fingers is the story of a child prodigy who is forced by his family's hapless fortunes to abandon all hope of a career in serious music in favor of a quick and easy buck. As it turns out, the glitter-and-be-gay world of the movies is just what he always wanted. The mousey, mild-mannered little fellow becomes the talk of tinsel town and before long he's rich and famous and happy-ever-after. Who needs Mozart anyway?

André is fifteen. We see him hunkering down into the weave of the back seat of a car. It's his Uncle Charlie's Plymouth and Charlie's up front with Papa Jack. The man with the Brooklyn accent is convincing the man with the German accent that this is really the best thing that could happen to his boy. Look what the film business has done for me, Uncle Charlie is saying, and look how your boy Steve is coming along. He's a full-fledged film editor now; give him half a chance and he'll be producing his own movies one day. And look who's going to be at this audition. (The car is turning into the MGM lot now; the boy in the back seat is bug-eyed.) None other than Joe Pasternak. *Pasternak*, for Pete's sake. The guy who made Deanna Durbin * * DEANNA DURBIN * *. And now that new kid, Margaret O'Brien. Pasternak could do the same thing for André. Start him out in one of those Garland-and-Rooney "Andy Hardy" pix, the kid who'd rather practice his piano than play football with the gang, right?

In the back seat, pressing his music to his stomach to keep from being sick, André hears the names go by and imagines them shimmering high above him, Pasternak . . . Durbin . . . Garland . . . Rooney . . . O'Brien . . . Previn? Not likely. His mind flashes back to his one chance to break into the movie business, the day he was hired to play the piano in that old theater that still ran the silents. D. W. Griffith's *Intolerance* was the feature and there he was banging away at *Tiger Rag* when he heard the theater manager bellowing, charging down the aisle like a bull. "Look at the screen, dummy! Look at the goddam screen!" How was he supposed to know that right in the middle of "Hold that tiger," the scene would cut to the Crucifixion? He'd been thrown out on his ear.

Uncle Charlie is talking about money, about Papa's meager income from teaching piano. That's where Brahms and Schubert'll get you, he says. And Charlotte selling cheesecakes to make a few extra bucks! André hears his Papa give a long sigh.

"Go on, go on. They are all waiting." Papa's voice seems to come from far away, but feeling the gentle shove against his shoulders André knows he is standing behind him. He takes a deep breath and steps out onto the stage. To reach the piano, which is downstage center, he must wind his way through chairs and music stands that are set up for an orchestra, a rather large one. He is in Recording Studio One and he knows that this is where the music is made that one hears in movie theaters. There are microphones all about and he very nearly trips over a cable. Looming above the orchestra, to its rear, is a movie screen. Blank, expressionless, it is like the face of an oracle whose silence is its most profound message.

Below the stage are other faces. André recognizes none of
them except Uncle Charlie's, which is grinning and winking
like a semaphore. The other faces belong to MGM's three
most prestigious producers of musicals, Joe Pasternak, Jack
Cummings, and Arthur Freed. Also in attendance are two
composer-arrangers, Johnny Green and Roger Edens, a studio
pianist named Lela Simone, who is married to film composer
and conductor Franz Waxman, and an assistant to Jack Cummings is also there. No one has put up the piano top, so André
does it himself. Then, as though there were no one there at all,
he sits down and begins to play.

From Johnny Green, whose memory for details is startling in
a man over seventy, we know what André played that afternoon: pieces by Bach, Chopin, and Stravinsky, sections of concertos by Tchaikovsky and Beethoven, even a few things he
had composed himself. It was a successful audition, even
though it did not lead to the sort of keyboard-Deanna Durbin
career which Uncle Charlie had envisioned. The producers saw
nothing magic about the cool, methodical little piano wizard,
no "camera presence," let alone "star quality." No, there
would be no movie called *The Boy with the Magic Fingers*,
not even a bit part for André in an "Andy Hardy" flick. But
everyone there that afternoon knew the boy had talents which
could be put to valuable use *behind* the cameras. Johnny
Green knew.

> He gave us all goose bumps that afternoon. I was ab-
> solutely fascinated by the kid's very sad look. He was
> terribly sad and quiet. In his playing he was like a lit-
> tle iceberg up there, not at all nervous. When he
> spoke, which wasn't often, it was all very polite and
> monosyllabic. Sure, I found out later when he came
> to work for us what a marvelous sense of humor he
> had and what an unbelievably quick mind that was,
> but I sure didn't see it that afternoon. What I saw
> was a quiet little prodigy who was about to be
> exploited in a big way.

When it was over I took Pasternak and Cummings aside and I told them what neither one wanted to hear. I recoiled from the idea of bringing a young genius into this kind of atmosphere. He shouldn't be going anywhere near the screen. I told them he ought to be left alone, to study and go to the great teachers. That's where he belongs, I said, not here, not subjected to the likes of you guys or, God forbid, Sam Katz* or Mr. Mayer. I lost and they signed him to a per-film contract.

Pasternak put André right to work, on a film called *Holiday in Mexico*, not a musical, but one of those heavy-handed comedies that was weighted down with music, in this case supplied by Ilona Massey, Xavier Cugat, a screen debutante named Jane Powell, and pianist José Iturbi. It was for Iturbi that André went to work.

Iturbi had been capital-D discovered in 1942, in a film called *Thousands Cheer*. A truly first-rate musician who brought class to movie houses, Iturbi knew almost nothing about "pop" music or jazz. For some reason, known perhaps to a few habitués of early-morning television movies today, the find-a-wife-for-father plot, set in Mexico, called for Iturbi to play jazz-like variations on "Three Blind Mice."

That was André's big break in the movie business: writing jazz variations on a nursery song. Pasternak's reasoning was faultless. The Previn kid knew something about popular music, plus he could write the stuff out in a way that Iturbi could read, classical-style. André labored over the assignment for days. When it was finished it sounded a little bit like jazz and hardly anything like "Three Blind Mice." Iturbi loved it. Pasternak loved it. Director George Sidney loved it. Even Music Director George Stoll loved it.

"Terrific," Pasternak said to André. "Now, Georgie, you get it orchestrated and we're in business."

"I can do that, Mr. Pasternak."

They were all astounded to hear anything more from André.

* Katz was Louis B. Mayer's head of production.

"Do what?"

"Orchestrate it. I wrote it, I might as well put the other instruments in."

André's future at Metro-Goldwyn-Mayer was assured. Not only could the kid play and "compose," he could orchestrate too. Even better—especially in light of MGM's badly slumping profits then—the kid came cheap. He was part-time and underage, so the studio could get away with paying him below scale.

He went at "Three Blind Mice" as seriously as though he were Johann Sebastian Bach writing out parts for the *St. Matthew Passion.* Today he laughs at it:

> It wouldn't have been acceptable to anyone who knew anything about genuine jazz—or, for that matter, to anyone who knew anything about genuine orchestration—but for what it was, an unmitigatedly revolting moment in a decidedly unimportant film . . . I suppose it must have been acceptable.

"Three Blind Mice" put André through the isinglass window into that Easter-egg world he'd gazed at in wonderment. On the set of *Holiday in Mexico* he sat down to sandwiches with Walter Pidgeon and Ilona Massey, with Roddy McDowell and Jane Powell. Suddenly the notion of his name up there with theirs on the silver screen seemed not quite so farfetched. From the beginning he developed a warm admiration for sixteen-year-old Jane Powell, who was just as new to the movies as he was.

> It wasn't that I found her voice interesting and I don't suppose you could call her a great acting talent, but within the confines of those awful movies, by God, here was a professional. Even today, I think, if I added up all the great artists I've worked with, in every medium, she'd come out in the top five among the professional-behaving people I've encountered. She was always *prepared* when she walked in, and the others were not. When she came into a recording session she knew just what she wanted to do and how to get it done.

It is typical of André that he should have learned something of value from this otherwise absurdist encounter. Proper, thorough preparation has become almost a fixation for him, just one of the many values he would later transfer from one incarnation to another in his karmic progression toward Success.

In 1945, success could have seemed no more than being precisely where he was. He'd spent nearly half his life, all those impressionable years since the onset of puberty, in the shadow of the giant film industry. Passing through the gates of Metro-Goldwyn-Mayer must have been like passing some tribal test of manhood. Now, for a few hours each week, he could sit in the warriors' lodge. He was, in his own metaphor, "a kid set loose in a candy store."

After school each day he would report to the Music Department compound for assignment. Georgie Stoll or whoever happened to be in charge that day would tell him, "Go on down to Studio C. They need two and a half minutes for Esther Williams." And there, on the set of *This Time for Keeps*, curvaceous Esther, the stuff of boyhood fantasies, would be stretched out beneath the noonday arcs. There would be the puckering school of chorus girls, each in her own swimsuit trying to impress whoever might be looking with her own set of curves. There would be a frazzled music director with a scrawled-out tune that needed arranging and, "Keep it nice and lush, okay? Esther's got to swim to this for three-twenty." Off he would go, pencils and staff paper in hand, to the nearest piano, thinking liquid thoughts. And in the evening he took the bus home, humming the music director's melody but hearing his own harmonies, satisfied with himself. And on the weekend there was money in his pocket.

> It didn't occur to me for years that they might have been taking advantage of me, paying me far less than the union would have demanded. I was still making a whole lot more than a kid my age deserved to be making and, on top of that, I could mingle with all those fascinating people. Unless one had already become a totally dedicated child artist, which I suppose I had not, it was an environment which would have

been very, very hard to resist. So I didn't; I stuck
around for a while.

He could have spent even more time at the studio if he'd
wanted to. After a few months they offered him a full-time
contract, but he turned it down. Accepting it would have
meant finishing his high school requirements at the so-called
school the studio maintained for its child stars. Elizabeth
Taylor "studied" there and so did Judy Garland, but André decided and his parents agreed that it would be better for him to
graduate from Beverly Hills High. "I realized there was no way
I could go to class with Margaret O'Brien and Butch Jenkins.
No way. The contract could wait."

He waited no time at all for his second assignment, and this
time it was a step up from "Three Blind Mice." He was told to
orchestrate the main title music for *Undercurrent*, a film that
starred Katharine Hepburn and Robert Taylor and whose
music director was dean of MGM's composing college, Herbert
Stothart.

Stothart had been around MGM since before movies made
noise, arriving in Hollywood in 1927 when the studio was making a silent film out of *Rose-Marie*, the operetta on which he'd
collaborated with Rudolf Friml. Two years later Stothart went
to work for Metro as composer of one of the very first screen
musicals, *Devil May Care*. He would subsequently add to his
notoriety by rewriting some of Giuseppe Verdi's loveliest music
to fit the screen requirements of *Camille* and by custom-tailor-
ing innumerable pages of Victor Herbert to fit the talents of
Jeanette MacDonald and Nelson Eddy. (A favorite tale among
old soldiers from the MGM Music Department concerns
Stothart's cagey labeling of those MacDonald-Eddy scores as
having been composed by "Herbert-Stothart." Quite often the
hyphen would be mislaid, sending Victor Herbert's rightful
royalties to Herbert Stothart.)

Stothart was well on in years and experience by the time
André encountered him. He affected a leonine head of white
hair and a majestic presence on the podium, a cross between

Liszt and Wagner, except that he did not quite share their comprehension of music, according to André.

> He wrote overlush, heart-on-the-sleeve-ish music, melodies which, judged strictly as music, were nothing short of reprehensible. But played behind pictures of leading ladies in flowing gowns sobbing on moonlit balconies, those melodies were sensational.

Stothart's melody for the main title music of *Undercurrent* turned out to be "adapted" from a cello theme in the third movement of Brahms's Third Symphony. André was a bit concerned at first, wondering how, even with an entire orchestra, he could possibly be expected to improve on Brahms, but Stothart told him exactly what he wanted. "Four minutes long I need. And make it big. I want it really BIG."

André set out to write the BIGGEST music he'd ever heard, all for a film which even Robert Taylor buffs would be hard pressed to remember in not too many years. He didn't stop until he'd written a part for everything, including the instrumental version of the kitchen sink. "Stothart told me I could use a chorus, an organ, anything I wanted. So I went home and wrote four minutes of *The Pines of Rome*. It had everything, even tam-tams, going all at once by the time I got to the end. I knew it wasn't any good, but by God it was loud!"

When it came time for Stothart to record the sound track, the orchestrator was required to sit at the base of the podium, score in hand, while the music director conducted from a piano reduction. He had to be there in case something went wrong and the so-called composer didn't know how to fix it.

Looking up, André watched Stothart's arms sweep the orchestra into the music, like a locomotive gathering momentum. As measure built upon measure, sound came cascading from every section, gushing from the strings, oozing from the woodwinds, frothing from the brass. The production staff looked on "in conclaves of admiration." Layer upon gratuitous layer of music piled up until, just before André's tower of music would collapse of its own weight and come crashing to an end, Herb Stothart leaned down to look at André. His eyes were glistening with emotion and pride shone in his face. He shouted a question that could not be heard above the din, but André saw the old man's lips move and knew what the words were. He was asking, "Did I really write this?"

There was a lot to laugh about at the MGM Music Department in those days. André encountered another so-called composer "whose lack of musical knowledge was awe-inspiring. He played the piano not with just one finger, but with just one *thumb*. It was creepy to watch." On one occasion this composer—whom André will not name—gave André a melody to be arranged "with lots of trumpets." André watched as the man thumbed his little melody an octave and a half above high C. "But Mr. ———, trumpets can't *play* that high." To which the unabashed composer replied, "Look, kid, you do your job and the trumpets'll do theirs."

A favorite Music Department alumni story goes back to 1936, when a notice was posted on the department's bulletin board. The notice was ordered by one of MGM's top brass who'd been offended by a phrase of music he'd heard in a biblical epic. "It's nothing but a minor chord," the composer had explained. The notice read: "From this date forward no MGM score will contain a minor chord." The story may be apocryphal, but André swears the notice was still there when he arrived in 1945.

After the better part of a year André was a member in good standing of the Music Department, his assignments growing in importance as producers found they could count on the skinny kid with the long nose. He was put to work as a pianist in his first musical, *It Happened in Brooklyn*, which starred Frank Sinatra, Peter Lawford, and Jimmy Durante and which was filled with Jule Styne–Sammy Cahn standards like "Time After Time." A young Kathryn Grayson was called upon to please the carriage trade by trilling a bit of Mozart and Delibes; André played her accompanist—but only off-camera.

His pianistic talents were in demand again for *Fiesta*, André's second helping of Hollywood con carne and a musical belch of the first magnitude, even more absurd than *Holiday in*

Mexico. This was Ricardo Montalban's Hollywood screen debut and he played the last in a long family line of bullfighters. He becomes the black sheep by pursuing a career as a composer and pianist. For love interest there was Cyd Charisse, who danced, and the unsinkable Esther Williams, who played a lady bullfighter. It was all based on a book called *Fiesta Brava.*

Jack Cummings, the film's producer, had a flair for music and, when the originally assigned composer for *Fiesta* missed the kill, Cummings got an idea. He tried to hire composer Aaron Copland to rewrite his orchestral score *El Salón México* into a piano concerto for Ricardo Montalban. Copland did not shout *ole!* at the suggestion. However, he agreed to sell Cummings the right to adapt *El Salón México,* provided his old friend Johnny Green were assigned to do the work. Green decided he would do the piano concerto, provided the playing of it were left to the only person on the lot he felt could handle it, André.

Though Copland's orchestral work was, in Green's words, "the most unpianistic piece I could imagine," and though *El Salón México* had to be cut by a third in order to fit the time requirements of the script, it nevertheless became *Fantasia Mexicana.* As Green had promised, the piece was outrageously difficult to play, but André recorded it and the Copland-Green piano concerto helped make Ricardo Montalban famous.

Hollywood had no qualms whatsoever when it came to improving on the creative efforts of great composers. A producer once asked André to come up with some suitable chamber music for a drawing room scene and he suggested the first movement of Robert Schumann's Piano Quintet. After first disappointing the producer by telling him that his favorite instrument, the harp, would not be involved, André showed him what the piano part sounded like. "Terrific. Very pretty," said the producer. "So we'll have five guys in the scene, right?" "Right." "Okay. But we need a big sound here, so you'll have to put a full orchestra behind them." When André bolted at the suggestion of orchestrating the quintet, both he and Schumann were taken off the film.

André's refusal to toe the line for the MGM lion might have had serious consequences, but his reputation for reliability and efficiency was already sufficiently established that the gust of outrage soon blew over and he was back in the studio's good graces. In addition, his bargain-counter rates continued to be a major asset in 1946, when MGM found itself dropping behind Paramount, Warner, and Twentieth Century-Fox in profits. He was by now a fixture at the studio, a jack of all musical trades who "did everything but fetch the coffee."

The Publicity Department at MGM helped build his reputation by hiring him out for parties, and word that he was available and cheap quickly circulated through the other studios. It was from the Publicity Department at Universal that the request came for him to play at Mary Pickford's home. So it happened that André could boast of having a conversation with his ultimate employer, Louis B. Mayer, a man whom many senior members of MGM's Music Department had never even seen.

Mayer's remark to André that evening, that Jascha Heifetz could hardly be considered great without film credits, sounds like rampant, unbridled parochialism today. It can easily be argued that Heifetz's reputation and name have far outlived those of some of Mayer's biggest stars. And faces familiar to millions of moviegoers now have no names attached in our memories. Who, for example, was that remarkably durable dowager who provided Groucho's love interest in nearly all the old Marx Brothers films? Movie trivia buffs may be the only ones who remember her name was Margaret Dumont. On the other hand, Louis B. Mayer may have had a point.

In the 1930s, '40s, and '50s, the sound tracks of MGM musicals certainly reached more ears in a single evening than would have encountered a Beethoven symphony in the space of a year. In 1946 only the elite few could repeat a melody by Robert Schumann, but the movie-going masses could hum "Look for the Silver Lining" by Jerome Kern, simply because Judy Garland had sung it to them in *Till the Clouds Roll By*. And if Louis B. Mayer wanted those same masses to have Robert

Schumann, then, by God, they *got* Robert Schumann. The very next year, in fact, Paul Henreid played Robert and Katharine Hepburn played Clara Schumann in *Song of Love*. If Louis B. Mayer had wanted to, he probably could have "made" Jascha Heifetz too.

In terms of film music, MGM set the pace for the industry. When André arrived on the scene there were twenty full-time composers on the staff, twenty-five arranger-orchestrators, forty music copyists, and an enormous library staff. Under the leadership of legitimate composers, such as Miklós Rózsa, Alex North, and David Raksin, film music had become something of an art form in its own right, notwithstanding the denigration by most of the world's best musicians, who agreed with Sir Thomas Beecham when he said, "Film music is noise."

Certainly the quality of the music was of very little concern to the movers and shapers of MGM; it was simply part of their entertainment software package. André observes that "the Music Department was no more nor less important than the Department of Fake Lawns." Perhaps, but while a lot of films got along without plastic sod, hardly an MGM frame passed through the projector gate without its moment of music.

That moment was usually an individual moment, written for the specific purpose of accompanying that individual frame, not the way it's done today, with a film's "theme song" repeated ad nauseam, slowed down or speeded up to fit the mood of the scene. At MGM there were usually fifteen different films in production on a given day, each one under the supervision of a music director. But there was far too much music per film for any one man to handle, so the less important work, including most of the orchestrating, was farmed out to André and the other sharecroppers on the plantation. He might be working on a New York cafe scene one day, a western hoedown the next, and a Louis XIV drawing room scene the day after that.

> We shaped up at the Music Department each day like truckers waiting to see who has tomatoes to be driven to Chicago or furniture for Delaware. We

never knew who might need what. If some composer
was in trouble with a prize-fight film that had to be
finished immediately, we might all be rushed over to
that set to pitch in for a few days.

Inevitably, being in the company of older men, André fell
under the influence of a number of MGM composers and musicians. One of these, a man he took to from the start, was
Lennie Hayton. Something of an iconoclast, Hayton had the
gossip columnists buzzing because of his involvement with
black singer-actress Lena Horne, who had created her own kind
of sensation three years earlier with MGM's *Cabin in the Sky*.
Hayton added to his notoriety by traveling with Lena as her
accompanist and, eventually, by marrying her. André apparently was quite impressed with Hayton, spending a great
deal of time with him and even emulating his style and mannerisms. At one point Jack Previn expressed fear that what he
considered Hayton's loose morals might rub off on André.

But there were others, men like Johnny Green, Conrad
Salinger, and Miklós Rózsa, each a serious musician in his way,
from whom André could and did learn a great deal. One of the
things he evidently picked up early on, perhaps even from Max
Rabinowitsch, his old piano teacher, was the heavy burden of
guilt and sometimes frustration that classically trained musicians bore in Hollywood. Johnny Green is now still a would-be
conductor of Mozart and Mendelssohn who usually must settle
for Gershwin and Kern when he accepts guest conducting
offers. Salinger was an extremely talented composer, self-exiled
in Hollywood, who also happened to be an avowed homosexual
and was given to fitful bouts of drinking. Later, on his sixtieth
birthday, he committed suicide. In those early days, however,
those older men set aside their cynicism for the pleasure of ob-
serving and nurturing what they considered to be André's remarkable talents.

> His prodigious sight-reading (says Green), that in-
> credible coordination of eye, brain, and fingers, that
> was a special gift. He gave me a musical inferiority

complex and I never knew whether I wanted to kiss him or kick him. But also, he had a lot to learn and he realized that. At first transposition puzzled him. He was bewildered, for example, by a bass clarinet sounding a ninth lower than the note that was written. So he would sit for hours, poring over my scores or Salinger's or somebody else's, devouring our music, just trying to understand. And quickly, I mean, incredibly quickly, a door opened somewhere in his mind. It was suddenly like he'd had four years of advanced composition at Juilliard. He absorbed it all.

Budapest-born Miklós Rózsa recalls that "everyone was like a big family in the Music Department. It was like a Broadway crowd, with laughter, play, fun and jokes," but Rózsa recognized immediately that André was "not one of the boys. He was the only one there I could have a real musical conversation with."

Rózsa was not yet under contract to MGM when André signed on in 1945. In fact, the two came together twice before Rózsa joined MGM in 1948. On one occasion they met at the Hollywood Bowl; the other occasion was when they worked together on a film that André's superiors at MGM knew nothing about.

André was under exclusive contract to MGM and could have been fired for working outside the studio; perhaps it was his brother Steve who talked him into it. Steve had left Universal and set off on his own as an independent film cutter. He happened to be working on a film called *The Other Love* for which Rózsa happened to be writing the music. In the film, Barbara Stanwyck played a pianist who was called on to play a bit of jazz (shades of *Holiday in Mexico*) and composer Rózsa had an absolute aversion to jazz. The film was at a standstill. Steve heard about the dilemma and suggested André. The extra money, along with guaranteed anonymity, prompted André to accept and he dashed off the pieces. There was already a pianist engaged for the recording sessions, Ania Dorfmann, but Miss Dorfmann's hands did not photograph at all like Miss Stanwyck's. It was somehow discovered that André, still very boyish in appearance, had hands that looked very much like those of Barbara Stanwyck, so much so that when Steve spliced the film together, you'd swear it was really Barbara playing. So it was that André Previn's hands made their on-camera debut in an independently produced film, *The Other Love*.

The footnote to the story—which Rózsa never confessed to André—is that on his first day at MGM Rózsa unthinkingly spilled the beans about André's breach of contract. The head of the Music Department was incensed and might have dismissed André on the spot but for Rózsa's impassioned plea for leniency.

"Working at MGM," André reflects, "was like being enrolled in some huge, demented conservatory. It was sensational, thrilling, and between classes I could drool over all the pretty girls." Demented though it may have been, the studio provided a learning experience that perhaps no young student of serious music ever shared. As he learned orchestration, by trial and error, André also learned the unique abilities and the unique limitations of each instrument in the orchestra. He learned it by himself, autodidactically, without professors, without textbooks. Again, Johnny Green was impressed by André's uncanny powers of absorption.

> Today there are all those books on film scoring, but back then they weren't even written yet. You worked with sprocket holes and frames-per-second in your head and with a stopwatch in your hand. André's adroitness with timing seemed inborn, and that was the hardest thing for most of us to learn. I found it all very curious since he seemed to me like a kid who'd have to call in Tom Edison if he needed a lightbulb changed.

Film is a confining medium for a composer, referred to by some of them as "the celluloid straitjacket." The mood of a film score, its message if any, its length to the second are all predetermined by the time a composer is called in. After the composer decides what to play when, there's not a whole lot of creative input left for the arranger. André had little choice but to follow the rules and do as he was told; he did just that, much as his father had done years before in Germany, waiting for the law to let the family emigrate. André worked and waited and learned.

In the area of music theory, the film studio had a distinct advantage over any real conservatory, no matter how less depraved. That was the ability of a student to hear the fruits of his labors and to hear them almost instantaneously. Each of André's "exercises" had a very nonacademic purpose and, in the managerial eyes of the studio, André was just another worker on the music assembly line, adding another piece to the product that needed quick finishing. Hardly had the copyist's ink dried on the score pages than one hundred top-rank musicians were assembled to lay down a track on full-coat film. You knew what you did right and what you did wrong without a teacher having to tell you:

> I'd sit on that scoring stage, hearing music I'd written down earlier that same week. I'd hear those strings and horns playing *my* work. I'd tick off the moments in my score as they went by, "yes, this works" . . . "no, this is terrible" . . . "this you could learn something about" . . . "*never* do this again."

It wasn't "art for art's sake," no matter how loud the lion roared under that satirical motto of MGM's. Profit was the motive and production was the byword. Produce. Produce. Produce. There was no time for puerile self-doubt or school-day laziness. Other ears than André's were listening to every bar he wrote and other tastes than his demanded catering to.

Maybe it was not what he should have been doing, but at sixteen André was learning the structure of music, from the inside out, like a student artist learning to mix his own colors from the reds and greens of nature. He learned how the building blocks of the orchestra could become complementary elements in the manufacture of pleasing sound.

> When I put together four bars that were homogeneous-sounding; when the composer wanted something that "sounds like Ravel" and I managed a recognizable ripoff, I was thrilled to bits. I thought it was a major accomplishment . . . And I'll tell you something, I guess it *was* a major accomplishment.

V

Lotte Lehmann came to MGM late in 1947 to do a film called *Big City*, in which an orphaned waif (Margaret O'Brien) is befriended by an Irish Catholic cop (George Murphy), a Jewish cantor (Danny Thomas), and a Protestant minister (Robert Preston). Naturally, Mme. Lehmann was supposed to sing, but nobody could make up his mind *what* she should sing. André was summoned from the Music Department so that the soprano could "run through a couple of your tunes for us." She sang the songs of Schubert, Schumann, and Wolf, music which had made her known to generations of music lovers but which, to Joe Pasternak, were "not quite right for this piece." Her patience a bit frayed, Mme. Lehmann suspected a bit of humor was called for to relieve the tension. "Well," she said with a shrug, "I guess we could always do the Brahms Lullaby."

"Sure, sure," the producer nodded. "That I took for granted. I mean, you made the song *famous* for crissake."

Ironically, it was through his studio connections that André found a teacher to replace his father's choice, Ernst Toch. From his musician friends at MGM he learned that everyone who was anyone in Hollywood music studied, at one time or another, with Mario Castelnuovo-Tedesco.

Tedesco was a Jewish Italian with a sunny, Florentine dispo-

sition. After André's chill experiences with professors from
northern and central Europe, here was "one of the kindest,
gentlest, most adorable men I ever met." The serious musicians around Hollywood knew him for his classically oriented
work; the others knew him for his film scores. "Studied under
Mario Castelnuovo-Tedesco" was a virtual requisite for California musicians, even for jazzmen like Shorty Rogers and for
bandleaders like Paul Weston. When Tedesco, at a banquet of
the Screen Composers Guild, jokingly referred to himself as
"the father of West Coast jazz," he was very nearly telling the
truth.

To André the man was "a walking encyclopedia. There was
nothing he didn't know. You could ask him what was the
lowest possible shake on the oboe d'amore and he wouldn't
have to look it up."

More inclined to the writing of operas than of film scores,
Tedesco never really fit in the convertible-and-chorus-girl play-
ground he called home. His eyesight was so poor he couldn't
quite make out the images on a movie screen, let alone drive a
car. His glasses were misplaced with laughable regularity and
he frequently went around with his shirt buttoned wrong and
his tie off center, the archetype of the absent-minded professor.

One evening, as André was sporting around with the convertible and chorus girl he finally was able to afford, he spotted
Tedesco at a bus stop, nose buried in an imposingly thick
book. "Can we give you a lift home?" he shouted. After assuring himself that he was indeed going home and that he did indeed know the driver of the car, Tedesco climbed in. "Been
waiting long?" the girl asked. Tedesco squinted at his watch.
"My goodness. Has it really been two hours?" He'd been so
lost in Gibbon's *Decline and Fall* that a good twenty buses
must have passed him by.

Time could be just as relative at one of Tedesco's lessons. A
paid-for single hour of his time might easily be stretched to
two hours, and that was good for the pupil of the moment. For
anyone whose own lesson was supposed to have started forty-
five minutes earlier, it was not so good. But one generally
found cookies on the foyer table, with thick black coffee or the

maestro's homemade raisin wine. To an Italian time is never so precious that a moment can't be found to reminisce about old friends, friends such as Ottorino Respighi and Manuel de Falla, or to visit with an unexpected guest such as Andrés Segovia. The atmosphere was casual, one of mutual enjoyment of music, the antithesis of Joseph Achron's rigid discipline. Time spent with Tedesco was so free of all the accustomed pressures and pace of his daily routine that even today André looks back on it wistfully: "I really took to it. I took to it very much."

Generous with his compliments, Tedesco also could see right to the heart of a pupil's weakness. He continually accused André of being too facile, too quick a study; that, he said, "makes you lazy." He spent far less time mastering difficult assignments than other pupils did and Tedesco would have egged him on to greater accomplishments. But André resisted and Tedesco let it go at that, perhaps realizing that the prodigy was yet a child, already burdened with too many responsibilities.

Rarely did anything drive Tedesco to distraction. André saw it happen only once, when he took on as a pupil a middle-aged man who wore all the ribbons of success as a film composer but was rumored never to have written a note of his own. It was said he paid ghost writers to do each of his films and signed his own name to their work.

This self-styled composer (now as nameless as all those who did his work) must have heard the gossip, for he suddenly decided that he needed to maintain a modicum of respectability; he needed to be able to write "studied with Mario Castelnuovo-Tedesco" behind his name, just as the real musicians did. Tedesco seemed suspicious from the start, but he accepted the man as a student and gave him the same assignments he gave others. At his second lesson the man returned with a piano piece by Debussy, now diligently, beautifully orchestrated. Tedesco was impressed.

"Look here," he said, "if you can do work like this you don't need me. We're both wasting our time. It's all here." The fellow answered unctuously that from such a maestro as

Tedesco one might always learn. Tedesco was not satisfied and after the man left he began to look more closely at his work. There was something about the feel of the music, something in the musical handwriting that Tedesco recognized. He went through stacks of former students' work and came up with a very close match.

On the telephone, the former pupil was astonished. "I thought he wanted that Debussy for some film he was working on." The following week the "composer" came in at the end of André's lesson with another of "his" arrangements. Without even looking at the music, Tedesco flew into a rage, screaming and cursing in Italian. He tore up the pages of music and all but threw the man out bodily.

The instrumentalists who played the works of these Hollywood composers and arrangers were, for the most part, graduates of good conservatories, had played under important conductors with top-flight orchestras. They worked in Hollywood because the pay was better and the work was year-round steady, but they never stopped thirsting for the purer waters of the classical tradition. Thus Los Angeles and its environs never lacked for players ready to make "good" music at the drop of a baton. The older generation spawned new musicians, all eager to make their own marks, desperate for opportunities to perform, and to meet that need the California Youth Orchestra arose.

The California Youth Orchestra was the prototype of the earnest and hard-working student orchestras which later sprang up in cities all over the United States. The vision and the supervision were provided by Peter Meremblum, another member of the East European horde that swept over southern California in the first half of the century. Meremblum was a fanatic on the nurturing of young talent and the organization he founded gave young players a firm, first foothold in the music profession. André was only one of many CYO players who would one day rise to the upper levels of the profession. He joined in 1945 and got his first taste of playing piano concertos with a full symphony orchestra.

By bus and car caravan the California Youth Orchestra

would travel to outlying gyms and bandshells. André first performed the first concerto of Beethoven in a high school gym, Rachmaninoff's Second in a sweltering town meeting hall. Even Jack Previn couldn't say anything bad about the repertory, but as he drove home from a concert at a particularly underwhelming seacoast town he remarked, "Well, it wasn't Boston, was it?"

Since a youth orchestra was still a novelty in those days, the CYO got a lot of attention in the newspapers and among the music community. Peter Meremblum was able to coax fairly well-known music figures to conduct or play at Saturday morning rehearsals and, occasionally, even to help out with the concerts. So it was that André found himself playing the Tchaikovsky Piano Concerto No. 1 under the baton of Sir John Barbirolli.

It was his first experience with a conductor of international stature and maybe it is too bad it could not have been under some more exacting taskmaster. Never the sort to inspire genuflecting obedience among his players, Sir John more or less let André have his head with the concerto rather than bend him to the will of experience.

Years later the two would meet on more equal footing and André would remind Sir John of that concert that meant so much to him as a teenager. The occasion was completely erased from Barbirolli's memory and only André's time-tattered program convinced the Englishman that he'd ever led one of André's performances in California.

Even though André got to perform his share of Tchaikovsky and Rachmaninoff, repertory was a distinct shortcoming of the California Youth Orchestra. To Peter Meremblum, the "classics" were the works he'd digested as a steady musical diet in turn-of-the-century Moscow and they had as little resemblance to Mozart and Beethoven as borscht has to apple pie.

> The repertoire that Meremblum taught us was quite funny. Here we were, a lot of wildly talented youngsters sitting in an orchestra for the first time, and Meremblum would come striding into the auditorium for a rehearsal at precisely 10 A.M. on Saturday morn-

ing. He'd tap his baton on the music stand and say,
"Okay. Glazunov Eighth." He turned out a lot of
young Californians who had an amazing grasp of
Balakirev but who'd never seen a score of Mozart's
Jupiter. Still, it was an amazing thing he did and he
left quite a legacy.

The California Youth Orchestra was only one outlet for
André's talents outside the walls of MGM. He joined more
advanced musicians in a concert series originally called "Evenings on the Roof," but later moved indoors and called
simply "The Monday Evening Concerts." These were devised
by the enormously energetic Lawrence Morton, another pio-
neer who realized early on that the key to success to southern California was novelty. Californians were willing to try
anything, provided it hadn't been tried first somewhere else.
Thanks in part to Morton's groundbreaking, many large American cities have societies devoted to obscure music, but in the
forties that sort of thing was as novel as the youth orchestra
and much of the music performed by the Monday Evening
Concerts had never been heard on this side of the Atlantic.

In the Monday Evening programs there was something for
everybody (or nobody if you were Jack Previn)—everything
from Gesualdo madrigals to Stravinsky premieres to first hearings of works with the ink still wet on the pages by composers still wet behind the ears. Larry Morton's budget favored
music written for small ensembles rather than large orchestras
and consequently good pianists were in demand. André found
his way to Morton through members of the MGM orchestra
who knew of his increasingly uncanny ability to sight-read
modern music, a priceless asset considering the unpredictability
of Morton's programs and the meager rehearsal time his
budget permitted.

Like most of the hard-core Monday Eveningers, André
found the opportunity to hear new music almost as irresistible
as the chance to play it. So if he wasn't being paid to perform
on a given Monday he usually paid to sit in the hall and listen.

"I used to go quite often," he recalls, "not just when they asked me to play, because you could hear such extraordinarily obscure music. I can remember an evening of chamber music by Igor Markevitch. God Almighty, I even remember hearing a chamber opera by Boris Blacher!"

One never knew who'd be in the audience on a given evening. It might be an unexpected colleague or an old teacher or even somebody famous. André recalls one evening when he and another young pianist, Lukas Foss, were scheduled to perform the difficult, 1935-vintage Concerto for Two Pianos by Igor Stravinsky. As he strode out onto the stage he stopped dead in his tracks, Lukas very nearly bumping into him. There, in the third row of the theater, was Stravinsky himself, with a man sitting next to him who could be none other than Aldous Huxley: "an extraordinary thing to look out upon."

> After the concert we were backstage and there was the usual backslapping and horsing around when in walked Stravinsky and Huxley. Stravinsky took Lukas' hands in his own left hand and my hands in his right. He examined them meticulously and then he looked us in the eyes and said, "You both have wonderful fingers." Then he turned and left. To this day Lukas and I have never decided whether that was a compliment or a put-down.

It was easier to read his father's judgment. Jack had very little good to say about André's headlong plunge into the icy waters of the musical twentieth century. "Where is Brahms, where is Schubert?" he would ask rhetorically whenever André practiced one of the pieces he was scheduled to play at a Monday Evening Concert. Nor did Jack miss an opportunity to remind his son that not only did this esoteric music demand too much of his overcrowded schedule, it also paid damned little. And much of Los Angeles' musical establishment was indifferent to the Monday Evening series.

> At the time I guess the musical community took it all pretty much for granted. Nobody realized how much

work went into those concerts. But I can tell you that
as a pianist I was kept very, very busy. I played chamber music by Jolivet and by Kent Kennan. I accompanied Ives songs and I played all manner of wildnesses
by Rolf Liebermann.

Through it all, André never paused to consider his father's
legitimate question: Where are Brahms and Schubert? Jolivet,
Kennan, Ives, and Liebermann could hardly be considered the
stuff of a solid repertory foundation.

I guess I had no system; I simply played what was put
in front of me. At age sixteen I'd recently been se-
duced by the film industry life and I was very, very
busy. I had no friends with whom I might have gotten together to have that sort of endless chamber
music evening, exulting in Mozart and Haydn. Except for those few times I actually got to play it with
the Youth Orchestra, most of the standard repertoire
was virgin territory for me. When I was invited to
play chamber music it was always Harris or Copland.
Nobody *asked* me to play Brahms or Schubert. And
why should they have asked me? After all, there were
an awful lot of better piano players around, you
know.

André was indeed becoming identified with modern music
and not merely in the eyes of others. He was impatient with
the predilection of his teacher, Tedesco, toward more traditional composition, disturbed that "if a student wrote something that was far removed from his own line of thinking
Tedesco wouldn't know how to deal with it, except on purely
technical terms." It even made him a bit of an elitist. When
Miklós Rózsa showed him his finished First Piano Sonata, already labeled modernistic, André sloughed off the work as
"well, a little bit old-fashioned." André was very close to walking into a musical cul-de-sac, thanks to his sight-reading prowess; but that same prowess rather dramatically opened a new
door back into the sunlight of the classics.

The principal cellist in the MGM studio orchestra was Willem Vandenberg, also first cellist and assistant conductor of the Los Angeles Philharmonic and a well-known soloist. At the studio one afternoon Vandenberg asked André if he'd like to play some chamber music with him and a violinist friend. The friend was vacationing nearby and had been sent a newly finished trio for violin, cello, and piano. Since it was one of those outlandishly difficult modern pieces, they needed a pianist who could sight-read the contemporary styles or they'd be forever trying to work out the piece. Mindful of his father's criticism of how he spent his time, André was on the point of turning down the offer when Vandenberg dropped the name of his friend the violinist. It was Joseph Szigeti.

André drove with Willy Vandenberg down the coast to where Szigeti was spending a sabbatical in an aerie above the rocky beach. The new trio was, as promised, "a particularly hair-raising piece" by a young composer from Szigeti's native Hungary. After doing close combat with raging dissonances for the better part of an hour, Szigeti called a time-out and suggested they relax with a bit of Beethoven, much as a runner cools down by jogging or walking after a long race.

"How about one of the Beethoven trios?" the violinist asked, looking at André. "Which is your favorite?"

To break what he knew might become an embarrassed silence, André stammered, "Well, I . . . I, uh . . . I don't really know the trios."

"No, I don't suppose you could have played them often enough to make up your mind. How about you, Willy, which is your favorite?"

Under other circumstances André might have played along, but he knew he'd never bluff his way through Beethoven without the two senior musicians guessing the truth. "No, that's not what I mean," he broke in. "I mean, I've never played any of the trios. Never."

"Good God!" Szigeti was incredulous. "A boy with your talent has never played a Beethoven trio?"

"No, sir."

"Then why are we wasting your time with this?" Szigeti

collected the Hungarian manuscript. "You know the Schubert trios, I take it, and the Brahms?"

"I played a Brahms concerto once, but . . ."

"But not the chamber music?"

"No, sir."

"Mozart then?"

"I guess I've just never had much chance."

Szigeti looked at Vandenberg and both men shook their heads. "I find that the greatest disgrace," said the violinist, "inexcusable. It must be remedied. Willy, you've got to bring this boy back every Monday night for as long as I am here. We are going to play through all the Beethoven trios, all the Brahms, all the Schubert, all the Mozart, until you know them all."

> That was the kindest thing, in terms of musical education, that's ever happened in my life. It's the most overt act of kindness I've ever seen. At that time, of course, I had no idea of what it truly meant. I thought it was very nice of Szigeti. I thought, well, now I'll have to miss the Monday Evening Concerts for a while. It was only much later that I realized just what that man offered me and how much it must have taken out of his time.
>
> By God, the experience was unforgettable. For about twenty weeks I went there every Monday night and we'd play. We played for two hours, took a break for supper, then went back and played for two more hours. What Szigeti didn't know about chamber music playing is not worth knowing. The education I got at his hands I'd never have gotten at any university in the world. I'll never forget what he did for me.

It was the sort of favor a person yearns to repay, but the only chance André ever had to repay Szigeti came too many years later and fell somewhat short of the debt. It was at one of the Monday Evening Concerts, ironically enough, for which Szigeti had agreed to perform the three sonatas of Charles Ives. Even though he had other commitments, and even though he had little affinity for Ives, and even though the sonatas existed then only in facsimile scores of Ives's barely legible scrawl, André leaped at the chance to accompany Szigeti. ("Simply another incredible experience. It seems to me that I learned a lot of marvelous music by sheer accident.")

A piece of marvelous music he almost didn't learn, according to a tale told by MGM's Johnny Green, is the *Burleske* of Richard Strauss. To appreciate the story it is necessary to know that the protagonist was Franz Waxman, best remembered today for his scores to films like *Sunset Boulevard, A Place in the Sun,* and *Rebecca.* Waxman was yet another in that long line of film composers who longed to do something "more meaningful" with their lives. In Waxman's case that something was the founding in 1947 of the Los Angeles Orchestral Society. That Society's purpose was the annual staging of a Festival of Music devoted to the airing of still more new and unheard music. It was for one of his early spring concerts that Waxman called MGM and asked if he might hire their talked-about young pianist. Johnny Green takes up the story:

By this time I'd been made music director at MGM so I was André's boss. He was under contract to the studio and he had to get permission from me before he accepted any outside work. I said, "The Festival? Okay. What are you going to play?" He told me the Strauss *Burleske.* I said, "You've *got* the Strauss *Burleske?*" Because I had never even seen a score of the thing. He said he hadn't seen it either and I told him, "You know, that's not an easy piece to bring off. When the devil are you going to start working on it?" He said, "I don't know. You've got me working on a picture now. I'll get around to it." I said, "Wait a minute. Franz is a friend of mine and you're going to be in some pretty fast company at his festival. Don't slough it off."

Well, the weeks went by and the festival got closer and he still hadn't started looking at the music. I called Franz and I said, "You'd better start whipping my boy Previn 'cause he still hasn't looked at your

Strauss." He said, "My God! I'll talk to him." Then finally André got down to work. But by that time he was already busy recording for the picture and doing half a dozen other things.

I called him into my office one day and said, "You know, I wouldn't really be offended if you came in some lunchtime and played a little of that *Burleske* for me. Who knows? I might even have a suggestion or two." "Well," he said, "it's not ready for that yet." "Well, when are you going to learn it," I said, "after the concert?" We always had a wonderful rapport and I could laugh even when I was mad at him. Right now I was *very* mad. He just gave me a look like, "Don't push me," and he never did come back and play it for me.

Finally comes the night of the concert and I'm sitting in the audience with my wife, at Royce Hall on the UCLA campus. The previous orchestra number is over and here they come wheeling the big piano out onto the stage. One guy pulls the music rack out of the piano, sticks it under his arm and walks off with it. I'm thinking, "Oh no! He's gonna lay the music out on the top of the piano like a guy in a dance band." Next thing I know, out walks Previn and Waxman and my heart jumps into my mouth: *André isn't carrying any music.* I lean over to my wife, Bonnie, and I say, "I know it now, the kid's crazy. He never had a chance to memorize this piece." But I watch him walking out like a cucumber, so cool. He bows nicely and sits down at the piano and off he goes, playing like a goddam little god. Remember I said sometimes I didn't know whether to kiss him or kick him? This was the night I kicked him. I walked backstage after it was over and said, "Bend down. You've had this coming for a good, long time." And I kicked him nice and hard, right in the bobo.

VI

"I needed a job and I was willing to work for anyone. If someone was willing to put up with me I was very flattered." That
was André Previn's career, in his own nutshell, from 1945 to
1950. For all his forays into highbrow piano playing, it was his
arranging for MGM that paid the bills. He was a studio hack,
the same sort of musician of whom he later said, "Whoever
has their price they'll orchestrate for. Whether it's rewriting
Copland or scoring a short subject on pottery-making, what
difference does it make? You can't say you won't work on it because it's not a good film. You try to do the best job you can."

He finished Beverly Hills High School in three years thanks
to the waiver of foreign language courses; there was no thought
of continuing his formal education beyond that. In 1946 he
signed with MGM a "fairly fraudulent and fearsome contract,"
heavily weighted in the studio's favor, which indentured him
to Louis B. Mayer for at least another three years at a salary of
$250 a week.

His handful of school friends left behind, André devoted
himself full-time to the studio. He was assigned a two-room
bungalow near the Music Department, with a piano in one
room and a desk in the other. His friends became the other or-
chestrators and the studio musicians, "very rarely the people
for whom I worked." He became a member of the Arrangers
Society, made up of the people who actually wrote down the
music which was played in the films, "men who had studied

very seriously, then found this comfortable way of life. They were the people I respected in Hollywood, the people I admired, the people I hung out with. The Society would meet once a month to have a large drunken dinner somewhere."

At one of these monthly shindigs André met Leo Arnaud, "a French musician of the highest elegance." Along with Conrad Salinger, who once studied with Paul Dukas in Paris, Leo Arnaud contributed immeasurably to André's fondness for French music and to his understanding of the way French composers manipulated the instruments of the orchestra to achieve that peculiar Gallic sound.

Arnaud also contributed to André's simmering stockpot of cynicism when it came to anything involving the film industry, especially its mercenary approach to music. Sometimes the musical frustration built up a head of steam that was best released in a practical joke. The butt of one of these jokes was George Stoll, then head of the Music Department at MGM, a man André describes as "an adorable, sweet human being of no musical learning whatever."

> Leo and I were assigned to do some last-minute work on one of Georgie Stoll's pictures on which the music was overdue. We got Stoll's material so late that we decided just to take it over to Leo's apartment and work on it nonstop. Then Leo decided we really ought to do something to get even. We would stall, drag our feet with the arrangements so there'd be no time to have the lead sheets made and poor Georgie would have to conduct from the score. He hated to use a score and when he did he'd just follow the treble clef line wherever it took him.
>
> Somehow that didn't seem like sufficient revenge, so we got the idea of writing everything, every instrument's part, in a transposed key or a clef that was foreign to that instrument. It took hours longer, but we sat there like two scheming schoolkids, putting the cellos and the oboes and the trombones in the tenor clef, putting the trumpets in F and the horns in D and the clarinets in A . . . anything so long as it went

against the traditional way of doing things. Finally we finished and called a copyist to come get it. Then I fell asleep on Leo's couch, sometime after the sun came up, until the phone started ringing.

It was a frantic call from the studio. The recording session had started, then ground to a screeching halt almost immediately. Mister Stoll wondered whether the two of us might kindly come round to the recording stage. Leo and I were exhausted but delirious with laughter, so we got dressed and went down to the studio. Then came that tremendous surge of satisfaction as we walked onto the stage knowing there was nobody in the recording studio who didn't know that *we* were the writers of that music and that the head of the whole Music Department couldn't figure it out to save his life.

It was like that in all of Hollywood's Music Departments, with so many gifted people placing their talents in the service of an industry they didn't really respect, laboring over music they neither wanted nor were able to sign their names to, kowtowing to leaders less capable than themselves. The members of the Arrangers Society were a disillusioned lot who had discovered "that it was possible to be a rich, famous, highly considered, award-winning figure in Hollywood's musical world and still not know a goddam thing about music."

Even today André suffers from what he calls a "retrospective disdain" for anything touched by Hollywood, yet for years he stayed on there. He explained it to Dick Cavett in 1978: "I stayed because I had a great deal of fun and because the work, in a cheap way, was glamorous and thrilling. I suppose I should also mention greed and stupidity." He might also have included the fact that in those first five Hollywood years he was a teenager, with very little experience of the real world and with virtually no pressure to alter the course of his young life.

His MGM salary was twice what his father was bringing home as a "serious musician" and $250 a week was far more than a teenager in the 1940s had any right to be earning. That and the side money he made as a pianist brought him almost up to the level of those Beverly Hills High schoolmates he'd once thought of as decadently rich. His secondhand convertible, his expensive suede sport jacket, the fast talk he picked up from older companions, all gave him easy entry into that circle of starlets and chorus girls that had dazzled him when he first walked through the gates of MGM. "It was every young man's dream of the candy store. Who's going to turn down that kind of life? Who's going to say, 'Sorry, not tonight. I have to stay home and practice the Hammerklavier'?"

It never occurred to him that he should be making plans for his future. Perhaps it was because of his immersion in the Land of Make-Believe or perhaps it was that nowhere in that landscape was there anything to look up to, nothing like what we'd call today "role models," not for André.

> I never took any long and hard looks at those un-
> disputed leaders of the film composing field, people
> like Alfred Newman and Max Steiner. I never looked
> at them and said, "Ah, *that's* who I want to be when
> I grow up." I never thought about emulating them
> and spending the rest of my life around a film studio.
> In fact, it never occurred to me to think about the fu-
> ture at all; I just enjoyed myself a lot.

Stricter parental guidance at this stage of his development, guidance of the sort one would expect from Berliners like Jack and Charlotte, just might have altered the course of André's life. But their own uprooting seemed to have left his parents with an insecurity that weakened their influence over the children. Certainly they disapproved of André's life-style but neither of them knew how to change it.

> My mother was strongly maternal, but she was never
> ambitious for me. She didn't care whether her son be-
> came a famous musician or not. She never said any-
> thing about the life I was leading or the company I
> kept; she just wanted me to be happy. If that's what
> it took to keep me happy, fine. I've always been grate-
> ful for that.

As for Jack Previn, he seems to have had his head so buried in his own music that he could not see what was becoming of all the lofty ambitions he'd formulated for his younger son. Six days a week Jack gave piano lessons; on the seventh day he rested by listening to radio broadcasts of concerts, the one nostalgic reminder in this new land of what life had been like before the upheaval. As he listened to the sounds of the New York Philharmonic coming over the Emerson in their tiny living room he could follow along in his four-hand score and pretend that he was back in their home on Innsbruckerstrasse.

The rare evening out for Jack would invariably be spent at a concert. Once in a while he would take Charlotte and Leonore to one of André's Youth Symphony concerts or a Monday Evening Concert and on a few occasions he even attended one of his son's film recording sessions at MGM. None of it, however, impressed Jack favorably.

> If I was doing a film he'd say, "Well, it's nothing serious, is it?" If I played a chamber piece or even a concerto he'd say, "Pity you couldn't have conducted it." When I finally did begin to conduct my own film scores he'd say, "Now then, you haven't quite written another Beethoven Ninth, have you?" I couldn't win.

For all his pecking away at his son's confidence, Jack never sat André down for a long heart-to-heart talk about the future. He never said, "Look here, this film business is not good enough for you. Stop wasting your time and get on with serious music." All Jack's efforts in that regard seem to have stopped with his selection of André's first two music teachers in Los Angeles, first Joseph Achron, then Ernst Toch. Indeed, it's at the very point of André's breaking off from Toch that Jack's breaking off of discipline and guidance comes, almost as though he washed his hands of his son's career when André deserted a strict, classical German instructor for an easygoing, film-oriented Italian, Castelnuovo-Tedesco.

Or perhaps André's action had nothing to do with Jack's abdication. It could be that the father felt some sort of unassuageable guilt for having brought his son to California in the first place and then having placed him in the film studio environs. Whatever the cause or causes, Jack Previn simply stood by and watched his son skip merrily down a road which he felt certain would lead to ruin. "What's he going to be," Jack once asked Miklós Rózsa, "another Lennie Hayton?"

The absence of discipline was amplified by Jack's unabated negative reinforcement. Just like an old second-string varsity man whose son fails to make all-pro quarterback, Jack let André know time and again how he was letting the old man down. Jack's disguise as a musician fooled everyone but himself: he knew damn well he was simply a lawyer who idealized the music profession. The only way he could fulfill his dreams of music greatness was through his son, through André, and when he saw those dreams evaporating Jack resorted to the bitterest cynicism.

> I'd have to say he was pretty passive about the things I did, except for shooting me down. He was rather like a sniper; I never expected his remarks when they came, though I suppose after a while I should have known they were coming. That sort of thing, when you're very young, doesn't serve to goad you on to more and more work; it only enriches your resentment. Now my mother tells me he was extremely proud of me, but he never told me that himself. Nor did he really lay out his concerns about what I was doing. I suppose if it had been in his personality to say, "Enough. Stop wasting your time," I might have paid attention. After all, he *was* my father and I loved him a lot.

For kudos André had to look to MGM, where there was mounting evidence that they loved him a lot, even in 1948, when it was mighty hard to find love objects in the film business, when sales of television sets were quadrupling depressingly and when MGM profits dipped to a Depression-level low of five million dollars. Even then they loved André enough to entrust him with his first full-length film score.

The very first movie of his own was *The Sun Comes Up.* That its music director was only nineteen years old was far from being the quirkiest thing about this film; for starters, it co-starred Jeanette MacDonald and Lassie. The script for *The Sun Comes Up* had been turned out by Marjorie Kinnan Rawlings, whose novel *The Yearling* had been a deer-story success story for MGM at the box office. But this one was a dog story and a dog: embittered singing widow eventually opens heart and home to orphaned boy and to a canine companion that had accidentally caused her own son's death.

It may have been that producer Robert Sisk felt the film just couldn't miss with a plot like that, with Jeanette MacDonald and Lassie too, and so he could afford to take a chance with a novice music director. Once again, André's budget rates may have been a factor, since the movie required more than the usual amount of music.

One of the stars of *The Sun Comes Up* could only bark, the other could only sing, and what went between the barking and the singing was primarily hundreds of feet of lush background footage, a travelogue of the Ozarks. All told, more than an hour's worth of the ninety-minute film required music. At the time it seemed tailor-made for André. Thirty-odd years later, he is proud only that *Sun* rarely comes up, even on the late-late show, and that his contribution to it is therefore rarely remembered.

It all might have gone to his head in 1948, though, were it not for Lassie's keen powers of observation and sense of the Hollywood pecking order. At a meeting in the director's office, dog trainer Rudd Weatherwax gave the shake-hands order to his canine transvestite. (Although he could be a bitch to work with, Lassie was in truth a laddy.) Lassie offered his paw to the producer first, then to the director, then to each of the actors in order of billing. But when André proudly held out a hand to take the silken paw, Lassie did a 180-degree turn and made his exit.

"I suppose I should have been grateful, as Mike Nichols says, that the dog didn't piss on my leg. I didn't understand that Lassie was trying to tell me something, that a musician has no place in Hollywood when he can be snubbed by a collie colleague."

It should be pointed out that in 1948 André's star was on the rise while Lassie's and Jeanette MacDonald's were on the decline. In fact, the only reason *The Sun Comes Up* is recollected by film buffs is that it happened to be Miss Mac-Donald's last picture. Instead, it should be remembered as André Previn's first picture as a music director, the first occasion on which he stepped onto a recording stage not as an apprentice arranger but as a conductor.

The MGM musicians, for the most part, felt warmly toward the "wonderkid" and they wished him nothing but success in his budding career. Naturally, the atmosphere around the studio being what it was, they made a lot of jokes about his approaching the new assignment so seriously. After all, this was the kid who'd hoodwinked Georgie Stoll with the crazy clefs. For André's conducting "debut," they cooked up a scheme of their own.

There were great butterflies lurching through his stomach as he mounted the studio podium for the first time, self-consciously fingering the baton he'd been given. He was facing not simply an ensemble of experienced musicians, but a group of friends. He knew he had to strike a balance between camaraderie and authority, but he'd no idea how to do that, so he simply rapped his baton on the desk and asked the oboe for an A. That was the moment the orchestra had been waiting for: the oboist hit an A-flat instead.

André recognized the false note immediately and was somewhat nonplussed to hear the rest of the orchestra meticulously tuning to it. If they did that they'd be playing his music in the wrong key, a half-tone flat. He was on the verge of stopping them when his eye caught that of one of the tuba players: there was a twinkle in it and the man averted his gaze instantly. He looked around the string section, where the players had no mouthpieces to help conceal their smiles, and he caught on. He stared down at his music until they were quite finished, looked up, then rapped his baton again, feeling a sudden surge of confidence.

"All right, now," he said in a clear, crisp voice. "Everyone transpose a half tone up." And without another word he brought his arms down in the first beat. Most of the players burst into laughter and were unable to play, then someone started applauding and the rest of them picked it up. By that single gesture André had won the undying confidence of his first orchestra.

Appealing like that to their sense of humor as well as their musical sensibility was a stroke of genius. These men had played under the best, Toscanini included, and they had very little respect for most of the men who came before them at MGM. They knew the fellow waving the stick often had to lean on André for the answers to their questions; they had watched André mature as a musician; they knew about his work with the Youth Orchestra and with Tedesco and on the Monday Evening Concerts. They knew he was a player like themselves who understood what players could and couldn't do, who wouldn't call on the trumpets to hit an A above high C. They knew he had mastered that basic but often ignored art of transposition. They knew that, even though he was young enough to be their son, in some cases their grandson, he deserved their respect.

> On that day and on subsequent days, those musicians saved me from making a fool of myself. On that first picture I knew damned near nothing about conducting and they were kind enough to let me get away with it. But I'll tell you something, after two days of waving that stick at a bunch of musicians, I knew what I wanted to do with my life. The way I had felt hearing an orchestra for the first time, it all came back to me. I knew that my life belonged to conducting.

It soon became apparent around the studio that André and conducting were meant for each other and several members of the orchestra approached him to ask whether he might like to conduct them after hours sometime, when they got together just for the fun of playing "real" music. Of course André jumped at the offer. There were several of these makeshift jam-session orchestras around Hollywood, each a grab bag of players who thirsted for the mother's milk of the classics from which the film industry had weaned them. The groups were informal, democratic, and under no pressure to perform or to please anyone but themselves; they were musicians playing to empty halls just for the delight of making good music together.

More often than not the repertoire was chosen according to what they could *not* play, owing to an acute shortage of one or more instruments. The instrumentalists did so much playing around town they could never say with certainty whether they would attend the weekly session, so they might gather for an evening to discover they were blessed with seven trombones but no clarinets. André would come ready to conduct one thing and have to substitute another. "Still, there was always something we could manage. And no matter how unprepared I was or how badly I might conduct they always played well and I never failed to learn something from them."

At long last there seemed to be an emerging purpose to André's life. He was only nineteen but he already knew things, had already experienced things that most fledgling conductors would have to spend years learning. He even seemed to be on the verge of pleasing his father, who had never disguised his ambition to have a conductor in the family.

Proudly, with a sense of filial fulfillment, André invited Jack to one of his "rehearsal" sessions with the MGM musicians. Luckily it turned out to be a night when most of the musicians showed up and André could conduct the piece he'd planned on conducting, Brahms's Fourth Symphony. He wanted very much for his father to be pleased that night. Jack sat alone in the dimly lighted school auditorium as André led his men in and safely out of the Brahms Fourth. As they left the building, having heard nothing from his father, André could contain his curiosity no more. "Well, how was it?" "Fine, fine," Jack answered, "but of course it's not the Boston Symphony, is it?"

Again André had to look to his peers and superiors at the studio for encouragement. His efforts on *The Sun Comes Up* were rewarded with ever-expanding responsibilities. He was now an official composer-conductor, no longer relegated to the hackwork. He still worked on assignment but the assignments came from producers, not music directors. The music tracks of the films he worked on were his responsibility.

He didn't write every note in a film, no more than any other music director did, and he is quick to give credit to those arrangers, nameless and unrecognized outside a fifty-mile radius of Los Angeles, who gave him the same kind of backup he'd so recently been called upon to provide for other music directors. André was climbing the Hollywood ladder step by step, toward some end he steadfastly refused to question, becoming more and more like people he didn't admire. But even if he couldn't see that he was different, there always seemed to be someone like Miklós Rózsa around to remind him:

> In those days I think there must have been only two composers in Hollywood who conducted from an orchestra score, Bernard Herrmann and myself. Everybody else used a piano reduction, which was called a PD, from the old vaudeville days. Most of them had never set eyes on a score in their lives; they could follow two or three staves of music and that was it. I'll never forget the awakening I had when I wrote my first music for Paramount, just as an arranger of course. I was sitting there listening and I heard the conductor ask the orchestra, "Now who has the F-sharp?" The conductor has to *ask?* Well, I found out that's what they all did. But when I saw André imitating what he saw, conducting from one of those PDs, I had to step in and give him hell. I got him in my office and I said, "No, not for you." He said, "Ah, but it's so cumbersome to use a score." I said, "It is not cumbersome. You just have to get used to it. These other idiots maybe can't do any better, but you can." From that day on he used a score. He wasn't a technician like most of the others. He was a musician.

In 1949, the year of MGM's twenty-fifth anniversary, André's films included two murder thrillers. One was *Tension,* produced by Robert Sisk, who'd given him his first major assignment the year before. The second was *Scene of the Crime*, which starred Van Heflin, Arlene Dahl, and Gloria De Haven. He was picked as music director for that picture by producer Harry Rapf, but Rapf died during the early stages of production and Louis B. Mayer gave the picture to a personal friend of his. The new producer may not have known much about music, but he sure knew what he liked. He summoned André into his newly acquired office and told him just what he wanted for his main title music and theme:

"I can't remember the name, but you know it. It's that Spanish song that goes ah-YA-da-da-daaah, da-da-YA-da-da-daaah, da-da-YA . . . What's the name?"

"Sounds something like 'Cielito Lindo.' "

"That's it. Yeah. See, I knew you'd know it. Now I want you to kind of slip that music in all through the picture, okay?"

When his music director expressed a degree of wonderment at the thought of a Mexican love song "all through" a violent crime drama set in the streets of New York, the producer shrugged and said, "Who cares why? I like it a lot. It's my favorite song. Use it." André used it.

It seemed as though MGM wouldn't release a picture in those days unless it contained at least a song or two, as though the studio were constantly reminding the public that *it* was the studio that gave them all those great musicals. Musicals were indeed the hallmark of Metro and it was probably inevitable that a composer with as much talent as André was showing would sooner or later be assigned to one. The picture was *Three Little Words*, produced by one of the men who'd auditioned André nearly five years before, Jack Cummings.

André's only previous encounter with a musical had been *It Happened in Brooklyn* in 1946. Curiously enough, that one was a musical about songwriters and so was *Three Little Words*. The plot was based on the real-life team of Bert Kalmar and Harry Ruby. Fred Astaire was Kalmar, Vera-Ellen his wife and dancing partner, and Red Skelton played Ruby, with

Arlene Dahl as Eileen Percy, the silent movie star who became
Mrs. Ruby. The young dance team of Debbie Reynolds and
Carleton Carpenter made its first film appearance in *Three Little Words* and gorgeous Gloria De Haven was cast as her own
mother, who had been a star of Broadway.

Though overshadowed and outweighed by MGM's release
that year of *Annie Get Your Gun*, the film became a hit at the
box office, with the audiences and even with the critics. The
success of *Three Little Words* has to be credited in some degree to André Previn, since there was scarcely a frame in the
film that went unscored, it being a musical about music. He
managed to integrate no fewer than fourteen Kalmar-Ruby
standards into the score, turning several of them into brilliant
dance numbers for choreographer Hermes Pan. He left very little room for doubt that his rightful place at MGM was the
musical factory.

Three Little Words did something else for André: it gave
him the opportunity to work once again with Gloria De
Haven, with whom he had struck far more than a working relationship during the production of *Scene of the Crime*. In fact,
André and Gloria were an "item" around Hollywood. She was
the first in a long line of famous, sometimes controversial fe-
males with whom his name would be linked in the gossip columns.

Gloria first passed through the MGM gates in 1940, when
she was a very young, but already well-developed teenager. Her
movie debut that year was *Susan and God* and there followed
a string of relatively unsuccessful roles in relatively obscure
films. By 1943, however, her curves were even curvier and she
was given the chance to show them off in the featured dance
numbers of three films, *Thousands Cheer, Best Foot Forward*,
and *Broadway Rhythm*.

By 1949, when she was dating André, Gloria's figure had ma-
tured and she was no longer an ingenue. The once shoulder-
length, brown hair was now bobbed and blond; the image was
sultry but playful, not a far cry from the look Marilyn Monroe
would make famous. For the publicity cameras on the occasion
of the MGM twenty-fifth anniversary, Gloria gave the lens a

direct, come-hither stare; among the fifty-nine "Silver Jubilee Stars of Metro-Goldwyn-Mayer" she is pictured just below Katharine Hepburn and just above Lionel Barrymore. MGM had her pegged for stardom.

But the very next year she bowed out of the studio in *Summer Stock*, the film that was also Judy Garland's last, for Metro. Chances are, her exit from MGM would have ended her romance with André anyway, but outside forces had already conspired to break them apart.

Even as *Three Little Words* was entering the final stages of production, André received a notice from the Los Angeles draft board. Studio executives pulled strings and André was allowed to stay on until the picture was completed, but just as his first musical was being released to movie houses around the country, André Previn was boarding a train to khaki obscurity. In 1945 Papa Jack Previn and Uncle Charlie Previn had agonized and argued over whether they should involve young André in the movie business; in 1950 it looked as though Uncle Sam might have the last word.

VII

They had a farewell luncheon in the MGM commissary for André, complete with bad jokes from the boys and tears from the girls. After all, they all assumed that his eventual destination was Korea. To the studio crowd he was still a boy, with his slightness and almost studied timidity, even though he'd already celebrated his twenty-first birthday.

In some ways he was still a child. The wild-party-and-chorus-girls fantasy notwithstanding, André really understood very little of life out beyond the walls of the studio. And on the morning after the farewell party, standing alone on a train platform in the predawn chill and peering down the tracks toward the vanishing point, the future seemed very uncertain.

He traveled to the United States Army training facility at Camp Cook where older men who were professional soldiers began his instruction in killing, survival, and abject obedience. His war was against drill sergeants. His most grueling survival tests involved calisthenics, forced marches, inspections, potato peelings and chipped beef. He had followed rules before, at MGM, but in the Army there was no prize of music.

It is doubtful that any of his superiors at Camp Cook had any idea he was a musician, not at first. At the moment his name might have been flashing across the silver screens of America, but in the Army he was just another buck private, another serial number. Some of the officers carried batons; he carried a mop or a shovel.

"Hey, Previn."

André straightened up and peered into the broiling sun from the ditch he was digging. There was the silhouette of the corporal who worked the HQ desk.

"Lieutenant's lookin' for you."

"Be right there." Looking for *me?* He turned over in his mind all his minor infractions of the past week, wondering which one he'd been caught at. "What's he want?"

"Somethin' about a telegram for you."

Telegrams meant bad news. He pushed his shovel into the sandy bottom of the latrine he was composing and pulled himself out. His father hadn't been feeling well. His mother was broken up by his departure . . . What else?

At the lieutenant's desk he managed a stiffer salute than he normally gave and barked out, "Sir, Private Previn reporting, *sir.*"

"At ease, soldier." The lieutenant was working on some triplicate papers and didn't look up for a minute, merely flicked his wrist in answering salute. He shuffled through a pile of papers on his desk and drew out a folded yellow sheet. "Got a telegram for you here, says you been nominated for a, uh, what was it? Oh, yeah, Academy Award."

André almost lost his composure at that one: the only status symbol that meant anything in the film industry. He took the telegram from the lieutenant, stammering his thanks as though the officer had had something to do with the nomination. He was told to get back to his duties and was dismissed.

He'd actually been nominated for his first musical, for *Three Little Words.* He wanted to run and tell someone. How did he go about reserving a seat at the presentation? Then he was back at his ditch, looking down at his shovel, remembering there was no one there to tell and no way he'd be going to the presentation. He was a buck private digging a latrine. The Army had a nice way of putting things into perspective.

As it turned out, the only thing André missed by not attending the Academy Award ceremonies was the disappointment of hearing his name read out only once, as a nominee. Someone else's picture got the award for best musical score. His condition improved slightly when basic training ended. He was made a private first class and sent to a remote base in the state of Washington, near the Canadian border, a way station on the journey to Korea. Rigor became mere drudgery and suddenly he found time on his hands, time to read some of the books on music he'd brought along or which had been sent from home.

> During those hours of enforced boredom I suddenly realized that there was nothing musical I *had* to work on, that I did not have to put in all those prescribed hours of musical activity. Suddenly I began studying seriously for the first time. All that time that could have been spent drinking beer at the PX I spent coming to grips with the fact that music was not simply making a noise. I read for the first time John W. Sullivan's *Beethoven—His Spiritual Development*. That was an eye-opener. I studied pocket scores in my bunk and I finally got around to reading my old teacher Ernst Toch's book on the shaping forces of music.

One book he did not get around to reading was a volume his father had sent him for Christmas, Hector Berlioz's textbook on the fundamentals of orchestration, a trade he had already plied for five years with a certain amount of success. "Of course it interested me, but when you're young and you've been working a lot of hours at a craft, then somebody gives you a book on how to do it, you don't recognize it as a reference book, you take it as a put-down. I had the rug pulled out from under me momentarily, again by my father." This is not to imply that André had anything against polishing his skills. Several years later Leo Arnaud made him a present of a long out-of-print book on orchestration by Widor which contains an appendix listing "every double, triple, and quadruple stop on every string instrument and tells you which ones are easy, which ones are difficult, and which ones are impossible. Now there's a practical book."

At any rate, during his Army days André seems to have come to an appreciation for the first time of the value of study

for study's sake. At the same time, he began to begrudge the
Army all the time he had to spend away from music and he
began to look around for a way to make music and the military
less incompatible.

He'd noticed there was background music on most of the
training films shown at Camp Cook and he began to wonder
whether there might be an alternative to Korea. He found out
that the films were produced at the Army Signal Corps' huge
motion picture factory on Long Island, just outside New York
City. André figured that if he could set a murder mystery to
"Cielito Lindo," he ought to be able to create the perfect
music for the Army's films on C rations and venereal disease.

His application for transfer was summarily turned down.
Later he found out that the officer in charge of the Long Island studio had once been turned down himself by Hollywood
and so had nothing but disdain for "Hollywood people." He
wanted none of them in his outfit. That was the first time
André really experienced the use of the word "Hollywood" as
a pejorative.

The application for transfer did set his credits circulating
among the top brass and soon he got another offer, from
Washington, D.C., where the Army conducted a music school
for leaders of all the military bands it maintained around the
world. At last someone in the Army had recognized that rifles
were not his forte; he was invited to accept a commission as a
second lieutenant and teach music. The offer sounded too
good to be true, and it was.

The string attached was three years long. In order to teach,
you had to be an officer. In order to become an officer, you had
to sign up for an additional three years of Army life. André
had nearly completed the first year of his two-year hitch and
he felt like a prisoner being asked to extend his own sentence
for good behavior. He knew it would mean a bearable existence, a raise in pay, a job in music, and an apartment off base
in a civilized city. But somehow he felt there was just as great
a chance of being sent to Korea as a second lieutenant; in fact,
the chances were about two years greater. He pictured himself

André (age eight) with Jack.

André and Betty, Carmel, 1953.

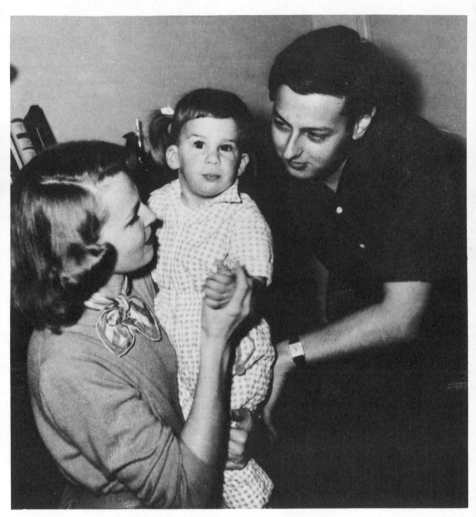

André, Betty, and Claudia, 1956.

Festival Hall, London (Claudia, Papa, Alicia), c. 1964.

Dory Previn. *(Courtesy Wide World Photos)*

In the late 1960s with the London Symphony Orchestra's General Secretary, Harold Lawrence. *(Courtesy Mary Lawrence)*

Itzhak Perlman (second from right in front row) sits in with the violin section at a London Symphony Orchestra rehearsal.

A bearded Previn in Romania in 1970 with writer Anthony Hopkins. *(Courtesy Harold Lawrence)*

At a post-concert reception with Mia Farrow and Maestro and Mrs. Carlo Maria Giulini. *(Courtesy Mike Evans)*

relaxed moment in rehearsal with
ac Stern (note the message on
ern's sweat shirt).

Backstage with Isaac Stern moments before they go onstage.

With members of the London Symphony Orchestra boarding a flight on tour.

as leader of a company band on the front lines and turned
down the offer.

In the Army one does not refuse a commission without
reprisal. To the professional military man, that was like slap-
ping Uncle Sam in the face. For the next several months
André felt he was back in basic training, pulling KP and
guard duty with astonishing frequency. On Thanksgiving
night, in 1950, Pfc Previn stood in wet falling snow, an M-1
rifle slung over his shoulder, guarding an almost deserted base
against no one in particular and feeling very sorry for himself.

Through the snow sloshed the only creature more pitiable
than himself, a bone-soaked dog wandering through the night.
There was an old jeep parked just inside the gates, its canvas
top in place, and André decided he'd get the dog inside the
jeep. That way at least one of them could dry out. But no matter how loud he whistled and clucked at the dog, the dog only
stared at him. He decided he'd have to carry the dog to the
jeep.

"Okay, boy. Good dog." He tentatively scratched the soggy
hair behind an ear but got no reaction from the dog, so he
bent down and wrapped his arm around the animal to pick
him up. Unfortunately, André's recognition factor among dogs
had, if anything, deteriorated since his snubbing by Lassie, for
this time the dog actually bit him.

Eventually the United States Army decided that ungrateful
Pfc Previn had suffered enough and he was elevated to the
rank of corporal, which only meant that he had to pay someone to sew stripes onto his sleeves, since he hadn't the faintest
idea how to manage a needle and thread. More importantly,
someone decided it was time to make use of his musical skills,
so he was transferred from the holding tank in Washington to
the Sixth Army Band at the Praesidio in San Francisco.

"Welcome to the unit, soldier. What's your instrument?"

"Piano, sir."

"No good."

"No good, sir?"

"Dammit, man, what are you going to do with a piano on a
parade ground? Carry it on your hip like a snare drum?"

"No, sir."

"We'll have to find you something else, soldier. You willing to take up another instrument for your country?"

At this point André was thinking very little of his country and a great deal of guard duty, KP, and M-1s; he'd have played ocarina if the captain had asked him to.

"Flute. You look like a flute man to me."

But his looks were deceiving. He labored at it until his fingers ached and his lips had a permanent purse, but it was no good. Then he heard that the captain was looking for band transcriptions of a few symphonic pieces. Ignoring Basic Rule No. 1 of military life, André volunteered for arranging duty. The lack of a portable instrument was forgotten and André was left alone with his pencils and staff paper, turning out band arrangements of everything he could get his hands on.

> I did it all. Of course, there were the predictable marches from operas and such, but I also did band arrangements of things like Chabrier's *España* and even the Shostakovich First Symphony. Now how's that for pointless endeavor?

Before long he was planning band and ensemble concerts for special events such as generals' wives' birthdays, and often he would conduct as well. There was even an international meeting of heads of state in San Francisco that year, hosted by the music-loving Harry S. Truman. As part of the entertainment package André was asked to plan a program with Norman Carol, a violinist when he wasn't marching. The catch was that the President's protocol advisers insisted on a nonnationalistic program. One would hardly want to offend the Chinese by playing something Russian, and so on.

"I've got it then," said André, giving Norman Carol a wink. "We'll give you an evening of Swiss music."

"Perfect," said the President's top man. "The Swiss aren't coming and they're neutral anyhow."

Everyone shook hands and parted friends, but when they got outside Carol turned to André in a panic. He didn't know any Swiss music.

"Neither do I," said André.

"Well, how in the hell are we going to play it?"

"We're not. We'll give them German music and French music and Russian music and any other kind of music we feel like playing. We simply won't tell anybody the titles of the pieces and they'll never ask."

They never did ask. Norman Carol, by the way, survived the experience and the Army and went on to become concertmaster of the Philadelphia Orchestra.

There were other serious musicians in the Sixth Army Band, soldiers with whom André would get together for chamber music sessions. Through them he was introduced to the man who would continue his music education where Mario Castelnuovo-Tedesco had left off.

Pierre Monteux was at that time music director of the San Francisco Symphony and also was holding conducting classes for advanced students on the West Coast. Quickly André became one of his star pupils and he no longer spent his passes traveling down to Los Angeles; he wanted to absorb everything Monteux could give him. Once again he was reminded that conducting was his true vocation.

Most of Monteux's lessons were private, in the Frenchman's living room, but on occasion some of the privileged students were allowed to conduct a rehearsal orchestra made up of San Francisco Symphony players and student musicians. Monteux would sit in the rear of the hall, making corrections when necessary.

Once I was conducting one of the Haydn symphonies. I don't remember which one, but it had one of those typical Haydn last movements that sort of rollicks along. When it was done Monteux called me over to him and said, in his wonderfully thick French accent, "Tell me, Monsieur Previn, in the last movement there, did you find the orchestra was playing well?" I had to stop and think for a moment, for I felt certain I was about to step into a trap, but finally I had to say, "Yes, maître, I did think they were play-

ing rather well." "Good," he said, "so did I. Next
time they're playing well don't interfere with them."

I tell you, that message should be hammered out in
brass and hung up in every conductor's dressing
room: "When it's going well, don't interfere." There
were so many important things Monteux said, things
said almost in passing but things I've never forgotten,
things I've used every day since. For example, he had
a predilection for rhythmic clarity which has become
a part of my own philosophy and has stayed with me
all these years. He was a truly venerable person, Monteux, the kindest, wisest man I can remember.

Monteux was concise and incisive about conducting but he
could be rather obtuse when it came to matters other than
conducting. André recalls and often recounts the story of his
arriving for a lesson one morning, crestfallen at the rumor
that his unit was about to be shipped to the Far East. Monteux did his best to console him and to set him straight.

"Why are you so unhappy today, my boy?"

"I'm about to be sent to Tokyo," André moaned, wringing
his khaki cap. "And you know what that means, maître."

"Sacre! You must not go there."

"I don't believe I have a choice."

"No, no, no. I fell for that once myself. I was talked into
going over there to Japan. But let me assure you, that Tokyo
Orchestra is no good."

"But it's not the orchestra that . . ."

"What's more, the experience will do absolutely nothing for
you. The strings, maybe, are not so bad, but the winds are
hopeless; you can do nothing with them. That is one offer you
must turn down. It's a great waste of time. Besides, there's that
war going on not too far away and it could be dangerous."

As it turned out, André's fears of being sent to the combat
zone continued to plague him for his entire two-year hitch, but
he never was sent overseas. The war in Korea went on without
him and he was promoted to first sergeant before his discharge
in 1952. His parents expected him to return immediately to

Los Angeles but André decided to stay on with Monteux, knowing there was still a great deal to be learned.

More than ever now, he knew he had to conduct and Monteux's granary of musical knowledge seemed inexhaustible. He rented a room above a garage, floored with linoleum, the hills and valleys of which might have tested the torque of San Francisco's trolleys. The nearest bathroom was down an outdoor flight of stairs in the garage. He lived on his savings from MGM, plus whatever he could pick up by playing piano and making arrangements for a local radio station that still clung to the tradition of live music broadcasts. "Somehow I kept it all together. Even when you're broke, San Francisco is a wonderful city. I enjoyed myself a lot and I made a lot of friends."

He took in whatever he could afford of the city's culture, finding it vastly different from Los Angeles. He roamed the art galleries, haunted the theaters and concert halls, spent late nights in its clubs and coffeehouses. He also perforce discovered every cheap, hole-in-the-wall eatery that San Francisco had to offer, since even this period of "la vie bohème," did not prompt him to learn what he has never learned: how to cook.

"I am," André confesses, "perhaps the only guy in the world who can ruin a sandwich." It may be a throwback to his mother's early resistance to culinary efforts, though even Charlotte learned how to cook when she had to. André, instead, sought out girls who would cook for him or, if worse came to worst, give him step-by-step instructions.

> One night I was working at home and I really wanted a steak. At that moment that was what I craved more than anything else. So I went out and bought one, then wondered, now what do I *do* with the damned thing. It was just sitting there all red and floppy. I called a lady friend and said, "Now don't laugh, just tell me how to make it edible." After finding out what equipment I had and how I liked it cooked she guessed I should grill it for about nine miuntes on each side. I thanked her and slapped the steak on the grill, only then remembering that my watch was out for repairs. Suddenly it came to me that I knew a

piece of music that ran just about nine minutes:
Berlioz's *Roman Carnival* Overture. So I stood there
in my little kitchen, going through *Roman Carnival*
in my head. When I got to the end I flipped the
steak and hummed it again, just like turning over a
record. The steak was perfect.

Whether it was flipping steak or swinging a baton, André
gathered the expertise he needed from whatever sources presented themselves. So it happened that when Leonard Bernstein brought the Israel Philharmonic into San Francisco
André was in the audience, eager to learn.

His only previous encounter with Bernstein had been in
1949 when Bernstein was in Hollywood working on *On the
Town* for MGM. "It was at a party at Gene Kelly's house,"
Bernstein recalls, "and André was introduced to me. Someone
said he was a German kid, about fifteen or sixteen, I think [in
point of fact André was twenty], who was trying to make his
way in Hollywood as a pianist. For some reason he knew my
Age of Anxiety."

Bernstein's still-new composition was difficult, though on his
Monday Evening Concerts programs André had been called on
to play far more elusive and out-of-the-mainstream music. At
Gene Kelly's house, André found himself in the old role of
sideshow attraction, amazing the guests just as he'd wowed
them in Berlin by reading from Gibbon. Most impressed at the
way André's fingers found their way confidently about the keyboard was Bernstein himself. "He just sat down and played it
and he knocked me out."

It would have been nice if that initial encounter between
the "enfant terrible" of classical music and the film industry's
"Wunderkind" had led to something. A "Young People's Concert" or a summer concert with the New York Philharmonic or
a guest appearance in Israel might have cleanly and quickly
broken the spell of Hollywood. But André never asked for that
sort of favor and Bernstein never offered it.

It may simply have been the first instance of André's being
snubbed by the musical establishment because of his Holly-

wood lineage. Certainly Leonard Bernstein wanted nothing more to do with the film industry after *On the Town*. Thirty years later he is still bitter about that experience: "Roger Edens, an associate producer who fancied himself a composer, decided to put six of his own songs into the film, including one called "On the Town." I was young and naïve of course, but the fact remains that there are six songs in that picture which are not good and are not by me, yet people assume I wrote them. I resent that." (Bernstein's single encore in Hollywood was the score for *On the Waterfront*.)

André, after that initial meeting, grew to admire Bernstein's work on records and, when the opportunity came at last, he looked forward to hearing and seeing him conduct in person. And with Bernstein, especially in those days, *seeing* was an integral part of believing.

> He was still very young then and fifty times more balletic than he is today. When he came out to that podium, he just electrified the audience with, I think it was the Schumann Second Symphony; well . . . It was the best thing I'd ever heard or seen. I thought: that's it.

The serpentine arms, the whiplash movements of the head, the tap-dancing feet were all part of Lenny's music. He made music with his whole body and it all worked to draw the music out of the orchestra. André decided it would be well nigh impossible for a group of musicians to play under those circumstances in any manner other than what the conductor wanted.

In those days the icon was Toscanini, who used only his right hand, flicking the baton like a lion tamer gesturing with his puny whip, daring his charges to defy him, staring them down with unswerving eye contact. Lenny was the seeming antithesis of all that, the iconoclast. Had he been born with a third arm or four feet, he'd have used them all. Nor did he hesitate to shut his eyes when the spirit moved him. To many young conductors of the fifties, Bernstein was the Messiah. André that night in San Francisco became an absolute and abject disciple.

I was so knocked out by what I saw I went to another
of his concerts the following night in Berkeley, then
to another one the night after that across the Bay.
For three days I sort of bathed myself in Bernstein
and after that I felt as though I'd been baptized in
the One True Technique.

André could hardly wait for his next session with Monteux,
bowled over as he was by his conversion. It turned out that the
next session was his turn to conduct the rehearsal orchestra.
With the image of the dancing divinity graven on his memory,
he awaited his old master's call.

"Monsieur Previn?"

"Oui, maître?" At last.

"Give us the Brahms Fourth, s'il vous plaît."

He ascended the platform, feeling positively aglow with rec-
titude, then launched into the fiery sermon of a symphony, giving himself over entirely to the music, lunging with it, breath-
ing with it, undulating and palpitating and . . .

A soft clapping broke the mood.

He stopped, opened his eyes and turned around. Monteux
was beckoning from the rear of the hall. Why, he wondered,
after only eight bars? He stepped down from the podium,
scratching his head with the baton as he walked up the aisle.
The old man signaled to him to bend down closer so that he
might speak softly, privately.

"Oui, maître?"

"You went to see Bernstein last night." It was not a question.

"Yes?"

"Go back up there and do it again, please."

No further words were spoken and none were needed. André
felt ashamed of himself for violating one of Monteux's credos,
that a conductor's duty was to the music, to the orchestra, and
to the audience, in that order. What they all wanted was not
showmanship but rhythmic clarity: tell the musicians when to
hit the notes, how long to hold them, and how loud to make
them; that's all the conductor's up there for. The fiddlers and
horn players and Brahms will take care of the rest.

In later years the experience would be turned into one of André's favorite anecdotes, assuring him of a laugh from interviewers and television audiences, but there was nothing funny about it at the time. He must have felt shaken and humiliated, suddenly unsure what basket his eggs belonged in. The rebuff from Monteux was no doubt quite correct, and it laid the foundation for a philosophy that has grown into almost a mania for André Previn the conductor. Though he tries very hard not to denigrate other conductors who do not share his philosophy, Bernstein and Mehta for example, he insists that showmanship has no place on his platform, that by attempting to add one iota to an audience's appreciation of the music, or even to an orchestra's appreciation, a conductor in fact detracts from the music itself.

> I guess you simply don't study with someone good and not try to emulate him. I admired Monteux, I adored him. I saw the results he achieved with his precision and with that self-effacing podium style of his. "Self-effacing" only stands to reason because, after all, *you* didn't write the piece, did you? At the same time, I disagree with people who criticize Lenny for his "balletics" and his "gymnastics." That's nonsense. His personality is best expressed by what he does and the musical results he achieves are a direct result of that. He doesn't say to himself while he's conducting, "Now I'm going to jump six feet in the air because it will look good." If he jumps it's because it comes out of his own musical thinking and there's nothing wrong with that.

As he came to see it, Bernstein's style was a suit of clothes tailored for someone else; André's own personality was less demonstrative, more introspective, more controlled. That was the reasoning process, André says, and somehow it sounds just as premeditated—just as contrived?—as if he'd done it the other way around. "I used to be all over the shop, as they say in England, really flying around. But I discovered that by leaping into the air you don't really make the sforzando come out any louder."

So he continued to study with Monteux, remaining in San Francisco for the better part of a year after his discharge from the Army. It was enlightening, it was enriching, it was invaluable. But it was taking him nowhere. There was no diploma, no "terminal degree" he could hope to take away from it, nothing he could use to gain magic admittance into the ranks of professional conductors, which was what he wanted most. No one was standing by with a satchel of contracts waiting for Monteux's best students. Nor was he suited to the contemplative life of the long-term student. True, he was at the same time gaining increasing prominence as a jazz pianist, but for three years now he'd been away from the business of music, at which, since his childhood, he'd been grinding out a living, performing or composing or conducting.

It was time for André to go home again, to Hollywood.

PART TWO

The Jazz Life

VIII

In San Francisco it is that time of day when the morning fog has lifted and the afternoon rain is waiting to begin. On a Saturday in the early fall of 1952 two young men are leaving a cheap hotel looking for a cheaper coffee shop. One of the young men is André Previn, at twenty-four an emerging sensation of the West Coast jazz scene. The other man is Lenny Bruce, comedian of outrage. The conversation, as remembered nearly three decades later, went something like this:

PREVIN: God I'm hungry.

BRUCE: Me too. Is that the sun? What's it doing up at this time of day?

PREVIN: Are you kidding? It's almost lunchtime.

BRUCE: Since when do you eat lunch, André? I don't know about you—all I need is coffee. That should be pretty easy to find around here. What time did you get to bed?

PREVIN: Oh, maybe three o'clock. What about you?

BRUCE: Who knows? But it had to be pretty late because I was worn out. That's the only reason I was able to sleep in that bed. Do you believe this place?

PREVIN: I've been in worse.

BRUCE: In my room the rug and the pillow have one thing in common: they both smell the same.

PREVIN: What were you doing with your nose on the floor?

BRUCE: There was no grindstone around.

PREVIN: (Stopping, pointing to storefront display) Say, look at that.

BRUCE: Look at *what?*

PREVIN: I don't believe it. Twenty-five dollars!

BRUCE: Believe *what*, André?

PREVIN: Those books. The three big ones. That's the Emily Anderson translation of Mozart's letters. A teacher of mine had them once. That set looks used, but still at twenty-five dollars they're hard to pass up.

BRUCE: If you don't have the twenty-five dollars, you've no choice but to pass them up.

PREVIN: You're right. The price might as well be twenty-five *hundred.*

BRUCE: (As they walk on) You're really bugged, aren't you?

PREVIN: Jesus, I'd love to have those books. They're a steal.

They go into a coffee shop, filled with tables filled with crumbs and not another customer in sight. They select a table with crumbs but no ashes and André sits down.

BRUCE: I'll be right back. Do me a favor and order me a coffee, okay?

PREVIN: Where you going?

BRUCE: Don't worry, I'll be back before you can say "Emily Anderson." Don't forget the coffee.

Lenny Bruce is gone, out the door, leaving André puzzled. Why the hasty retreat? But as he muses, the waitress materializes and André orders the coffee. Lenny has never before pulled a disappearing act like that. What can he be up to? And why the mystery? In his act Lenny Bruce is famous for doing the unpredictable, but not in his camaraderie with André. He toys with the idea of getting up and walking out, but the waitress is returning with two cups, coffee slopping over into the saucers. Moments later Lenny appears in the doorway, looking over his shoulder. As he approaches the table there is a wide grin on his face. The three volumes of Mozart letters are held firmly under his arm.

PREVIN: Lenny, how in the name of God did you get these?

BRUCE: Elementary, my dear Previn. You acted as though

they were the Gutenberg Bible, or something. You said
they were a steal . . . so I stole them.

PREVIN: Are you out of your mind?

BRUCE: If you believe the papers, I am.

PREVIN: But this is *really* crazy, Lenny.

BRUCE: Wait a minute! You want them, don't you? You can
use them, can't you? So just letting them sit there gathering mildew in that store window, that would be crazy.

PREVIN: But if I were that desperate, I could come up with
the money, Lenny. I mean . . .

BRUCE: Look, do me a favor. Just take these heavy books and
put them under your chair or something before the guy
who runs that lousy bookshop comes running in here
screaming all kinds of obscenities.

PREVIN: I don't think you're listening to me, Lenny. I . . .

BRUCE: I don't think you're listening to *me*. Look, if someone
has twenty-five bucks to blow and spends it on a friend, so
what? I mean it, what's so great about that? But here I
go and put my whole career on the line for my friend and
what does he do? He reads me the Ten Commandments.
Suppose I were to get busted for shoplifting, then what?
Then it's printed in every newspaper up and down the
West Coast, I get fired from the club, and I can't get a
job anywhere for at least a year. Those books are a *real*
present.

PREVIN: That's the most convoluted philosophy I ever heard.

BRUCE: You've got to be kidding. Yours is the most ungrateful
reaction *I've* ever heard.

PREVIN: Hey, hey. Don't go playing hurt on me. Outraged
I can take, but not hurt.

BRUCE: Say you're grateful.

PREVIN: I'm grateful, I'm grateful.

BRUCE: Say you love those big fat books.

PREVIN: I love them. Only you didn't sign them. If you give
someone a gift of books, you have to autograph them.

BRUCE: I like that. You want me to sign them? That's like
John Hancock stealing the Declaration of Independence
before he signed it. Okay, give me a pen.

Opening Volume I, Lenny begins to write on the flyleaf. He seems to be thinking about it a great deal. At last he finishes off with a flourish and hands the book to André.

PREVIN: My God, Lenny, it looks like a monologue.
BRUCE: Read it.

ANDRÉ sees a column of figures, a descending scale of prices, with an X through each but the last figure:

> "$25.00" crossed out.
> "$17.50" crossed out.
> "$10.00" crossed out.
> "$5.00" crossed out.
> "$.75 crossed out.
> "Take it, friend. Nobody's looking."
> "Love, Lenny."

Of course today those volumes are highly prized among André's impressive collection of books, rarer even than some of his autographed manuscript scores. It's probably safe to say that André is the only person in the world who can so vividly recount anecdotes about Lenny Bruce on the one hand and Sir William Walton on the other. In a way, you might say he owes that distinction to a blind black piano player, Art Tatum.

It's an oft-repeated story and, by all accounts, a true one that when Thomas "Fats" Waller found out that Art Tatum was in his nightclub show he stopped playing and addressed the audience. The quote is: "Ladies and Gentlemen, I play the piano, but God is in the house tonight." That, from a pianist who was himself a legend in his own time, gives an idea of the reverence in which Tatum was and still is held in jazz circles. If other pianists were virtuosos, then Tatum was *two* virtuosos, for sometimes he sounded as though he had four hands. André discovered jazz the day he heard Tatum play for the first time.

Much as he'd formed his first impressions of other aspects of American life, André got his first ideas about jazz from the movies. He thought a jazz musician was "a guy in a hotel dance band with a white tuxedo and a funny hat." He did not question his father's disdain for this brand of music until he was fourteen years old and, for the first time, a scratchy, out-of-print recording of Art Tatum fell into his hands. The tune was "Sweet Lorraine" and it sounded unlike anything André had ever heard. He "just fell apart. It was unbelievable." Rather quaintly, he assumed some of the credit must go to the song's composer.

> This was wonderful piano playing. The music was harmonically fascinating and the man's technique was impeccable. I thought, what a song! So I went around looking for the sheet music of "Sweet Lorraine" and, when I found it, here was this pleasant, folksy little tune. Where the devil had all those notes come from? Then it dawned on me that this Tatum fellow must have arranged it all himself. He'd taken that puerile thirty-two-bar melody and made ingenious music out of it. Suddenly I became very interested.

Haunting the record shops of Los Angeles, André soon came up with a beginner's collection of Tatum. He gave up trying to buy the sheet music, since what he admired was Tatum's arrangements; the only way he'd be able to play them would be to notate each song from the record, note by note. So he did, blunting several packets of old-style cactus phonograph needles in the process.

That process was a long and a painstaking one, for Tatum's playing was crammed with fists full of notes and harmonic changes that might look like mistakes on paper if you hadn't heard them first. Here was a musical magician whose illusions remain to this day something of a mystery to his fellows. No less a jazz pianist than Oscar Peterson, a man André calls "a pianist of blinding virtuosity," tells of being stunned by his first hearing of a Tatum record; Peterson at first refused to believe anything but that he'd heard two pianists and a bass player, not just one man on one piano.

Yet André had so keen an ear that he managed to ferret out Tatum's notes and chords from the records. Soon he had pages and pages of handwritten music, each song in the Tatum version requiring many times more sheets than the simple tunes on which they were based. Sometimes just a few bars would be so overflowing with notes and movement that they'd need an entire page just for themselves. André went on with this arduous, monk-like work until he'd copied out all the music. Then he began learning to play the pieces à la Tatum. Throughout, it never occurred to him that Art Tatum might simply have been making it all up as he went along.

> After I had them all written out note for note I started teaching myself to play them, like you'd learn a composition of Mozart's. I simply didn't understand what jazz was all about. I figured this was the way it was done and I wanted to take a crack at it. Finally I learned to play Tatum's pieces and I practiced them for hours on end. Slowly it began to dawn on me: the trick was not to *play* this stuff but to make it up as Tatum had done. A jazz player had to be his own composer and play not premeditatively but make up his music on the spot. Improvisation. *That's* what jazz was all about.

But André kept making wrong turns in his exploration of jazz. Now that he had the Rosetta stone of improvisation, he misread the matter of style. Rather than striking out in his own direction he tried to follow the fingerprints of Tatum. He bought sheet music for other popular songs, sat them on the piano and tried to play them the way he thought Tatum might have played them. Except of course he couldn't, and he finally realized the odds against successfully imitating Tatum were overwhelming. So he began listening to other pianists, Teddy Wilson and Bud Powell and others, musicians who were successful not because they imitated Tatum or each other or anybody else, but because each had his individual style. He started out trying to copy them, but after some time he got the point and started working on playing his own way.

Part of André's misconception of jazz was that his interest in it developed concurrently with his swift immersion in the film industry so that, one way or another, his ideas of jazz were bound to be influenced by the movies. In the forties and fifties movie music could not have escaped the influence of jazz. Often film composers consciously evoked the spirit of jazz, although a Music Department like MGM's could hardly be seen as in the mainstream of jazz activity. If a movie scene called for "jazz" underlining, the music had to be written out carefully so that a hundred players could play it together and there *had* to be strings. The result was that the music coming out of the speaker system at the movie theater in Sioux Falls may have sounded like jazz, but it wasn't.

André's lack of gut appreciation of what jazz was all about was bound to be felt by other musicians who *had* that gut appreciation. Consequently, when he began playing seriously what he thought was serious jazz, André was not taken seriously. Being taken seriously did not happen, if it truly ever happened for André, until sometime in the mid fifties, after his military service and his exposure to the jazz scene in San Francisco. Nevertheless, during the preceding ten years André had carried on a love affair with jazz.

In the beginning he developed, if not a personal style, an excellent ear. He listened mostly to the studied improvisations of the big bands, whose records were commercially successful. He got to know the styles of Benny Goodman, Lester Young, Count Basie, the early Woody Herman bands, and Duke Ellington. Theirs was the music people were buying and it was music André could master technically, even if he "didn't play anything personal for a while. And by personal I don't necessarily mean good."

Impersonal though his jazz playing may have been, it helped land him his job at MGM when the studio needed a "classical" musician who could write "jazz variations" on "Three Blind Mice." Then, through his expanding contacts at MGM, André made his way into the recording studios.

Other than those early chamber music recordings he'd made with the UCLA group, André's first 78-rpm recordings were produced by a company called Sunset Records. The initial session of October 13, 1945, produced a single disc of "Blue

Skies" and "Good Enough to Keep." It was by the André Previn Trio, the sidemen being John Simmons on bass and Dave Barbour (Peggy Lee's first husband) on guitar, both acquaintances from the MGM studio orchestra. An interesting sign of Art Tatum's influence was the absence of a drummer.

The following March, André did another session for Sunset using the same instruments but different instrumentalists, Irving Ashby (guitar) and Red Callender (bass). This time six sides were pressed and Sunset released an album. André and his trio of pickup sidemen began appearing at local coffeehouses and concerts. Their fame spread and they began traveling out of town on weekends, as far afield as Phoenix and Seattle. One of their appearances in concert, a "Just Jazz" concert in Los Angeles, was recorded and released on the Modern label.

Trying to get closer to the commercially successful big band sound, he formed the André Previn All-Stars, in which he was joined by a trumpet, three saxophones, bass, and drums. The All-Stars cut two singles for Monarch, including Johnny Green's "Body and Soul" and Morgan Lewis' "How High the Moon," toward the end of 1946.

Much of this nascent jazz activity took place while André was in his final year at Beverly Hills High School and his initial year at Metro's Culver City studios. How he succeeded in doing so many things at once is not clear, but it established once and for all the breathtaking pace he has maintained ever since.

Among his peers, both in school and in the studio, the records, even though they had limited sales success, set him apart. In movie-jaded Los Angeles the mere fact that he was a sixteen-year-old working in a film studio meant nothing. But the records were something else. At MGM, producers took notice. At Beverly Hills High School he became a Big Man on Campus and the girls started paying attention to this slim, physically unexceptional boy almost to the same degree that they fawned over the captain of the football team. More significant than any of this is the fact that he now had a foot on still another branch of the entertainment tree, one which ultimately would mean a great deal to his career.

Sunset, Modern, and Monarch were not exactly major labels, being neither widely distributed nor wildly profitable. But they and other hole-in-the-wall companies provided a wellspring of new talent for the Columbias and Deccas and Capitols. André's efforts on those labels were by his own account highly unoriginal, yet they showed a keen awareness of the music and the instruments as well as a sophistication, despite his youth, that was to become André's hallmark as a jazz interpreter. Those qualities caught the ear of Walter Heebner, an artist-and-repertory man for RCA-Victor's popular music division. Heebner decided not to sign André to a multirecord contract but to try him out on a session-by-session basis.

The first album for RCA was called simply *André Previn*. It consisted of four 78 discs, all standards, performed by the André Previn Quartet, another ensemble of studio musicians from MGM. Al Viola played guitar, Jackie Mills the drums, and bass duties were shared by Charles Parnell and Lloyd Pratt. The eight sides were "But Not for Me," "This Can't Be Love," "Should I," "I Didn't Know What Time It Was," "My Shining Hour," "Hallelujah," "Just One of Those Things," and "Mad About the Boy."

For a reason or reasons which today André cannot explain, the record-buying public *was* mad about the boy. The album sold like hotcakes. In the days when best-seller lists were based on actual sales as opposed to "projections," *André Previn* was the Number 1 album in the United States for a couple of weeks. Suddenly the music world, or at least a certain segment of it, had no choice but to notice the boy wonder from Hollywood. At the time André was just as impressed with himself as everybody else was; later he came to see the album as just another in a long line of artistic cop-outs.

Those early recordings are nothing more than popular material played by a pianist with good technique and a kind of glib ear who managed occasional flashes of

imitation Tatum. They had little if anything to do
with jazz, except for the fact that they were improvised. I played with sidemen who were studio musicians, people accustomed to a role of subservience.
No matter what I was doing, be it good, bad, or
indifferent, they weren't going to egg me on to be
adventurous. Still, people bought them.

Sales reached 200,000 copies and in the forties that constituted a major success for anything that went by the name of
jazz. So Walter Heebner was quick to get André's signature on
a contract that tied him up, at least for recordings outside the
range of the film studio (where he was the exclusive property
of MGM), for two years. His next album for RCA brought in
a string section to play arrangements that sounded very much
like one of André's youthful film backgrounds. This was a de-
vice he would employ for many years and which inevitably
stained whatever claim he might otherwise have held on jazz
purism.

None of the series of albums he recorded for RCA in those
two years achieved anything like the spectacular success of the
first one, despite the fact that their formula was pretty much
the same: sophisticated, easy-to-take improvisations on standard tunes. Worse, "chasing after the success of the first one" in
an effort to fill RCA's coffers resulted in André's failure to go
on from those pleasant imitations to develop anything like a
style of his own. "Had that initial album been only moderately
successful," he laments, "maybe I could have talked the RCA
people into something different. But the best-seller's format became André Previn's magic formula. By all rights, the success
should have been repeated with the next records, but nobody
bought them."

No wonder RCA dropped André's contract in 1950, figuring
that he was only a flash in the pan. The company took one
more ore sample in 1953, after André's course through the
mainstream of San Francisco, but he allowed himself to be
talked into the same fool's-gold formula, even though by then
he had a much better idea of what jazz was all about.

IX

"Until I went into the Army my idea of jazz was dangerously close to the kind of music provided as inoffensive background music in bars." A typically self-effacing Previn remark, despite the grain of truth it contains. If his music bore a resemblance to that kind of gin-and-tonic playing, it was due more than anything to its old-fashioned taste. Throughout the first ten years of his jazz discovery André was never in the company of young jazz musicians who might have helped him wade into the mainstream. The studio men who knew or played jazz and who worked with André were all ten years or more his senior. Their heroes were Les Brown and Benny Goodman and André accepted their standards as his, as the standard of jazz in the forties. And on the turntables of mid-America, so it was. But right under André's ear, on the West Coast, there was brewing a minor revolution in jazz. Bebop. It shocked André out of his lethargy in 1950.

> Those were the days of Charlie Parker, of Milt Jackson and Dizzy Gillespie. When I got into the Army, suddenly I was thrown together with guys my own age who had been listening to that stuff. They knew I was a jazz musician and they tried to get me to talk about *their* heroes and I hadn't even heard of them. Suddenly I began listening to other people's records and realized I was in the dark. I simply had no idea what Charlie Parker was doing in that music of his. I

took up the challenge and turned myself into one of
the Coast's most rabid beboppers.

To turn himself into a bebopper, André had to turn off all
the influences under which he'd been playing for ten years. It
is one of his most telling traits, an imprint of his Teutonic heritage perhaps, that his approach to work is deadly serious. Methodical. Meticulous. He completely swore off playing jazz as
he knew it for an entire year just so he could educate himself
in the intricacies of the new wave. He did it, he says, "to as-
similate what was going on around me. The change was fascinating. I thought, here's somebody playing jazz in a way you
don't know anything about. You will now learn it."

Shortly after that stringent commitment was made, André
was transferred to San Francisco, the right place at the right
time, 1951. Carrying enough of a calling card to be admitted,
but with sufficient anonymity to be left alone, he tried his new
wings.

San Francisco was rife with jazz clubs then and I just
started going down whenever I could get off the base
and asking if I could sit in. Just to see what happened. I felt as though I'd assimilated something and
in my private playing I'd gotten loads of compliments
from my Army buddies, so I said, let's see if it works.
Well, it wasn't exactly *Young Man with a Horn*, but
it was a hell of a lot of fun. They let me into their
club. I belonged.

You know, you listen to those old records now and
they sound so . . . sweet. So naïve and funny. But
back then we thought we were really blazing the trail
of music. It was such a gas.

One of the top spots in San Francisco was the Black Hawk,
a steamy little club thick with smoke and elbows and knees,
the prototype of Hollywood's version of the jazz club. Big
names played the Black Hawk: Gillespie, Shorty Rogers, Dave
Brubeck, Oscar Peterson. André spent his weekends there,
grooving on their music, engaging in serious discussions about
it and often joining in on the piano.

The more he hung around, the more he established himself as a member of the inner circle. Soon he was going with friends to the "after hours" clubs, the smaller spots that stayed open until the morning and where the big-name players would often gather to drink and celebrate after their own gigs ended. It was a local radio announcer who became friendly with André and introduced him to this subculture and who, on an early morning in July of 1951, took him to a place called Facks's. There was a promising young singer the announcer wanted André to hear. Her name was Betty Bennett and André was instantly taken with her style. They talked. Miss Bennett was flattered by the compliments he paid her, but she had no idea that thirteen months later she would become Mrs. André Previn.

> I had the dim impression that morning that André was a British pianist. I'd heard him play a few times and I don't recall being especially impressed. My musical interest at the time was exclusively jazz. But somehow, when he came in to hear me sing, as near as I can remember it was love at first sight.

Betty had promised to perform later that morning for a group of soldiers just returning from Korea. André said he'd like to accompany her and her own accompanist was only too happy to call it a night. They had breakfast, then went down to San Francisco Bay to watch the sun come up. They made their first music together a few hours later when the troopship came in. As the song goes, who could ask for anything more?

> André is a formidable courtier, complete with lovely bouquets of roses, theater tickets, long drives in the beautiful countryside surrounding San Francisco. Add to that his considerable charm and who could resist him?

Betty Bennett was born in Lincoln, Nebraska, and brought up in Hamburg, Iowa, where her father was the local baker, her mother the local pianist. Betty recalls being taken along on her mother's musical engagements, social functions, and accompanying at Hamburg's silent-movie house, from the time she was six. Her mother loved the music of Basie, Ellington, and Waller and she communicated her love of jazz to Betty. She learned to sing along as her mother played and they shared the secret language of "jazz talk." Childhood was wonderful for Betty because she had such a "sensational" mother.

Betty went on to become one of those perennially budding songstresses who performed so regularly and all but anonymously with the big bands. "And now," the leader would say, "here's our own Betty Bennett . . ." and Betty would get up off her stool to play second fiddle to a trumpet or a clarinet in a number, then retire to her stool until once again the lyrics were thought needful of rendering. She sang with the biggest: Woody Herman, Stan Kenton, Charlie Barnet, Benny Goodman, Charlie Ventura, and Alvino Rey. In 1951 she struck out on her own and the gig at Facks's was her first solo. Shelly Manne heard her there and thought she was "a marvelous jazz singer." André found her "absolutely superb."

> She was the most musicianly jazz singer I ever met. An unsung singer, you might say. I was crazy about her singing and then I was crazy about her. She seemed like a thoroughly admirable lady with a highly developed sense of humor. That's important. I think if you meet someone with whom you can laugh a lot that's an extremely good sign.

They enjoyed each other's company a great deal during the next year in San Francisco as André finished up his service obligation and then stayed on to work with Pierre Monteux. In San Francisco's jazz circles they became, as Betty says, "an item." At that point Betty knew many more of the important jazz musicians than André did and by introducing him to her friends she helped him find work and thereby support himself in San Francisco. The more André listened to those musicians and the more he performed with them, the better he became, until "he became a first-rate jazz pianist. He had incredible facility," Betty continues, "and he was able to play like absolutely anyone he heard. As far as accompanying, he was and is the best accompanist there is." If not for this sojourn in San Francisco André might never have developed as he did, either in jazz or as a conductor. That he was able to make a go of it, André credits in large measure to Betty:

> Through Betty I met some of the really famous jazz musicians, people who for the first time would *push* me. I never became what the books would call an important jazz pianist, but I enjoyed myself and had a measure of success and there were some very good people who enjoyed playing with me. Without Betty's help I never would have met a lot of the people with whom I eventually wound up working.

André's career, in 1952, might have spun off in either of two directions. He might have devoted all his energies either to jazz as a pianist or to classical music as a conductor. Instead he chose to continue along the path of least resistance and economic certainty, returning to Los Angeles and to MGM. It was a practical move, since he and Betty had decided to get married and start a family.

They were married August 24, 1952, in the home of André's once-again studio mentor, Johnny Green. The Greens, Johnny and Bonnie, had seen André through a succession of girl-friends. Now they asked each other whether Betty was finally the right match, whether at last their adopted prodigal son would settle down. Johnny wasn't sure:

> There had been a series of improbable ladies in André's life, one of them Gloria De Haven. To us Gloria hadn't given the impression of being deeply substantive. Sure she was charming and pretty as a picture, but nowhere near as intellectual as André. I remember another one, a singer-type lady who did those Hunt's-for-the-best radio commercials for the tomato sauce. She was older than André. Betty I never had heard of until André told us they were going to get married. Bonnie suggested we give them the wedding as a present.

The ceremony, a civil one, was held in the Greens' enormous living room, where he happened to have a complete recording studio set up. Betty recalls that she was in a daze as Green walked her down the "aisle," toward a fireplace, not an altar. There was a combo playing the Wedding March and as they walked Green kept gesticulating with his hands, up and down. It took Betty a while to realize he was giving cues to the musicians and to the recording engineer. The judge read from a prepared text, which included the traditional warnings about all the little unpleasantries that one must expect in a marriage. But the bride and groom were not paying attention. They were staring at each other with stars in their eyes, though it was midafternoon.

There was a buffet on the lawn afterward and a great deal of dancing and singing and kissing and mingling among the forty or so guests. The Danny Kayes were there, the Previn family of course, Lennie Hayton, Betty Comden and Adolph Green, the Bronislaw Kapers. All the right people to make all the right columns. A few weeks later the newlyweds presented Johnny and Bonnie Green with a loving cup for giving "The Best Wedding Ever." With the hindsight of nearly thirty years, André is not so sure about that.

"We were such good friends," he observes. "We got along so well. The one thing we should not have done was get married."

X

André returned to the business of scoring films, "grinding out the work at MGM," as he puts it. But his musical heart seemed to be pining after jazz and "all those adventurous people" who were blazing the trails. At first, Los Angeles offered only opportunities to listen, and even for listening it was nothing compared to San Francisco.

But this was California, where even the musical establishment can come off as being disestablishmentarian. Even the Los Angeles Philharmonic began sharing its home with the combos in a series called Jazz at the Philharmonic. André found this a novel idea, even though his only entrée, at first, was the price of a ticket.

> I went only occasionally, because of the format. I just couldn't seem to get turned on by a whole evening of jazz with endless variations by trumpeters and saxophonists. Each set became a half-hour jam session on a concert stage and I wasn't exactly thrilled by it. But this was the format of Jazz at the Philharmonic, so I only went to hear specific artists: Dizzy, Charlie Parker, Benny Carter, Johnny Hodges, Oscar Peterson.

As a jazz performer André was still not in the same league with those men. He was a Los Angeles hometown boy who worked for the movies. Norman Granz, producer of the Jazz at the Philharmonic series, could not have been persuaded to give André one of the main concerts. However, André's return to LA coincided nicely with Granz's decision to start a touring jazz troupe and André fit in there quite well.

As a pianist with the Jazz-at-the-Philharmonic All-Stars, André went on the road and got his first real taste of what eventually he thought of as "a stupid and stupefying life," an endless round of planes, trains, buses, taxis, cheap rooms, and expensive meals. In the beginning, though, it was a lot of fun. And there was a lot of music to be learned, much of it from two men who shared the All-Stars' piano with him, Russ Freeman and Jimmy Rowles.

The early fifties held perhaps too many learning experiences for André. In jazz he was still an eclectic drifter, deriving both enjoyment and inspiration from such disparate sources as, for example, Lester Young and Jack Teagarden. "I was really impressed by Teagarden," admits André. "I found him elegant even though he was dated." He discovered Nat "King" Cole, "a wonderful pianist sadly remembered more for his voice. Most people don't realize how truly great a pianist he was." But soaring above them all was the Bird, Charlie Parker, the alto saxophonist who led the revolution in jazz. George Wein, producer of the Newport Jazz Festival, has called Charlie Parker second only to Louis Armstrong in his influence on the course of jazz. When at last he got to accompany Parker, André felt he had arrived.

> I guess it's pretty difficult to describe now the awe in which Bird was held in those days. Charlie Parker was a messianic figure. Nobody approached him. One of my most indelible musical memories is of the two nights I sat in as a substitute pianist with Charlie Parker.

In terms of his jazz experience, though he eventually mingled with all the great ones, only one other memory comes close to that one for André. It is of a night when he and Betty and some friends found themselves stopping after an already late evening at an out-of-the-way after-hours club in Watts, a place called Brother's. Known as a gathering place for jazz musicians, Brother's boasted three grand pianos which were kept in tune and in shape—a small wonder for a small jazz club.

Brother's was especially popular among local black musicians and there were two of those on hand that night to join André at the keyboards. Their names were Nat Cole and Art Tatum. Though he claims he avoided getting into a one-on-one session with "God," André's recollections of those small hours are blurred and mystical. He actually remembers clearly only that the music-making ended about 6 A.M. and that afterward the pianists and their various entourages all went out for breakfast. "It was," he smiles, "quite an education."

Thanks largely to Betty's way-paving, André was in the best company. Thanks largely to an influx of extraordinary jazz musicians into the orchestras of the film studios, André was able to put together a company of his own, a trio that bore little relation to those hastily formed combos of his pre-Army days. Like a group of chamber musicians, the members of a jazz combo are required to be a close-knit group, sharing the most intimate musical thoughts, needing to think alike and act alike. Because of his studio work and theirs, André was never able to form the sort of indestructible bond that seemed to exist among other jazz combos as, for example, Brubeck put together with Norman Bates, Joe Morello, and later Paul Desmond (though in time even the Dave Brubeck Quartet would go through personnel changes). What André did instead was to find two drummers and two bass players with whom he could work, confident that one of each would be available when he needed them. The bassmen were Red Mitchell and Leroy Vinnegar, the drummers Frank Capp and Shelly Manne. Their association began in 1955 and would stretch over the next ten years. Of all of them, it was probably Shelly Manne to whom André was closest.

I met André when I first came to Hollywood and settled down and started doing studio work, first for MGM and later for the Goldwyn Studios. At MGM

André was known as a big jazzman and he would use
jazz musicians and jazz-oriented music in his films
whenever he could.

I found out quick enough that as a player he had
all the chops in the world and he seemed to have a
pretty good conception of what jazz was all about.
But I guess he was really more a fan of jazz than a
player of it. He played *at* it, you know? But he always
kept in touch with the jazz people and he always was
very interested in what we were doing. He wrote
album liner notes for a lot of us, me included.

On one liner, in 1956, André wrote what Shelly would always cherish as "probably the nicest thing anybody ever wrote
about me." The comment concerns Manne's construction of a
three-minute drum solo, using his fingers and no sticks or
brushes to create what André called "tom-tom glissandi." He
had a way of using the language of classical music to legitimize
jazz in the eyes of those who played it. It happened during a
Bud Powell tune called "Poco Loco," a cut on Contemporary's
The Swinging Sounds of Shelly Manne album. André went on
to say:

> Shelly, with his constant awareness of form and dy-
> namics, builds a set of variations which would be
> amazing enough had they been written by one of the
> acknowledged masters of modern percussion music
> such as Bartók, Varèse, or Chávez. Considering that
> they are wholly improvised, they constitute one of the
> most amazing solos in recorded jazz.

Clearly André was listening to and playing jazz with the ear
of a classically trained musician and that, for better or worse,
set him apart from many of his contemporaries. It was that
"musicianly" quality he looked for in other jazz performers. It
was what had attracted him to Betty Bennett and it was at the
base of his attraction to Shelly Manne, the son of a symphony
musician who'd been raised among the classics and who

believed in his heart that drums were musical instruments, not just loud timepieces. As Shelly puts it:

> A lot of jazz musicians were simply playing things that would astound people for the sake of astounding them and not for the sake of the music itself. We didn't feel that way. I think that's one of the things that's always been a binding force between André and me.

Shelly and his wife Flip became two of André's and Betty's closest personal friends. They spent a lot of evenings together, making not only music but also conversation. Shelly remembers having some good times at the Previns' home on Mulholland Drive and he remembers with special fondness the time they tried to take a vacation together in Palm Springs.

They had rented a huge and expensive house in the resort town, complete with its own palm-tree oasis and swimming pool. After a long drive to get there they went to bed early, planning a morning assault on the pool. They were awakened during the night by a fierce windstorm and heard furniture blowing and bumping around the yard but couldn't tell the extent of the damage until the sun came up. They found a palm tree uprooted and the swimming pool half filled with sand, the other half with lawn furniture. They spent the rest of their vacation cleaning up and never did get to enjoy the pool. "I wish I could remember what André said when he saw that mess," Shelly says. "I know it must have been something funny. The guy's got a great sense of humor."

It required a sense of humor in those days to be a jazz musician. In order to build and keep a reputation you had to be constantly on the go, hopping from club date to club date, college campus to campus and East Coast to West. Especially in the colleges there were legions of foot-pounding, screaming fans of the new-wave jazz. Bebop (though that name soon gave way to simply "modern" or "progressive" jazz) was to the students of the fifties what the big bands had been in the forties and what ersatz folk music of the Peter, Paul and Mary genre would become to the students of the sixties. In California, the most sought-after musicians on college campuses were the three- and four-man combos, possibly for economic reasons, and the most sought-after of those combos were those of Brubeck, George Shearing, and André Previn. To André the most sought-after commodity was a decent night's sleep.

> I have to laugh today when musicians complain to me that they have to eat their meals in the dining room of a hotel and can't get room service. Room service! Back in the fifties, in the hotels we frequented, you were ahead of the game if your door had a lock on it. If the desk clerk would let you register for the whole night it was a triumph! For me it was like a boot camp and a sense of humor was indispensable.

Shelly Manne remembers a big laugh he got at a concert at Loyola University of Los Angeles when Joe Mondragon was filling in on bass with them. The students were encouraged to ask questions between numbers and, when a question was directed to Shelly, he naturally stood up to answer. Actually, he didn't quite stand up. Instead he half-leaned with one knee on his stool while he gestured with his drumsticks to drive home a point. He forgot that he'd been pushed back against the rear edge of a ten-foot-high platform and that there was nothing behind him but air. He also forgot that the seats on drum stools are made to spin.

Shelly lost his balance and began to tip over backward, his right foot lodged gracefully behind his left knee. He instinctively called out to Mondragon for help, but Joe just as instinctively thought first of his instrument as he saw sticks and cymbals flying into the air. Mondragon picked up his bass and scurried to the forward edge of the stage. By now Shelly had disappeared from view and a hush had fallen over the crowd.

André calmly rose from his piano bench and walked to the rear, looked over and saw Shelly picking himself up, dazed but to all appearances in one piece. He walked back to his piano and looked in the direction from which the last question had come. "What Shelly was about to say," he told the audience, "is that while each of us must always be conscious of what the others are doing, we do our best not to interfere when the other guy is having a big moment . . . as, for example, Shelly's big moment just now."

A comradeship existed among jazzmen that André had yet to experience in film music or classical music. Not only his sense of humor but also his dedication were appreciated by his fellow musicians. They enjoyed arriving early at a hall and finding André already at the piano, working on some composition of Ravel or Bartók, and they never failed to ask him to go on, to play some more for them. As Dizzy Gillespie inimitably remarks, "André had completed the course prescribed by both jazz and the classics. I could dig that."

And likewise could André dig the fact that his '50s counterparts had taken jazz into previously uncharted areas of "popular" music, harmonically, rhythmically, and technically. Musicians like that, he thought, had to be "at least unconsciously interested in what was going on in the more complex forms of music." And that went even for such apparently a-serious musicians as Gillespie.

> Dizzy talks like a clown and knows everything. Most people have no idea he's one of the world's great nonprofessional chess players. As far as classical music goes, Dizzy understands a lot. So do a lot of those guys. Oscar Peterson, for example, is an inveterate concertgoer and classical record collector, though I don't believe he's interested in anything from, say, late Stravinsky on. But he can talk intelligently about the impressionists, and even Bartók.

If André's classical background made him appreciated by his jazz peers, his film background made him invaluable. Aside from being able to hire jazz players for his film orchestras, as Shelly Manne pointed out, he could also handle work for them as an arranger, when that sort of thing was required.

André's arranging business outstripped his performing and recording schedule at some points. He remembers fondly a three-plex apartment building which he and Betty shared with two other arrangers before they bought the house on Mulholland Drive. On one side was Stan Kenton's arranger Pete Rugolo. On the other side was Skip Brown, who arranged for Les Brown. In the center was André, who wrote for nearly everybody, being a jazz pianist who "happened to know his way around strings and wind sections."

This building was like a crazed fraternity house. Copyists would arrive at all hours of the night and indiscriminately ring a doorbell. They could never tell who might be finishing up the piece they'd come for. One of us was always calling one of the others at midnight to say he'd overextended himself again. "Look, I've got this whole album to do for Doris Day (or Mel Torme or whomever) so can you take a couple of the tunes for me?" And we'd just do them for each other, not for money or album credit or anything, but just to help out. That building was finally torn down. I'll bet if someone had kept track of all the pages of music that came out of that place it would make the *Ring* look like an encore.

Among the jazz notables for whom André made arrangements was Benny Goodman, who took André's orchestrations along when he took his band to the Brussels World's Fair. There had even been a time, in 1954, when André and Goodman made a record together. It came out of a strange encounter in New York that illustrates the famous Benny Goodman style. The André Previn Trio (with Red Mitchell and Frank Capp) was playing a gig at a club called the Round Table when in walked Benny Goodman, apparently for the express purpose of speaking with them, causing a stir on the bandstand as well as among the tables. In 1954 Benny may not have been the idol he once was but, as André quips, "even Kojak would be impressed if Sherlock Holmes walked in."

Benny just walked up to the bandstand between numbers and said, "Say, would you guys like to cut an

album with me?" How could we refuse? He asked us
to come to his place in Connecticut to go over the
material. We said, "Sure, what time?" and he said,
"How about nine-thirty?" We told him we'd be playing here again tomorrow night and he said, "No, nine-
thirty in the *morning*." I said, "Benny, Connecticut
isn't exactly uptown, you know. And we don't get
finished here till almost four." He just said, "Well,
then you better head straight for your hotel after the
gig."

So anyway, we got there and found he had this
phenomenal music room set up in the basement of
his house. There was only one problem. It was the
middle of January and the room was *freezing*. I mean,
this was the kind of cold where you actually cannot
even speak for your teeth chattering, let alone play.
We managed to hang in for about an hour before I
finally took him aside and said, "Say, Benny, you
know it really is too cold in here to be playing." He
kind of looked around for a moment and nodded and
said, "You know, you're right. Thanks." And he went
out and put on a sweater.

Now when you hear that story you might be
tempted to think, what an unfeeling bastard. But no:
that's Benny. He genuinely thought we were concerned for his health and was grateful we cared about
him. So the three of us just laughed and froze and
kept on playing.

Benny invited André to appear with his band on television.
This was only one of many such TV appearances for André as
the fifties wore on. Music specials and variety shows were a staple of the early television viewer's diet and André's playing was
heard on many of them. He accompanied Ella Fitzgerald and
set Marge and Gower Champion dancing across the tube. No
one ever asked him to say anything, which fit his image of
being withdrawn and nonpublic. He was quite content to let
his fingers do the talking.

In those days I was a mute. No one let me say anything, which I didn't mind at all. I was still very shy about speaking as a performer, be it for twenty people or six million. It wasn't until much later, when I got my confidence in the career I *really* wanted, that I began to try speaking on television. Eventually I actually came to enjoy it and to think of it as the easiest part of TV. But in those days I'd be introduced, play my number, bow, and disappear through the scrim at the back of the stage.

When it came to playing, though, there was no longer any shyness. Even if, as Shelly Manne says, André was only playing *at* jazz, he knew he could do it with authority and no one would question that authority. There were, and would always be, those who doubted André's right to play jazz, but not Dizzy Gillespie:

He has the flow, you know, which a lot of guys don't have and won't ever get. Yeah. I heard him play and I knew. A lot of guys, they have the technique, the harmonic sense. They've got the perfect coordination. And, yeah, all that's necessary. But you need something more, you know? Even if you only make an *ooooooooooooo*, like that, you got to have the flow.

XI

With something called the LP or long-playing 33⅓-rpm disc, the word "album" took on a new meaning in the record industry, no longer the bulky photograph-album-like set of 78s or 45s but a neatly stored single record that contained as many as fourteen or sixteen "sides." This created virtually a new medium that saw countless minor-league recording companies trying to take a slice of the new bigger profits. Virtually every jazz musician who wanted to record could find a label of one kind or another, even though its margin of profit might be slim indeed.

One of the first LPs after his Army service was an off-the-wall album called *André Previn Plays Fats Waller*. It was recorded in 1954 and was released on two labels, Tops and Zenith. Sales were not spectacular.

There followed a series of recordings for Decca with a quartet that included guitarist Al Hendrikson. These albums are not particularly noteworthy except that they marked the beginning of André's working relationship with Red Mitchell and Shelly Manne. The noncontractual arrangement with Decca lasted less than two years and was followed by an association with a smaller but perhaps more ambitious company called Contemporary Records. In August 1956, André and Contemporary helped put each other on the map.

The small company was owned and operated by the late Lester Koenig, whom André describes as "an intellectual, erudite man who was mad about jazz and had sunk all his money into it." He operated out of a tiny office on Melrose Place in Los Angeles, with the recording studio in a large room behind the office. There the musicians had to make room for themselves among the stacks of records and boxes waiting to be shipped out.

Recording for Les Koenig was an informal affair and was often done at night, after the musicians had finished whatever activity it might be that paid their bills. Les made the coffee and periodically sent out for hamburgers and about the time the sun was rising there would be enough music laid down on tape to cut a record. The musicians earned union scale for the session, plus a share of whatever royalties there might be.

Since the leader of any group earned an extra hundred dollars for such a session, André, Shelly Manne, and Leroy Vinnegar had agreed to alternate as leader. In August the short straw fell to Shelly, so the André Previn Trio became, for the sake of the record, Shelly Manne and His Friends. That meant Shelly had the responsibility of choosing the music for the album and as he was setting up his drums it dawned on him that he hadn't the slightest idea what he wanted to do. It was Koenig who suggested starting with a couple of tunes from *My Fair Lady*.

This was the new Broadway show that everybody was talking about. Since its opening earlier that year, *My Fair Lady* had been drawing SRO crowds at the Mark Hellinger Theater and looked as though it might be on its way to becoming the biggest hit since *The Merry Widow*. The two songs from the show everybody knew and liked were "I Could Have Danced All Night" and "On the Street Where You Live." Initially there was no thought of going any further with *My Fair Lady*. No one had ever tried selling a jazz album devoted to just one show. But as they played, group leader Manne liked what he was hearing and wanted more.

> They were nothing but "head arrangements," of course, made up as we went along. We had never got together and rehearsed these numbers or anything. André would say, "Hey, this might sound better as a

ballad. What do you think?" Or, "Maybe we ought
to swing this into a different tempo." When we realized we had come up with a whole new way of
approaching those two tunes than had ever been done
before, we just decided to do the whole damn show.

Trouble was, nobody knew the whole damn show. They
couldn't just run out and buy the sheet music, since by this
time it was nearly eleven at night. No one could think of a
friend who might have the score—if indeed it had been published that soon. Then Koenig remembered the record store
that stayed open till midnight and that might just have the
original cast album. He sent one technician after the album
and another after sandwiches. André remembers a feeling of
excitement, like kids with a new toy, when the album arrived
and Les placed it on a turntable.

We listened to one cut after another and I scrawled
out the chord changes. Then we fooled with each
song until we had an idea we could all agree on. We
laid it down, then we went on to the next cut on the
record. When we got finished sometime that morning
I closed the piano and said, "Les, you now have the
most expensive party record ever made." He said,
"What are you talking about?" I said, "Well, you're
never going to sell it because there's no way Lerner
and Loewe are going to be happy about what we've
done to their nice tunes and they'll probably fight the
distribution."

André was wrong. Four months later Lerner and Loewe
bought enough copies of the record to give them as Christmas
presents to the cast, staff, and stage crew of the Broadway production. In its own way, *Shelly Manne and His Friends Play
My Fair Lady* was as big a hit as their play. In a matter of
weeks the album was out of stock in Les Koenig's studio–ship-
ping room and new pressings began falling way behind the orders from record stores. The album climbed to the top of all
the charts—at a time when it was almost unheard of for a jazz

album to be *on* those charts—and it stayed at the top. *My Fair Lady* became the biggest-selling jazz album in history and it held that title for many years. Since, in a jazz trio, the lion's share of credit for that kind of success would rightly go to the pianist—no matter whose name came first on the album cover —André's career in jazz was made.

Re-released by Contemporary in 1979, *My Fair Lady* still sounds fresh. Only the recording techniques date it. It must have sounded fresh indeed in 1956 and maybe that's what made it catch on, that unmistakable "head arrangement" quality. Maybe it was that the musicians had hit upon a fail-safe formula by exploiting music with which the public ear was familiar but not yet jaded. Maybe it was simply good playing of good tunes.

But lots of musicians had done all those things before. For a clue as to why it was *My Fair Lady* and not a dozen other jazz albums of the period, you have to credit André Previn's acumen. After ten years of working in the movies he had an insight into the public taste, an insight many jazz musicians would have found undesirable. Whether or not he found it abhorrent or even admitted the fact to himself, André was acutely aware that a musician playing to himself is like that tree falling in the forest with no one around to hear: it doesn't matter how big a noise you make. He may not have had the "purity" of a Charlie Parker, but he knew how to get a jazz message across to large numbers of people, people who might have said, "I don't like jazz." André was able to break down those barriers with the songs from *My Fair Lady*. No wonder he says, "That's a nostalgic record for me."

When it came to jazz, though, André's proclivity for imitating proved to be his Achilles' heel. He started out trying to imitate Art Tatum and he wound up trying to imitate himself. Just as he'd done with his first successful RCA album, he attempted to recapture the success of *My Fair Lady* by doing another one just like it. There followed a whole string of Broadway hit albums for Contemporary: *Bells Are Ringing, Pal Joey, Li'l Abner, Gigi,* and *Camelot*. There was only one that came anywhere near the success of the first, the only other one that

André looks back on with musical approval. That is Leonard
Bernstein's *West Side Story*, played by "André Previn and His
Pals." As in the case of *My Fair Lady*, *West Side Story* contains excellent material performed with excellence and originality. The classic "America," for instance, contains hardly a
trace of the Latin beat Bernstein gave it and the simple melody is not even stated until about a third of the way through,
well after Previn, Manne, and Mitchell have made their
thoughts about the music crystal clear.

André's warm association with Contemporary lasted until
1960, when he entered into a more lucrative arrangement with
Columbia. But most of his best jazz playing came during the
years on Contemporary. There was a clever double-entendre
disc called *Double Play* which saw André teaming up with his
fellow pianist from the Jazz at the Philharmonic All-Stars,
Russ Freeman, along with Shelly Manne. They played songs
associated with baseball. Another interesting album was *Four
to Go*, in which the trio was joined by the great jazz guitarist
Herb Ellis. There were also a number of albums in which
André appeared only as accompanist, backing up several of the
fine instrumentalists who recorded for Contemporary.

Never losing sight of his idol, Art Tatum, André also did
several piano solo recordings for Contemporary, even though
piano solos were not exactly the rage anymore. Much later,
when he went with RCA, he tried something even more novel
on an album called *André Previn All Alone*. He went into the
recording studio and rifled through a stack of sheet music
pulled at random by the producer. When a tune struck his
fancy he immediately sat down at the grand and improvised.
The engineer recorded that take and André never did a second
one. In three hours he'd laid down twenty-two cuts, then he
left and let the producer select the twelve he liked best for the
album. That *All Alone* album remains one of André's senti-
mental favorites and is another of those that wears well.

By the late fifties André had become internationally known
as a jazz pianist, his records selling as well as or better than
those musicians he considered his betters in the field. His trio
was in great demand on campuses, in clubs, and at jazz festi-

vals. Television appearances were coming with increasing frequency. Indeed, as the sixties dawned, mention of the name Previn would have conjured up an immediate word association: jazz. Yet André persists in the declaration that even at the height of his powers and popularity in the field, he never was more than an honored guest at the table of jazz.

> You've got to understand. I was interested in jazz and I was allowed in because I was facile and fairly clever. I played with a lot of interesting people. But I was never a jazz musician by singular profession. I didn't consider myself one and the other musicians didn't consider me one. I met a lot of great people through jazz and made a lot of lasting friendships. But I was truly only a guest. Tolerated—gladly tolerated, I like to think—but never an important jazz pianist.

One can argue in circles over the interpretation of the word "important" in that context. If André means to say that he did not have the pivotal influence of a Louis Armstrong, Art Tatum, or Charlie Parker, of course he is correct. On the other hand, the number of well-known jazz artists who did not play that kind of role is legion. What about Art Blakey, Charles Mingus, Ahmad Jahmal, Sonny Stitt, to conjure up a few names? One could hardly call them *un*important. Yet it can be argued that none of those musicians made any greater contribution to the progress of jazz than did André himself.

André's self-deprecation as a jazz musician rests solely on his failure to devote his entire life to that form of music. The argument is specious; one might as well call Harry Truman an unimportant President because he did not devote his entire life to politics. The fact is that André was a gifted musician who applied the full range of his talents to film composing and thereby became an important film composer, and when he applied those same talents to jazz, he made himself a jazz musician in the fullest sense of the term. Here is the opinion of one noted jazz critic, Doug Ramsey:

> It has always seemed to me that Previn was judged too harshly in the 1950s when he was doing all that

jazz recording. The term inevitably used by the critics who pilloried him in those days was "eclectic," written with a sneer, as if to be eclectic was to lead a life of dishonor. Previn was a jazz pianist of well above average ability and creativity. He had detectable influences. He never melded them into the highly original style of a Tatum, a Powell, or an Evans, but he was certainly not a mimic. He had taste, technique, compendious knowledge of the jazz piano tradition, and he could swing.

He was also an admirable accompanist. I think he often played better on other people's records than on his own. For instance, on the Benny Carter *Jazz Giant* and Helen Humes albums on Contemporary. It must be conceded that there was a detachment and coolness on some of his trio records. But in an era remarkable for its great number of insipid or mechanical jazz pianists, singling out Previn for not being a master improviser amounted to a bum rap. He was not in the first rank of jazz pianists, but he was certainly well into the second.

André himself has done so much breast-beating over his lack of commitment to jazz that it's small wonder the criticism is repeated by close friends like Shelly Manne, who professes to be "a lot more liberal" than other jazz people in this regard.

A lot of jazz musicians who didn't know André personally resented him 'cause they thought he was just dabbling in it. They're not convinced he ever was a dedicated jazz musician. Well, so he wasn't a dedicated jazz musician and he did dabble in it. But during that period he was doing an awful lot of jazz, and when you do something a lot it's only natural that you get better at it.

For me, knowing André was a very important part of my life. His musicianship, as a player, was definitely an influence on me. Just by keeping my ears open, listening to things he played and wrote and

said. We've always had warm feelings for each other,
not just as musicians, but as persons.

There are drummers in this world who would aver that if
André Previn was that important to Shelly Manne, then he
was important enough to jazz.

He was also important to another Hollywood musician, John
Williams. Like André in many respects, though a few years his
junior, Williams went from arranging to composing to conducting in films. Like André, Williams also might have had a
career as a jazz pianist. Instead, he focused his attention on
film composing and eventually achieved a sensational kind of
fame as the composer of the score of *Star Wars*, topping that
off in 1980 by succeeding the late Arthur Fiedler, a man it was
said could never be succeeded, as conductor of the Boston
Pops Orchestra.

John Williams pays homage to André as one of the pivotal
influences of his career in music, declaring that "as a youngster
I tried to emulate André Previn, to the extent that I could, in
the breadth of his view and the breadth of his ability." Yet
Williams agonizes over André's shortcomings as a jazz artist:

> By the time I met him, when he was playing jazz in
> his early twenties, he already gave the impression of
> knowing everything. He could play you sixteen bars
> of Art Tatum's version of anything you could name.
> Somewhere along the line he had learned much more
> *about* jazz than I would ever know about it. Yet
> somehow I thought I was a better jazz *player* than he
> was. This is where the frustration comes in: since he
> knows, intellectually, more about the thing than I do
> or anybody else does, and since he far surpasses the
> rest of us in his powers of recall, what is there about
> André's jazz playing that isn't quite satisfying? Far
> lesser musicians were able to communicate far more
> using far fewer notes. With André you're always left
> just faintly dissatisfied.
> Maybe it's just that he wasn't born an American.
> Or maybe it's the rhythm, a little too much forward

pressure in his playing, where you are in relation to
the beat, how much ahead or how much behind and
when to be exactly on-the-spot with it. The great jazz
artist does that intuitively, you can't teach it. If you
have too much pressure at the wrong moment, or too
much relaxation, something's disturbed.

I keep coming back to the word "impatience."
André is impatient with lesser people, and that happens to include most of us. He wants to get on with
it, get it done. It's that same pushing forward, when
something may need a little more time to make it
live. Anything—a person, a relationship, anything
from eating to sex to music—you've got to have a
sense of how long a thing should take. Five minutes
or five and a half? It's an instinct, I guess, a sense of
the rightness of time.

Does a song need five minutes or five and a half? Does a
marriage need five years or five and a half? André's instincts
seem to have failed him there too, if one can judge by the fact
that he put the coda on his marriage a few months before
Betty bore their second child.

XII

"If I could personally get to everyone who is going to read this book," said André Previn to the authors in 1979, "I would show them pictures of my kids for two hours straight. That would be the extent of my talking about my private life. The rest is nobody's business."

It does no good to remind him that even he has remarked on the impossibility of knowing a man's music without first knowing the man, no good to point to his unlocking many of the secrets of Beethoven's symphonies by reading John W. Sullivan's book about Beethoven's spiritual growth. Couch personal questions in the cleverest circumlocution and André will see right through it and swear that there is simply no way to pry out of him any of the intimate details which might add another dimension to his own music.

"The things that happen between two people, I will never discuss with anybody," he insists. "Not even with friends. It's simply nobody's business. To rehash what happened as much as three decades ago, to relive it all, for me is totally pointless."

As André says, even his closest friends have been sealed off from this inner sanctum of "personal life," so their observations are no more than the observations of outsiders. John Green can tell you that "Bonnie and I got to know Betty casually well. She seemed like a very pleasant lady, but when we pondered out loud whether they were really in love, we couldn't be sure." Shelly Manne reminisces about evenings together with Betty and André, at their house or at the movies or restaurants. "It seemed like a happy marriage to us. They certainly were getting along very well the whole time we were together. Of course, you never know what goes on between two people when they're alone."

Apparently it wasn't so much what went on when they were alone as what did *not* go on, all the important things that were left unsaid in the hope that they would go away. Betty claims she never saw their breakup coming, that there was never any indication from André that a thing was wrong. Perhaps when André said he would never discuss personal matters with anybody, not even friends, he should have included "or wives." If that was truly the case, then Betty was just like everyone else before whom André stood in his armor of rose-colored glass. As far as she was concerned, he was living the life he wanted, a carefree life of movies and jazz. He was "a wonderful husband, very attentive and very funny." He seems not to have discourage Betty's pursuit of her own career. Rather, as she had introduced him to the musicians who were on the front lines of jazz, André introduced Betty to influential Hollywood people who had the wherewithal to help her, though apparently they did not have the motivation.

> Though I did very little professional singing during our marriage—outside of recording a couple of albums with André—I did work a few local clubs with a trio. André did our arrangements and rehearsed the trio, but he didn't play for me. At Hollywood parties, however, we were a very big duo. I used to be discovered once a month.

Betty recalls one party at which she was trying very hard to impress Ira Gershwin. One of her big numbers with André was "Over the Rainbow," which she sang quite freely, retaining hardly any of the original melody line. Johnny Green took umbrage at this and asked Betty why she didn't feel Harold Arlen's melody was good enough for her. "I was desolate," says Betty, "because besides Ira there were a lot of other influential people there and naturally I wanted them all to like me." It was not André but Ira Gershwin who gallantly stepped in: "Well, Johnny, I think we are all very much aware of what the melody is. I think it's wonderful to hear what a jazz singer can do with it." Betty declared herself president emeritus of the Ira Gershwin fan club.

As far as family finances were concerned, there was no need for Betty to work, so André felt no need to push her into greater prominence as a singer. Instead he devoted himself to his wife's education, finding her deficient in the areas of classical music and literature. Betty's reaction to music appreciation in Hamburg, Iowa, was essentially the same as André's had been in Beverly Hills, but for Betty the result was a complete turning away from anything remotely "highbrow" and a full commitment to the slang music of jazz. Now André wanted to turn that around and he made it a point to take her to every concert in town as well as to spend hours listening to and discussing recorded music. As for literature, Betty was Zelda Fitzgerald to André's F. Scott.

> From the time I was able to read I'd been an avid reader. But during all those years I'd spent on the road with the bands, the paperbacks I could pick up were never particularly enlightening. Through André my choice of reading material improved about one hundred percent. He used to laugh at how I couldn't put anything down once I'd started. Even such heavy stuff as *War and Peace*, which he confessed that even he had trouble getting through. I owe him a tremendous debt of gratitude for improving my taste.

A great change came over their life together in 1954 when Betty gave birth to their first child, a daughter they named Claudia. Inevitably the change was the greater for Betty. Her infrequent club dates ground to a halt as she threw herself into the role of mother. For André the child meant not so much a new responsibility or a turning point as a confirmation that he was in the right place doing the right thing at the right time. A baby meant permanence and the establishment of one's own traditions, no longer depending on those of parents and ancestors. His commitment to Hollywood was renewed. "Claudia's birth," he says, "was an enormous event. We were very happy. I was fulfilled. I thought it was the best thing that ever happened to me."

For a while the baby brought André and Betty closer together than they had been since the early days of their marriage. With dreamy fondness Betty recalls long evenings at home as a family, André helping with the dinner dishes and then playing with the baby while she napped on the living room couch, exhausted but very happy. They went out seldom during Claudia's infancy, not eager to trust her to sitters. Finally Betty's parents (who had moved to Los Angeles from the Midwest) talked her into leaving the baby with them periodically so that she and André could enjoy an evening out.

Claudia retained vivid memories of her early childhood. Lying on her mother's lap on those late-night rides home from her grandparents' house, the streetlights blinking past. Christmas tree lights playing brilliant colors over the living room as Mama and Papa (the names they gave themselves, in recollection of André's own childhood) sang and played Christmas carols. A rocking horse on springs that took her on bouncing rides through the meadows of her imagination. A tricycle that came with strict warning not to ride near the steeply sloping driveway. A house full of good feelings.

"My mother and father always seemed to share a lot," reflects grown-up Claudia. "They got along well together." As Claudia remembers it, her parents shared everything. As Betty recalls, they shared humor, music, literature, and the joy of quiet contemplation. But André says, "Outside of our enthusiasm for jazz, we didn't have all that much to share."

> It was all very nice. But it was all wrong for our eventual life and happiness. We would have driven each other mad. As it was, the marriage lasted five or six years. As to why it broke up, most of it was my fault. My ambitions were pretty relentless in those days.

As to the nature of those ambitions, André is evasive. They seem to have centered around his film career and the winning of Academy Awards (both of which he would later deride) and the making of money (which now seems to have little meaning for him). Certainly his serious music ambitions were only dimly in the picture at that point and Betty could only have helped him get ahead in jazz.

His "relentless ambition" of the mid fifties was most likely nothing more than a gnawing dissatisfaction with the life he was leading and with the man André Previn was becoming. A quarter of a century later, with that life and that individual well behind him, his churning ambitions for himself in the field of serious music require that he blame "Hollywood" for his personal shortcomings—whatever they might have been, since he will not dwell upon them. At the same time, since "Hollywood" is no longer a part of his life he can use it as a sort of spare room or attic in which to shove any niggling detail of his past on which he'd now rather not reflect. But his past will not go away; interviewers and the public will not let him forget it. In defense, he takes a page from literature, from Nathaniel Hawthorne. He wears a scarlet *H,* for Hollywood, and will not discuss it. This is part of me. I do not repent it nor do I excuse it. Is it my sin or yours?

Neither "ambition" nor "Hollywood" explains what went wrong with their marriage, and neither does Betty's revelation of "another woman."

André confesses that immediately upon leaving Betty he went through "a series of ill-advised attachments." Betty says those attachments were antecedent to and a factor in the breakup. She and the Hollywood gossip columns of the day cite specifically his attachment to singer Peggy King, a gifted entertainer and aspiring actress who was involved in making a film when she became involved with André in 1957. In defense, or at least by way of explanation of his "ill-advised attachments," André cites his immaturity. "It was," he says, "the kind of thing you usually do when you're eighteen, but I'd been working so hard I'd had no time for that kind of mistake." Actually, André was twenty-eight and a man who, at least in the eyes of his friend John Williams, "gave the impression of already knowing everything." To Betty, he gave the impression of being a faithful husband and a loving father, right up until the time she discovered she was going to have another baby.

> In addition to the improvement of my literary taste and opening up the world of classical music to me, André constantly bolstered my ego by telling me how pretty I was, how funny I was and how bright. Perhaps this, more than anything else, explains why his departure—when I was three months pregnant with our second child—came as such a shock.

André had been keeping his own counsel. Whatever his dissatisfaction with the marriage, whatever his ambitions, whatever his yearnings after other women might have been, he never let on to Betty. "In those days," he explains, "the secrecies and the guilts were enormous. Nowadays, no one would blink."

Not only were the newspaper columnists blinking, they were beginning to stare. Now that Betty knew the truth, or enough of it, André made no attempt to conceal the new object of his affections, making things that much harder on Betty. The publicity, she says, "was very painful, since I was in no condition to compete in my pregnant state. Nor would I have attempted it. Yet I've never mentioned, in all the years since the breakup, that André actually left me for Peggy King . . . That 'other woman' number was never a favorite of mine, so I just never spoke of it." By comparison with Betty's wound-opening account, André's comments on the dissolution of the marriage sound almost clinically detached:

> In retrospect, I don't believe I behaved very well. Betty is an absolutely sensational lady and the marriage was breaking up as she was about to become a mother again. As far as what happened to make it go wrong, I won't talk about the details. It's true that when a marriage goes wrong it is the fault of both

parties, but with the intervening years it is consistent
with reality and also perfectly normal to take the
blame on oneself. It probably *was* my fault. We split
up much too quickly afterwards, in terms of humane
behavior patterns.

Over those same intervening years, Betty has had occasion
to ask herself what went wrong. She too has found it "consistent with reality" to shoulder at least part of the responsibility.
As she sees it, the major problem was that "we never really got
to know each other. We both played whatever roles best suited
the situation. It was only years later that we finally talked
about this and I was just as surprised at some of his complaints
about me as I know he was with mine about him. Many of
those complaints were so simple and silly and would have been
so easily adjusted."

"We were such good friends," André told Claudia some
years later, "it's too bad it didn't work out. If we were smarter,
we might have made an entirely different marriage." But emotional thought processes are not André's usual style and he will
not indulge himself in them for long. Instead he dissects his
own actions with the same cool detachment he applied to dissecting the music of Art Tatum and Charlie Parker.

With twenty-twenty hindsight you can save every broken marriage. I'd like to think that as the years go by
we all get smarter, more used to life and more able to
cope with its problems, so that looking back on those
problems seems insanely trivial, even though they
once may have appeared insurmountable. Of any marriage, of any friendship, you could say that if only the
two people involved could have sat and talked it out
at the time—not by way of a third-person analyst, but
between themselves—then probably two thirds of
those marriages could be saved. But none of that does
you any good when you're going through it, when
you're emotionally immature and unprepared to deal
with life. It's no good to be retrospectively dismayed,
because none of that can help.

And so the marriage ended, for reasons however unspoken or ill-defined or immature. It ended in a way that would repercuss through at least four lives and that would deeply scar at least one of those. Yet, André says, "I didn't *choose* to leave when Betty was three months pregnant. It was just that all at once everything came to an absolute cul-de-sac."

XIII

As far as MGM was concerned, André's three years in the Army and in San Francisco had been lost. But he had left behind in Hollywood a good reputation and an Oscar nomination, so he was cheerfully welcomed back into the fold. With the ceaseless outpouring of movies from all the studios in the early '50s, composers were in greater demand than ever and André went back to work with a vengeance, "doing endless films, some good, mostly awful."

One of his early efforts in this "second" Hollywood career and a personal as well as a critical success was his score for the film *Bad Day at Black Rock*. André's use of pregnant silences kept the audiences guessing as to what Spencer Tracy and Lee Marvin would be up to next and when the next shattering outburst from the orchestra would assault them. It hurt André's reputation not the least that the film happened to be a runaway success at the box office.

He had returned still cherishing the thrill of *Three Little Words*, caring to work on nothing but musicals, but the studio told him to expect a musical on the average of every third film. The next musical to come his way was *It's Always Fair Weather*, a film that by all rights should have been a hit but that somehow missed.

The critics loved the Arthur Freed–Gene Kelly production. They loved André's snappy score and they loved the lyrics by Betty Comden and Adolph Green. But for the most part the audiences ignored the film, feeling perhaps that they'd seen and heard it all before. In terms of plot, *Fair Weather* was nothing more than a G.I. version of the three sailors out for a good time in *On the Town*. The script even called for a long ballet sequence for the opening—shades of Bernstein's *On the Town*. No matter, André threw himself into that long opening number, creating a fine musical montage that swept the dancing actors along from setting to setting and mood to mood. No one doubted that it was André's best film work to date.

It's Always Fair Weather was not destined to bring André an Academy Award, however. Just as MGM had destroyed his chances in 1950 by releasing *Three Little Words* the same year as the heavyweight *Annie Get Your Gun*, so it did in 1954, giving *Fair Weather* unfair competition in yet another servicemen-on-leave story called *Hit the Deck*, which got the promotion and the publicity as the studio's BIG musical that year.

If not an Oscar, at least there was the reward of working with so talented a pair of songwriters as Comden and Green. Up to then André had only scored songs or written around them, but now he had the chance to compose actual song melodies and in *Fair Weather* there were at least two potential hit numbers in "I Like Myself" and "When the Time Has Come for Parting."

Adolph Green got the idea that "I Like Myself" would be a natural for Frank Sinatra to record, so he got Gene Kelly to set up a meeting with Ol' Blue Eyes, who happened to be working on *High Society* on an adjoining sound stage. The singer agreed to meet André and Adolph in his dressing room after lunch that day. They found the star's dressing room next to that of Sidney Blackmer, who was playing one of the heavies in *High Society*. They paced the hallway, music in hand, for the better part of an hour. Finally they spotted someone approaching, but it turned out to be Blackmer, not Sinatra. After a while Green decided the singer must have forgotten the appointment and they might as well get back to work.

"Wait a minute," André said. "As long as we're here, why don't we play it for Blackmer. Maybe he'll record it."

Every one of André's friends and fellow musicians has a favorite André Previn story. That one happens to be Adolph Green's.

Despite Sinatra's snub and the lack of enthusiasm on the part of moviegoers around the country, André's gift for songwriting was not lost on Arthur Freed, who happened to be an ex-lyricist with a lot of big hit songs under his belt. The arch-producer of MGM musicals felt that all André really needed to take off as a song composer was the luxury of his own personal lyricist, someone with whom he could work steadily, perfecting his craft as he perfected their songs.

It happened that at about that time a New York friend of Freed's sent him copies of some lyrics he'd come across by an unknown, a girl who was supposed to be (but actually was not) involved in the songs for Leonard Sillman's *New Faces* series on Broadway. Freed thought this girl, Dory Langdon, had promise and might be just the partner for André. He wired an airline ticket in care of his friend and told him to get the girl out to Los Angeles for a trial stint as a junior writer working out of his office. It turned out that the girl (actually a woman over thirty) was terrified of airplanes but she was so enthusiastic over the chance to work in Hollywood that she gulped down a handful of tranquilizers and boarded the flight.

There were only two small flaws in Freed's plan. One was that he had André committed to a string of musicals (the one-out-of-three rule having been abandoned in the wake of success) which had no need of Miss Langdon's services. The other flaw was that he neglected to tell André about the plan.

> There was this strange young woman who sat in Arthur Freed's outer office and who, whenever I came through, would jump up and say politely, "Mr. Previn, do you think you could take a look at some of my lyrics now?" Well, I was working on two or three films at once and I would say to her, "Of course I'd love to look at them, but you'll have to excuse me now. I simply don't have the time."
>
> After this happened a few times I finally said, "Arthur, who the devil is that girl out there who

keeps thrusting bits of paper with lyrics in my face?"
He said, "Oh, right. Her name's, uh, Dory Langdon.
She wrote some lyrics in New York and I brought her
out here to be your collaborator. I think she could be
terrific and maybe you two could do some songs together." I told him the least he could have done was
introduce us.

Later on I got her number and called her to explain and we had a good laugh over the whole thing.
I told her we'd get together and write some songs as
soon as I finished the films the studio had me working on.

That André had no time to spare for a lyricist is forgivable.
He was then involved with *Kismet*, *Invitation to the Dance*,
and *Silk Stockings*, all simultaneously. One day he might be
surrounding Howard Keel with his harem girls and their "Bau-
bles, Bangles and Beads," and the next be waltzing Cyd
Charisse around Paris in her silk stockings. Meanwhile he was
composing a full-length ballet for Gene Kelly's experimental
no-dialogue *Invitation to the Dance*, which eventually merited
a special award from the Screen Composers Association.

It should have been a carefree time, filled as it was with such
happy music. The fact that none of his work in those months
reflects in any way the strain of his personal life serves only to
cast a harsher light on his marital problems. How does a person under such emotional strain manage to occupy himself
with such pleasantries? In answer André falls back on one of
his leitmotivs, a recurring theme with deep resonances and
jarring overtones:

> If I'm in a state of confusion, whether small or large,
> I never let it keep me from enthusiastically pursuing
> my work. Sometimes I'd rather do anything in the
> world than start a rehearsal, but once I'm there with-
> out any conscious effort at all I turn into this *working*
> person. Then I'm off the hook. It's okay.

As long as he placed himself in the hands of the film studio,
André could stay off that hook. Now Arthur Freed was start-

ing production on what would be the most lavish, highest-grossing musical of his long career, and he wanted André to do the music. As soon as he finished recording the track of *Silk Stockings,* André packed his bags and took off for France and the set of *Gigi.*

For virtually everyone who came into contact with it, *Gigi* was pure gold. Not only was it opined to be one of MGM's most delightful movies ever, it was in fact the studio's financial savior, single-handedly restoring fiscal creditability after the first money-losing year in MGM's thirty-four-year history.

Gigi also restored pride to the old lion. At the 1958 Academy Awards presentations the film danced off with a total of ten Oscars. Arthur Freed got one for producing the year's best film; Vincente Minnelli got one for the best direction; Joseph Ruttenberg got one for the best photography; Alan Jay Lerner got one for writing the best screenplay; Lerner and his partner Frederick Loewe got one for their song "Gigi"; Adrienne Fazan got one for her editing; Cecil Beaton got one for his costumes; William Horning and Preston Ames got one for their Art Direction; Maurice Chevalier got an honorary one for being the world's favorite seventy-one-year-old heart throb. And, at the age of twenty-nine, after thirteen years in and out of the film business, André Previn got his first Oscar for the score of *Gigi.*

> If you stuck around long enough you'd eventually do some good work or be assigned to a good picture and sooner or later you were bound to be nominated. Sooner or later *everybody* gets nominated. I think in the end I wound up being nominated fourteen times. Actually winning one was something else.
>
> From a purely venal point of view, winning an Oscar was helpful because every time you won one your price shot up. Once you set foot outside Los Angeles you could not fail to realize the honor really

meant very little, but there, every year, within that
tiny industry, there is a feverish gold rush. Everybody
clambers over everybody else to win one of those
garish awards. And I fell for it as much as anybody
else, I guess. I'd be nominated and I'd want to *win*.

The night he finally won was April 6, his birthday. It would
have been nice to stay out all night celebrating, but instead he
had to rush from the ceremonies to the airport, where he
caught a plane for New York, due there the following morning
to rehearse a television special. Hopping cross-continent and
over oceans was still quite a novelty in those days and André
recalls the astonishment on the face of Eli Wallach, whom he
ran into at a Fifty-seventh Street coffee shop: "Say, André,
didn't I see you on the Coast at the Oscars last night on TV?"

Rehearsals for the television program were at Nola Studios,
then located in an old building across from Carnegie Hall,
cubbyholed with rehearsal rooms and said to be haunted by
ghosts of audition losers from seasons long past. The rehearsals
were going along in typical confusion when André was summoned to a telephone in the hallway.

The call was from Los Angeles; the connection was not good
and the band was rehearsing a noisy number through open
doors a few feet away. André cupped a hand against one ear
and pressed his other ear into the phone. He recalls his attention flitting to the shapely legs of a dancer who was limbering
up nearby and to graffiti scribbled above the telephone: agents'
telephone numbers, theater addresses, audition times. He apol-
ogized to the caller for not being able to hear. He was in the
middle of a rehearsal. Could the man possibly call him later at
his hotel? But the voice on the West Coast kept shouting
something and, from the East Coast, André kept shouting
back that he couldn't hear. Until, finally, when a pause in the
music and a break in the static came together, the words came
through loud and clear: "YOUR SISTER IS DEAD."

Leonore had been in and out of the hospital for most of the
last year. André and Lolo had been very close and her illness

was a deep personal difficulty for him. As with the difficulties of his marriage, he would not discuss those emotions then or later.

There seemed to be some dour angel lurking over André, guarding him against self-satisfaction and complacency. The pell-mell music education of his childhood had broken on rocks of racial persecution. His first Oscar nomination had slid into an Army latrine. His superficially idyllic marriage had tripped over indiscretion. Now that long-coveted award lay forgotten somewhere, the moment of glory swept away by a wave of pain. He might have let himself be swept away too into the self-pity of cynicism. Instead he went back to Hollywood and resumed his role as Working Person. But this time his work did not protect him from personal relationships; rather, it led him into one.

Some months later, on a Monday morning, André walked into Arthur Freed's office all smiles. Vincente Minnelli was there and he casually asked whether André had had a pleasant weekend.

"Very pleasant," answered André and then, turning to Freed, he said, "Remember that girl you brought out here to work with me, the lyricist?"

"Sure," said Freed, "Dory Langdon. Whatever happened to her?"

"Well," said André, "over the weekend she married me."

XIV

Dorothy Langan was born on October 22, 1925, in Rahway, New Jersey, a doleful point on the map some twenty miles outside New York City. The chief landmark of Rahway, just off the grim Jersey Turnpike, is a state prison.

Dory broke out of Rahway to become an actress on Broadway or, failing that, a tap dancer. Succeeding in neither profession, she determined to make herself into a songwriter. After just four months Fate stepped in; somebody showed her lyrics to Arthur Freed and Dory was on her way to Hollywood. It might have been a Cinderella story, but Dory's guiding spirits were malevolent leprechauns, not fairy godmothers.

In 1979 she declined to be interviewed for this book, saying that Doubleday would soon be publishing her autobiography, *Bog-Trotter*, which would contain everything one might care to know on the subject of her marriage to André Previn. *Bog-Trotter* is Dory's third book about Dory, following *On My Way to Where* and *Midnight Baby*, and like its predecessors is less autobiography than autoexorcism, an effort to free her psyche of its ravaging demons by loosing them on an unsuspecting world. The books are either astonishing or disconcerting, depending perhaps on the reader's own mental stability, and they tread cautiously through a mined no-man's-land between fact and fiction, Dory describing herself in *Bog-Trotter* as a woman with one head in reality and a second in fantasy.

Michael Langan, Dory's father, was in her estimation a "madman," gassed in the First World War and subsequently eaten away by depression and rage. Florence, her mother, was a "martyr," steeling herself with forbearance for her husband. Once, for a length of time that is unclear but which seems to have been at least several months, Dory, her mother and baby sister were restricted to one room of their house, the boarded-up dining room, simply because Mike Langan did not want to set eyes on what he considered to be his shame. Langan was convinced that the mustard gas had left him sterile and that the two children were proof that he had been cuckolded. The memory of those months releases torrents of bitterness in Dory's books, but she leaves us to guess whether the greatest resentment is felt toward her father, toward her mother for putting up with the confinement, or toward herself for not simply leaving by an open kitchen door. Dory's dark history included two abortions and an annulled marriage, so that the normal pursuits of love, sex, marriage, babies, family were all mined with booby traps in her mind. She was well along the way to her first in a long and ugly series of sanatorium confinements when, in 1956, she signed a Los Angeles hotel register as "Dory Langdon."

As a struggling actress–tap dancer–lyricist in New York, Dory had picked up extra money by baby-sitting. The very last time she did that, watching television as her charge slept, she happened to see a variety program taped in Los Angeles. Her favorite performer on the show was a pianist named André Previn and she thought she might like to meet him some day. A few months later she'd be hired to collaborate with him and in less than three years she'd marry him, but none of that found its way into her imagination that evening when she saw him on television, an uncontestable Somebody. So far her only encouragement in the struggle to rise above shanty Irish Nobody status had come from a kind soul who'd written in the Woodbridge *Independent* that Dory was "destined to reach greater heights in the theatrical world." That had been on the occasion of her greatest honor to date, first prize in the Perth Amboy, New Jersey, Talented Child Competition.

Some years later, however, Dory's options of ladders for scaling greater heights were very much in question. By the time André returned from France and *Gigi*, the songwriter from New Jersey was nowhere to be found. She had been fired or, more precisely, the studio had declined to pick up her short-term contract option. After all, in her brief time at the studio she had failed to write a single usable song. Still, her MGM "credit" got her a foot in the door at UPA, the company that produced movie cartoons, and for a brief period she did write lyrics for two-dimensional performers.

If her career lacked direction, so did her life. Dory fell in love with a married man who refused to seek a divorce from his wife. Dory sought the help of an analyst, but it came too late to prevent a nervous breakdown and she landed in a sanatorium. Upon her release she found part-time employment as an office clerk, working on her lyrics during her spare time. With understandable trepidation she got in touch with André at MGM and, at last, he found time to read what Dory had written.

> She wrote extraordinary lyrics. You might say they tended to be downbeat and the words were a bit too multisyllabic for the period, as well as too intelligent. They were the kind of songs that are very much in vogue today but which at that time were hardly the things you'd want recorded by, say, Doris Day. Still, I was crazy about the way she wrote. I just couldn't believe that Arthur Freed had brought this girl clear across the country to work with me and then forgot to tell me about her.

The first of Dory's lyrics André chose to set was called "My Heart Is a Hunter." Like virtually all of Dory's published and recorded output, this is about Dory, casting a narrow-beam searchlight into the caverns of her self. The lyrics describe a heart's hunting through "the vast unknown" for permanence, for a home. To Dory it had already begun to seem that in André she had at last found her destination: he was the com-

bination father-lover-soulmate for whom she'd been searching
so long.

Their collaboration—the musical part of it at any rate—
seemed tailored to success. André and Dory finished a group of
songs and then quickly cut a demonstration tape, with Dory
singing and André playing the accompaniment. Dory found a
record producer who agreed to distribute an album but he
could think of no "name" singer who would touch the material. He suggested that Dory sing it herself, but only if André
would accompany her on the finished record, to supply the
name appeal that might sell a few copies. Dory anticipated rejection, but she asked and André agreed. The title of the
album, which the producer picked from one of the song titles
over Dory's objections, was *Leprechauns Are Upon Me*.

About this time André did something he'd never done
before—he decided to take a vacation. Dory might have gone
along, but her fear of travel, particularly in airplanes, was too
strong. So he went alone to England, a place he just had an
itch to visit. It was, he says, "the classic American tourist trip.
I wanted to *do* England. Well, I did it and I fell in love with
the place instantly and I promised myself I'd return." He
would, but not for several years. Meanwhile, it was back to
Hollywood and more of the same, "grinding out four pounds
of music a week" for the films. No longer, however, would he
work exclusively for MGM.

The only visible rift between André and Metro happened in
1958 when he was assigned to a film called *For the First Time*,
an ironic title since it marked Mario Lanza's first return to the
Culver City studios since he made *Because You're Mine* six
years earlier and since it turned out to be the last film Lanza
made. In Hollywood there was a good deal of resistance to
working with Mario Lanza and André was only more vocal
than many of his peers when he called the tenor "offensive and
boring." He refused to work on the film and the studio placed
him on suspension. That amounted to no more than a wrist-

slap since "three days later they discovered they badly needed me to work on another picture."

Clearly, though, it was time for André to sever his exclusive ties to MGM and to begin working as an independent composer. With the *Gigi* Oscar and his other credits he could earn more by offering his services to the highest bidder. His first free-lance assignment came from the Goldwyn Studios where André was named music director of the very costly and very successful screen version of *Porgy and Bess*. In 1959 that score would bring him his second Academy Award and catapult him into the first rank of film composers.

Containing as it did some of George Gershwin's finest and most recognizable music, *Porgy* presented a ticklish problem to André for the first time. He was not sure just how much of the film score should be Gershwin and how much Previn, how much of Gershwin's own orchestration he could "rearrange" to fit the requirements of a film; but he found his answers in the original score parts, which had been measured to fit the instruments of a Broadway "pit band." André's requirements were something else entirely.

> Gershwin had been stuck with the physical limitations of his orchestra pit. Had he been writing for a larger group he'd have written it differently, because what is orchestrated for thirty men is not necessarily going to sound good when played by one hundred. I had to deal with the facts of life in the late fifties, the days of the new screen processes like CinemaScope and Todd-AO and VistaVision. The screen was getting wider and wider and the music was getting louder and louder, coming at the audience from more and more channels. The producers wanted a rich sound and there was no way I could give it to them without reorchestrating that score.

During his work on *Porgy and Bess* André was provided with a choice bungalow on the Goldwyn lot where Dory would visit him frequently and where they would refine her lyrics and try out his tunes. It was "mainly for the pleasure and experience of working together," Dory writes. "We dreamed of our first million seller. Of some day writing a film musical. Perhaps even a Broadway show." It was all very much a labor of love, as André concurs:

> We wrote a lot of songs that never saw the light of day. We wrote three complete scores to musicals that we couldn't get anybody to produce, despite the fact that there were some very, very good songs in them. Dory seemed to me a very interesting combination: a genuine lyricist who understood the wedding of words and music, as well as an extremely well-read, erudite lady whose vocabulary was infinitely more extensive than that of the usual lyricist. I found her to be the most wonderful craftsman.

Neither André's spoken words nor Dory's writings about those months of working together say anything about falling in love. Nevertheless, one must assume it happened. Dory hints that for much of the time she secretly cherished a dream of someday becoming Mrs. André Previn, but André will say nothing about the processes of thought and emotion that led him to take the marriage vows for the second time, especially in light of Dory's prior and subsequent mental problems. She was thirty-three years old (four years André's senior) and not likely to mature suddenly on her wedding night. According to Dory's account in *Bog-Trotter*, André entered the marriage with his eyes wide open:

> Before we tied the knot I told André I'd had something called a nervous breakdown. I was afraid to go too deeply into details and was relieved when he seemed disinclined to go any further with the subject. In fact he avoided the subject as much as I.

Dory's fear and André's reluctance to go into "personal" details to any depth provide the key to understanding. This was a marriage founded on a failure to communicate adequately. In fifties California, especially in and around Hollywood, "nervous breakdowns" were all the rage. Anybody who was or wanted to be anybody was having one. Psychoanalysis sat on the throne that would come to be occupied by cosmetic surgery in that kingdom of insecurity. Dory's casual mention of her mental problems led André to believe they were simply signs of the prevailing times. Today he maintains that had Dory volunteered a few of those details into which she was afraid to delve, he would have "thought long and hard before asking her to marry me."

> There was simply no hint of the problems to come, from the time we met to the time we married. I knew she'd had a very rough time, but I thought she was finished with all that. She thought, possibly mistakenly, that she didn't have to tell me much about it. When it so vehemently overcame her later, I suppose it must have been as much a shock to her as it was to me. But I simply didn't have the faintest warning about it.

So it happened that on an otherwise unmemorable day late in 1958, in an unmemorable civil ceremony, the tap dancer turned actress turned songwriter, Dory Langdon, became the second Mrs. Previn. The marriage must be credited with helping André to a lamentably late discovery of himself and his true talents, but the marriage was also greatly to blame for Dory's eventual total mental collapse.

XV

if he should hold me fast
and whisper will it last
i'll tell him yes
i'll tell him yes . . .

Unless, the song continues, he should ever suggest it might be time to end the relationship; then Dory would tell André—for the lyrics were certainly about them—"no." The lyrics of "Yes," the first she dedicated to André, imply a naïve belief on Dory's part that whatever evil might befall their marriage, she would simply deny it and it would go away.

Eventually Judy Garland would record "Yes," as would André himself, with a female chorus singing Dory's heartfelt lyrics. It was one of their earliest collaborations and she was still using the name Langdon when it was written. It was not until 1962 that she accepted the fact of her anonymity and wrapped herself in the stylish cloak of the name Previn. As she says, she took André's name and *used* it. "Previn as a label opened doors and charge accounts," she writes, "slightly lessened the feeling of intimidation by headwaiters and got me past the cop at the studio gate."

Unquestionably, by the early sixties any studio gate in Hollywood would open to the name of André Previn. He'd hit his stride as an independent film composer and it would be hard to call any of his films after *Gigi* unsuccessful. As Miklós

Rózsa found out one evening in Paris, even awful films can have exemplary music tracks:

> I was in my room with nothing to do, so I turned on the television and began watching a movie which had already started. I noticed immediately that the music was extraordinary. The dialogue was in French and failing to see that it was dubbed I assumed it was a French film. But the music was certainly not like most French film music, which is not taken very seriously. I tried to think of every composer in France who might have written this score and none of them could have. The story was terrible, but I had to know, so I stayed with it until at last the credits came on and I discovered who it was.

Of course the composer was André. The "terrible" film was MGM's remake of *The Four Horsemen of the Apocalypse*, released in 1961. The score remains one of André's personal favorites, though it was attached to what he terms "a hilariously bad film." Only a small segment of the film-going populace paid to watch it and it turned into a six-million-dollar loss for MGM, besides lingering on as a late-night television embarrassment for Glenn Ford, Charles Boyer, Paul Henreid, Lee J. Cobb, Vincente Minnelli, and a host of others. Aside from the music, perhaps the best thing to be said for *Four Horsemen* is that it is only half as bad as it might have been due to the studio's decision to cut it from four hours to two before it was released. Unfortunately the surgery created some new problems.

André tells the story of one of the film's most dramatic moments, with the music building to a shattering climax as the heroine screams at the hero, standing on the Pont Neuf: "THEN TAKE YOUR *KEY BACK!*" On that cue the orchestra went berserk and the audience sat bewildered. The scene in which he'd given her the fatal key had been excised. *The Four Horsemen of the Apocalypse* produced much red ink and many red faces and it may be seen as a tribute to the power of André's music that MGM decided to release a sound-track album of the score despite the standing-joke status the film had attained within the industry.

Another memorable flop of the early sixties, and another MGM film, was *The Subterraneans,* based on one of Jack Kerouac's beat-generation best-sellers. Since the setting required a jazz-oriented score, it was only natural that the studio should hire André to write it. Since the screenplay called for some recognizable jazz musicians on screen, it was only natural that André should appear playing his own music.

The Subterraneans was hardly the Andy Hardy screen debut Jack and Charles Previn had envisioned for young André fifteen years earlier, but there he was, bigger-than-life on the silver screen, floppy sweater, skinny tie and all, looking very beat. With Gerry Mulligan, Carmen McRae, and others, André was in good musical company and the picture also afforded another opportunity for him to work with the charming Leslie Caron. Unfortunately, *The Subterraneans* turned out to be just another of those films nobody went to see.

Elmer Gantry was altogether a different story and holds much fonder memories for André. The subject inspired André to experiment with the music and so he settled on an orchestra composed only of strings and brass—a departure from the norm for which he'd have been taken to task not so many years earlier. But by this time producers and directors were far less likely to bridle at his winning imagination.

Gantry was indeed winning for Burt Lancaster, to whom the Motion Picture Academy gave the Best Actor award for his portrayal of the mesmerizing preacher. However, there was no Oscar in 1960 for André. He was beginning to think that his second Academy Award would be his last, no matter how often his scores were nominated. In fact in 1963, when he was once again nominated, for *Irma la Douce,* he seriously entertained the notion of just staying home and watching the boring awards presentations on television. He'd gone to them so many times that the glamour of it all, the faint aroma of mothballs from the annually exhumed tuxedos and the requisite ogling of the beauty queen *du jour,* no longer sparked images of victory in his brain. Especially for *Irma la Douce.* It was a cute picture but he gave it about the same chance of success as that oft-cited snowball in hell. Boycotting the awards was the chic thing to do: Billy Wilder wouldn't be there, Shirley MacLaine wouldn't be there, and neither would Jack Lemmon. But none of them had a mate who also happened to be nominated, as André did.

The word "disaster" is flung around in cavalier fashion by the chroniclers of the motion picture industry. It has been applied here and elsewhere to several of the films on which André worked. Even *It's Always Fair Weather* and *Invitation to the Dance,* both good enough films in their way, have been referred to as box office *disasters.* The word is hackneyed and there surely ought to be another—"debacle," perhaps, or "cataclysm"—reserved in movie parlance for special films and only taken out of a storage vault once in a very great while. For films like *Pepe.*

Pepe came about for the sole apparent purpose of Columbia's attempting to turn Mexican comic star Cantinflas into an international superstar, duplicating and even redoubling the success MGM had had with Ricardo Montalban. Cantinflas had proved lovable enough seven years earlier as Passepartout in Mike Todd's *Around the World in 80 Days,* but neither Todd's nor Jules Verne's spirit was there to lift *Pepe* above the banal.

It was one of those cameo-role films, another borrowing from *Around the World,* and went a long way toward eliminating the unemployment problem in Hollywood. For *Pepe's* music, Columbia opted for a similar casting technique. The studio's Music Department chief was named music director of the film, but André was commissioned for several specialty numbers, including one of the movie's big moments, an entertainment-within-the-entertainment in the form of a huge ballet sequence. The ballet was to be a Mexican gang fight, a south-of-the-border version of the ballet in *West Side Story.* In addition, a spotlighted song, which Judy Garland herself had agreed to sing in the film, was assigned to André. The division of responsibility was then multiplied by the announcement that the original music director of the film had been canned and *Pepe*'s score handed over to André's ex-MGM boss, Johnny Green, by now himself a free-lancer.

It may have been due to the prevailing mood of confusion at Columbia Pictures that André succeeded for the first time in bringing Dory into a film as songwriter. Until *Pepe*, all their work had been for the pleasure of working together or for Dory's unspectacular recording ventures. This time André opened an important door and Dory was in. Not only did she write the lyrics for André's blues number, but she also collaborated with John Green on a title song (which, incidentally, made it into the film only as an instrumental).

The song she wrote with André was called "The Faraway Part of Town," a plaintive ballad of a young girl (ultimately played by Shirley Jones) who gazes longingly from her home on the wrong side of the tracks toward the bright lights and tall buildings and excitement glittering just out of reach.

The autobiographical content is unmistakable, Dory writing about Dory. Judy Garland also may have heard an echo of herself in the song because she liked it a great deal and sang it better than anything she'd done in recent years. She sang it unseen because of what the studio considered her deteriorating physical condition. Both the song and the score were hailed in Hollywood as not-quite saving graces in a film that was depressing to the industry, a film whose colossal failure came into focus early on, at the party following its world premiere in New York, a party attended by hardly a soul not directly connected with the studio. As survivors of this Hollywood holocaust, Johnny Green, André, and Dory were nominated for Academy Awards. Had it not been for Dory's starry-eyed anticipation, André surely would have skipped the awards in 1963. As far as he was concerned, *Pepe* had even less chance of winning anything than did *Irma la Douce*. But Dory was confident that nothing could go wrong. She had her acceptance speech ready.

It was a year of unusually stiff competition. From United Artists alone had come—besides *Irma la Douce*—*The Great Escape*, *The Manchurian Candidate*, *Dr. No*, and *Tom Jones*. From other studios had come films of the caliber of Fellini's

8½, *The Longest Day*, *Gypsy*, *The VIPs*, *Days of Wine and Roses*, and *Lilies of the Field*. With all that competition it was coincidental that André and Johnny Green found themselves vying for the same award, best score adaptation, since the scores for both *Irma* and *Pepe* were derived from other sources.

Green that evening was conducting the pit orchestra at the Academy Awards ceremonies, a post André had filled on several earlier occasions and a nerve-jangling one. The conductor must have himself and his musicians so well drilled that as he hangs on every breath of the award presenter, arms raised and ready, they are prepared to launch into the opening bars of any of five possible pieces of theme music for each category.

It was Sammy Davis, Jr., who presented the music awards that night for best song, best score adaptation, and best original score. As André tells the story, when the award for best adapted score was announced, "it was a name other than mine, which didn't surprise me in the least, since I hadn't expected to win." As it turns out, we also have the story from that graciously unnamed colleague who became the butt of an unintended joke that evening.

What Sammy Davis said when he opened the award envelope was: "AND THE WINNER IS, JOHN . . ."

At which point Johnny Green's assistant conductor pushed him from the pit and launched into the theme from *Pepe*.

"Oops," said Davis, "wrong envelope." The security man from Price-Waterhouse had handed him the envelope for the winner of the next category, best *original* score, the winner of which was John Addison for his music for *Tom Jones*.

"Oh-oh, wait till the NAACP hears about this," Davis quipped. The laughter from the audience covered the comedian's embarrassment but served only to exacerbate Green's as the correct envelope was brought out and Sammy Davis read that the winner was Green's onetime apprentice, André Previn.

"Was I surprised when it turned out to be me," André says. "It was fun." Hardly fun for Johnny Green though, as he retrieved his baton and gave the musicians the cue for the theme music from *Irma la Douce*.

Losing that way to André, thinking you hear your own name then hearing somebody else's, made it much tougher to be graceful about it. I was happy for André but lumpy in the throat for me. I never did the exit music. When the presentations were over I handed the stick to my assistant and left the pit. André was the first one to meet me backstage and there he was holding his damned Oscar. He put out his hand and said, "I'm sorry about what happened." I told him I was happy for him and he said, "Are you really?" I said, "André, don't be so goddamned analytical. I'll see you at the party." It was a rough moment for me.

Sometimes a story can be interesting because of what the teller says, sometimes for what he does not say. Green makes it clear that this was the beginning of an awkward rift between him and André that would grow into a feeling of rejection on the part of the older man. André chooses not to mention Johnny Green by name and says nothing about the unpleasantness of bringing discomfort to an old friend: he will not deal in emotions. Nor does he mention an even closer, more upsetting disappointment that evening, that of Dory's failure to win in the best song category for "The Faraway Part of Town."

Dory does not mince words about her feelings, writing that when she realized she hadn't won, her first impulse was to shout an obscenity and storm out. Like her husband's story, Dory's *Bog-Trotter* account is revealing for what she leaves out, the fact that André *did* win an Academy Award that evening. They seemed to be working together and living together, yet somehow living quite separate lives.

Despite the significant success of their collaboration (in that the song from *Pepe* was at least nominated for an Oscar), rather than cementing their partnership the experience portended imminent doom. Others might have read the augury and striven to thwart fate, but André and Dory either failed to notice or refused to believe the warning signals. They chose rather to float along on the surface of their marriage, buoyed by the hollow trappings of André's fame and financial success.

They moved into a beautiful home in Bel Air, on Stone Canyon Road. It was a long low New Englandish house that lay snugly concealed up a bushy curving drive and which, while not so large as its neighbors, could respectably rub lawns with those Movie Star homes and take status from their proximity. To furnish their new home Dory applied what André calls "an impeccable eye" to make it at once unusual for the visitor and comfortable for the occupant. Some years later Dory would express her feelings for this Bel Air house in a song, seeing it as an extension of André and a locus at which and through which she was bound forever to him and, she thought, he was bound to her.

Together they turned the house into a private art gallery, filling the walls with twentieth-century American paintings that spanned the Ashcan School through the late forties. Dory was initiated into this shared passion by André, as Betty had been led into his love of literature. For his own appreciation of modern art André gives partial credit to his sister Leonore and her ceaseless dragging of him through the galleries of Los Angeles. Another of his mentors in this regard was Billy Wilder, director of *Irma la Douce* and, in André's estimation, "a man of enormous erudition."

> In the middle of preparing a script or going over takes, Billy would say, "Enough of this shit. Let's go look at the galleries." And everyone involved would hop into cars and drive downtown to look at paintings. I enjoyed working with him and I miss his company. He was really entertaining to be with.

André became a compulsive buyer of paintings, haunting the galleries of Los Angeles, San Francisco, and New York. He and Dory compiled a collection of what today would be called incredible bargains, works of Georgia O'Keeffe, Marsden Hartley, Arthur Dove, John Marin, John Sloan, and others which now command astronomical prices but which were then still affordable to a man of André's means.

It was wonderful because in those days you didn't have to own a string of banks to buy a painting. It was possible for me, with the indulgence of gallery owners, to pay off a painting as one pays off a Frigidaire purchase. To be always in debt yet always have pictures about. And the gallery owners on both coasts were quite used to sending me notes saying, "You have now sent us your last payment and are free to go into debt again." Then we would go rushing to that paid-off gallery to buy another picture.

Over a few years the Previn collection grew to such dimensions that it was viewed with envy by those same gallery owners and by museum curators. Eventually both the Santa Barbara and Los Angeles County Museums held showings of the collection and now, nearly twenty years later, its value has very likely increased by several powers. André jokes about a day in early 1980 when he stopped in a Chicago gallery owned by a dealer who had once been to their home in Bel Air. The dealer asked whether a certain painting was still in the collection and, when André replied that it was, the dealer told him eagerly, "Well, I now have the pencil sketch from which that painting was made. Would you care to see it?" The sketch was tiny and faded, a mere suggestion of what the finished work had become, yet the sketch carried a price tag of twenty-five thousand dollars. He and Dory had paid exactly twenty-five *hundred* dollars for the completed painting.

In the early sixties the paintings and the house itself were very nearly destroyed by a forest fire which swept out of the hills to ravage Bel Air. André remembers vividly the fire coming ever closer through the hills, the air black and malignant with cinders, and the moment of admission that their cherished home would not be spared.

I remember quite clearly the sight of the house in flames. I had thrown as many paintings as I could into the back of the car and, at the last possible moment, we got in and drove away. Dory was in shreds and tears, quite understandably. As we reached the bottom of our driveway we saw a crew of television newsmen. The cameraman yelled at me, "I didn't get a shot of you coming down the drive. Could you go back and do it again for me?" At which point I actually tried to run him down.

We went to a hotel and twenty-four hours later the police allowed us back into the neighborhood. We discovered that the fire had been rather quixotic, demolishing one house and skipping entirely the house next door. At our house the roof had been burned off almost as though somebody had sliced it away, and half of the walls were badly charred. But a lot of the insides were intact, almost as though nothing had happened. The rooms that were gone were the back rooms, mostly bed- and bathrooms, the rooms that did not contain much in the way of books or manuscripts or scores.

Nearly all of André's treasured possessions had been spared, including his prized collection of Aldous Huxley, one of three complete collections in California of everything ever published by Huxley. Weeks later the author tracked down André by telephone to ask whether the collection was intact and André could assure him that it was. Not all their friends were so lucky. Lukas Foss and his wife lost everything in the fire; all that remained of their brand-new house was the chimney. Foss recounts with affection the story of his answering the door of their hastily rented unfurnished apartment to find two deliverymen and a large round table. It had been sent by Dory and André, "to eat on and to compose on." The gift, says Foss, "was so nice, because even though they had been hurt they realized we had nothing."

The fire left an unprecedented demand for builders and building materials in southern California and it would be nearly a year before the Previns could look forward to returning to the house on Stone Canyon Road. In the interim, André rented a small townhouse apartment that had only a narrow driveway separating it from the apartment next door.

They were not long in discovering that their new neighbor was another Bel Air resident displaced by the fire.

> I had bought an upright piano for the apartment and had it placed next to this particular window where the light happened to be best and that's where I did most of my work. One day I looked out the window and across the way, in the house next door, there was someone I'd never met but recognized instantly as Andy Williams. He was quite obviously in his bathroom shaving, and as he shaved he sang. Well, I liked the song and I liked his voice, but I thought he really needed an accompanist. So I ducked down beneath the windowsill and started playing along, accompanying him through the open windows. The singing stopped and I sneaked a look. There was Andy, gazing around in disbelief, unable to see me or my piano from where he was standing. He shook his head and went back to shaving and singing, and I went back to playing.
>
> I found out pretty soon that Andy Williams sang whenever he was in the bathroom, for whatever purpose. Whenever I'd spot him through another window heading toward the can I'd drop what I was doing and rush to the piano to accompany him. Finally one day he got the direction pinned down, leaned out his window and said, "All right. Who lives over there?" I waved and we went outside and introduced ourselves. I understand he's still fond of telling that story.

Hollywood could be a lot of fun, but the bontemps was growing stale for André; being music-maker to the stars had lost its glitter. Looking into his own bathroom mirror he saw a man of more than thirty years who'd written music for more than fifty films, a man who was more than a little close to becoming the next Max Steiner or Alfred Newman. He did not want that, had no desire for their sort of fame. There were only a handful of those fifty-odd film scores that contained music he felt proud of and even those few were individual only in that they tended to evoke Prokofiev or Copland rather than Steiner or Newman. It was music that *sounded* good but that had little of what he would call substance. As a film composer he was as burned out as Bel Air.

The face in the mirror told André it was time to get on with what he knew was his true calling: conducting. It was past time to take seriously the advice he'd received a few years earlier from Schuyler Chapin of Columbia Records, that he should leave Hollywood and take to the road as a traveling conductor of serious music. He looked in the mirror and knew it had to happen soon or it might never happen.

XVI

It was in 1961 that Schuyler Chapin, head of Columbia Records' classical music division, Masterworks, first heard André conduct a symphony orchestra. He knew, of course, of André's many years of film conducting, but what he heard that day was something quite different and unexpected. André was conducting once again that rehearsal orchestra of studio musicians who played their symphonies for pleasure. Though the circumstances may not have been "professional," Chapin detected an unmistakable aura of professionalism about André's leadership and he felt certain that with time and experience—he guessed about ten years' worth—André could become a classical conductor of the first order. This opinion would have been challenged by some of André's Hollywood peers, not all of whom are as outspoken as Johnny Green:

> If someone had asked me then what was André's métier, I'd have answered, any one of the facets of his musical activity . . . except conducting. I thought of André as a brilliant pianist, as a potentially important composer, once he got rid of his inhibitions. Certainly he had the world of commercial music as his oyster if he wanted it.
>
> His conducting seemed workaday, a serviceable tool. I found it dull and mannered and I was too immature myself to realize that those faults were com-

pensatory; they were all on account of his own lack of experience, never having worked in any capacity as an assistant conductor. Okay, sure, he studied with Monteux. Sure, he got himself a stick and developed all the trappings of a conductor. But if anybody had asked me in those days, "What's André Previn going to be?" I never would have answered, "A conductor." And I'd have been as wrong as it is possible to be.

What Green had failed to observe in André was the change in style and intent that manifested itself at MGM after his return from San Francisco. But if the change was not obvious, it was as much André's fault as anyone's. Having sidestepped the traditional assistantship route, André assumed he was not on his way to becoming a conductor, no matter how he would have liked to be one. That vocation was apparent to Schuyler Chapin only years after André's work with Monteux, but film composer Miklós Rózsa spotted the difference immediately.

Meeting Monteux was the great good luck of André, otherwise I don't know what would have happened. He might have come to serious music sooner or later, but probably later. He came home after his studies with Monteux and went to work on his first film and I wanted to be in the recording studio on the first day he conducted because I wanted to see for myself whether there was any real difference. Up until then it had been the usual studio beat, just like all the others. But as I watched from the booth it was like a miracle. Suddenly, there was a *conductor*. From that time on he was much more interested in doing serious music.

Rózsa had been paternally solicitous about André's development since their first meeting, even before the incident of André's hand stand-in for Barbara Stanwyck. It went back to the summer prior to the start of their MGM colleague-ship, at the Hollywood Bowl when André was nineteen. He was guest soloist and Rózsa guest conductor for Rachmaninoff's *Rhap-*

sody on a Theme of Paganini. Rózsa recalls that after going through the music a couple of times with André, "it was the easiest thing to conduct. He was so musical. I knew the boy was in the movie business, but at that moment I also knew that he was not 'one of the boys.'"

What the composer grew to admire most about André was his versatility, particularly in the post-Army days when André would step from completing a film score on Thursday afternoon to playing jazz on Thursday night to conducting the MGM Orchestra on Friday to performing as a classical pianist Friday night to accompanying Betty (and later Dory) on Saturday. It was the immersion of André in music of whatever sort that astounded Rózsa, even though some of that music, notably jazz, was outside the limits of his appreciation.

> That jazz was bloody nonsense. Deedlee-boom-boom-boom. And everyone but me in ecstasy. But from that to jump into Grieg is quite a jump and André did it splendidly. I remember a concert of his I conducted at the Bowl, with the Los Angeles Philharmonic in the Grieg Concerto. He had never played it before and I found his attitude about late Romantic music ambiguous. In the beginning, at rehearsals, I don't think he liked it. But before long he fell in love with it. It was simply that he'd never had it in his hands before. Now that warm music was talking to him, especially after all the cool jazz he'd been involved with.

Rózsa's bungalow at MGM was the starting point for many famous European musicians—and some notable Americans as well—who came for one reason or another to tour the Culver City studios. For each of his distinguished visitors the itinerary included a private concert by the resident prodigy, whom Rózsa loved to put through his paces. According to the composer, the only one of these visitors who failed to be impressed by André's virtuosity was Eugene Ormandy. Rózsa says Ormandy listened dutifully to André's playing and then sniffed, "Well, I realize he's young of course, but he hasn't got the faintest idea how to play the piano." (Years later in Philadelphia, says Rózsa, Ormandy stoutly denied ever having heard André play.) But most of the visiting musical firemen reacted more in the manner of André's onetime Paris organ instructor, Marcel Dupré.

> Dupré was an old friend of mine. He also happened to be the greatest improviser who ever lived. I don't know what was in his brain, but what the fingers could do was incredible. I asked André to have lunch with us and afterwards took the Duprés into a studio to hear him play. I had an appointment and when I came back, more than an hour later, he was still entertaining them. Dupré was tremendously impressed and when I drove them home he and his wife talked the whole way about André and how that boy should go very far. I said, "Well, he's doing everything, you know. He's composing, he's conducting, he's playing jazz . . ." "Mais quoi? Le jazz? Ce n'est pas concevable!" I said, "Yes, but that's what he's doing."

As the sixties wore on, "le jazz," as "le cinéma," held diminishing fascination for André. Jazz, he came to feel, is "young man's music." His jazz friends were still his friends, his jazz heroes still his heroes, but jazz was moving on and he had little liking for the course it was taking. Peterson, Gillespie, Manne—Previn—were becoming elder statesmen, tolerated in much the same fashion as he and they had smiled ten years earlier at the old guys from the swing era. His interest in that kind of music was fading along with his enthusiasm for staying out till four in the morning in smoky clubs. Time was becoming far too precious and jazz far too expendable.

> Just as I never considered myself a "movie composer" but a composer who liked doing movies, so I always thought of myself as a musician who liked jazz and could play some of it but not as a "jazz musician." And I surely couldn't see myself doing any of that for the rest of my life. What I really wanted was to con-

duct, not just film scores and rehearsal orchestras, but really *conduct*. Instead, I found myself doing concerts in the classical field not as a conductor but as a pianist. I did it whenever anyone asked me and I could make time for it, but even then it was usually a *Rhapsody in Blue* or a Gershwin Concerto.

In whatever medium, breaking into classical music was bound to be difficult for a best-selling jazz pianist with three Oscars. Either impresarios and music directors viewed him as an interloper who'd not yet paid his dues (he had, of course, but not to their union) or they sought him as a gimmicky attraction to draw crowds on "pops" evenings.

Whether or not he approved of his image, André was a glamour figure, a child of the media at home among the squiggling threads of light of movie sound tracks, in front of television cameras, along the spiraling groove of a phonograph record. Standing before a proscenium in white tie and tails or seated stiffly at a concert grand, André Previn became a novelty act.

Not surprisingly, André saw that he could use his media connections as a means of breaking down those attitudes. Television as a tool would come later and film had to be abandoned eventually, but the phonograph record was malleable and its industry rulers accessible to him. Like a good military strategist, he chose the path of least resistance, Contemporary Records and Lester Koenig.

Despite Koenig's inevitable protestations that such a small-scale project was beneath him, André involved himself in a series of recordings by "The Society for Forgotten Music," produced by composer Vernon Duke. Los Angeles' tireless espousers of musical esoterica always seemed ready for André's sight-reading talents and he always seemed to find glimmers of commercial appeal in the darkest obscurity. Salability was hardly a factor, however, in the first of his Forgotten Music recordings in 1957 when, with violinist Nathan Rubin, André performed William O. Smith's Capriccio for violin and piano. Many were pressed but few were distributed.

The following year André tackled the less offbeat Piano

Quartet in A major of Ernest Chausson, joining members of the Roth Quartet with whom he had taken his first tentative steps into classical music recording many years earlier. There was even more déjà-vu when André sat down with his old tutorial nemesis, Ernst Toch, to prepare Toch's Piano Quintet for recording. It was on this occasion that Toch could not recall having encountered André ever before. Which was probably all the better for the recording sessions.

The last years of the decade saw a flurry of collaboration between André and Contemporary, for despite André's cooling affair with jazz, he and Koenig were both hell-bent on duplicating the success of their *My Fair Lady* album. When, in 1959, they came very close to doing that with *West Side Story*, André and his pals were quick to land a better contract with Columbia Records, a company that could guarantee their jazz efforts far wider distribution.

As part of his contractual agreement with Columbia, André secured the promise that he would be allowed to record some solo piano albums in the Masterworks series. So it was that in 1961 Schuyler Chapin came to Los Angeles to see what could be done about fulfilling that bargain and so it was that Chapin chanced to attend the orchestra rehearsal and proceeded to advise André to abandon all his other careers and concentrate on conducting. In 1961 André was not quite ready for that sort of commitment, though he felt even then that the time was not far off. Meanwhile, Masterworks was a classical bird-in-the-hand.

André's first recording for Masterworks was a pairing of Hindemith's Piano Sonata No. 3 with Samuel Barber's *Four Excursions* and the Prelude No. 7 of Frank Martin. That was, as André ruefully acknowledges, "not exactly the sort of repertoire that gets listeners beating down the doors of record shops." But it was a foot in those doors and it was good music played very well. André's unflagging willingness to cope with contemporary piano music showed how firm a foundation had been laid in the Monday Evening Concerts of his adolescence. That even as he was learning that extraordinary repertoire for Masterworks he was also putting together a commercially successful album for their Popular division must have made André's signing seem like a stroke of genius to the Columbia staff. Though perhaps not classical, the commercial album is truly a classic, a teaming-up with the preeminent jazz trombonist, J. J. Johnson, for *The Theater Songs of Kurt Weill*.

The Weill album was a cagey and inspired bit of self-marketing on André's part, what with Weill's identification with serious music. Moreover, the album contains so much originality and serious music-making that it was bound to attract a certain amount of crossover buying by non-jazz-oriented modernists who could derive at least intellectual pleasure from something like "Mack the Knife's Morität" played from start to finish in diametrically opposed keys—the trombone in C, the piano in G-flat.

The next four years saw André continue his work as a pianist in obscure music for Columbia Masterworks. The best of these recordings may be his pairing of Poulenc and Roussel, especially in light of the jazz inflections in both works. The disc also began a record of success for André in the recording of French music, perhaps traceable to that brief and sunny childhood stay in France. At any rate, André established early on a solid base of French music on which he would build an extensive repertoire.

In the last month of 1962 André began an album eventually released by Columbia as *Piano Pieces for Children*. The material for side one, works by Mendelssohn, Mozart, and Mussorgsky, lay around for almost a year until one day André sat down at the studio piano to sight-read, just for amusement's sake, a group of satirical pieces by Goddard Lieberson, chief of Columbia Records in America. With a musical wit that infected all present, André breezed through the four sections: "Piano Pieces for Advanced Children or Retarded Adults," "Five Songs with Mendelssohn," "Six Technical Studies (Which Teach You Nothing)," and "Eight Studies in Musicology (Which Will Teach You a Great Deal)." André had no idea the session was being recorded or that it would wind up as side two of his Mozart-Mendelssohn-Mussorgsky disc.

Whatever artistic success André had with his playing for Columbia Masterworks, those efforts could hardly be considered financially successful. As films they would have been labeled "box office disasters" or at least "flops." Yet within the serious music world they were noticed. They *had* to be noticed and that was part of André's strategy. The works were so obscure, most of them at any rate, that to hear them one had to listen to Previn's playing.

There was one occasion in 1962 when the young Soviet pianist Vladimir Ashkenazy, then blazing his own trail in the music world, gave a recital in Los Angeles and afterward was introduced to André at a party. "I remember asking him for a copy of one of his records," Ashkenazy says, "because I was just out of the Soviet Union and I didn't realize you could just walk into a record store and buy one. But for some reason he never sent it to me." It develops that this was a quaint turnabout to the Eddie Duchin–André Previn encounter of some twenty years earlier; this time it was André who was reticent in the presence of the other fellow because he thought Ashkenazy played so much better.

Actually it is unlikely that Ashkenazy could have walked into any record store and bought one of André's Columbia Masterworks releases. They were in and out of the stores faster than the latest Beatles album, though they were not sold but returned. There was simply too small a market for that repertoire. Then Columbia hit upon a plan to exploit commercially André's classical ambitions, without sacrificing his Hollywood jazzman image, by releasing a record of André performing the Gershwin *Rhapsody in Blue* and Concerto in F. To enhance further the commercial appeal of the album, André Kostelanetz was flown out to the West Coast to conduct a pickup orchestra. The recording was made in two days in the dreary but acoustically viable American Legion Hall on Holland Avenue and it gave Columbia Masterworks division its first Previn hit.

The Gershwin album helped entrench André's reputation as a pianist of extraordinary ability and a performer of magnetic appeal, to be sought after on the concert stage at least in the light-classic piano repertoire. It also helped Leonard Bernstein remember André as the kid who'd played his *Age of Anxiety* for him on the West Coast. He hired André to play the Shostakovich Piano Concerto No. 1 in a televised "Young People's Concert" of the New York Philharmonic. Ultimately the concerto was cut from the television show but was subsequently recorded by Columbia. Trumpet soloist William Vacchiano matched André's brilliance and Bernstein's enthusiasm, and the recording remains a delight to the ear.

Another work, like those of Gershwin and Shostakovich, which André had performed occasionally in his sporadic and slow-growing concertizing career was the *Burleske* of Richard Strauss, that piece he had memorized practically overnight for the performance in Franz Waxman's festival. The *Burleske*, with its faintly suggestive title and its lighthearted nature, seemed material well suited to André's Hollywood notoriety and Columbia decided the combination might have mass-market appeal. In order to give the still seldom-recorded piece a touch of legitimacy for the cognoscenti, however, André and Schuyler Chapin agreed that they needed a proper conductor. The perfect man for the job would be George Szell. It happened that about this time Szell arrived in Los Angeles to conduct the Philharmonic and Chapin arranged a meeting with André in the conductor's hotel suite. He went forewarned that Szell might not accept him as a colleague.

> Szell answered the door wearing an immaculate unwrinkled suit. He looked phenomenal. The room itself was too orderly for anyone to have been living in it. He was very nice as we sat down and talked about the *Burleske*. He asked me why I wanted to record the piece and I told him that I liked it very much. He asked me whom I'd worked with as a pianist and I answered, "Well, most recently Lenny Bernstein." That only got me a lecture on what was wrong with Lenny's conducting. I managed to mention that I'd studied with Monteux and that was a point for my side. At last he said, "Well, let's go through the piece." Relieved, I got up to go to the piano, but I couldn't see one.

Not to worry, said Szell. He knew the piece quite well and needed only to "hear" me play it on the tabletop. "Sit down here and play me the beginning," he said. Well, I was still young and inexperienced, I suppose, and in awe of the great conductor, so I didn't walk out. I sat down and started whacking away at this table in the Beverly Wilshire Hotel. After no more than a few moments he stopped me and said, "No, no, no. It needs to be faster," without a trace of a smile. At that point I felt incredibly stupid. I said, "Well, maestro, the reason it sounds so slow is that I'm simply not used to this table. My dining room table at home has much better action."

He looked at me coldly and said, "I don't consider that funny, young man. You may go." I laughed about the incident all the way home, but the next morning Szell called Columbia and said he would not be making any records with Mr. Previn because I was not a serious-enough musician. The whole *Burleske* project just went down the drain.

So it was that André's concerto-playing career with Columbia Records ended with the Gershwin and Shostakovich discs. The company simply had more than enough good pianists to accommodate the standard repertoire. But André's name continued to be a drawing card at live concerts. He played a series of "imitation Promenade Concerts" in Los Angeles, he played with Kostelanetz in the New York Philharmonic's springtime series, he played once for Arthur Fiedler in Boston despite the fact that his face was covered with chicken pox, and he continued to play "with horrendous regularity" at the Hollywood Bowl. Asked how the concertizing career evolved, André laughs:

It didn't *evolve* at all. It just happened. There was no method to it. If somebody said they'd like me to play the Gershwin Concerto I'd say, "Fine." If they asked me to do the *Age of Anxiety* I'd say, "Fine." The

Grieg Concerto? "Fine." *Rhapsody in Blue?* "Fine." I
just wanted to play and I was too stupid to do it with
any rhyme or reason.

The fees he commanded as a pianist were better than average since they were based on his Hollywood-cum-jazz appeal
rather than his limited exposure as a classical pianist, and those
fees, along with payment for his jazz gigs and royalties from
jazz recordings, would have amounted to a substantial income
in themselves. But as long as he could count on the revenue
from motion pictures, everything else was just gravy. The
films were there as long as he wanted them and part of his rationale for continuing to want them for so long was that as a
film composer he could help Dory with her career.

The second film on which they worked together, after *Pepe,*
was *Two for the Seesaw* for United Artists. Ironically, the title
of the theme song was "Second Chance." The music was excellent—André still rates it among his favorite scores—and
"Second Chance" brought Dory her second nomination for an
Academy Award. Again Dory got her hopes too high, again she
went to the presentations with an acceptance speech in her
head, and again she was disappointed.

Still, two nominations out of two pictures is an achievement
in itself, but Dory felt that she was not getting the recognition
she deserved. André continued to meet with resistance when
he tried to bring her into a film and Dory blamed this on the
industry's male domination, the two notable exceptions of
Dorothy Fields and Betty Comden only serving to prove the
rule that writing lyrics was a man's occupation. Nevertheless,
André managed to involve Dory in at least one film project a
year. They collaborated on *Goodbye Charlie, Who Was That
Lady?,* and *Inside Daisy Clover.* Their song "You're Gonna
Hear from Me" from *Daisy Clover* actually enjoyed a brief season of popularity on the charts.

One of their jointly dreamt ambitions was a film musical
version of *Goodbye, Mr. Chips,* a project they began in
sheerest speculation in 1961. Over the next couple of years the
project took shape and gathered momentum. MGM bought
the idea and assigned Gower Champion to write the screen-

play. Months of haggling ensued with much disagreement over Dory's lyrics. At last she was judged "inappropriate" for the film. If Dory went, André threatened, he also would walk off. The studio made no objection and replaced them both with Leslie Bricusse. Champion, who was a friend of André's, quit in sympathy and the screenplay was given to another ex-dancer, Herbert Ross, who, Dory says, had been brought to Hollywood at her suggestion as choreographer for *Inside Daisy Clover*.

The experience could hardly have been pleasant for anyone, certainly not Dory. She thought of André as a winner and she began to fear that she was holding him back. All their work on *Goodbye, Mr. Chips* went for naught, to be filed and forgotten.

Their disappointment over *Mr. Chips* was not much eased by MGM's disappointment when the film finally made it to theater screens in 1969, eight years after its inception, quickly assuming the epithet "disaster." Though it may have given Dory some small satisfaction to read reviews which blamed much of the film's failure on the songs of Leslie Bricusse. That satisfaction was far down the road in the early '60s as Dory kept on dreaming of brilliant success shared with André and kept on writing gloomily prophetic lyrics:

> they're going nowhere
> their dreams are packed
> but going nowhere
> and that's a fact
> their hearts are ready
> their hopes are high
> but going nowhere
> their lives a lie

"Going Nowhere" is from another of their discontinued dreams, a stage musical version of Jean Anouilh's *Thieves' Carnival*. The songs from this unproduced play were, according to André, among the best work he and Dory ever did together. "I still like them a lot," he says. "But no one ever looked at them." The lyrics from *Thieves' Carnival* show Dory at her best. In such songs as "Here Am I" and "The Old Soft Shoe" she is both incisive and revealing of the course of their life together. But from all indications they never intended and never read those lyrics as autobiography, not even the long and masterful monologue "To Find Myself," which one can imagine coming from the lips of either André or Dory, in which the principal character wonders whether he'll ever find out who he is.

They both seemed to be running a race against time to find themselves. André was trying every key in his pocket in every door he could find that might open for him the world of serious music, with yet a suspicion that perhaps that world would not welcome him. Dory's success was limited and suspect because much of it stemmed from André's influence. She felt unwanted in Hollywood, yet clung to it; as her husband's career pulled him away from Hollywood she began to feel less wanted and needed by him.

More and more, as the decade of the sixties waned, André was finding his identity in conducting. His contacts at Columbia Records, the contacts he'd made as a pops soloist with numerous orchestras, these were beginning to pay off in the form of occasional calls to fill in for suddenly ailing conductors. Still the repertoire tended to be Gershwin and Porter nights, evenings on Broadway, and music from films, but he was conducting. And once in a great while a Mozart or a Brahms symphony or overture would turn up on a program. Inevitably reviews of those concerts would identify him as "Hollywood's André Previn."

> If I did a piece with two harps it was instantly a "Hollywood" performance. That was written so often I stopped taking the reviews seriously. I knew that if the critic had heard the very same performance on a record, with the label torn off, he wouldn't have had the slightest idea which set of pejoratives to apply. The opinions were preset. But I knew when a performance was good or bad.

For the moment there was nothing André could do to shake the Hollywood image, which was just as well for his sake. Not having a manager, it was all he could do to bring in those early conducting engagements. So he clung to that image and to his dependency upon the film industry, to Dory's relief but much to the dismay of his ailing, aging father.

Broken and embittered by the death of his only daughter, Jack Previn had become an old man overnight. Now he almost never came out from that shell of cynicism which had sheltered him in the years following his flight from Germany. Jack spent long periods confined to bed and André grew increasingly concerned for his father.

One night I'd just finished playing the Rachmaninoff *Paganini Rhapsody* with the L.A. Philharmonic and as soon as the applause ended I walked offstage and went to a telephone so I could check on him. Before I could say anything about the performance I'd just given, with the applause still ringing in my ears, he said, "Tell me something. When is that Schumann you're supposed to play in San Francisco?" I said it was in about six weeks and he said, "Ach! You'll never have it ready in time."

What André perceived as a possible breakthrough, one that might satisfy even Papa as to his intentions, came in the fall of 1962 when he was called at the last minute to conduct the St. Louis Symphony in a program of serious music. Though hardly a first-line American orchestra, St. Louis had gained national recognition first under Vladimir Golschmann, then under the energetic Brazilian conductor Eleazar de Carvalho. Carvalho had fallen ill and manager William Zalken wanted André to fill in.

Eager to convey personally to his father the news of his most prestigious conducting assignment to date, André rushed to Jack's bedside. The words were barely out of his mouth, André recalls, when "he looked at me with the sin of pride written all over my face and he said, with a sigh of finality, 'Well. You can't get Boston.'"

It was a series of heart attacks which finally claimed Jack Previn in 1963. At the time the word "career" could not yet have been attached to his son's stubborn efforts at conducting.

A father of vision or even with a little optimism might have caught sight of that career lying just around the next turn in André's fortunes. But in his last days Jack Previn was no longer the visionary who'd enrolled his little boy in the Berlin Hochschule, no longer the optimist who'd listened to his teenaged son's first audition for a film studio. What Jack saw of André's life, up to the age of thirty-four, served only to convince him that as a father he had failed. He somehow had given the wrong advice, somewhere had not applied the stern hand; the child prodigy had become the prodigal son, squandering his talents and wasting his life. Jack died too soon, leaving André to make the burial arrangements. Steve was away in Europe, working on a movie.

> I was devastated by his death and suddenly, without knowing quite how I'd gotten there, I found myself in Forest Lawn Cemetery, amid tastelessness and tactlessness of such a monumental nature that it somehow transcended grief and brought me to another plane, one of comic wonderment.
>
> When I arrived, my name was dutifully checked off a registry and a soft-spoken receptionist asked me to take a seat and my grief counselor would be with me in a moment. *My grief counselor?* Pardon me? But she steadfastly refused to say "mortician." That gentleman, when he arrived, asked if I would like a moment alone with the makeup lady and then suggested a blanket of red, white, and blue flowers for the coffin. I explained that my father had been neither an actor nor a general.
>
> By the time he took me to pick out the coffin, the gallows humor had worn thin and I only wanted out of there. I was beginning to feel claustrophobic. But in the coffin showroom I was taken to what he assured me was the Rolls-Royce of coffins, complete with rosewood finish and gold-plated handles.
>
> This was all a waste of time. I told him I would simply walk to the coffin I wanted and that would be the end of it. Instantly his tone of voice changed.

"*Well*," he said, "if that's what you *really* want. But you're *crazy* to turn down the rosewood like that. I mean, don't you realize that Harry *Warner* was buried in one just *like* it?"

André claims he heard another voice in his ear, distant but clear, perhaps the voice of his father calling one last time from beyond. *There. That's Hollywood,* the voice said. *Get out now. Go.* But where? St. Louis? Where was he going to find the kind of security he'd built for himself in California? He couldn't get Boston, or Philadelphia, or New York, or Cleveland, for that matter. But didn't they call St. Louis the Gateway to the East?

XVII

"A shrewd, generous, kind, and disorganized man" is André's description of William Zalken, former manager of the St. Louis Symphony. "He's the first one who told me to go ahead and do whatever I wanted to do: Mozart, Brahms, Beethoven, Britten, Copland, Shostakovich, whatever. And he invited me back three years in a row."

Present at a rehearsal for one of his earliest concerts in St. Louis happened to be Schuyler Chapin. He'd flown out from New York to nail down with André details of an album of Fauré and Mendelssohn piano trios. This time Chapin was even more impressed with André's conducting skills than he'd been the previous year in Los Angeles.

> I sat through one two-and-a-half-hour rehearsal for this huge program and I saw that day the most extraordinary example of using minimal time in a maximum way. As I watched him work I had the gut feeling that here was a major talent for whom nothing yet had been possible in the classical field. I felt he could do it, even though there were built-in problems because of his background and because of the innate snobbishness of those people who would not want a person well known in his field to cross over into theirs.

What followed was a series of fortuitous coincidences, kneaded together by Chapin's desire to help mold André as a conductor. Half-jokingly, André asked Chapin whether he might not be allowed to make a record for Columbia as a conductor. At first the Masterworks executive smiled patronizingly and proceeded to rattle off that well-known list of conductors to whom his firm was already bound by contract, a formidable array even without the recently deceased Bruno Walter: George Szell, Leonard Bernstein, Eugene Ormandy, Igor Stravinsky, Aaron Copland, and the young Thomas Schippers. There would be little chance of getting an orchestra for André to conduct, let alone finding a market for his work.

Then Chapin remembered a contract which Columbia had signed some years back with this very orchestra, the St. Louis Symphony, whose players and manager seemed so taken with André. A call to New York confirmed that there was one record remaining to be made under the contract, which would soon expire. Chapin had intended to let the contract lapse without that final release, since the arrangement originally was made so that Columbia engineers could test out the acoustical properties of an old St. Louis brewery. Now, if the orchestra agreed, Chapin was willing to use the beer factory once again as a trial forum for conductor André Previn.

Zalken and his orchestra were only too glad to comply and a recording deal was struck. Zalken found a date in the spring when André could return to work with the orchestra again prior to the recording date. Unfortunately, there was no matching the repertoire of that spring concert—Brahms and Beethoven—with Columbia's requirements. As in the past, if André wanted to make classical records he would have to work outside the basic repertoire. This time, however, he was not dealing with a company like Contemporary, willing to settle for a tiny share of the market with almost unmarketable music; this time all concerned were interested only in a record that would net respectable sales.

The choice of material turned out to be surprisingly easy. On his first concert in St. Louis, André had conducted Benjamin Britten's *Sinfonia da Requiem*, an excellent and deeply moving composition of 1941. The music was of great interest to André, and what appealed to Chapin was the fact that the only previous recording was one conducted by the composer in monophonic sound.

As for the other side of the disc, there is disagreement about who proposed Aaron Copland's orchestral suite from the film score of *The Red Pony*. André maintains it was the recording executive's idea but Chapin claims he thought it would be a "dreadful combination" and fully intended to come up with an alternate proposal to be recorded later. But after *The Red Pony* was recorded Chapin's evaluation turned full compass to "tremendously exciting" and the Britten-Copland pairing was released.

From the critics, that minuscule portion of the small segment of the populace which pays any attention to classical recordings, the immediate reaction was surprise. Most of the music world had no inkling that André had designs on a conducting career outside the plush and pampered repose of movie scoring. Virtually none of the critics was prepared for the thoughtful, credible readings he gave to the *Sinfonia da Requiem* and *The Red Pony*. Even with an orchestra like the St. Louis, taxed to the limits of its skills and experience, André's energy, understanding, and firm hand all came through on the recording. Despite the predictable murmurings of Hollywoodishness—the ready rationale stemming from the Copland work's filmic genesis—a small thrill of promise shot through the classical music world.

The release of the "*Red Pony* record," as it has come to be called by followers of André's career, was unquestionably the breakthrough for him. For starters, it helped lead him to a manager. Until that point André had managed, or mismanaged, his own career. Rather surprisingly, no Hollywood agent had signed him to a long-term contract, but then in Los Angeles he didn't need an agent to find more work than he could handle. Conducting was different. If he was going to succeed as a conductor he would need someone to look after his interests, to find, select, and secure for him the right opportunities with the right orchestras. It had to be someone who knew the strings and could pull them, for there were neither

opportunities nor orchestras enough for all the young conductors who wanted them.

Nor did André have time to waste on mistakes. At age
thirty-four he was not exactly young to be "starting out" as a
conductor. Someone who knew the business would have to
step in quickly and take advantage of André's gathering momentum or the parade might quickly pass him by, leaving him
to slink back into the miasma of Hollywood. Both William
Zalken and Schuyler Chapin thought they knew the right man
for the job. Independently and unbeknown to each other, they
contacted Ronald Wilford, vice-president of Columbia Artists
Management, Inc. and a man of considerable influence among
American orchestras. According to Wilford, it was Zalken who
called first:

> Willy Zalken and I were very close then, doing a lot
> of business together, and on the phone one day he
> told me about André Previn. What impressed Willy
> was his knowledge of the score, his presence on the
> podium, and his basic conducting abilities. On top of
> that, he said the musicians liked him—and I don't
> mean just *liked* him; he got them to rehearse the way
> he wanted them to and they were sufficiently
> impressed at that to give him a good performance.
> Well, I considered Zalken a phenomenal judge of
> conductors, so I'd already made up my mind to get in
> touch with Previn when, the following week, who but
> Schuyler Chapin called and said, "Would you be in-
> terested in meeting André Previn?" I told him that
> indeed I would.

That meeting was set up a few weeks later in the Edwardian
Room of the Plaza Hotel in New York, attended by one of the
reigning lords of the classical music business, the overseer of a
major classical record label (and future General Manager of
the Metropolitan Opera), and the Hollywood composer-
pianist, no longer a wunderkind, who wanted to conduct orchestras. It was a fateful meeting, yet none of those in attend-

ance can recall a feeling of being present at the creation of a new career. Rather, it was a dry and business-like conversation over lunch. The conversation can be pieced together from their various recollections.

"If what Schuyler tells me is true," Wilford began, "you have the makings of a pretty good conductor."

"Well, it would be nice to think so."

"You can believe it," Chapin interjected.

"Of course I haven't seen you conduct, but I've heard you play and you're a dandy pianist."

"Thank you."

"Then there are lots of dandy pianists, aren't there? And there are not all that many good conductors. The question is, how to get people to take you seriously as a conductor, given your background."

"Granted."

"Quite obviously you're going to have to give up your other activities entirely, both the Hollywood business and the jazz."

"I've all but given up the jazz anyway, but the movies are a different matter. They're paying the bills."

"How about if he gives up *most* of the film work?" asked Chapin hopefully.

"Say I do eighty percent conducting for you and twenty percent film work."

Wilford ruminated for a moment over a bite of lunch before responding. "The films pay well, don't they?"

"Extraordinarily well. Shamefully well, as a matter of fact."

"Then one film a year should carry for a while. I'll let you do one film a year for the time being only. Eventually all connection with Hollywood must be severed."

"One film a year, eh?"

"Only under that condition can I take you on. It can't be a hobby for you. It's got to be your profession, your *job*, even though you'll make little or no money from it at first."

Chapin asked what sort of orchestras Wilford had in mind for André's first season and the manager replied, "Orchestras he's never heard of. Maybe orchestras *you've* never heard of, in cities you can't even fly to directly from New York."

André bridled a bit at that suggestion because he felt he'd already risen above that sort of thing. After this meeting, for example, he would be leaving for Philadelphia and a pops concert Chapin had arranged through Roger Hall, then manager of the Philadelphia Orchestra. He wondered aloud how it would look for him to be conducting one day orchestras of the Philadelphia's stature and the next some civic symphony in Kalamazoo or in Elkhart, Indiana, or Jackson, Mississippi.

Wilford pointed out that it was precisely the repertoire he'd be conducting in Philadelphia that André wanted to escape. "And you'll never get back to Philadelphia with Beethoven unless you first do Beethoven in Kalamazoo. If conducting pop concerts is what you want to do for the rest of your life, then you don't need to be paying me twenty percent. If you want Beethoven and Brahms and Mozart, then you'd better start building up your repertoire in the hinterland, because I can assure you Roger Hall's not going to let you do it in Philadelphia. Nor would I, because you'd be eaten alive by the critics."

"Let me have a little time to think about that."

"All right. You think about it and you let me know. If you decide this thing is really what you want, then we'll try it for a year. I'll run you around the country as much as I can during that year and you may squeeze in whatever film work you find time for. At the end of one year I'll let you know whether or not I think you really are a conductor. If the answer for both of us is in the affirmative, then you will conduct to the exclusion of every other activity. Agreed?"

"I'll let you know."

Hindsight has allowed André to scoff at his recalcitrance, but it must be pointed out that Wilford's proposal came at the very time Hollywood offered him a hand in what was sure to become one of its most successful and profitable ventures ever, the movie version of *My Fair Lady*.

Nearly a decade after André had surprised and delighted Lerner and Loewe with his jazz rendition of their Broadway score, they insisted at Warner Brothers that André was the only music director in Hollywood they would entrust with the task of transforming that same music into a film score. Since that first encounter André had collaborated successfully and happily with Alan Jay Lerner on *Gigi* and now "there was no way for me not to be flattered" when Lerner and Loewe demanded his presence in the most expensive film musical ever produced.

André succumbed to the flattery, perhaps to the good of all concerned, certainly of the moviegoer. Certainly too of Warner's stockholders, since *My Fair Lady* brought in roughly seventy million dollars. It also swept the Academy Awards of 1964, earning Oscars for director George Cukor, best actor and actress for Rex Harrison and Audrey Hepburn, and best score adapter for André Previn.

Fond of quoting Woody Allen's now anachronistic line about California's only advantage being the legality of a right turn on a red light, André has grown caustic in his criticism of Los Angeles. Orange juice, warm weather, and sunshine, he maintains, inspire one only to indolence. But that secure, comfortable life had earned him a great deal of money and a comfortable home; it had brought him a wife on the verge of her own Hollywood success and had kept him near his widowed mother and two daughters. His Hollywood friends were not the glamour people with their "lives of improvised morality," but real, influential, and interesting people like Billy Wilder, Richard Brooks, Miklós Rózsa, Lennie Hayton, Alex North, Johnny Green, Shelly Manne, John Williams, Lionel Newman, Jerry Goldsmith; people who counted, people who would be surprised and perhaps shocked if André simply dropped out of their world. Besides all that, he never for a moment discounted the value of what Hollywood had taught him.

> I learned a tremendous amount there. I learned, for example, how to orchestrate, and that taught me the limitations of every instrument. I learned how to get along with and among professional musicians. I learned what orchestra players would stand for and what they wouldn't. I learned how to psych myself into standing up many times a week in front of an orchestra of first-rate musicians—albeit with third-rate

music—and how to sight-read, rehearse, and record very quickly. I learned a lot there. But I stayed too long.

In his travels André had endured in countless hotel rooms many of the films on which he'd worked in the forties, during his earliest years in Hollywood. His name had not been included in the credits of those films, but he recognized many of the names that rolled by on the way to the next commercial. Some of those people were still in Hollywood, still doing much the same work they'd done twenty years before: makeup men, wardrobe mistresses, gaffers, grips. Music directors.

There were also many names in those credits of people he'd lost track of. What had happened to them all? Were they truly dead, he wondered, or just professionally dead? "It seemed spooky the way that industry just seemed to eat up the people who worked within it," he says, searching no further than his first film for the perfect illustration: "José Iturbi. The fact that someone of his stature could fall for all of that is very sad. To think that he ruined his career, maybe his life, just for the sake of playing a piano at the edge of a pool so Esther Williams could have music to swim by. That frightened me."

Even worse, at least in retrospect, was the fact that the element of fear was otherwise totally absent from his work in Hollywood.

I think there's a kind of complacency that comes from doing work that you know you can do well and that never worries you. It's the biggest cul-de-sac of any professional life. Here I was, putting in a great many hours every week, working very hard at film scores and the rest, but never even secretly worried about whether it was going to be all right. It just did not *frighten* me.

I knew that not to be challenged was a dead-end street, that for a musician to do his best he ought to be really cold with fear at the prospect of a new challenge. I was always technically adept enough that whatever was demanded of me in films I could han-

dle. I don't mean that what I did was always good,
but it never frightened me. I never had that problem
with my conducting. From the beginning, every single
concert scared me to death.

Still André agonized over the decision to plunge into conducting to the depth of Ronald Wilford's demands. He would
make great plans one day then abandon them the next. He
would weigh carefully the pros and cons, alone on the freeway
and in conversations with Dory that ran well into the early
morning, then by the following noon he would be undecided
again. Ultimately, he says, it was an incident straight out of an
absurdist drama that shocked him into a decision.

He was about to start a new film for Twentieth Century–Fox, dealing with a producer whose misunderstandings
about music were deep and chronic. After many hours of conversation over André's plans for the music track, the producer
told André he'd like to see his ideas on paper. Accustomed to
meek compliance with the whims of producers, André went
home and got to work, turning out a five-page typed proposal
for dealing with what he felt were the film's musical requirements.

The next morning I walked into his office and
handed him the memo. He said—and these were his
exact words—"Stick around, kid, while I read this
over." So I stuck around and watched him. There he
was, this great man in a great studio, sitting behind a
desk you could have staged the *Ice Follies* on, and I
suddenly realized: My God, he's moving his lips as he
reads!

It probably sounds like a small quibble, but all at
once it came to me that I was desperately unhappy,
working on music I didn't believe in, trying to
impress my musical values on a man who moves his
lips when he reads. "Excuse me," I said as I rose to
my feet. "You aren't going to understand this, I
know, but I've decided I'm not going to do your
film."

"What the devil are you talking about?" he demanded, and I said, "Well, we really haven't signed anything yet and although you've been very nice I'm just not going to do it." And so I walked out, fully intending never to set foot in a film studio again.

On his way out, André looked at a clock and saw that he still had time to drive home and call New York before the end of the business day there. He told Dory he had made up his mind and then he called Ronald Wilford.

XVIII

André's most ticklish problem, to Ronald Wilford's thinking, lay in getting serious audiences to take André seriously. Specifically, the new manager's chief task was to "sell" André as a Hollywood celebrity and then convince his buyers that the Hollywood label was nothing more than a come-on. What they wanted was the *real* André Previn.

There was simply nothing to be gained from Wilford's attempting to build the new career without leaning on the old. Any such attempt very likely would have been doomed from the start by public apathy, even if it had been possible for him to change identities in an instant. At least for the moment there was a certain attractive notoriety about his Hollywood image, even to snobbery's elite. As Shelly Manne puts it, "The jazz albums, the pop albums, the films all made him popular. His name was being bandied about a whole lot. Sure, people didn't know whether André Previn was any good in that other kind of music, but when he started waving a stick in front of those big orchestras, they wanted to be there. They wanted to see what the hell was going on."

Wilford acknowledges that the energy which had propelled André through fourteen years of phenomenal activity in several spheres of music could surely be transferred to this new sphere, at least in sufficient quantity to give his conducting career the kick it needed. "Very few conductors have started out with his kind of celebrity interest," he observes. Yet he was concerned that many music-lovers would greet André with a stony show-me countenance.

Conductors are always going to be criticized for *who* they are, regardless of what they do. The jazz part of André, the Hollywood part, those were just incidental. The serious part was what he really was trained in. When you study his career you realize that it was Hitler and the War that created the extraordinary circumstance of his being raised in Hollywood. So here he was, a celebrity. Now we had to get him past the purists before he could be accepted.

Getting him past the purists meant clearing the high hurdle of his repertory limitations. As a conductor André still had very little music he could call his own, disregarding the "pops" material which, it was agreed by all parties, he would refuse to conduct, no matter how prestigious the offers might be. He turned down "Gershwin night" appearances with the best orchestras in the land—New York, Philadelphia, Cleveland, San Francisco, and more—determined not to be saddled the rest of his life with that sort of repertoire, in the manner of a Johnny Green or even of an André Kostelanetz.

His poor track record as a conductor of serious music was offset somewhat by his limited but notable successes as a serious pianist. Wilford's idea was to begin by selling André as a pianist who would conduct from the piano, and that worked like a charm, though it added to the pressure on André. In order to minimize the strain, they settled on two piano concertos, by Mozart and Mendelssohn, one of which would constitute one half of every program André performed during that initial year of concertizing. That was presented to each prospective employer as a given and the rest of the program, says Wilford, "I made sure was right up his alley. It worked. Right from the beginning, it worked."

So André took off, to Kalamazoo, to Elkhart, to the civic auditoria of America's heartland, to Holiday Inns and all-night diners, on a schedule as unpredictable as the health of all the other conductors. He filled in at the last minute for the indisposed great and the indisposed small, for Sir John Barbirolli in Houston and for William Steinberg in Pittsburgh, and everywhere he went Ron Wilford worked the telephones to nail down scheduled return engagements.

Everywhere André conducted, the audiences were exhilarated and the critics—when they weren't snorting "Hollywood!"—admitted to being impressed. André occasionally voiced the complaint that his manager, secure in a Manhattan office and sleeping nights in his own bed, seemed concerned only whether his client could make the next plane and whether that plane would make its next connection.

The increased travel meant longer separations from Dory, adding immeasurably to the strain on their marriage. Though her fear of flying was born of circumstances in her life long before she met him, still she blamed André for it. He imposed too many conditions on her travel, told her how much luggage to bring along, insisted upon her remaining in the background at rehearsals, changed his itinerary without warning, warned that he would be unable to meet her at the airport in person. Of course she put it all down in a song some years later. Occasionally they would travel together by train, when Wilford left sufficient time between engagements. But André's schedule only grew more crowded and eventually even railroads filled Dory with stark terror.

Her grasp on reality was beginning to slip noticeably. With André, her father-substitute, so frequently away from her, Dory leaned ever more heavily on her psychiatrist. This led to periodic confinements for "observation" or "rest" in a sanatorium and that trend was unsettling to André, despite his vaunted ability to keep his personal and professional lives on separate tracks.

On one occasion, in a dressing room of some forgotten auditorium far from home, he received a deeply upsetting phone call from Dory only moments before he was due to take the podium in a performance of Brahms's Fourth Symphony. As he conducted, he poured all his anxieties, frustrations, and unhappiness into the music. He felt more than heard what was coming from the orchestra and he knew it had to be the best Brahms Fourth ever played.

To André's lasting gratitude, this happened to be one of the concerts Ronald Wilford managed to attend and the manager was standing in the wings to meet his conductor as he staggered offstage, glowing from the Refiner's fire and limp from the catharsis he'd achieved. "Would you mind telling me," said Wilford, "just what the hell you thought you were doing out there? That was one of the most disgusting performances I've ever heard in my life."

André shouted insults, accusing Wilford of absolute ignorance where music was concerned, then stormed out of the theater determined to find himself a new manager. But the performance had been taped for broadcast and the following morning André decide to listen for himself.

> It was disgusting. Ronald was absolutely right. I had done the one thing you just never do, I had put myself, the performer, ahead of the composer. My puny problems suddenly had been imposed on the Brahms Four. It was excess upon excess, just awful. In my inexperience I hadn't learned that there is no room for improvement in a piece of music. You can add musical thoughts but you can't let personal emotional problems override Brahms's genius.

There were quite naturally other mistakes along the way for André and that was precisely why Wilford had insisted that all his wing-trying be done in out-of-the-way places. As months passed and mistakes mounted there were moments of self-doubt. Had he really made the right decision? He might have been tempted to turn back for Dory's sake, since he was beginning to realize that his new career was unraveling the fabric of their already threadbare marriage. But he also realized that there could be no turning back. He needed the time to mature as a conductor and was determined to give himself that time, despite a profound understanding of what his future in Hollywood would be if things turned sour in serious music.

> I'd have been in frightful trouble, because the loyalties in the film business extend, with luck, to about nine days. Had I failed to accomplish anything as a

conductor after being away a couple of years, I could not have gone back. I don't think I'd have wanted to anyway because I'd be too disheartened at having to return to something I no longer wanted. I'd have had to find a totally new direction for my life. I knew it would be a truly diabolical situation if I failed and I spent more than a few sleepless nights thinking about that. But confidence always won out and I decided I *would* succeed. But I also knew it might easily take me a decade.

In a way I suppose I was naïve. I was old enough to understand I was well past the normal starting age for conductors, but I was young enough not to be concerned with mortality. On the one hand I knew I had to get going with this thing, but on the other hand I never stopped to think that it might be too late. As for money, the fees I got from some of those orchestras quite literally did not cover the expense of travel and accommodations. But I luckily had enough salted away to support us—though hardly in the style to which we'd become accustomed—for at least a year and maybe a little longer.

Then, you see, I was so extraordinarily lucky, because it all happened so quickly.

Success did not need a decade. In less than a year from André's total commitment to conducting he signed a conducting contract with a major record label. This truly was the sine qua non, the one element above all others without which his career quite probably would have ground to a halt. That the record company was RCA, which recently had intensified its recording activities in England, where orchestras were far less expensive, turned out to be an incredible stroke of luck.

André's exclusive recording contract with Columbia still had several years to run, but both Schuyler Chapin and Ron Wilford were aware that Masterworks was no place for a beginning conductor. Wilford put out a feeler to RCA, whose Red Seal division was now under the direction of Roger Hall, who not long before had championed André's cause as manager of the

Philadelphia Orchestra. Hall's initial response to Wilford was an extremely positive one. That put the ball into Columbia's court.

Chapin could not simply release André from his contract. For one thing, to do so was not in his power. For another, the principal agreement in that contract was not with him but with Irving Townsend of the popular division. For Townsend, André's recordings (in a style that moved steadily away from jazz into so-called "easy listening" music) were money in the bank. There was only one individual who could release André from that contract, Goddard Lieberson, Director of Columbia Records.

Perhaps Lieberson's decision had nothing to do with the fact that just a few months earlier André had unintentionally recorded Lieberson's Piano Pieces, only the second of his works to break into the record catalogues. Perhaps it was simply that Lieberson truly was, as André opines, "one of the best executives in the music business" who understood that an unhappy conductor could not be a happy pianist. Also Lieberson had a reputation of going out on limbs to help fellow musicians. He went out on a costly limb for André.

> Goddard told me that I should first get a clear commitment from RCA that they were ready to sign me to record as a conductor. He told me that if conducting meant that much to me then he would hate to make me sit at Columbia and tread water for three or four years, even though I was in the middle of my piano project for Masterworks and even though my jazz records were selling a hell of a lot of copies for them. It would have been easy for him to say, "Tough luck, kid." I can think of several others in his industry who would have. Instead he said, "Find out if RCA wants you and if they do I'll let you go." That was an act of genuine altruism and it was awfully good of him.

At Columbia Masterworks it had been Schuyler Chapin's idea to use André's skills as a pianist to build his reputation and following among buyers of classical records. At RCA

Roger Hall turned that around, aiming to use the work of other pianists to establish André's conducting credentials on records. He sent André to London to record concertos with Lorin Hollander and Leonard Pennario.

Chapin, who at this point retires to the sidelines to "watch with tremendous satisfaction André's career go up and up," is unsparing in his praise of Roger Hall. "Roger believed strongly in André and put a lot of RCA's money where his belief was."

Indeed this was a considerable gamble on Hall's part since at the time André's abilities as a conductor remained largely unproved. Still more uncertain was the degree to which record buyers would accept his conducting after the initial curiosity wore off. The question of public acceptance would linger but, with the release of André's first two RCA recordings, there were no more doubts about his capability.

Both albums were recorded with the Royal Philharmonic Orchestra in London's Walthamstow Assembly Hall. Lorin Hollander's pieces were the concerto of Aram Khatchaturian and the previously unrecorded *Scherzo Fantasque* of Ernest Bloch, neither of which André had encountered before. Leonard Pennario was far more experienced at recording than young Hollander and his pieces came from the standard repertoire, the first and fourth piano concertos of Sergei Rachmaninoff. The recording sessions with Pennario were uneventful and the performances revealed on André's part a firm grasp of the subtleties of the Russian composer, with whom he would later become closely identified.

The Khatchaturian concerto, in its slow movement, calls for an optional flexatone, a novelty instrument that might best be described as an electronic musical saw. When used properly it can add an eerie, surreal quality to the movement. Never having heard or heard of a flexatone, André asked the Royal Philharmonic percussionists to dig one up and bring it in for a rehearsal. The RCA engineers taped the run-through and, upon hearing the flexatone played back, André remarked, "My God, that's awful. That truly is one of the ugliest sounds I've heard in my life. It sounds like an instrument somebody picked up at Woolworth's. Let's forget it." The recording went ahead sans flexatone and fifteen years later André still had not heard the concerto played with one, though he says he will give the instrument another chance when he records the Khatchaturian again.

At the time they were made those two records were momentous events in André's life; he has come to consider them musically unimportant.

> No, I don't think they were good records. But I'd been waiting so long for that kind of chance that I'd have accompanied anybody doing anything. I proved I could do it. I proved I enjoyed accompanying and that soloists enjoyed working with me. Also the RPO took to me fairly well and that didn't hurt a bit.

Not a bit, certainly not in London, where the competition among five major orchestras is so keen that the music grapevine is virtually a spy network. Word was soon out that this fellow from Hollywood could hold his own with a fine orchestra. Nor did it hurt André's cause that he had so many good things to say about England.

Roger Hall didn't know it but in that ticket to London he had presented André with a gift beyond price. A resolute Anglophile since his first trip there as a tourist in 1958, André found London a three-ring circus of musical activity, a dream after the comparative stagnation of America's West Coast. The sheer availability of music in every form, the endless round of concerts, operas, and recitals, made London a terrestrial Elysian Fields. The British people with their dry, acerbic, unanticipated wit—so like André's own—and with their readiness to accept strangers seemed infinitely more civilized than the rough-edged denizens of the film studios. Underpinning this newfound life of England was a love of long standing for English music, a case of love at first hearing for André.

The very first recording of twentieth-century music he'd possessed was English music. It was a 78-rpm album "so old it didn't have a picture on the cover" of Sir William Walton's Viola Concerto, played by Frederick Riddle. "I really just went 'round the bend listening to it," he recollects. While that recording was also partially responsible for André's headlong plunge into modern music, it also began a tempestuous love affair with British music, which transcended time and national boundaries. The Walton discovery was followed closely by his first experience, via a radio broadcast, of the then brand-new Sixth Symphony of Ralph Vaughan Williams. That inspired work put the seal on his youthful enthusiasm for English music. "For some reason which I cannot explain," he muses, "under all those palm trees and all that sunshine, English music beckoned me loud and clear."

Such a predilection could hardly have brought him commercial success in the United States, where English music was usually brushed aside as being merely parochial. Yet for perhaps twenty years he clung to his vision and when time and fortune offered an opportunity at last to conduct classical music on record it was Englishman Benjamin Britten's *Sinfonia da Requiem* that he chose. Even granting the fact that by 1964 the expansion by American companies into British recording halls had begun, there was still something fatalistic in Roger Hall's sending André to Walthamstow Assembly Hall for those first RCA efforts.

Though it was readily apparent to Hall that neither of those two records was going to be a runaway best-seller, there also was no reason to suspect he'd made a bad bargain. Having supplied André with a calling card as a serious conductor, RCA now had to get his work onto the world's turntables. Two ingredients were necessary: first, an orchestra of high and marketable caliber and, second, a strongly appealing repertoire, most likely romantic or modern, that would command the attention of all those younger generations of record buyers who would recognize the Previn name from his exploits in other fields.

Together, Hall and Ronald Wilford approached Ernest Fleischmann, then manager of the prestigious London Symphony Orchestra. The LSO's recording dates in 1965 were not yet all assigned to conductors and repertoire, so one or more recording dates with André would be possible. Thanks to London's heavy traffic in musical espionage, Fleischmann knew ev-

erything there was to know about André's smooth handling of
the RPO and his rapport with the members of that rival orchestra. Now he let the two Americans convince him, at least
partially, that he could snatch this potential major attraction
away from the RPO and at the same time get in on the
ground floor of a major conducting career. The three men settled on two dates in late summer, again in Walthamstow for a
pair of recordings. The repertoire would be Russian: Shostakovich's Fifth Symphony and Tchaikovsky's "Little Russian"
Symphony No. 2, to be filled out with Anatol Liadov's *Eight
Russian Folk Songs* for Orchestra.

The players of the London Symphony who were part of
those sessions in August of 1965 say there was an immediate
affinity between orchestra and conductor. André makes the
same statement, declaring that this was certainly the best
group of musicians he'd ever faced. No one seems to remember
any anecdote from those sessions, no typically wry Previn
remark that served to put the musicians instantly in his camp,
no mischance from which he smoothly recovered, to their instant admiration. The men (for there were no women in the
orchestra) all simply enjoyed making music together. And that
may well be the highest compliment one musician can pay another; it is certainly the highest an orchestra can pay a conductor.

The two recordings were well received by the public, as they
were by the critics. Both were reviewed enthusiastically by the
influential British monthly *Gramophone*. There André's readings of the two much-recorded symphonies were compared favorably to previous recordings by such "name" conductors as
Bernstein, Ormandy, and Giulini. Several critics hailed André's
unusual treatment of the Largo section of the Shostakovich
Fifth. That movement contains—in André's estimation—the
essence of the entire symphony and he took it at a slower pace
than could be found on most previous recordings, revealing
nuances seldom heard before and firmly establishing his credentials as an interpreter of serious music, not simply a time-
beater.

First reports of record sales were good, but even more important than sales or reviews was the proof of André's ability to hold up under the potentially hostile scrutiny of world-class symphony orchestras. He went so far in convincing the LSO of his credentials that Ernest Fleischmann invited him to return the following season for a series of concert appearances and, with Roger Hall's enthusiastic approval, to record as well.

Certainly André greeted the prospect of spending more time in London with great relish. More than ever now Ronald Wilford was running him around the United States on a breathless itinerary. His first season of committed conducting had ended with both manager and artist convinced that they were on the right track and that, despite a ninety percent drop in André's income that year, there was little reason for his spending any more time in the film studios.

Nevertheless, even as his first recordings with the LSO were finding their way to the better record shops of Los Angeles, André was back there in his customary role, doing a film for Universal Studios. He told Wilford that it was a commitment he'd made several years earlier to Julie Andrews and now the promise had to be kept. A few columnists sharpened their told-you-so blades on him, but André's score for *Thoroughly Modern Millie* was a thorough success with its sparkling, clever use of Roaring Twenties instrumentation and material and it did nothing to stunt his growth as a serious conductor.

In fact, in some American cities André's multimedia pattern of successes only served to enhance his appeal to the culturally omnivorous people who move and shake their local gentry into action. Houston was one such city. André had visited Houston as an emergency guest conductor and discovered that their beloved music director Sir John Barbirolli had made of the symphony board a group of Anglophiles almost as dedicated as he. Suddenly, in their minds, André was elevated to a higher plane than most young American conductors because of his recording associations with two important British orchestras.

In 1966 the Houston Symphony moved into a new home, Jesse Jones Hall. With the orchestra's reputation in ascendance, Sir John picked this time to inform the Houston Board that he would no longer be able to spend so much time away from his beloved Hallé Orchestra in Manchester, England. Although Barbirolli's decision to resign his Houston post was not yet publicly known, feelers were going out for his replacement as early as the grand opening of the new hall.

Coincidentally, a guest at the gala opening was Hollywood's Johnny Green, a confidant of Ima Hogg, heiress to a vast Texas fortune and primary benefactress of the Houston Symphony. "Miss Ima's" references to the subject on that occasion were oblique, but in a later meeting she came right to the point with Green:

"What do you think of André Previn? As our principal conductor?"

Still entertaining serious doubts about André's abilities in this regard, Green was caught off guard. He himself had long dreamed of one day conducting his own orchestra; now here was his onetime assistant, with only a comparative handful of professional concerts under his belt, under consideration for a position he hungered for. And he was being asked to advise and consent.

Aside from those serious doubts about André's vocation, Green also wondered how he would manage to fill a season with the amount of music he knew. "He may have known the entire standard repertoire as a listener," Green remarks, "but to know it from the point of view of the guy on the podium and to get first-class musicians to play it according to an effective plan, that's something else."

Green tried to beg off, claiming that while he knew André as a film composer he really had no frame of reference in which to judge his abilities as a music director. Besides, he told Miss Ima, "I'd rather put my arm in a threshing machine than evaluate a colleague."

Not to be put off so easily, the astute Miss Hogg pressed for an evaluation of André's repertoire and experience. Clearly her concerns were not far from Green's own. "We used to say at MGM that you could never walk past André Previn with a score under your arm unless you wanted him to play it from memory the next day. That little monster can sit down at a piano with a 36-line orchestra score and reduce it at first sight.

The guy is so brilliant that if he didn't know all nine Beethoven symphonies last week, he probably does by now." Green hoped the lady could recognize hyperbole when she heard it.

"What do you think of him as a person?"

"As a person? I love him like a son. Bonnie and I have three daughters and André. He's our son."

Ima Hogg cut him off abruptly. She was not talking about pleasantries but about his ability to socialize with the moneyed gentry when called upon to do so, to "fit into the community." Houston wanted neither a radical nor an isolationist for its music director.

Again Green hedged. He knew full well that André had a stubborn, standoffish streak that could be interpreted as shyness or elitism. But he also knew that his protégé had for several years been eager for an opportunity like this and that he was clever enough not to antagonize the first community that made him such an offer. "It was a very uncomfortable conversation altogether for me," Johnny Green says. "I think she considered me evasive. I *was* evasive."

Not so ambivalent was Sir John Barbirolli. He had met André and enjoyed talking to him about Mother England. He would be returning often to Houston and thought that having André take over in his absence would be jolly good. Ultimately both the orchestra committee and Miss Ima Hogg agreed. André's only question was, "Where do I sign?"

> If someone had offered me an orchestra in the Outer Hebrides I'd have taken it. I desperately wanted my own orchestra. I was knocked out by the idea. I hardly remember signing the contract, but I do remember walking alone into Jones Hall after the deed was done. There was no one else there, but the stage was set up with chairs and music stands for that evening's performance. I walked to the back of the theater and just stood there for a few moments, reveling in the most extraordinary feeling of elation. This was it. This was going to be *my band!*

Mia Farrow, André, and babies. *(Courtesy Wide World Photos)*

Shaking hands with Sir William Walton in the U.S.S.R. following the performance of one of his works.

With Artur Rubinstein during a rehearsal break in London. *(Courtesy Mary Lawrence)*

With Leonard Bernstein and an unidentified visitor in Israel, 1973.

Catching forty winks on a tour flight in the seat next to violin soloist Kyung-Wha Chung.

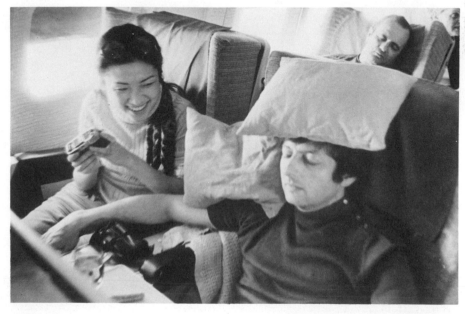

Deep concentration with pianist Vladimir Ashkenazy. *(Courtesy Allan D. Cisco)*

Listening to a recording playback in a cold EMI control room with Dame Janet Baker (foreground) and producer Christopher Bishop. *(Courtesy Roy Round)*

With H.R.H. Prince Charles and André's guest, Heather Hales.

A moment of levity just prior to a television program with the London Symphony.

With Sir Benjamin Britten and soprano Elisabeth Söderström following a performance of Britten's *Our Hunting Fathers* in 1976. *(Courtesy Nigel Luckhurst)*

A friendly coffee break with Howard Snell thirty thousand feet aloft. *(Courtesy Mary Lawrence)*

The principal conductor (r.) congratulates guest conductor Edward Heath (the Prime Minister) at the London Symphony's Gala Concert in 1971.

Committee Chairman Anthony Camden presents a photo album signed by all the members of the orchestra commemorating André's tenth anniversary as the London Symphony Orchestra's principal conductor.

XIX

"One day I just looked around and he was gone. To *Houston*."

So Shelly Manne describes André's abdication of his Hollywood attachments, but Houston was less than half of it. Indeed, the Los Angeles newspapers were peppered with comments about André's new role and his desertion of their Mecca
for the cultural wasteland of east Texas. Less noticed but ultimately far more significant were the tightening ties to England
by virtue of his recording successes with the London Symphony Orchestra.

The sessions of 1966 produced two records which became
the high-water marks of André's conducting career to that
point. The recordings were of Sergei Rachmaninoff's Symphony No. 2 and the First Symphony of Sir William Walton,
the composer whose work had set André on his pursuit of English music.

RCA's readiness to press and market the Rachmaninoff dis-
played utter confidence in their new conductor. In the first
place, it is a difficult piece which requires a firm hand to protect it from incohesiveness; in the second place, it is a familiar
work which already was in the RCA catalogue in an excellent
rendition by Sir Adrian Boult and the London Philharmonic, a
disc to which the Previn-LSO rendition was bound to be compared. In André's favor was the fact that techniques had improved considerably since the Boult-LPO version was made in
the early years of the stereophonic process. Also, André was

most eager to take advantage of the fondness and, he believed, the special feeling he had for Rachmaninoff, developed during his studies of the piano works.

That special feeling came through in the recording, more than justifying RCA's faith in André. Sales were excellent and so were most of the reviews. Particularly pleasing to British critics was André's restraint in never allowing the music to stray outside the boundaries of good taste. Where Rachmaninoff's melodic rhapsodizing was often demeaned by excess emotionalism, André applied cool intellectual brakes and his carefully thought-out treatment from beginning to end gave the symphony a continuity not always found in the Boult version. Soon after the Second Symphony's release Roger Hall and Ron Wilford began negotiations for André and the LSO to record the Rachmaninoff Third Symphony the following year. That probably would not have happened had the Second not been such a dazzling success.

The choice of the Walton First Symphony gives further evidence that RCA was applying the sink-or-swim philosophy to André's conducting career, quite the opposite of Columbia's depressingly cautious approach earlier. For an American conductor, particularly one so tainted by Hollywood, to try to sell himself as a bona fide interpreter of English music was tantamount to an American beer salesman trying to peddle his wares in Shropshire pubs. Worse luck, he was up against the stiffest competition possible: the release at precisely the same time of the same symphony on a rival label by a rival orchestra under a staunchly British conductor.

Sir Malcolm Sargent, the other conductor, was a recognized master at interpreting the compositions of his good friend Sir William Walton. He had given the premiere performances of a number of Walton's works and the public was eagerly awaiting the release by EMI/Angel of his reading of the First Symphony with the New Philharmonia Orchestra. Knowing of course of the RCA project, EMI laid on a heavy advertising budget to promote the fact that *their* version was the one personally sanctioned by the composer.

All of those potentially threatening factors played right into

André's hands because, as it turned out, his record was generally judged to be the better of the two. With unpredictable unanimity the London critics gave their blessings to his reading of the symphony and the record took off, especially in England, where the market for English music is insatiable. In time even Sir William Walton would be heard to say that the Previn version was his own preference.

In a virtual coup d'état, André captured the imagination and affection of music-loving Britain. He was a Yankee who loved their music as much as they did. His name already was well known throughout the Isles through his jazz records. In the pre-Beatlemania fifties the British devoured American jazz records, among which André's cool piano style stood out for its almost Anglican reserve and erudition. Now, ten years later, that familiar name leaped out of the inside headlines in a brand-new context. Now he was sought after by producers of radio and television talk shows and the British audiences began to perceive him as the very antithesis of the brash young Hollywood-person they'd imagined him to be.

Harold Lawrence, successor to Ernest Fleischmann as manager of the London Symphony Orchestra, recalls that from the first there was a possessiveness toward André on the part of Englishmen, as well as a tendency to glamorize him as a sort of media event. One could find even then references to him in the press as "the British Leonard Bernstein," and according to Lawrence the public was ready to believe that:

> There was something about André's personality which strongly appealed to the British. A diffidence, not exactly a shyness, but a *normal* way of speaking when he was interviewed. A lack of pomposity, a humility in the best sense of the word. Then there was his quick and ready sense of humor. In his early TV appearances he impressed the general public in a profound way.

Success with the Walton First Symphony put André right where he wanted to be, in demand as an interpreter of British music. At RCA, Roger Hall was well aware of André's aspirations in this vein, so RCA made a quick decision and an announcement to the press, timed to take advantage of their new conductor's publicity momentum. André, leading the London Symphony, would record all nine symphonies of Ralph Vaughan Williams, possibly England's favorite musical son. That such a project was being undertaken at all made it a landmark in the record industry. That it was being taken by an American company and an American conductor caused a great flurry in the British music sphere. Maintaining that he felt "pursued by good fortune," André declares that the whole thing was Hall's idea.

> Roger, quite correctly, was concerned about my recording repertoire. But he wasn't about to give me the nine Beethovens and the four Brahmses. One day he said to me, "You know, Lenny (Bernstein) has made an enormous thing out of Nielsen and Ives. Have you got anything like that up your sleeve?" I thought for a moment and told him I'd always been crazy about Vaughan Williams and that I'd love to do a couple of his symphonies, maybe the Second, Fourth, and Fifth. Roger said immediately, "No. You're going to do them *all.*" I said, "But, Roger, I don't even know them all." And he shot back, "Well, you're not going to record them all in one year, are you?" So I learned them all.
>
> This announcement had enormous impact on the British record-buying and concert-going public. Suddenly I was no longer the visiting and faintly curious American, but someone who had a rather unusual predilection for English music, someone who took it seriously and who did it all the time. For them to learn I would be the first conductor to do all nine Vaughan Williams symphonies on stereo LP records made quite an impression.

The announcement made quite an impression also on the executives of EMI Records. The London-based company had in the works its own plan for recording the entire Vaughan

Williams cycle, a plan which called for dividing the symphonies between its two prestigious British conductors, Sir John Barbirolli and Sir Adrian Boult. EMI had been burned once by RCA and this upstart Previn in the recording of Walton's First Symphony; it would not happen again. The company scrapped that plan and, in what amounted to throwing down the gauntlet, announced that its Vaughan Williams cycle would be conducted entirely by Boult, with the London Symphony's almost bitter rivals, the London Philharmonic and New Philharmonia orchestras.

The parallel projects would take several years to complete and in the end both record companies, along with music lovers, would be richer for the effort. André was first out of the gate with the *Sinfonia Antartica*. Once again the British music press waxed ecstatic. In *Gramophone*, Robert Layton wrote:

> There is in Mr. Previn's approach to modern English music an uncommon freshness, urgency, and sympathy that makes one feel that he is encountering the music for the first time. He is attentive to detail without ever sacrificing the spirit to the letter and I know of no artist born outside these shores who shows so keen an idiomatic instinct in this area.

That sort of praise, though with diminishing wonderment, kept coming for the Vaughan Williams cycle during the four years it eventually required to complete. For some conductors that would have been the *only* recording project in those four years but not for André. Even as he was preparing the *Sinfonia Antarctica*, his all-important debut in the VW series, he was working on another project which would be his debut in three other areas at once: his first Mozart on record, his first opera as an established conductor, and his first collaboration with Dory in the field of serious music.

The project sprang out of his and Ronald Wilford's mutual desire to forestall quickly any impression of André as a specialist in Romantic and Twentieth-Century music, a pigeonholing that could prove almost as deadly as his earlier identification with movie music. The fact was, however, that at this point André *was* largely a specialist. A vast expanse of Classical, Renaissance, and Baroque music constituted a gaping hole in his repertoire. He was working feverishly in Houston to remedy that situation, but something had to be done immediately on records, where people would notice. To record something by Mozart would cut right to the heart of this budding criticism and Mozart's music always had been dear to André.

But Mozart posed a particular problem. There were conductors who specialized almost exclusively in Mozart and whose interpretations had been declared near-definitive. For André to compete with those specialists in something as familiar as, say, the *Jupiter Symphony* could backfire fatally. But Roger Hall knew an area of the Mozart repertoire that had been largely ignored by the major record companies. He asked whether André was familiar with "any of those little Mozart operas." André replied that his only experience in that arena had been conducting an aria from *The Impresario*.

Hall decided that *The Impresario* (original title, *Der Schauspieldirektor*) would be ideal, particularly since its brevity would allow for a single-disc recording, far less expensive than most operas. The only catch was that RCA wanted the comic opera in English, so that American and British audiences could laugh at the jokes. But the only thing funny about existing translations were the translations themselves. André suggested that, given a good literal translation of the German, Dory should be able to fashion an English libretto that would be both humorous and singable. The husband-and-wife gimmick delighted the RCA publicity department.

For the first time since his initial collaboration with the LSO, André recorded not with that orchestra but with the English Chamber Orchestra. In the recording sessions, he was delighted with the musicians as he was with the singers, sopranos Judith Raskin and Reri Grist, tenor Richard Lewis, baritone Sherrill Milnes, and narrator Leo McKern. In fact, André's sole disappointment with the project was that Dory's fear of flying prevented her from attending the recording sessions of her witty libretto at Kingsway Hall. As for the finished project, "Well, it's not exactly the *Ring,* you know, with an overture and five arias. Still, I thought it was very good. Dory's libretto is still used by a lot of schools even though the record's been out of the catalogue for years. It never sold anything."

A more financially successful collaboration of that year, 1967, was his album called *Right as the Rain,* with soprano Leontyne Price. This was an effort to better a 1962 attempt, with Eileen Farrell on Columbia, at combining an operatic voice with "jazz" music. The word is in quotation marks because in neither case—though perhaps a bit more arguably so in Miss Farrell's—could the resulting music be catalogued as jazz. The Farrell-Previn album, *Together with Love,* had been organized by Schuyler Chapin. It utilized André's talents as composer, arranger-orchestrator, conductor, and pianist in jazz and pop standards, along with a few of André's and Dory's own songs. The Price record for RCA employed precisely the same formula and was better planned and engineered. Also, since the Metropolitan Opera star was at the apex of her fame, it was far more easily promoted and sold well.

Of course, none of the publicity that attended his various recordings hurt André a bit in impressionable Houston where, in the fall of 1967, he began his tenure as music director and principal conductor. The "y'all come" Texas charm grew to panting anticipation and helped André feel that at long last his career was getting under way. He had ambitions of the highest order for the Houston Symphony, despite attempts to cool his fever by Ronald Wilford. "Remember," his manager cautioned, "the world's music is not made in Texas." André's private answer was, "Not until now."

He arrived in Houston, found an apartment and got to work. "Whether I had any right to be a music director in those days I didn't really know. I was certainly old enough." He now encountered the problems of a music director for the first time, problems he'd never faced as a guest conductor, such as planning an entire season of concerts. There was also the matter of that security-blanket repertoire Ron Wilford had devised. It now had to be cast off with no show whatsoever of concern for stepping into new fields of conducting. Besides providing him with that sheer terror he'd so pined after in Hollywood, this suddenly expanded repertoire brought other shortcomings into focus. He'd never before faced the question of which edition of a score to use, had never dictated the bowing of an eighteenth-century composition. The solitary advantage in all this was that the very music he needed to learn was the music the Houstonians loved to hear.

For André to consider himself competent in a particular work, say a Brahms or a Beethoven symphony, he needed to play it over and over again, so he scheduled those works not only in the regular Jones Hall season but on the orchestra's whistle-stop tours as well. Also, in studying the programs of Houston's recent seasons, he discovered that several of the "warhorses," like the Tchaikovsky Sixth Symphony which he wanted dearly to conduct, had been absent from Houston for years. "There were a lot of those gaping holes in the repertoire," he recalls, "and I worked hard to fill them."

André quickly discovered the importance of good principal players and he did everything he could to make the Houston principals happy. When one of these, cellist Shirley Trepel, informed him that she was being wooed by the Cleveland Orchestra, André promised that if she would remain just one more season in Houston he would write a cello concerto for her. She agreed and he kept his promise, with the happy result that the Cello Concerto has remained one of his most important compositions. To another section leader, concertmaster Raphael Fliegel, André gives credit for "teaching me an awful lot about bowing." With the help of such members of the orchestra André was able to make good music in Houston.

I worked *very* hard and I like to think that some of it must have been good. But I'll tell you, we did local radio broadcasts of some of those concerts and a couple of years ago I came across the tapes in my study. I put on one of them and listened to it, but not for long. There can't have been more than eight consecutive bars I'd now consider doing the same way. Wilford tried to calm me down about Houston but I was exploding with enthusiasm and I just wouldn't listen.

Meantime I built up my repertoire. I had done most of the Beethoven symphonies before, but a couple of them never. I'd never conducted the Tchaikovsky First or Third, none of the Mahler symphonies or any big Strauss work. I'd never done an oratorio or the Beethoven Ninth because I couldn't get my hands on a chorus; in Houston I found an excellent one. I set myself the near-impossible task of performing in my first two Houston seasons fully half the "standard repertoire" works I didn't know so that I could learn them. It was a hair-raising struggle to cram all that music into my head. It took a lot of temerity and gall.

Of course I did my best not to let the people in Houston know all those were my *first* performances. If that raises any eyebrows now, well, how many conductors do their first *Carmen* or *Aïda* at the Met? A lot of them. Or their first Beethoven Nine with the New York Philharmonic? Too many of them. If the public found out, those conductors might be booted from the hall. The thing is, ours is the one musical craft that can't be practiced at home. You need an orchestra. You're going to have to do every piece of music for the first time *somewhere* and it might as well be in Houston as in London.

In the beginning André encountered no friction with the moneyed gentry who pulled the purse strings of the Houston Symphony. He smiled at the dowagers, he went to parties given by oilmen, and he kept to himself when he could. He recounts with ironic pleasure an incident at one of those Board parties when he was invited on a guided tour of the host's private wine cellar. The assumption was that since André was a man of some culture and refinement then he must know a great deal about wines and must be very interested in them. In fact, he did not and was not, but he went politely along.

"Ah always wanted a wahn celluh that *looked* lak a wahn celluh," grinned the host as he flicked on the lights and revealed a vast and formidable array of bottles, nestled like lay-ing hens in their rows and rows of racks. The host boasted about how much it had cost and the fact that it had only just been completed in time for this party. If that were the case, André wondered aloud, how had all those cobwebs been so meticulously spun in every corner of every shelf? The Texan explained, with no small display of wonderment at his own resourcefulness, that in pursuit of authenticity he had commissioned a New York theatrical house to spray his cellar with imitation cobwebs. "Ain't nothin' but rubbuh," he said. "Ah c'n git 'em changed any tahm ah want."

Having spent so much of his life in Hollywood, André's only surprise at this Houston display of wealth gratia wealth was that it could thrive outside the atmosphere of southern California. Once he got past the occasional puff of provincialism, André's real problems with the Board of Directors began. He found his ambitions for the orchestra continually crashing into a wall of resistance to change. That single factor, despite all the backslapping praise of his work, ate like acid at his enthusiasm and quickly turned all the ayes of Texas into resounding nays.

The disagreement first manifested itself when André mentioned in an interview his intentions of approaching RCA with a plan for recording a series of contemporary American works with the Houston Symphony. He now sloughs that off as "a new music director making music director noises," and it is true that the plan might have run afoul of RCA's financial considerations, but it never got that far. In order to record contemporary music the orchestra would have to play the works in concert and the Board of Directors did not want to hear any contemporary music, especially American contemporary music.

André never blamed the orchestra. Though they had almost never coped with such music as a group, "they took to it very well" as André made his first stabs at contemporary programming. Nor could he in good conscience blame the audiences who reacted with stiff politeness. Rather, he blamed the orchestra's previous music directors for not chipping away at the resistance, for failing to prepare his audiences for anything later than the music of Prokofiev. His immediate predecessor,

Barbirolli, "never touched the stuff." The man on the podium
before Sir John had been Leopold Stokowski, a champion both
of contemporary music and of American music. But in Houston, Stokowski had capitulated and pretty much programmed
his concerts away from controversy.

André got a firsthand appreciation of the depth of the problem early in his first season, while Barbirolli was still very much
a presence at Jones Hall. He had programmed *The Unan-
swered Question* of Charles Ives, a piece composed in 1908, and
was going through it with the musicians when Sir John ambled
into the hall. He stayed until time came for the musicians to
take a break and André walked over to pay his respects.

"What was *that?*" asked Sir John, gesturing disapprovingly
toward the stage.

"Sir John, that was Ives."

After a thoughtful moment the Englishman rose from his
seat as though to leave. "So that's Ives, is it? You know, I've
never heard any of his music before. Absolutely disgusting."

Resistance to new music ran high in Houston, but it was no
more than symptomatic of the general and ill-considered im-
mutability which frustrated André's attempts to better the orchestra and, in turn, to better himself as their conductor. The
first blowup, a hint of things to come, occurred when he returned from his first tour with the orchestra and vented his
anger in print. To newspaper reporters André proclaimed the
tour "a farce" and "a waste of a lot of good musicians' time."
The plain truth, said he, was that on the tour "nine tenths of
the time nobody gives a goddam whether we're there or not."

> The tours we took were figured out not musically but
> according to which towns had Holiday Inns. It was
> simply a way of keeping the orchestra going. The the-
> aters we played were mostly disgraceful. We managed
> to do a couple of concerts in Washington and New
> York, but at the time I really wanted to take them to
> London, Paris, Rome. And the more ambitious I got
> with the programs on those tours the more I came to
> grief. I think I was up to the music, but not up to
> being a music director.

Perhaps if Houston had been André's only concern during
that first season of 1967–68 he might have made himself happier but, as he puts it, "outside the orchestra I found the city
stultifying" and he did have a number of other things on his
mind. For one thing, there was his recording career, blasting
off in London. For another thing, there was Dory.

Their only collaboration after *The Impresario* recording was
on the songs for the Twentieth Century–Fox production of
Jacqueline Susann's *Valley of the Dolls*. André does not talk
about this film or say why he chose to work on it in 1967, considering his commitment to leave Hollywood behind him and
devote all his energies to serious music. One may reasonably
conjecture that the collaboration grew out of a husbandly urge
to help Dory in any way he could. Her grip on reality was
growing weaker.

The theme from *Valley of the Dolls* has a halting, stum-
bling lyric which, Dory writes, is taken directly from her own
experience as a woman hooked on pills. That is also the main
concern of the film. André's melody is strangely, hauntingly
fitted to the words, as though he knew from his closeness to
the situation in his own household just what was going on in
Dory's mind and in the minds of the women in the film. Originally the theme was to have been sung in the movie and
recorded by one of its stars, Judy Garland, but she was fighting
for sanity herself and simply not up to the assignment. Lionel
Newman, head of the Fox music department, signed Dionne
Warwick to record the theme and gave André and Dory Previn
their first million-seller. Success in the pop music field brought
an offer from Broadway but there was no way Dory could accept; even the train was too much for her now. André went to
New York alone to begin working on the show, a musical biog-
raphy of Coco Chanel. His lyricist was Alan Jay Lerner.

In *Bog-Trotter*, Dory writes of increasingly frequent and
longer stays in the sanatorium, stays which still were referred
to as breakdowns. She describes in unhappy detail André's
horrified discovery of the nature of her illness, which till then
had been sugarcoated for them: he accidentally read the word
"schizophrenia" written on a page from her file in the doctor's

office. She recalls, too, André "conquering his own apprehensions to play the piano in the day room for the crazies while they twitched and picked at themselves. To this day I don't know how he stayed so long." You have to wonder. In the face of such adversity, while he was engaged in a tooth-and-nail battle for professional survival as a conductor, why on earth did he try so hard to keep his marriage to Dory going?

> A marriage that is working on many levels yet not working on one level has to be worth keeping alive. It was the beginning of my career, my first year as a music director in Houston. I was traveling a lot and even though she was not hospitalized all the time, she was afraid to travel and it would have been dangerous anyway for her to be away very long from the people who were taking care of her. She never went with me and I had to go.
>
> Dory really wasn't very well and when we were together our marriage seemed to degenerate into a sort of patient–male nurse relationship. It was beyond her to help it. A life together, especially since it was childless, began to seem like a rather pointless endeavor. Still, we kept it going. I felt terrible about the fact that it wasn't working and I kept thinking well, maybe I should be doing something more or something differently.

Whether or not André consciously used his work and travel as an escape from this situation, the fact is that he enjoyed such escape and did so at every opportunity. It was on one of his hopovers to London, late in 1967, that he renewed an old acquaintance and thereby eliminated whatever slim chance there might have been for patching up his marriage to Dory.

It happened that his brother Steve was in London then, working on a film. Steve was still a bachelor and had remained, in André's words, "a film person through and through." He'd come into the business as a mailboy at Universal, then worked his way up through the ranks as film cutter, editor, director, producer, and finally executive of American National Pictures.

Having moved his base of operations to Europe, Steve found it far easier to spend time with his brother when André was in England than back home in the States. On this particular occasion Steve picked up André at Heathrow Airport and, on the drive into London, invited him to a party that evening. André groaned, but he was too tired from the flight to put up much of an argument.

> It was absolutely the epitome of a bullshit publicity party. Hundreds of people were milling around pretending undying love to one another whereas in truth they either loathed each other or hadn't seen each other in twenty years and would knife each other in the back if given an opportunity. It was everything I'd missed least about Hollywood for the last couple of years. To an extent I did enjoy seeing a few people I knew and I was glad for a chance to visit with Steve, but he kept being dragged off into film conversations. I began feeling very hemmed in and I didn't feel like standing around in that room any longer so I went out to breathe some air on the sidewalk. I turned around and there she was. Mia Farrow.

It was hardly the first time they'd met. André remembers being introduced "some years earlier" in Los Angeles by her godfather, George Cukor, but their paths had crossed on numerous occasions. Mia was a child of Hollywood. John Farrow, her father, was an MGM director. Her mother, Maureen O'Sullivan, made a long career for herself at Metro after being cast as Jane opposite Johnny Weissmuller's first Tarzan in 1932, after which she and Weissmuller were as inseparable on the screen as Cheeta and his banana. In July 1966, her elfin young daughter, Mia, earned headlines and the hatred of thousands of ex-bobby-soxers by becoming Mrs. Frank Sinatra. That marriage was on the rocks by the time she renewed her acquaintance with André in 1967.

> I said hello to her and she remembered me. I asked her why she was leaving the party so early and she

said because she couldn't stand it in there. I said, "Well, that's interesting because I can't stand it either. How about going out to have dinner?" She agreed, so we went out to dinner. That was it.

Should André ever have designs on a writing career, he might take a few lessons from Dory, whose description of Mia is far more vivid than his own: "The skin was translucent," she writes, "as though she were still wrapped in the gauze of her placenta." The two women met rather frequently and Dory says she was flattered that Mia Farrow Sinatra wanted to be her friend. She urged Dory to conquer her fear of flying so that she could spend more time with her husband, if not in London then at least in Houston, but Dory could not overcome the anxiety that gripped her. So she stayed in Los Angeles, near her analyst and her sanatorium. It was Mia who went to Houston to be with André.

In the beginning it was a working relationship. André had agreed to do an updated version of *Peter and the Wolf* that would attract young people, something in the style of the Beatles. After a great deal of discussion and indecision on the question of an appropriate narrator, André is reported to have said, "Look, I don't know the lady all that well and I'm not certain she would do it, but I do know she's a hell of an actress: Mia Farrow." Frank Sinatra's wife? How could Houston say no. A chance to work with André? How could Mia say no. Not long after *Peter and the Wolf* the rumors about André and Mia began.

André denies that she represented to him any sort of escape hatch from his own sinking marriage to Dory. At any rate, he says he never considered her in that light. As to what the feelings were, what conflicting emotions he might have had for these two women in his life at this difficult time, he will only say, in no uncertain terms, "Uh-uh. Not me. Brick wall."

He was far less enigmatic about his feelings for the two orchestras in his life. As 1967 drew to a close André again found himself in London for a recording session with the LSO, happy to be away from Texas where, as Ron Wilford had warned and as he at last was beginning to see for himself, the world's music was indeed not made. During this brief stay he was invited to appear as the guest on a venerable and highly popular BBC Radio program called "Desert Island Discs." Near the close of the interview the host, Roy Plomley, asked a provocative question:

"Mr. Previn, if you had a magic wand that would give you the Berlin Philharmonic or the New York Philharmonic or the Philadelphia Orchestra or any other, which of the great orchestras of the world would you choose?"

André gave the answer without a trace of hesitation or of guile: "Absolutely no question about it, I'd wish myself the LSO."

A few months later he was handed that magic wand.

PART THREE

The Classical Life

XX

It was just after her London encounter with André in November 1967 that Mia left Frank Sinatra. That she would be entering into a new relationship with André was not immediately apparent to the outside world, which by now was glued to Mia's every utterance. For the time being they were two glamorous people with two sets of problems who saw each other on occasion. Also, there was a difference of sixteen years in their ages.

As 1968 began both André and Mia were quite busy, on projects which seemed to be pushing them in such opposite directions that they would never get together. He had his mounting responsibilities in Houston and in London, along with his time- and thought-consuming responsibility to Dory. Mia, meanwhile, continued to make headlines as the movie mother of *Rosemary's Baby*, whose sire was no less than the Devil himself. In her previous film pregnancy, *Secret Ceremony*, she played a prostitute who fantasized herself into motherhood. Small wonder she was feeling a bit disoriented, especially with packs of photographers, columnists, and autograph hounds on her trail.

"The last thing I want to be is someone's breakfast news," she told one reporter. "If I seem to be running, it's because I'm pursued. Ten thousand people march to get a paragraph in a paper, but I get pages. An inane actress girl talking about her great ideas on life. It bothers me. It offends me."

Mia searched for answers. Salvador Dali advised her to wear her shoes on the wrong feet for a couple of days. That gave her "unusual perceptions" and blisters. Dali attempted to shock her with "a real happening. Violence in a bottle." It was supposed to be a death match between a rat and a lizard, trapped inside a glass bottle, but by the time it got to Mia the rat was already lunching on the expired lizard. She still "had no roots. I was dangerously low." So she followed the Beatles to India, in search of the Maharishi Mahesh Yogi and answers.

She found the *paparazzi* of Bombay even more annoying and tenacious than those of New York and London, so she left her hotel in secret and alone to find the Maharishi. It took her three weeks. She joined an American hunting party but left them in disgust when she learned of their intention actually to shoot animals. She spent an evening around a campfire with a friendly commune of beggars only to discover the next morning that they were actually a roving leper colony. She is said to have danced on the banks of the sacred Ganges while singing "Goodbye Charlie," music by André, lyrics by Dory. Mia emerged from the jungle, she says, permanently changed and convinced that "the world is full of whirlpools; you've got to make your own."

Meanwhile, André was whirling around England with the London Symphony Orchestra on one of its railway coach tours of the provinces. On the stopover in Brighton an incident occurred which André believes may have had a profound effect on his career.

The program that evening included the Mendelssohn First Piano Concerto, the soloist for which became suddenly indisposed. André said that he would play and conduct from the piano. He canceled the usual afternoon rehearsal in Brighton and spent the entire day alone at the keyboard, reacquainting himself with the piano part. He even had his meals brought to him at the piano. When the change was announced that evening there was much ohing and ahing and applause from the audience, along with some little nervous jitters onstage, from the orchestra members as well as from André. However, the concerto began well enough and they all settled into playing the familiar work.

I was comfortable conducting from the keyboard and I was content with my playing, especially once we got past the first movement, which has an awful lot of notes in it. I felt a surge of relief when we came to that section of the second movement in which the orchestra rests and the piano goes unaccompanied for a long time. I really felt relaxed then. In fact, I was so relaxed that suddenly I felt my memory clang shut like a great iron door. I hadn't played this piece in nearly seven years and here I was without a score in front of me and my fingers on the keys and everybody expecting me to play. This was not simply a memory slip of the normal kind. I'd worked so hard that day that I really couldn't remember what piece I was playing. I knew only that it was Mendelssohn and that the next entrance was by the cellos in B major.

I gave the cello section a sheepish look which I hope conveyed the message that they should not count measures and I started playing, kind of making up Mendelssohn-things. I wandered around in phrases and decorations I thought sounded quite a lot like Mendelssohn. Mind you, lousy Mendelssohn, but Mendelssohn. I finally managed to get myself to an F sharp seventh chord, gave a firm nod to the cellos and they came in. My conductor-memory started working for me. They knew where I was and, more importantly, *I* knew where I was.

Afterwards the members of the orchestra congratulated me and told me how brilliant they thought I was. There is nothing more pleasing to an orchestra than to see a conductor in dead trouble and nothing they admire more than seeing him rescue himself. There were actually musicians in the audience that night who were unaware that anything had gone wrong. There was even one local pianist who wandered backstage and asked me what edition I had used. He never found out why half the orchestra fell down laughing.

Less than a month later, during an important general membership meeting of the self-governing LSO, someone brought up the incident in Brighton, pointing out that André first of all had agreed to perform the piece at the last minute and second had got himself out of a pickle without letting the orchestra suffer in the least. Said the player, "Maybe this is a good fellow to keep."

In 1968 the London Symphony Orchestra was at a crossroads, perhaps even a watershed, clinging to a quite precarious foothold on the shelves of London's musical supermarket. Some observers wrote that these were the most parlous times for the orchestra since its formation in 1904, the first self-governing orchestra in London.

During the sixty-four years of its existence the LSO had elected itself only seven principal conductors, occasionally going through periods during which there was no principal, but only a succession of guest conductors. Its first principal was Hans Richter. He was followed in 1911 by Edward Elgar, whose First Symphony the orchestra had premiered. Elgar's successor, Arthur Nikisch, elevated the LSO to new international stature and took it on the first American tour by any British orchestra. Nikisch also blazed British trails in recording (for Edison) and even in making music for films. Nikisch was followed on the podium by Sir Hamilton Harty, who led the orchestra until the outbreak of the Second World War. The next principal conductor, Josef Krips, was not appointed until 1950; he gave the orchestra distinguished leadership during his tenure. The post was filled in 1960 by André Previn's San Francisco mentor, Pierre Monteux, who, despite his eighty-five years, impishly insisted on a twenty-five-year contract with an option for an additional twenty-five years. When he died in 1964 the position was awarded to István Kertész.

It was not uncommon to read, in one of the fiercely competitive British newspapers, of a squabble between the LSO and its conductor of the moment, particularly when that conductor happened to be someone other than an Englishman. European maestri were unaccustomed to ochlocracy in their orchestras; they were more accustomed to batons in iron hands. But the LSO insisted on governing itself, making its own rules, voting democratically on where it would travel and what it would play.

No less chafed by this system were the LSO's managers, although their fallings-out with the orchestra were perhaps less well publicized than those of the conductors. Indeed, the LSO so balked at the idea of being "managed" that they refused to call their managers by that title. Rather, they were "general secretaries." In April 1967, Ernest Fleischmann resigned as general secretary; he later became general manager of the Los Angeles Philharmonic. The Orchestra Committee elected not to fill the post for the moment. A few months later came the final blowup with István Kertész.

The crux of the problem was "artistic control," a sticking point which had halted LSO-conductor relations often in the past and a phrase which is difficult to define because of its wide range of interpretation. For a conductor, artistic control meant the power to use every means at his disposal to mold the orchestra into a performing organism whose sound, spirit, and reputation reflected his own approach to music, his own *statement* about music, and his personal judgment as to the place of that orchestra in the music world. In short, artistic control to a conductor is the crown and the scepter.

The self-governing orchestra would argue that the only artistic control that matters is the freedom to shape a piece of music. It is only in performance, they would say, that the many wills of the players must bend to the one will of the conductor; the music, they insist, will make the only statement that needs to be made. They would point out further that the orchestra as an entity and they as its members will continue far beyond the relationship with any one conductor and that therefore it is folly to pin all their fortunes on any single man.

The orchestra was intransigent on this point. It had once

rejected an offer by Thomas Beecham to underwrite personally their salaries and expenses as principal conductor in exchange for artistic control. In 1967 the Orchestra Committee and István Kertész came to an impasse over artistic matters. Kertész issued an ultimatum: change the policy or I will leave. The Committee refused and Kertész informed them that 1967–68 would be their last season together. Somehow the Committee managed to keep the resignation a secret so that it was not widely known that the LSO was fishing for a new conductor.

By the time the fall season arrived, the orchestra seemed very much in danger of sinking under the weight of its own freedom. Important guest conductors for the next season had not been booked. A tour of Japan and an appearance at the Osaka Festival, carefully arranged by Fleischmann, had been canceled as too costly, generating equally costly international ill will. Sometime prior to Fleischmann's departure in the spring, all advance booking activity had ceased, a potentially disastrous lapse for an orchestra whose livelihood depends on its being kept busy three hundred and sixty-five days a year. By the fall they had not suffered yet, but they were about to unless something were done quickly.

With what must have been a feeling of urgency, the LSO went after a new general secretary and found Harold Lawrence, music director of Mercury Records, who had produced dozens of recordings with the London Symphony Orchestra. Lawrence knew he had the committee over a barrel and held out for the title of general manager, becoming the first person in the orchestra's history to hold that rank. Lawrence maintains that it was not until his arrival in London in December that he found out how bad things really were. "The LSO then was in a shambles," he later told a reporter. "There was dissension on the Board and it was in the red." Lawrence also learned about Kertész's resignation and that the orchestra had made no move to replace him. Immediate prospects seemed less than favorable to the new manager.

We were facing a 1968 with virtually no work for the orchestra, a canceled tour that meant more empty dates and a resigning conductor. My first recommendation to the Board was to have a principal conductor because I believed that without artistic leadership no orchestra can long survive, particularly ours, in this precarious financial situation. We had to act quickly.

I telephoned Leonard Bernstein to see if he was interested. He said he was honored but not interested. He was conductor laureate of the New York Philharmonic and that was that. I called Solti at Covent Garden and he said that the LSO hadn't even seemed interested in *booking* him for the next two seasons, so he'd filled up his calendar for the next two seasons. After that he might take the job, provided he could have artistic control. The orchestra of course said no to that. We approached Colin Davis, only to find that he had just taken the job as director of the BBC Symphony. Somewhere down the list of conductors who'd had a good association with the orchestra was the name of André Previn.

There was little doubt that André would take the job if it were offered. He had blurted out to the world over BBC Radio that conducting the LSO on a permanent basis would be fulfillment of his dreams. Lawrence, the self-appointed one-man ad hoc search committee, decided that under the circumstances he was not likely to find a heavyweight candidate and that his best move would be to step in quickly and recommend André to the Board. He drew up a thirteen-point proposal listing what he considered to be André's qualifications. Among these were that he was "the most talented conductor of his generation anywhere in the world"; that he did have an international reputation, albeit a reputation built on his accomplishments in the jazz and Hollywood fields; that even this "pop" reputation could be put to use to draw on a segment of the population largely unreached by classical music; that his steadily growing recognition as a "media personality" could be put to profitable use in audience development.

In March 1968, Lawrence coaxed the Board into a vote on

the Previn appointment. After a great deal of discussion on the matter, the vote was split, with the majority favoring André's selection. The Board told Lawrence that André would be recommended to the general membership of the orchestra. Lawrence begged them *not* to go to the membership with anything less than a unanimous decision, refusing to take any action himself without at least the solid support of the Board. Somewhat reluctantly the Board agreed to consider the matter further and at last resistance was whittled away; the vote was declared unanimous.

Lawrence was invited to address an "extraordinary general membership meeting" of the orchestra and again went through his thirteen reasons for selecting André Previn. Some of the players bridled at what they said was Lawrence's attempt to use them as a "rubber stamp," merely ratifying the decision made behind closed doors by the manager and the Board. But Lawrence had studied the LSO bylaws and knew his ground. The membership had the option of filing a petition to overturn the Board's decision on the matter, in effect to declare "no confidence," and to elect itself a new Governing Board. It could not simply conduct its own vote on the matter of principal conductor.

There were impassioned speeches from the floor, many beseeching the Board to offer them an older man, someone steeped in the tradition of Central Europe. Players rose to speak in André's behalf, citing their good experiences under his baton, such as the Mendelssohn incident in Brighton. Others foretold dire befallings to the orchestra's image if it elected a man who bore the taint of Hollywood. Several players actually threw back their chairs and stormed out in protest. As Lawrence recalls, "It was a very sober and solemn meeting, not at all happy. You might say it was less than an auspicious beginning for the relationship."

This all happened at a meeting room just down the street from Kingsway Hall, in which André happened to be recording at that time with the London Symphony for RCA. He was staying at the Savoy Hotel.

I was in my hotel room when this little band of
players from the orchestra committee trooped up to
see me. They were led by the chairman, Stuart Knussen, the principal bass. I had some tea sent up and we
all sat down and they presented me with the proposi-
tion: "How would you feel about being the eighth
principal conductor of the LSO?" My every instinct
urged me to bolt the door and refuse to let them out
until we'd signed a contract.

I later found out that there had been a good deal
of speculative gossip to the effect that I was being
considered for the job. A lot of people had been expecting the appointment. Itzhak Perlman claimed
he'd known about it for months. Well, by Jesus, *I*
hadn't known about it. Here was one of the greatest
orchestras in the world asking *me* to be their principal
conductor.

Much as he'd have been willing to sign in blood on the spot,
André was forced to withhold a commitment until he could
clear it with the Houston Symphony. The Board of Directors
in Houston, ever the Anglophiles and perhaps even a bit flattered that their man had been offered such a prestigious post,
voiced no opposition (a decision which would later stick in
their collective craw) as long as any schedule conflicts could be
worked out without inconvenience to the Houston Symphony.

Ronald Wilford went to work on the schedules with Harold
Lawrence and with Tom Johnson, the Houston manager, to arrange the London schedule in such a way that not even a rehearsal had to be moved in Houston. The only inconvenience
was to André, who would be working for at least a year at a
mind-boggling pace, making twelve Atlantic crossings during
that year just to be with the right orchestra on the right days.
There is no indication that either André or Wilford considered
Dory and her worsening condition in arriving at this schedule
of conducting by commutation, but then, how on earth could
André have passed up such an opportunity?

It did mean that I would be living in airports and aboard planes, but I'd have been willing to put on a diving suit and walk across the ocean twelve times to work with the LSO and all those great musicians. I mean, just as an example, Barry Tuckwell was the LSO principal horn player and Neville Marriner was leading the second violins. What an amazing orchestra! And what an astonishing gamble on their part to hire me.

Wilford and Lawrence negotiated a contract and it was smilingly signed in June 1968. Thus began one of the stormier conductor-orchestra relationships in the rough-and-tumble history of such affairs. Certainly the signing was historic as the first of its kind between a major British orchestra and an American conductor. Moreover, although few would have wagered on it at the time, the signing signaled the start of the longest tenure of any conductor since the founding of the London Symphony Orchestra.

XXI

On the first cross-Atlantic flight to conduct *his* London Symphony Orchestra, André made good use of his time. Having obtained a recent photograph of the orchestra, he matched faces and instrument positions to names in an extraordinary test of his mnemonic powers. Once past Heathrow Customs he was whisked straight to rehearsal, where he astonished the members of the orchestra by addressing each and every one of them by name, from concertmaster through third percussionist. When it was done he received cheering applause from the players.

Thus André's first rehearsal with the LSO broke what would become his cardinal rule: never waste time. He understood from the beginning the pressures felt by musicians in London, financial pressures which create extraordinary demands on their time and send them dashing from session to session, by Underground and motorcycle.

> My patchy past came into play, the built-in clock I developed during my days at MGM. I've watched many young conductors who were brought up the right way, not the wrong way as I was, rehearsing meticulously at the beginning of a session, overlooking little flaws in the middle, and racing through the final minutes, never playing the end completely and at a loss as to where to start correcting. I knew that with

the LSO every minute I could save was worth its weight in gold. Either they could use it to make a few more pounds or else just have time to exhale for a moment. I realized they were rehearsing on the fly, so very often I didn't stop when I heard a mistake but would just keep going and shout over the music, "Four bars after letter V, violas. That phrase has to come out more for six beats." The inside men would mark the spot on their scores as the outside men kept playing and that night at performance the correction would be made.

The first performances of his first season did have their problems, however. The misgivings concerning his "patchy past" and his lack of European prestige continued to smolder within the ranks of the orchestra. Press notices were mixed. André himself felt that the initial season was "pretty bad" and that hopes for a long relationship with the orchestra were on the verge of being dashed. Manager Harold Lawrence told André he was being "a bit harsh on himself."

It is true that there were times the orchestra was unhappy with his rehearsals and with his performances. It depended a great deal on the repertoire. André was very careful, generally, in the choice of repertoire and he wanted to build a solid relationship with the orchestra. Of course they did a lot of Vaughan Williams in the beginning because they were in the middle of the recording cycle for RCA. They also did Walton well together and later Shostakovich. Basically he tried to choose material which suited the virtuosic abilities of the orchestra as well as his own personal tastes and in the main he was very wise in his choices. Every concert was an occasion. I never felt as though he took anything for granted and there were some magnificent concerts during those first two years.

It is hardly remarkable that there were doubts and misgivings about André in those first seasons with his first world-class orchestra. Though he was nearing his fortieth birthday when he took over the orchestra, he was nevertheless the new kid on the block. His fame in England rested almost exclusively on his jazz accomplishments, even though the establishment eyebrows had raised at his recordings of the Vaughan Williams symphony cycle. He had to prove himself, with the audience, with the critics, even with his own orchestra, at every step.

> Let's face it, I had not done any major conducting in London, none outside the privacy of the recording studios, and no conducting at all over in Europe. Nothing I'd done on the far side of the Atlantic amounted to a hill of beans. If you work the circuit in America, whether with small or large orchestras, you're still a nobody. Unless you work Europe, they never heard of you. It was as though I'd been conducting on Mars.

The analogy is not so farfetched. If a Martian, of whatever musical persuasion, appeared on the London musical scene and suddenly began conducting one of their most prestigious orchestras, Londoners would turn out in droves to see how many arms he conducted with. If André suffered from his Martian obscurity, he also benefited from his Martian notoriety. As Harold Lawrence put it in another context, every concert was an occasion. It didn't matter why they came; the point was that they came.

André's ability to draw crowds was tested and found not wanting when the British soccer team made its way into the World Cup Finals at the height of the concert season. With the nation's attention focused on the playing field, a full house for an LSO concert of Mozart and Brahms the night of the championship match seemed like the remotest of possibilities. At the request of some of the players, André had two television sets brought in backstage so that the musicians who sat out the Mozart could watch and so they could all watch during intermission.

"There was a great deal of note-passing that night," André remembers. "Today I can't recall which team won, but I do remember our great astonishment at the concert being sold out. Even the press joked that any American who could sell out a concert on World Cup night had better be kept around."

Even as his star rose in England, it was falling in Houston. Nearly a decade later, a journalist would sum up the awkward two-year relationship between André and the Houston Symphony Orchestra in less than fifty words: "The Houston Board of Directors objected to his pop life-style, exemplified by his headline-capturing romance with actress Mia Farrow. They also cited his dalliance with the LSO at a time before Georg Solti and Pierre Boulez made jet-set music directors respectable."

That fairly well summarizes what was written in newspapers and magazines of the day, but it does not give an accurate picture of the falling-out. For that, one must go back to two remarks made even before André took over the Houston orchestra. First, there was the concern expressed by dowager Ima Hogg that André might not fit in with the city's preconceptions of a proper conductor. Second, there was manager Ron Wilford's caveat to André that "the world's music is not made in Texas." On both accounts, André Previn in Houston was a round musical peg in a square musical hole.

This was evident to André from the start but never was it more forcefully brought home than at the obligatory party after the opening night of his second season. He arrived at the hotel grand ballroom, cognizant that half the people in attendance had already forgotten the program, to discover that the lavish decorations were centered around a life-size statue of himself, in ice, in a conducting pose. He noticed that "I was cooling the champagne as I melted."

Also melting were André's once lofty dreams of using his Houston tenure as an opportunity to raise the orchestra to world-class stature. Between a Board which thought of him as a party centerpiece and an orchestra management with whom he considered himself incompatible, life under the Texas sunshine was swelteringly uncomfortable.

Where we came to blows was the difference in approach to newer kinds of music and in ultimate ambitions for the orchestra. My gung-ho attitude was misplaced in Houston. Barbirolli was smart. He put in his time there, got a lot of money, and they adored him. He wasn't going to blaze any trails for them because they didn't want that. It was simply not going to be the new Paris of the Southwest. That was nonsense, but I was determined. I came against a lot of stone walls for my trouble and I made a mess of it.

Ever the pragmatist, Ron Wilford never had looked on Houston as anything more than a way station to bigger and better things for André. The job had come along at the right time and he took it. He only smiled at his client's naïve efforts to make more of the Texans than they wanted for themselves.

The Houston Board was too antiquated, too provincial to get along with André. I remember he wanted to do preseason runouts to the suburbs and outlying towns where a lot of the poorer people lived, just to get the orchestra in top condition for the subscription season and to give those who couldn't afford a subscription a taste of what it was like. The Board wouldn't hear of it. They didn't want "those people" involved with their symphony. This was the way they thought.

Sir John really hadn't been a music director there. He just wanted to go and do his concerts and go home. This was André's first job and he wanted to be a music director. He was anxious to improve that orchestra and the Board didn't want it. They thought it was none of his business, yet the contract clearly stated that it was. Even then he wanted to start a television program. He wanted to expand the audience base with young people and others. But this was an elitist group. They couldn't understand why he wanted to meddle. It was a terrible situation and it had to end.

As for what Wilford calls "the Mia thing," that was as much a red herring as the business of André's spending too much time "dallying" with the LSO—which had been carefully cleared and negotiated with Houston before a London contract was signed. "If you wanted to look for something André was doing wrong," says Wilford, "you could pick on the Mia thing." And pick on it the Board of Directors and the Houston press corps did, because in southeast Texas the unconcealed affair between the orchestra conductor and the actress stood out like an upside-down oil derrick.

By the beginning of the second Houston season in 1968, Mia was no longer Mrs. Frank Sinatra, having been granted a Mexican divorce in August. Also by then there was little doubt about the object of Mia's current affections. André and Sinatra had known each other in the Hollywood days, both in films and in sporadic instances of André's working for the singer as an arranger or pianist. There was no common social ground, André says, because "I found his kind of power play a bit overwhelming." Though the two have never crossed paths in more than twenty years, the only concrete result of André's involvement with Mia was that "I came off Sinatra's Christmas card list."

But, as André quickly discovered, there was a certain amount of notoriety that went along with being Mia Farrow, whether or not she was Mrs. Frank Sinatra. A few months after the divorce, when she and André were being seen and photographed together with increasing frequency, and when André was trying to get his act together in London and hold it together in Houston, Mia was "making whirlpools." It happened in London, but they read about it in Houston as well.

The fracas occurred in a London municipal court, to which Mia had been summoned after being "boisterous" in a nightclub the previous evening and allegedly having directed the copulative pejorative to two police officers who attempted to remove her from the premises. When the magistrate asked her to step forward, Mia asked whether she might first take off her clothes. (That was the way it appeared in the newspapers. She later maintained she only asked if she might remove her *coat*.)

Having quieted down that commotion, the judge asked Mia whether in fact she had used "bad language" in front of the police officers. Mia took righteous umbrage at that. What constituted "bad language," she wanted to know. Did the judge mean bad as in "war is bad"? Doing his best to remain calm, the judge explained that he was referring to "obscene language." Did he mean "dirty"? Yes, he did. That placed him right where Mia wanted him. She asked innocently whether the judge was referring to the word "fuck," which certainly could not be construed as dirty since, she assured the judge, "it would probably be the nicest thing I could wish you."

It was, remember, a period in history when judge-baiting and holding outmoded mores up for contempt were all the rage. Mia was merely indignant, "upset that lovemaking, the very act we all owe our existence to, has been made a gutter word to be put in the bottom of a trash barrel and stomped around on." That was an unacceptable attitude in Houston in 1968.

It cannot be doubted that this sort of headline, along with photos of Mia and André together in London, circulated by the wire services and picked up by the local newspaper and television stations, did not sit well with the proper citizens who made up the Houston Symphony's Board of Directors. They found the sharing of hotel rooms by a married man and a newly divorced woman unacceptable, and they were outraged when, some months later, André and Mia actually began living together. Criticism there surely must have been, yet André maintains he never heard a complaint from the Board about his public private life.

> Mia did not bring about my problems with that Board. Whether there was any private censorship going on in their Texas minds I couldn't say, but if there was they kept it to themselves. I doubt very much if it made any difference to them. The issue was one of artistic disagreement, along with an enormous personality clash between the then-manager and me. By the time we were really along in my second season there it was pretty obvious to everybody there

would be no third. We knew we'd be glad to see the backs of each other.

Albert Camus wrote that "every act of rebellion expresses a nostalgia for innocence." One suspects that for André that may have been the case. For Mia Farrow there is no description if not "innocent." Her directors always have cast her as an innocent and Mia's own published comments on life, even if affected, support the image. André, on the other hand, could lay no claim to innocence.

He must have felt a bit like Dorian Gray. His public countenance continued to be one of youthful inexperience and exuberance, bursting as he had upon the classical music scene in the guise of an *enfant terrible*. Youth clung tenaciously to his features, and his trendy tastes in clothes—purchased in London and therefore even more avant-garde in the United States —abetted the disguise. Beneath the surface lay the experiences of several lives overglazed and cemented together by a patina of guilt with respect to his prior personal relationships. Rebellion against that presented and personified itself in the hell-raising innocence of Mia Farrow.

André spent the first three months of 1969 in London concertizing with the LSO. Mia shuttled between London and New York, where she was starring in the production of a film called *John and Mary*. On the eastern side of the Atlantic they were photographed together, André meeting Mia at Heathrow, the pair out for an evening of theater, embracing backstage after a Festival Hall concert. On the western shores reporters pestered Mia for the scoop on her future marital plans. In February she blurted that, marriage or no marriage, she'd been spending time in London with the one man she felt she could live with for the rest of her life.

In the race to bring Sinatra's ex back to the altar, the London *Daily Standard* asked the very next day, "Who is Mia Farrow hoping to marry?" Answering its own question, the newspaper narrowed the field to one, since André Previn "makes no secret of the fact that he and Miss Farrow are close friends." Just in case anyone had missed the point, André fueled the speculative blaze by jumping to Mia's defense in answer to another reporter's questions:

"People have a tendency to look at Mia and say, 'Look at those funny clothes and the way she acts and the things she talks about compared (let's say) with Debbie Reynolds. She's some kind of freak.' But I think Mia is the straight one. I think Debbie Reynolds is the freak."

In the late sixties the feuilleton had become the front page and persons who had no right to opinions beyond their own half acre of competence could be quoted as authorities on world issues. During his own quarter hour of notoriety, the painter Andy Warhol predicted, "The day will come when everybody will be famous for fifteen minutes." If that day had arrived, then Mia had far exceeded her time in the limelight. Since 1966, when she splashed onto the world's front pages and television screens with the announcement of her marriage to Frank Sinatra, Mia had been wrapped in a sort of transparent mystique. She wanted, or seemed to want, everyone to know her but no one to understand her. The result was that her every act and utterance was deemed noteworthy and therefore was noticed. By association with her, André had become a hot item in his own right, a household name far beyond the reaches of his music. Together, André and Mia were the world's "breakfast news."

In Houston, members of the orchestra Board bolted down their breakfasts and began publicly deriding their conductor. They let it be known that they had turned over their orchestra to him and he was quite apparently ungrateful. The chairman of the Board went so far as to denounce André for never having done a good concert thus far during his Houston tenure, a claim which lends credence to André's contention that "my living with Mia had nothing at all to do with the breaking off with Houston," no matter how certainly the media wagged their fingers at his "impropriety."

The Houston-Previn divorce had become a foregone conclusion months before the most glaring Farrow-Previn publicity. Moreover, the divorce was mutually agreed upon and the settlement was out of court, further supporting André's claim that "both sides heaved great sighs of relief when we decided to call the whole thing off." He turned his back on Houston, resolved never to darken that city's doorstep again. Coincidentally, it was about the same time, in May of 1969, that Mia became pregnant with André's child. Or rather children, since it later became apparent that Mia was carrying twins.

The pregnancy was still undiscovered when André received word that Dory once again had been nominated for an Academy Award for "Come Saturday Morning," written with composer Fred Karlin for the film *The Sterile Cuckoo*. From London he wrote Dory a letter of congratulations and she read the letter in her bed at the mental hospital in Culver City. In *Bog-Trotter* Dory maintains that André concluded this same letter by asking, in an offhanded way, whether he might have a divorce, the first time such a thing had been mentioned, according to Dory. André stoutly, almost emotionally denies this. He insists that any words about separating were spoken face to face and he blames Dory's unstable mental condition for the "confusion of facts."

It is not improbable, however, that Dory is remembering accurately when she states that the first word of Mia's pregnancy by André came to her via a cruel, impersonal source. She writes that she was telephoned in the hospital by a columnist "friend" who asked for her reaction to published reports that André would father Mia's child.

Some weeks later Dory secured a pass from the hospital to attend a recording session. Instead she boarded a plane for London. First she telephoned André from the airport and asked him to meet her at Heathrow, just as the newspapers told her he met Mia Farrow. But the arrival time conflicted with his rehearsal schedule and André said he would instead send a mutual friend, Robert Carrington. Carrington was there to meet her all right, but Dory did not disembark in London.

From a stewardess the friend learned that she had been taken off the plane before it ever left the ground in Los Angeles. She had stood up in her seat screaming as the Pan-Am jet taxied to the runway. Dory then had ripped off most of her clothes and had run barebreasted down the aisle of the plane, shouting threats at a priest who happened to be on board. The plane stopped and an ambulance was called to take Dory to Culver City Hospital. That may have been the beginning of her return to normalcy, but it was the finish of her efforts to save the marriage. André, of course, had stopped trying long before.

The shamelessness and openness of André's affair with Mia now traveled brazenly from England to the United States. During the final work on his musical, *Coco*, and for its Broadway opening, they lived together in New York, Mia's expectancy no longer concealable, what with her waif-like figure. A few months later, when he brought the LSO to America for an eighteen-city tour in the first weeks of 1970, André was grilled relentlessly about Mia. He politely told one interviewer in Connecticut that "on a tour like this everyone's personal life takes a back seat." But in the newspaper that statement came from "the father of Mia Farrow's twins," the customary label in those days for the man who'd made the unheard-of Great Leap out of the mire of pop music into the Elysian Fields of the classical world and who, at the same time, was the first American ever to lead a prestigious English orchestra. All his other accomplishments seemed as nothing compared to the fact that he had got with child the former wife of Frank Sinatra.

Mia's pregnancy was also the focal point of Dory's outrage and hostility, a happenstance which actually may have speeded up her recovery. She believed that Mia had gotten herself impregnated for the express purpose of stealing André from her. For the time, her life seemed to be sustained by the hatred she felt for Mia, for André, and for herself. From a distance André watched Dory retreat into the dungeons of her mind and, though he never let it crack his public façade of the mod roué, André staggered under a barrage of self-recrimination.

> The end of the marriage took a tremendous toll on me for a lot of reasons. I suppose I have not had the best of luck with marriages. I've been at fault or wrong twice. Dory was ill and I felt a tremendous

amount of guilt at abandoning her to her illness. In a
small way I actually was helped by her doctor who
told me I had to decide whether I was going to be
one lady's male nurse or another lady's husband. Still,
my actions made Dory feel terrible and it was a trau-
matic breakup of a marriage. When you consider that
in the long run I probably did her no good at all, the
situation was close to tragic.

Dory would eventually agree, but only much later, when she
would write that as Mrs. André Previn she had subjugated her
needs completely to his, had been absorbed emotionally and
professionally by André's stronger, more secure personality. She
lived in André's shadow and could never see her own identity
clearly enough to grasp it. In *Bog-Trotter* she even writes sym-
pathetically of André's role in the collapse of their marriage,
wondering how he ever managed to remain steadfast as long as
he did, nearly ten years. At least in an intellectual way Dory
has managed to shoulder some blame for the estrangement,
writing that long before André deserted her for another
woman, she had deserted the world to which he could relate in
favor of her own realm of unreality.

Dory now realizes, in retrospect, that no matter how
dreadful it was for her at the time it was to our mutual benefit to break up. Moreover, it was to our mutual salvation. Had we continued with what we were
doing to each other and what she was doing to herself, things would have turned into a genuine horror.
The proof of this lies in the fact that today she is
happy, successful, rich, and fulfilled in every way.

Far from happening overnight, that turn of fortunes for
Dory required the better part of ten years. It took that long before they were able to confront each other and what had happened to them openly and, in André's phrase, "to wish each
other well."

Perhaps in an effort to cut the cord that bound her to
André, Dory quit writing for films after *The Sterile Cuckoo*.

In fact, when she was offered the role of Nurse Ratchett in *One Flew Over the Cuckoo's Nest,* Dory turned it down. Instead, she concentrated her efforts on writing and recording her own songs, turning recording studios into electronic analyst's couches. Her first song, the music for which she cribbed from "The Whiffenpoof Song," was entitled "Beware of Young Girls." The young girl of the title was unmistakably Mia Farrow and so the song became an instant international hit. People on both sides of the Atlantic gobbled up the album, *On My Way to Where,* and listened in gaping astonishment to Dory's nightmare songs of terror and screams in the dark, of Marilyn Monroe's suicide and Jesus' crucifixion, of a small girl's sexual fantasies ("With My Daddy in the Attic"). Mia helped the record sales tremendously by responding to reporters' questions: the song about her was "tasteless." At last Dory was right there in the inch-high headlines with Mia and André.

She designed her own outlandish image, more than a match for André's Nehru jackets and Mia's mini-sacks, affecting a sort of post–flower child look, complete with auburn afro and superlarge eyeglass frames. She produced more albums, first *Mythical Kings and Iguanas,* then *Reflections in a Mud Puddle* and others. Each successive album, as each of her three autobiographies, can be viewed as being a step closer to the traditional viewpoint of reality, though application of the word "traditional" to Dory Previn seems rather oxymoronic.

In 1972 she told a reporter she never would marry again, never would "allow myself to be again in the position of a supplicant, an inferior." Nor did she intend to saddle another man with the burden of her love. "You pin everything on him. You tell him you are my God, my father, my angel, myself. No wonder they leave in droves." In 1979 she flew in an airplane.

XXII

In London, where his relationship with the LSO had gotten off to a conflicting start, André very much needed to shift public attention from his "scandalous" extramarital arrangement to something more positive. He knew full well he could not afford to become a recluse but must somehow use the maelstrom of publicity to cement his relationship with the orchestra and to sanctify its dependence upon him as its leader. The perfect opportunity arose in an offer from the British Broadcasting Corporation.

BBC Television producer Herbert Chappell first encountered André Previn in 1968, shortly after his appointment as principal conductor of the LSO. As a guest on the network's "Late Night Line-Up," a "chat show" as the British say, André was responding amiably and easily to questions about Sir Thomas Beecham. (A documentary about Beecham had just aired.) "It was my impression at the time that the LSO was just fencing with him, wondering if they could kill him in five minutes or would it take ten." Nevertheless, Chappell found the American charming and ingratiating, particularly in his praise for the BBC's production efforts. "In America," André told the host, "there are simply none of these programs which you in England take for granted."

Indeed, serious music had been an integral part of BBC programming since its earliest days as a radio network, and concerts as well as documentaries on musical subjects were ordinary fare on BBC Television. However there never had been an earnest effort to bridge the gap between audiences who wanted important concerts in their living rooms and those who used television exclusively as an entertainment medium, mostly because there was no musical "personality" around whom such a bridge could be constructed. Leonard Bernstein was such a personality in the United States, but no Bernstein had yet arrived on British television. Chappell and others found themselves wondering whether Previn was their man.

The job was very nearly botched at the beginning, when André told Chappell to "call me tomorrow at the Savoy." Chappell assumed André wanted him to "call on" him, rather than "ring" him on the telephone, as a Britisher would have said, and he found André stepping out of the shower and rushing to make morning rehearsal. André was brusque and nothing came of the meeting. Chappell, however, became more and more enamored of the idea and decided he would chance a trip to New York in an effort to set up another meeting.

> I arrived in New York at the most frenetic time, two days before the opening of *Coco*. They were rewriting and rescoring. Katharine Hepburn was nervous and Mia was pregnant and André's phone at the Algonquin never stopped ringing. I sneaked out of the suite and went downstairs and I bribed this Betty Hutton-sort-of switchboard girl fifty dollars to hold the calls. That was everything I had on me. I went back upstairs and at last André said, "All right, we can talk, but only for a few minutes because I'm expecting a call from so-and-so because they're in the middle of underscoring the dance numbers." So we sat and talked. The whole time Mia was walking around being Mia-ish and André kept glaring at the telephone, terrified that it wasn't ringing because he wasn't used to that kind of silence.

Together they formulated a plan for André and the LSO to do a series of nine programs over three years, each of which would be built around a theme and would feature André talking about the music as the program progressed, to a studio audience as well as to the audience at home. The object was to appeal to a mass audience without underselling the music or condescending in any way. The first three programs would draw on André's obvious areas of appeal: "American Music and All That Jazz," followed by a program on Vaughan Williams and one on the better class of film music.

Herbert Chappell returned to London "crowing, thrilled to bits." But when he gave the news of nine concerts in three years to Hugh Welton, the Welshman who controlled the arts output of the BBC, Welton scowled, "Nine over three years? Why not nine a year? Milk the butter dry." That would have been in keeping with television's tradition of inventing celebrities and dropping them but, as Chappell observes, "André was fifteen jumps ahead of us. He'd learned all about that sort of business as a kid."

With the negotiation of the BBC contract, another important development in André's career occurred. The negotiations were begun by Ronald Wilford with much correspondence between London and New York, but it quickly became apparent, even to Wilford, that what André needed was a London-based manager. For a while Wilford engaged Robert Patterson to handle his client's European affairs but, in Wilford's words, "that didn't work out. André needed a manager there. I couldn't do it from New York."

At a party in North London, André met Jasper Parrott, a young man as colorful and verbally gifted as his namesake, who was rapidly rising in the circles of British artists' management. For the moment he was an agent for Ibbs and Tillett, probably the most widely recognized agency in Europe. One of Parrott's clients was the emerging keyboard celebrity Vladimir Ashkenazy. An acquaintance and admirer of André's since their first encounter in California, Ashkenazy enjoyed being with the American conductor as much as he enjoyed working with him. It was he who had invited André to the party, alone since Mia was not in London at the time.

"After dinner," Parrott recalls, "one of those silly guessing games was played, one in which you identify pieces of music. I was lucky that evening and managed to guess some difficult things, which seemed to impress André." At the conclusion of the evening Parrott offered to give André a lift to the Savoy in his recently acquired Morris Minor, "a gift from someone who'd intended to scrap it, held together by bits of wire and string and not behaving very well at all. With a lot of coaxing I could get it up to twenty miles per hour."

After one look at the Morris, André said he would not mind at all taking the Underground, but Parrott dragged him along. At every stop for a traffic light André would put his hand on the door handle and attempt to convince his chauffeur that this was surely too far out of his way to go and that a taxi would be quite convenient. By fits and starts, with much time for musical conversation, they arrived finally at the Savoy. "By that time," says Parrott, "I'd made up my mind that I wanted to handle his affairs and I wondered whether this was the way to convince him. I could only hope that the situation had a sort of quixotic appeal to him."

Dissatisfied with the Wilford-Patterson arrangement, André was taken with Parrott's enthusiastic approach. And being with Ibbs and Tillett made a certain prestigious sense. However, the agreement with Patterson had several months to run and he would have to wait until that contract had lapsed before even talking about signing a new one. This was in early 1969 and André would not be a free agent in Europe until that November.

This coincided almost perfectly with Jasper Parrott's own plans. In October he split with Ibbs and Tillett and, with several other young hopefuls, started his own agency under his own name. "We had no proper offices, no money, and only about five artists." But one of those was Vladimir Ashkenazy.

Almost immediately Parrott confronted André backstage at a concert, reminding him that he had said to come see him again in the fall. "Well," said André, "I am going to be out of this contract in November and I'm going to need somebody, so . . . what the heck? I'll be with you."

Now one of Europe's most respected managers, Parrott looks

back on that evening with a sense of destiny-in-hindsight. "I couldn't believe my luck. Ashkenazy put us on the map because to get him certain important people had to deal with us. But André launched us. Suddenly there were television contracts, recording contracts, a hand in the London Symphony. With that kind of base we could afford to gamble on some other, younger people who were just beginning their careers, like Radu Lupu and Kyung-Wha Chung. By having that kind of intuitive faith in us as managers, André made all the difference. We could have gone down without a trace and his career with us. We would not have the business we have today if that hadn't happened."

Parrott saw in André a man who had suffered a lot and was pinning his hopes for his future happiness on his current situation. "He was very concerned to make a home for his future family and to make his coming marriage to Mia work." That sort of normalcy was still months away, the divorce from Dory tangled by her instability and lingering ambivalence to ending the marriage she had seen so long as her salvation. In the meanwhile, André and Mia set up housekeeping in a Belgravia flat to wait for the twins and the divorce, wondering which would come first.

The flat, near Harrods on Montpelier Square, was owned by the model Jean Shrimpton, who happened to be using only a single room of it, permanently locked up, for her clothes. The rest of the townhouse was sublet to André. "It had, without my usual habit of exaggeration, the smallest rooms I have ever been in, no bigger than railway compartments. The bedroom and the locked-up room were upstairs. Downstairs were the so-called living room and bathroom, with a doll's-house kitchen in the back. The worst thing about it was having to trudge downstairs in the middle of the night to use the loo."

The other disadvantage to the flat was that it was an easy target for tabloid and free-lance photographers, who hung around the place like gulls around a trawler. As André puts it, mixing his metaphors, "The gutter press corps were nesting in the trees." This was, as Mia saw it, "my press," the *People*, the *Evening Standard*, *News of the World*, the *Sun*, the *Mirror*, and the *Daily Mail.* Those were the ones in the trees. Had André gotten that sort of attention from "his press"—the *Times,* the *Telegraph,* the *Guardian,* the *Financial Times*—he might never have had cause to put an end to it. But Mia's press "was degrading. It was unbelievable. We would go to the market and there would be people behind us with cameras."

It got to the point where I looked out the window one morning and there actually was a man climbing into a tree with a telephoto lens to take pictures of us inside the house. At that point I'd had enough. I immediately went to the phone and rang Wendy Hanson (one of London's leading publicity agents at the time, who has since established her headquarters in New York) for advice. She told me to pick a photographer to do one session, then let him peddle it around and make lots of money. She brought in this gentlemanly, nice fellow named Terry O'Neill who was amused by the assignment and decided to do it all very formal, almost like a daguerreotype. He then went out and sold his pictures to everyone, including the Italian magazines.

O'Neill's photographs are incredibly tongue-in-cheek, most notably the one which appeared in the *Evening Standard* showing a solemn Mia seated primly in an armchair as André, paternally dignified, stands behind her, his hand on her shoulder. Beneath the photo is an article in boldface which begins, "The setting could hardly be more English: the early spring sunshine filtering through to a great (!) Belgravia drawing room . . . a painting over the fireplace; on the wall, a bell to call the servants. Miss Mia Farrow looks Victorian in the burgundy red velvet dress she designed herself. Only the bare toes reveal that Miss Farrow is a child of the times. Behind her stands André Previn. Miss Farrow is radiant looking. They say that mothers-to-be are often more beautiful. She is having a happy, relaxed time. Yesterday was her 25th birthday . . ."

Almost as silly was the two-page treatment in the *Sun:* OUR TWIN BABIES—BY MIA AND ANDRÉ. The largest photo showed

Mia in profile, wearing a lace-sleeved cotton smock, André's caring hand upon her protruding tummy. The photo editors had pulled out all the stops, with cutlines that read: "At play . . . Mia and André Previn enjoy a cozy game of draughts on a chequered rug," and "At rest . . . Mia and Previn snuggle up to share a book." The accompanying article, by Unity Hall, declaimed that "after seeing these pictures, no one could doubt the depth of feeling that exists between the delicate Mia and the father of her babies. They are members of the set that practises a new kind of morality. Where love is more important than marriage. Tenderness and care for each other, of more significance than legal ties." With syntax equaled only by taste, such blatherings achieved the desired end. The gutter press disappeared from the trees.

The twins, two healthy boys named Matthew and Sascha, were born a few weeks later, in February, but it was not until eight months later that André's divorce from Dory was finally official and André and Mia could get married. They did so on September 10, surreptitiously, to avoid publicity. Then they let it be leaked to the press after the fact.

> The whole thing had become an obsession with us. We had stopped going anywhere. We didn't go to the theater, except for my concerts; we didn't go to dinner. We simply stayed behind closed doors to avoid it, until even that didn't help. We were prisoners.
>
> Then after the photos appeared, it eased up considerably. After it became known that we'd married, we suddenly became boring establishment types and after that it would have taken clown makeup to get us into the papers.

The divorce from Dory meant that André could settle his affairs in Los Angeles, selling the house in Bel Air for a substantial profit and letting Dory keep the entire collection of paintings, an agreement which was painful but quick. He took the money from the California house sale and purchased the home he'd always yearned for, in the English countryside.

It may have been because of "having been chased all around the world by events in my childhood and later by my own doing" that André felt an urge to find "a place that really spoke to me." He had no clear vision of the place he needed, but he knew it had to be somewhere out of the hurly-burly of London and that it had to have trees. "Some people need mountains; some people need ocean; I need trees. Maybe it's some latent Teutonic genetic stream within me."

He subscribed to *Country Life*, a glossy pastoral magazine which features ads for country estates. He would select a house by its picture and, without the slightest idea where he was going, would jump into his unimpressive car, turn on his tape deck, and take to the open road. His shaky knowledge of British geography often led him leagues from London, as far as Northumberland, to look at houses that often turned out to be beyond his means. On other occasions he would get a call from a realtor and be shown "the goddamndest places, with indoor pools and projection rooms and the works. They knew it was for a conductor and a film star, so they assumed that we required the sort of home that had previously been owned by the Beatles' manager or something."

One bleak October day he was driven to a house in Surrey, midway between the small towns of Reigate and Dorking, each about five miles distant. The estate was entered through a gate and behind and around the large house André could see nothing but trees. "Twenty acres of woods," the realtor said, and to André that sounded as vast as the Black Forest. There was a small cottage off the main house, which André thought might make a fine study, but before seeing any of the inside he insisted upon a stroll through the chill and leafless woods. He knew at once that this place was "speaking" to him. There was even a pond with ducks that reminded him of his childhood days in the Tiergarten. He turned to the agent and said, "Unless the house is an absolute wreck on the inside, this is it. How much?"

At that point the realtor was forced to admit sheepishly that someone already had bid on the house and that his motive in bringing André to see it was to discover whether this was the sort of thing Mr. Previn had in mind. Before his client could find a suitable rejoinder or stout stick, the man managed to blurt out, "Of course, you might make a higher offer."

As it turned out, the early bidder was interested only in a summer home and had no intention of paying more than his first offer, so André's upping the ante by a mere five hundred pounds won him the house of his dreams. He decided to call it "The Haven." Mia fell in love with it at first sight.

At first the villagers were suspicious of their notorious new neighbors, but quickly they discovered that the Previns wanted no part of the publicity which hitherto had attended them and they grew rather protective. If some yellowish journalist wandered into the Seven Stars (*the* local pub in which *the* local telephone directory was kept) and began asking directions to the Previn house, the villagers were suddenly stupefied. When one persistent photographer actually found The Haven, the local constable pedaled out in answer to André's call and hinted to the photographer that on his next visit his camera might be invited into the pond.

It seemed that all the adversity in his life at last had ended, that André could settle down to work.

XXIII

"It took awhile for André to capture the enthusiastic endorsement of the entire orchestra," says former LSO manager Harold Lawrence. "There was a wait-and-see attitude which lasted the better part of two seasons." As responsible as anyone for taking the gamble on André, Lawrence looked on rather anxiously as the crucial year of 1970 approached. This would be the benchmark, especially in the case of a self-governing orchestra such as the London Symphony.

> The orchestra musicians look at a principal conductor quite differently than at a guest conductor. The guest conductor they really don't expect to get anything from, except for good rehearsals and good concerts. Certainly André had given them that. But a principal conductor is going to be a member of their family, which is something quite different. They liked him and respected him, but there were doubts. 1970 was the turning point.

It was a nervous time in the musical life of London. The orchestras were struggling to make ends meet, seeking out grants from corporations (a source of income the media held in suspicion and contempt). But without the money it received from Peter Stuyvesant, British Airways, Rand Xerox, and others, the LSO might already have gone under. With the pound sterling falling on international exchanges and inflation chewing away at the exchequer, government subsidies were being stretched thinner and thinner. The grant-channeling body, the London Orchestral Concert Board, was dividing among four orchestras (all but the BBC Orchestra) a grand total of £600,000. The *Sunday Times* pointed out that this was roughly equivalent to half of the city of West Berlin's grant to its one and only Phil- harmonic Orchestra. The London Arts Council studied the sit- uation and drafted a report recommending that all subsidies be concentrated on just two "contract orchestras," whose players would be guaranteed income security. The council did not sug- gest which two orchestras out of the LSO, the Royal Philhar- monic, the London Philharmonic, and the New Philharmonia should get the axe. A principal conductor's job in that situa- tion meant seeing to it that *his* orchestra worked its way to the top of the heap and stayed there.

The method André employed to achieve this goal was four- fold: first and foremost was television, with the LSO running away from the field in that medium; second, there was record- ing, the financial lifeblood of London's multi-orchestra system; third was the ever-necessary business of international touring, for if one could boast often enough and with success of being Britain's orchestral ambassador to the world, the audiences at home would begin to believe it and the corporate underwriters would flock; finally was the need for continuing the LSO's tra- dition of individual excellence among its players.

André had emphasized this latter point in a personal note he wrote for the recording of Rimsky-Korsakov's *Scheherazade*, made with the LSO before he became the orchestra's principal conductor. *Scheherazade* is full of prominent solos for the prin- cipal players of an orchestra, and André singled out for special praise concertmaster John Giorgiadis, and these soloists from the orchestra: Roger Lord, oboe; Gervase de Peyer, clarinet; Barry Tuckwell, horn; Roger Birnstingl, bassoon; Nelson Cooke, cello; William Bennett, flute; and Osian Ellis, harp. On television he made many of his players into recognizable "personalities."

"In America you're used to television as a tool for public relations," remarks Dame Janet Baker, "but in England we've always been very suspicious of that kind of coverage of anything serious. André got it started for orchestras. Many people will never come to music of their own volition, but he went out and reached those who were on the borderline, who maybe never had been exposed to it but didn't mind listening to the way he spoke to them. He looks like a person they wouldn't mind knowing. Probably the fact that he was an American let him get away with things an Englishman couldn't have. Because of that he became a tremendous influence on the course of serious music in England."

Part of the success in influencing the course of music had very little to do with André's skills as a musician. Rather, it was due to his emergence as a television *personality*, the very equivalent of what his father and Uncle Charlie had wanted for him on the first trip to MGM studios. The breakthrough there came when he was invited to appear as a guest on the annual BBC "Morecambe and Wise Christmas Show," perennially one of the BBC's highest-rated programs.

"If it had not been funny," André observes, "it would have dealt me a terrible blow. It turned out to be not only funny but *intelligently* funny." Millions of people who never had seen André Previn conduct watched him that night, in his deadpan clowning with the witty Morecambe and Wise. It was something Herbert von Karajan could not have done, but for André it worked.

> There were a lot of cartoons in the newspaper, of course, and I took on a role in the minds of the British public that had nothing to do with classical music. Suddenly I was the property of a much larger audience than had ever gone to a performance in Festival Hall. They couldn't have given a damn about the Beethoven program we'd done the week before, but now they thought, well, if this guy's a symphony conductor maybe we should go to a concert. I was a hero in the British pub.

His success on the comedy show spawned a rash of similar offers, but André turned them all down. "I said no all 'round and wouldn't touch them. I never did it again and there I was smart, I think." What he did not turn down was a suggestion from the BBC that he become the host of a new weekly talk show called *André Previn Meets . . .* , produced by Ian Engelmann.

In André's estimation, the first several shows were "lousy, because of my failures as an interviewer." But Engelmann found him "a skilled interviewer who draws out of people who might otherwise be reticent interesting and revealing things about themselves." He blamed the lack of "spark" in the first programs on his own choice of guests: Prime Minister Edward Heath, Morecambe and Wise, and Jonathan Miller. Declaring that he was "definitely not Johnny Carson," André gave the producer a list of candidates whom he knew personally, in some cases intimately, and suggested that he begin calling to see who was available. The result was a prize-winning series of interviews with the likes of Tom Stoppard, Janet Baker, guitarist John Williams, Julie Andrews, and even Mia Farrow. There were no scenarios for these interviews, no scripts, only conversation that turned out to be amusing, informative, and approachable. Engelmann decided, "He's a chat-show natural."

The talk shows were the icing, the music shows the cake. Beginning in 1970 André and the LSO began participating in television programs at the rate of about one a month. In that arena André quickly established what the LSO tuba virtuoso John Fletcher has termed "his credibility to ordinary people," a thing which "very few conductors have had." Managing the medium as skillfully as he wielded his baton, André made the same music that had always been bottled like medicine now seem like sugar candy. Says Fletcher, "He takes the upperclassness and high-altar quality of symphonic music *out* of symphonic music."

Producer Ian Engelmann recalls an instance which points up both the lengths to which André would go to achieve that effect and the extent to which he succeeded:

> We were preparing a program on British brass band music. A lot of our brass players today come from a tradition of brass banding in mining towns, colliery

towns, and mill towns. Each town has its own work-men's band and they get together for competitions. André was genuinely keen to find out about it per-sonally, talking to people in the bands and finding out what their life was like, even though this meant spending weekends with myself and a film crew in the north of England, in Lancashire and Yorkshire. I remember Colin Davis asking him where he was heading and he said, "I'll be in Ramsbottom." And Davis said, "Ah! You've hit the big time."

Well, we were in Middleton in Lancashire and we finished shooting around lunchtime. If I'd been look-ing after any other conductor, I'd have had to stage an elaborate lunch with wine at a hotel. With André we all just walked across the shopping precinct and sat down at a Wimpie Bar. It was far from grand. The waitress wiped off the counter, staring at him, and said, "Hey, you're André Previn, aren't you?" André admitted that he was. The waitress beamed and said, "I watch you all the time on the telly. Can I get your autograph?" So he signed the Wimpie menu.

On its annual tour through the British Isles, the London Symphony was greeted with similar enthusiasm. In small Welsh and Scottish towns the LSO concerts were sold out weeks in advance. "Not because they were dying to hear Brahms Four," quips André, "but because they considered us TV celebrities and wanted to see us in person."

André's programs captured the imagination of the public. On a show called "Who Needs a Conductor?" he answered the timeless question of why a man with a stick was necessary if all those other musicians knew their business. In the British Museum he came upon Beethoven's original sketches for the Ninth Symphony, including four different themes which the composer had tried and discarded as the setting for the Schiller "Ode to Joy" finale. André orchestrated each of the themes in the style of Beethoven and then did a program called "What

Price a Symphony?" in which he discussed the genesis of the
composition and what it might have sounded like had Beethoven traveled one of the roads not taken.

These thematic shows were roughly equal parts talk and
music. For producer-director Herbert Chappell, the main
difficulty with the format lay in controlling their content without disrupting their spontaneity. The first show, "American
Music and All That Jazz," was completely scripted, with André
using a teleprompter (or autocue, as it's called in England).
This proved a mistake and thereafter Chappell settled on a
method by which he did all the research and then did a preliminary script, complete with music cues, which André then
"tore apart" and rewrote. From that point on André never consulted the script, but saw only cue cards with distilled phrases
which led him along from musical point to point. Everything
else was ad libitum.

Ian Engelmann recalls his amazement at André's ability to
memorize the content of each cue card. "He'll look at a card
and halt everything to think for a couple of seconds. You'll ask
if he wants it on the autocue, but he doesn't hear you. Finally
he'll look up and say, 'Okay, I've got it. Let's do it.' And it will
work perfectly."

In addition to the straight "chat shows" and theme specials,
André began doing a series called "André Previn Music
Nights" featuring the LSO in concerts with distinguished guest
artists performing difficult music. The talk here would be restricted to intermission interviews between conductor and
guest. Soloists for these shows included Vladimir Ashkenazy,
Janet Baker, Kyung-Wha Chung, André Watts, and Pinchas
Zukerman. They were performed with as much intimacy and
informality as possible, in a BBC studio at first, but later, at
André's request, they were moved to a theater with a live audience.

Another successful—and concurrent—series was called "My
Kind of Music," in which André would chat with colleagues
such as Adrian Boult, Colin Davis, Yehudi Menuhin, and
Georg Solti about their personal relationships with music. The

guest would then perform or lead the orchestra in pieces which had meant a great deal to his personal growth or to his career.

Although André enjoyed the straight-out concerts immensely, he was "not that crazy about TV shots of orchestras playing." He felt the more effective programs were those which reached out less formally to the otherwise inaccessible Englishman away from London, "where people don't collect records or have a lot of concerts available to them. Suddenly, on the box in their living rooms, in direct competition with the police shows and the sitcoms, they found a great orchestra playing great music in a completely relaxed way, and they could be told about the music in unrehearsed, casual tones. It caught on and, to my immense gratitude, it stayed on."

For the BBC's Ian Engelmann, the success of the shows was due less to their format than to the personal magnetism of their star. Likewise behind the scenes, Engelmann points out, André was able to mix the seemingly incompatible demands of good music and good television.

> It is very difficult for things to go smoothly in a TV studio. André does not tolerate fools and he will not accept things going wrong about him. He wants to know what's happening and he likes people to move smartly. He doesn't tolerate incompetence. As a result, temperamental outbursts from him are not uncommon. If some piece of technical equipment fails he will understand, but if there's been a breakdown in communication between the director in the booth and the men on the floor, he'll go mad and bawl everyone out and we have to start over. But he never makes a session unbearable by harboring a grudge. He might throw the score down in disgust, but then he'll say, "Let's all go have tea in the Green Room." The result is that I've never met anybody, not even among the cameramen, who's worked with him once and who doesn't want to work with him again.

Important as television appearances were in placing the London Symphony Orchestra and its conductor at the head of

England's musical class, it was still the recording industry that kept meat on the tables of the musicians. After a 1969 that was comparatively devoid of recording dates, André and the orchestra recorded with a vengeance throughout 1970.

Continuing RCA's Vaughan Williams cycle, they did A Sea Symphony and the Symphony No. 5. Fast becoming another "specialty" composer for André, Rachmaninoff was represented by the First, Second, and Fourth Piano Concertos, with Ashkenazy as soloist in all three. In addition, they recorded Mendelssohn's "Italian" Symphony, Ruy Blas Overture and Piano Concerto Number One with Israeli pianist Joseph Kalichstein as soloist; Prokofiev's "Classical" Symphony and the Violin Concertos of Sibelius and Tchaikovsky with Kyung-Wha Chung as soloist. André's contract with RCA allowed him to record concertos on rival labels and the Ashkenazy and Chung collaborations were done for Decca/London.

In his choice of soloists—Ashkenazy, Kalichstein, and the twenty-one-year-old Korean Miss Chung—André opted for youth over experience. All three then were established concert artists, but they needed the solid recording base André and the LSO could give them. On the other hand, their relative freshness in the "meat and potatoes" repertoire gave André the chance to record in an area in which he still had to establish himself, so there was a certain quid-pro-quo. Likewise, it probably was no coincidence that both Ashkenazy and Chung were under contract to Jasper Parrott, the building of whose credentials was very important to André's own career.

The solo work of Chung, Ashkenazy, and Kalichstein was impressive on disc. So was that of Itzhak Perlman, who had made a Symphonie Espagnol/Tzigane recording with André and the orchestra the year before. A pattern was being established which, in coming years, would cloud the relationship between André and the orchestra. The more established, more internationally recognized, older artists—soloists as well as conductors—would begin to look upon the LSO as a bastion for youth. Gradually they began eschewing the LSO in favor of more traditionally bent London orchestras when it came to filling out their contractual recording dates. In the long run, André's youth movement would become an issue, but for the moment it proved an elixir for the London Symphony.

He was forty years old, and still very much identified with the "now" generation. Pushing that to its extreme, André brought out a record of one of his BBC film projects, a program called "The *Other* LSO," the ensemble of the title being the teenaged Leicestershire Schools Orchestra. The television program includes clips of André rehearsing the students in a frenzied run-through of Glinka's *Ruslan and Ludmila* Overture, during which the violins come out the losers in battle with a particularly difficult phrase. Without missing a beat, André turns with a smile to the first violins and says, "Better luck next time." Near the end of the show he tells the kids—and the television audience—about the differences he's noticed between their playing and that of professional orchestras. One difference, he says, is that while professionals have a gift for watching the conductor without ever seeming to take their eyes off the score, the students seem never to take their eyes off the conductor yet never actually *see* him. "Do take an occasional look," he exhorts them. "You'd be surprised."

A recording came out of this unlikely collaboration, released on the Argo label. The "Other LSO" performs zealously in the "Elegy" from John Ireland's *A Downland Suite*, along with an overture by Herbert Chappell, one of André's BBC producers, and a composition of André's entitled *Overture to a Comedy*. After hearing the recording some years later, he quipped that he still liked "approximately two dozen measures" of the overture.

For some reason, most likely having to do with its corporate revenue picture, the RCA management moguls in Rockefeller Plaza had fallen gradually out of love with André Previn. Roger Hall, who had brought him to the label, was no longer there. It was a time of belt-tightening, and André without his pop-jazz ventures was far less attractive than he had seemed in 1964, when the company was in an expansive mood. After six years, RCA opted not to extend his contract again. Ronald

Wilford got in touch with Peter Andry at EMI Records (released in the United States as Angel Records) and, as Wilford puts it, "Andry understood."

What there was to understand was that André was through forever with music in the popular genre, through with jazz and through with movie music. In the contract signed with EMI at the end of 1970 there was no mention of any work outside the classical range. Again there was a clause enabling André to conduct the LSO for soloists on rival labels, as well as the stipulation that he be allowed to complete the Vaughan Williams cycle for RCA, while EMI continued to release its own VW cycle under Sir Adrian Boult. Although EMI occasionally would suggest repertoire in an effort to supplement its catalogue, André would be left on his own for the most part when it came to calling the tune. It was a mutually happy agreement from the start, as well as one which had great potential of being mutually profitable, and the LSO breathed a collective sigh of relief.

There was a certain irony about the fact that EMI assigned, as André's recording engineer, Christopher Bishop, who happened also to be engineer on the Boult–Vaughan Williams project and who had grown accustomed over the past five years to viewing André and the LSO with a certain hostility. However, the two men soon came to get along famously.

Their first project together was the Sitar Concerto of Ravi Shankar. Again, there was a degree of irony in this choice for a conductor who was bending over backward to shake off his old labels. It was, after all, through popular music, notably that of the Beatles, that Shankar and his exotic music had floated into the sweet air that hung over British-American rock of the sixties. But as the seventies dawned, popular music seemed to have moved well beyond both Shankar and André Previn, enough so that André in his new identity could afford to espouse the concerto and thereby guarantee it a chic success. He conducted the work in performance at Festival Hall, Shankar and his table-tamboura consort seated cross-legged on rugs before the orchestra. It was a foot-stomping success and soon afterward the Sitar Concerto was committed to disc by EMI.

Judged by the standards of the Western masterworks, the Sitar Concerto has not a great deal to offer musically. But as a rare collaboration between two so dissimilar cultures, the concerto broke new ground. "Rather like hearing a Western orchestra through Eastern ears," the *Gramophone* critic observed. Perhaps its most significant musical moment comes in the fourth movement, during a marvelously intricate interchange between the sitar and the orchestra's flute and horn soloists. The success of that interchange, which involved Western instruments functioning in an Eastern idiom, grew out of a series of collaborations between Shankar and other virtuosos, most notably Yehudi Menuhin. EMI had reaped a substantial reward from the cultural mix since its first "West Meets East" release in 1967 and the Sitar Concerto recording only confirmed the company's sound judgment in this regard.

André's second release for EMI underscored their mutual desire to provide a strong financial foundation for their relationship at the very beginning, something which never had been a prime consideration in his work for RCA. Again the repertoire was music which the new André Previn had grown accustomed to shunning: Gershwin's *Rhapsody in Blue*, the Piano Concerto in F, and *An American in Paris*. It came, like the Shankar piece, at EMI's suggestion and probably the only thing that sold it to André was the idea that he would play the piano parts as well as conduct. He enjoyed playing and conducting the LSO in concert and this would be his first opportunity to appear in the dual role with his orchestra on record. Also, it would set a precedent whereby he might someday play and conduct more serious works, such as the Mozart concertos which he dearly loved. The recording was a huge success and the simultaneous release of a rival version by Philips only served to heighten critical interest in and preference for the Previn-EMI disc.

Despite his lingering fondness for playing the piano and even for composing, André was quoted in the *Evening Chroni-*

cle of October 23, 1970, as saying, "Conducting is the only thing I love doing." That was precisely the absolutist statement called for in this feuilleton headlined "In Praise of Older Men . . ." The woman responsible for the article placed André at the top of a list of over-forty celebrities which included a television star and a nobleman actor–turned–interior decorator. The article's premise was that successful older men "hold a fascination for women."

Listed at forty, though his true age at the time was forty-one, André's remarks were endearingly and typically self-deprecating. "I'm far from handsome," he said. "Perhaps it's true that talent is an attraction in a man, like prettiness in a woman."

Therein lies an implicit acknowledgment rarely admitted by André: that indeed women are attracted to him. Often these women are writers of one sort or another. Dory was one. Newspaper and magazine writers, assigned to interview, profile, or critique André, wind up fascinated by him, falling under some sort of spell which, as he says, cannot be accounted for by physical attraction. André simply is not dashingly handsome. Yet he is attractive to intellectually impressionable women. One he encountered at this point in his career was the music critic for the *Financial Times* of London, a woman in her midtwenties who certainly could list physical beauty among her own attractions, Gillian Widdicombe.

In her early reviews of André's work as principal conductor of the LSO, Miss Widdicombe was less than charitable toward the man she called "the biggest publicity magnet since Beecham." To her, André suffered by comparison with the great conductors; he had "none of the pungency that enables one to smell a Karajan, a Bernstein or a Giulini within a few bars." She mockingly described his conducting technique as "a kind of paddle." She seized on a quote by André in a rival paper, in which he had likened his new job to that of a traffic policeman. "Previn's traffic does not always obey his signals," she wrote, "and when the crunch comes . . . the result can be astonishingly untidy." As a listener, she preferred to leave André "hoist on his own publicity."

Yet within a few months, after she had gotten to know Previn the man, Previn the conductor was cast by Miss Widdicombe in an entirely different light. Sheathed was the rapier wit, cast aside the slings of comparison and the arrows of mockery. In a review of an LSO concert of the Vaughan Williams Fifth Symphony, one of her acknowledged favorite works and one with which she was familiar enough to be quite picky, she was the soul of tenderness toward her former "bête noir."

André's conducting of the Fifth Symphony was on a level with, perhaps even a step above, "the more familiar approach of Sir Adrian Boult." The pages of the *Financial Times,* once acrid with vinegar for André's supporters, were all at once coated with honey. "Previn fashions the dynamic detail with almost fastidious care." Previn "draws attention to the silky sheen of the string writing, the prettiness, the elegance." Previn "makes the most of those places of broad climax." Previn "gives rubato by the handful to all patches that are possibly romantic."

Romantic indeed, wagged London's rival publications, referring not to Previn's interpretation of the music, but to Gillian Widdicombe's interpretation of Previn. One gossip columnist called the relationship "a close friendship." The two came to be "seen out frequently together." Coy to the point of being cryptic, Miss Widdicombe told a fellow journalist that "I am not really saying anything to you. If we have been seen out together by people who say we are friends, then we are friends."

The friendship grew and with it a hostility between Gillian Widdicombe and Mia Farrow Previn. Even before her change of heart toward André, Widdicombe had sniped at "his unusual wife who occasionally comes to concerts." Whether to provoke a confrontation or to throw cold water on the enmity by pretending it did not exist, André took to inviting both women to semiprivate musical events, such as important recording dates. "It was a rather bizarre situation," observes one source close to the LSO, "with his wife and his girlfriend in the hall at the same time. To everyone's relief they just avoided looking at each other."

On another occasion, however, Mia somehow wound up with a seat for a Festival Hall concert which was directly behind the seat normally reserved for the *Financial Times* critic, Gillian Widdicombe. Seemingly delighted at a chance to make life uncomfortable for her rival, Mia slumped down in her seat so that she could dig her knees into Gillian's seatback, rocking forward as she did to minimize Gillian's chances of enjoying the concert. Perhaps she hoped Widdicombe would write a scathing review and thus provoke André's ire. At intermission both women went backstage and staged a shouting match over which of them should or should not be admitted to the conductor's dressing room. All of this was observed by members and staff of the orchestra and their only surprise is that none of it seemed to have any adverse effect on André's conducting. Typically, he was able to wall off his music from his personal life.

Equally typical is his aversion to discussing Gillian Widdicombe in any but professional terms. The two were thrown together on the LSO's 1970 tour of Russia and the Far East, with Mia back in Surrey, and the change in their relationship was immediately apparent to their co-workers in the worlds of music and publishing, but André dismisses the connection:

> The equation is not fair. She had written some extraordinarily adverse things about me, true, but she also had written some very nice things early on. She's a very intelligent woman who knows a lot about music and who writes very well about it. (This is distinctly atypical of André's opinions of critics.) She rarely takes kindly to an entire concert but always likes certain things and doesn't like other things. Yes, she did go to Russia and we did become very friendly, but that's all I'll say on the subject.

Whether or not it had any romantic implications for André, the 1970 tour had an enormous effect on his career, particularly on his relationship with the musicians of the London Symphony Orchestra. The season of 1969–70 had included André's first tours as principal conductor of the orchestra, successful tours to the United States, Romania, Czechoslovakia, and Hungary, but still there was uncertainty as to the permanence of André's position. As manager of the orchestra Harold Lawrence heard "doubts expressed by responsible members of the orchestra and its committee over his suitability as principal conductor." It was the spring of 1970, Lawrence believes, and the resounding success of the Russian-Oriental tour that brought "the turning point in André's relationship with the LSO."

The tour was something of a marathon event, with a total of eighteen concerts in seven cities in a period of less than four weeks. Included on the itinerary were Moscow, Leningrad, Tokyo, Osaka, Nagoya, Seoul, and Hong Kong. Had Mia gone along, as originally planned, Gillian Widdicombe might have been just another of the music writers in attendance, but one of the twins was taken ill and Mia stayed home.

Another writer in the entourage was the *Gramophone*'s Edward Greenfield. In his promotional book on André Previn for EMI's "Recordmasters" series, Greenfield remarks on the incredible energy level sustained on the tour by André. He seemed to get along with little more than three or four hours of sleep a night, between rehearsals and concerts managing somehow to squeeze in assorted diplomatic affairs, attendance at local music events, and writing a diary of the tour commissioned by *The New Yorker* magazine. At one point, says Greenfield, André dashed to a Leningrad jazz club with first horn player David Gray and there the two foreigners improvised into the morning to the enormous delight of the city's jazz establishment.

There were significant political overtones to the Soviet leg of the tour, particularly since André and Harold Lawrence had seen to it that the eyes and ears of Great Britain would be on them at every possible moment. To this end the troupe included England's most distinguished composers, William Walton and Benjamin Britten, as well as two of Russia's most distinguished soloists, Sviatoslav Richter and David Oistrakh. The grand curtain-raiser of the tour was a gala concert in Moscow involving all the celebrities.

"That was more than a concert," André reminisces. "It was the kind of howling success you dream about." The enormous Tchaikovsky Auditorium shook to screaming ovations for the orchestra, the conductor, the soloists, and the composers, and afterward they were mobbed by admirers wanting to shake hands and procure autographs. An old woman pushed her way through to André, tearfully clasped his hand and placed an orange in it. The gesture deeply moved André, for earlier that day he had noticed the long lines and the exorbitant prices at Moscow's fruit markets.

The stars of the evening gathered back at the Rossiya Hotel, hoping for a bite to eat, but the hotel's dining room was closing down for the night. They were told they might order vodka and nothing else. The interpreter assigned to the group by the Russian State Department attempted to intervene on their behalf, then Oistrakh and Richter joined in, creating a four-party shouting match which was totally incomprehensible to André and the others. All they understood was the headwaiter's immutable "*Nyet!*" Seizing a basket of bread from an uncleared table, André gestured with it, asking the interpreter whether they might be served similar baskets, along with some cheese. "Nyet." And André lost the basket before he had a chance to shove a partially eaten roll into his mouth. The orange in his pocket was beginning to take on an unsouvenir-like importance.

Suddenly someone remembered a large box of chocolates in the window of the lobby gift shop. A mad dash got them to the gift shop before it too was locked up for the evening and they bought out all the chocolate candy in the place. Those, along with four bottles of vodka graciously sold them by the headwaiter, constituted a meal for twelve hungry people.

The following morning André woke up feeling rather like the Russian Revolution had been fought in his stomach the night before. "I had overslept," he says, "and had managed to miss that seventeen-minute span in which a Russian hotel deigns to serve breakfast." He had to shower, shave, and dress in a hurry to make a 10 A.M. news conference at which he was supposed to be guest of honor.

I walked into this room and there they all were. Tass, *Pravda*, magazine editors, television reporters, lights, cameras, everything. And I was feeling rather fuzzy. I looked around for coffee, but instead they wheeled in this enormous carafe of iced vodka. I told the interpreter as graciously as I could that this would not do. I couldn't drink. Two drinks and I put on lampshades, I said. But she said, "I'm sorry but you'll have to. It's customary." So the vodka was poured and a toast was offered to my wonderful orchestra and how pleased everyone was and how marvelous we all were. I belted down the vodka and it hit me like a grenade. The interpreter said, "Now it's your turn, Mr. Previn."

I toasted the glorious Soviet audiences and started to sit down when somebody else toasted Walton, to which I countered with "Shostakovich!" belting down another vodka each time. "Britten!" somebody said. And we drank. "Rachmaninoff!" I said. And we drank. By ten-thirty I was just this side of catatonic. At last they began asking me questions about my background. I was none too careful about my answers, just trying to hang on to my senses. For some reason I made the mistake of mentioning my two years in the Army.

"You were in the American Army?"

"Yes."

"Can you tell us what it was like?"

"It was a waste of time," I said without thinking.

I saw thirty-six pencils move in unison and I realized I'd fallen into a political trap. All I could think about was my blinding headache, but somehow I pulled myself together and said, "It was a waste of time just as any army is a waste of time for a musician." Before the next press conference, in Leningrad, I made damn sure to get some sleep and some breakfast.

Aside from all the culture shocks of the tour, André suffered a few musical shocks as well, discovering that the Western music publishers upon whom he'd always relied had not been as faithful as they might have been to Russian composers. "We've been fooled," he realized, "by unauthentic editions." The initial discovery came in Leningrad where he attended a performance of the Fourth Symphony of Tchaikovsky, conducted by Yevgeny Mravinsky. He found the performance marvelously stimulating, yet it was not the Tchaikovsky Fourth he had known and conducted. "It was wildly eccentric. The tempo changes were, for the most part, sudden and unprepared." He discussed this with the conductor after the performance and Mravinsky urged him to examine a facsimile of the manuscript score, which André had never seen but which was easily obtainable in Leningrad. The next day he found one and saw that the Russian had conducted nothing more nor less than what the composer had written.

Even more startling was the discovery that the publishers had tricked him on Rachmaninoff's Symphony No. 2, a work which by then already had become a "signature piece" for André. His recording of the symphony four years earlier was a hallmark of his work for RCA Red Seal and it had become so popular in England that he had risked possible charges of bringing coals to Newcastle by daring to include the quintessentially Russian piece on his programs in Moscow and Leningrad. André had received some criticism for such temerity in the London papers before embarking, but it turned out that the symphony had been absent from major concert programs in the U.S.S.R. for many years and the Russians thanked him for reintroducing an old comrade.

> In later years we've gone on to play that symphony all over the world, the LSO and I, but the biggest success by far that we ever had with it was the night we played it in Moscow. Any arguments against nationalism in music were disproved that night. The Russians wept at the playing of our English orchestra as

though they were watching *King Lear*. People waited for us outside the stage entrance in the snow. Others ambushed us outside our hotel. It was one of the most emotional nights I've ever experienced.

André did not know until he got to Leningrad that he'd been playing less than the whole symphony. In his conversation with Mravinsky, the subject of Rachmaninoff Two came up and the Russian remarked that he'd heard and much admired André's recording of the work. "But tell me," he said, "why don't you play the whole thing?"

Up until then nobody in the West realized that the published score contained several cuts. There was nothing to indicate that cuts ever had been made. Everyone assumed that was the whole thing. Mravinsky got me a Russian score—which was printed on something like French money—and he showed me how much of what Rachmaninoff wrote had been left out. It amounted to about twenty minutes of music. Two years later we were able to record the whole symphony, uncut, for EMI and finally everyone got to hear it in its entirety.

As the tour progressed, the dispatches from Greenfield, Widdicombe, and the other reporters along, as well as the Russian reviews wired by Reuters, kept the British public well informed as to the acceptance of the LSO abroad. England was following the success of the orchestra much the way it followed the victories and defeats of national soccer teams on their tours of Eastern Europe and South America. Indeed, the headline-grabbing tour had all the trappings of an international sporting event and the LSO was treated as Britain's national orchestra team, coached and quarterbacked by the very winning André Previn.

The tour, the unmitigated success of the Vaughan Williams recordings, the imaginative programming of the Shankar and Gershwin discs by EMI, the growing presence of orchestra and conductor on television—it all combined in 1970–71 to set André's roots firmly in British musical soil. Beyond that, André's pluck and endurance, despite the rigors of touring, combined with the orchestra's brightening financial outlook to bring virtually all its members solidly into his camp. The probationary period was over.

XXIV

André's halcyon days with the London Symphony were during the first half of the decade of the seventies. With him the orchestra prospered, with few of the tensions that marked his early seasons in London and in Houston. Domestically, except for the flare-up over Gillian Widdicombe, his life seemed to be settling into as much a pattern of normalcy as is possible when one is an international orchestra conductor.

Within the walls of his 250-year-old estate in Surrey he lived like an English country gentleman, waking in the morning to the chattering of birds and insects, looking outside and seeing small deer grazing on the lawn. The thatched cottage in the rear of the main house had been turned into a live-in studio, where he could work late into the night on a television script or a score. Sascha and Matthew were developing real personalities now and he was proud to be called their "Papa," even though their mother insisted on being known to them as Mia. He told a visitor from the United States, "Often people say I must be mad to isolate myself like this. But in spring the brook runs and the grounds are a sea of daffodils, splattered with rhododendrons, hydrangeas, and begonias. At its most autumnal, it's a Monet-ic blaze. To see that is worth anything to me."

His expatriotism was fueled by the social and political contacts he made through his position as spokesman for the LSO. The former chairman of the orchestra's Board of Trustees, Edward Heath, had become Prime Minister. Suddenly André was hobnobbing with the leaders of government and thinking how this would have impressed his father, who had been so proud of his own familiarity with the government leaders of the Weimar Republic. Heath had been an organ scholar at Oxford before turning his talents to politics, and he had remained genuinely interested in music. He delighted in having André and Mia to 10 Downing Street and to the official country home, Chequers, for long talks about music. Despite his having to resign as Board chairman, the PM had remained vociferously loyal to the LSO. It seemed only natural, then for André to invite Heath to conduct the orchestra at its annual Anniversary Gala.

> Harold Lawrence said to me, "Listen, I know we have Isaac Stern playing the Sibelius Concerto and we have John Williams playing the premiere of your Guitar Concerto, but isn't there some sort of theatrical event, something unexpected we could pull?" I thought about it for a second and said, "What if we invited the Prime Minister to conduct an overture?"
>
> Harold laughed and told me I was crazy. The PM couldn't do such a thing even if he wanted to. But I went to see him at the House of Commons and he said he'd be delighted to do it. We settled on Elgar's *Cockaigne* Overture.

In Britain, of course, this was a publicity stunt nonpareil. Probably the only thing that could have topped it would have been the Queen herself on the podium. After only two rehearsals with the orchestra, Heath sat on the edge of his chair backstage as he listened to André make the introduction to a packed and glittering audience in Royal Festival Hall the night of November 25, 1971. "It is untrue," said André, "that I am now aiming to be Prime Minister for fifteen minutes."

Pink-faced and somewhat abashed by the applause, the Prime Minister and First Lord of the Treasury, the Right Honourable Edward M. Heath strode to the rostrum, bowed, and launched into the overture. No reporters other than the usual music critics were allowed into the hall, so theirs were the front-page and cover stories of the event. "The first test came in bar three," the *Gramophone* reported later, "when there is a tricky phrase to negotiate, and though his head was down in the score Heath managed it well . . . It was plain that this was no mere run-through and that he was putting over a very positive interpretation." By Christmas, EMI's "LSO Gala" recording of Heath's *Cockaigne*, backed by André conducting three "lollipops," Bernstein's *Candide* Overture, Vaughan Williams' *Greensleeves* Fantasia and Enesco's Rumanian Rhapsody No. 1, was a big-selling item. Even members of the opposition party bought it for their friends.

André's Guitar Concerto, another highlight of the LSO Gala, was recorded by Columbia, the company for which the guitarist John Williams recorded. The work justifiably holds a favored place among André's compositions for it contains a great many musical ideas, well planned and well executed. The moods vary considerably from movement to movement, with the central "Adagio" the longest and heaviest in content. The third movement introduces a jazz combo of electric guitar, electric bass, and drummer, which does its best to interrupt the conventional flow of the piece, but in the end the trio is overcome by the unrelenting stream of the classical tradition. It is, in a manner of speaking, an autobiographical composition.

One of the most important musical collaborations to grow out of this period was that between André and the composer Sir William Walton, to whom André felt a kinship and an allegiance ever since Walton's Viola Concerto had stirred his musical Anglophilia as a teenager in California. They had been introduced briefly and André had conducted the LSO in an RCA recording of the Walton First Symphony which was so successful that it overcame the composer's endorsement of the rival recording conducted by Malcolm Sargent. But it was not until the Russian tour of 1970 that the two men got to know each other. The deprivations of touring and the raucous success of the performances soon made them "Willy" and "André" to each other and at tour's end they continued their friendship, going to parties, dinners, and concerts together, visiting each other's homes and collaborating on musical endeavors. On March 29, 1972, Sir William celebrated his seventieth birthday, assisted in grand style by André and the LSO.

The concert began with a twenty-minute-long rendition of "Happy Birthday." André had asked ten of Britain's most prominent composers each to write a two-minute variation on the song and to conduct it that evening. The resultant collage was performed *attacca*, that is, without a break between "movements," so that as each composer-conductor's variation drew to a close, the next would step out onto the stage and would begin conducting when his music began.

Once the climactic applause for that brilliantly conceived effect had subsided, André conducted the orchestra in Walton's Second Symphony, followed by the composer himself conducting Yehudi Menuhin in the Viola Concerto. It was a huge program, climaxed by the addition of the LSO Chorus and baritone John Shirley-Quirk in a dazzling performance of Walton's oratorio *Belshazzar's Feast*. The performance was both expansive and incisive, precise and exuberant, and despite the lateness of the hour the Festival Hall audience was cheering for more when it was over.

Walton embraced André backstage and complimented him effusively on the *Belshazzar*, declaring that it was the finest interpretation he'd ever heard. Over the din of well-wishers and press, Walton asked André for his score and André pointed to a table where the score lay. The composer pushed his way to the score and leaned over to write something in it. Before André could see what he'd written, a reporter got hold of it and read aloud, "To André, King of Kings, with my thanks for the best performance ever given of this piece."

"Sir William," the reporter asked, "did you really mean that?"

Walton screwed down his thick brows and glowered at the reporter through thick glasses, "Of course not," he said, and André burst into laughter.

Since that time the relationship between the two men has deepened, with André becoming generally recognized as *the* interpreter of Walton's music. With the LSO he has recorded

Walton's *Improvisations on an Impromptu by Benjamin Britten* and *Belshazzar's Feast*, as well as the Violin Concerto with Kyung-Wha Chung. He premiered Walton's *Varii Capricci* and performed his rarely heard Sonata for String Orchestra. Through André's efforts Sir William became extremely well known to British television audiences; André also eventually became a champion of Walton's music in the United States.

> I started needling him about writing a Third Symphony and he said, "Oh, my God, a symphony? I'm never going to write another symphony." I said, "Come on, William, everybody's waiting. And your first two are so beautiful." Well, one Christmas I got a package from him and there was the first page of a score of Symphony Number Three with a loving dedication on it to me. I framed it and hung it in my studio. Periodically I ask him for page two. The last time I heard from him he said he actually had been working on it and had even finished one of the movements. Typically enough he said he didn't think he'd finish it. Also typically enough, I think he will.

With André's stock soaring in London it was only natural that one or another of the LSO's rival orchestras would try to lure him away. One rumor circulating throughout much of 1972 was that the London Philharmonic wanted him as principal conductor. The members of the LSO met, with a sense of urgency, and voted to offer him the unprecedented position of "Conductor for Life" of the London Symphony. Flattered beyond words, André suggested a compromise that would quell the LSO's fears without tying them to something they might grow to regret. He signed a contract with the orchestra that had no expiration date. If either party decided it was time to terminate, the other party would receive a *two-year* notice. The effect was of a self-perpetuating two-year contract and it spoke highly of the feelings that had grown between the musicians and their conductor.

"Sometimes they're like a marvelous racing car," said André of his orchestra in a 1973 interview. "You want to let it out and go as fast as you can and you know they just love playing in a bravura style." He was doing about seventy-five concerts a year with the LSO and felt he had impressed them with his stamp, helped make them into a homogeneous group "as opposed to a hundred wonderful instrumentalists who happen to sit in the same room."

In addition to André's concerts there were more than 475 other "working sessions" for the orchestra during the year, many of them André's rehearsals and recording sessions, the balance rehearsals, recordings, and concerts under guest conductors. The LSO players were averaging one and a half sessions per day, every day of the year, a punishing schedule but the kind of schedule they needed to ensure the highest possible income. One of their greatest problems in all this was the lack of a fixed rehearsal hall. London's rehearsal facilities were stretched thin among all the orchestras and chamber ensembles, so the LSO had to book space wherever it could be found. This produced the sight of musicians racing around town on motorcycles with cellos strapped behind. It was picturesque but hardly convenient. Conditions were so desperate that the orchestra quite literally might rehearse in the morning on one side of London, meet clear across town for a recording session in the afternoon, and be required to appear in formal attire for a concert at Royal Festival Hall that evening. Harold Lawrence called them "a band of gypsies."

In fact, said Lawrence, "the orchestra performs, rehearses, and plays concerts in about twenty-five different halls scattered around London. These working conditions will have to be improved. We're taking steps in that direction, but we also need financial help." He was referring to an effort launched by the orchestra trustees to find a permanent home for the LSO. The hall was still several years away from becoming a reality, but it did the musicians a world of good just to know it was on the way.

A source of tremendous pride was the invitation to participate in the 1974 Salzburg Festival. The LSO was the first British orchestra to receive such an invitation and André called it "a great feather in our cap." The *Times* of London called it "a signal compliment."

It was indeed a coup for the LSO and for André. Once again they were given the red carpet treatment by the media, cast in the role of Britain's "national" orchestra. At Salzburg the orchestra would be conducted by four internationally prominent conductors, in addition to André, and the LSO Wind Ensemble would have a concert of its own. The BBC sent a film crew to Austria to cover the event; Peter Andry of EMI made a speech; André and Mia held a joint news conference; Sir Jack Lyons, one of the trustees, was on hand to emphasize the importance of the LSO's "trying out its talents" on an audience that was "used to the best of everything."

André conducted what he thought was a very conservative program—Haydn's Symphony No. 87, Beethoven's Second Piano Concerto, and the Rachmaninoff Symphony No. 2—then roared with laughter when he read in the paper the next morning that he'd conducted three Salzburg Festival premieres. The wind might have been taken out of his sails somewhat by an incident at rehearsal. He was asked to move his rented Volkswagen from a privileged parking spot because Karajan would be arriving shortly and would demand the spot. But back home in London, the headlines said it all:

DEBUT OF LSO THUNDERING SUCCESS
AN IMMENSE JOY TO LISTEN TO
EVENING OF PERFECTION
ONE OF THE BEST IN THE WORLD

André and the orchestra returned triumphant, renewed in their commitment to each other. It seemed that way between André and Mia too. She had gone along on the Salzburg trip and there had been no suspicion of another woman. In Surrey, their family was growing.

The idea of adoption had been André's. In Korea in 1970 he had visited an orphanage for victims of the war in Vietnam. He did not consider himself an antiwar activist ("not to be confused with Vanessa Redgrave standing in Grosvenor Square on Sunday afternoon throwing rocks at the American Embassy") but he was moved by what he saw in Korea and the image of the war orphans stayed with him. It was not hard to convince Mia that they should adopt one of them. Kym Lark came to them in 1973 at the age of about two months.

> Meeting Lark was one of the extraordinary moments of my life. After months of struggling through mountains of red tape, we finally got a telegram saying that a Belgian nun would be conveying twelve orphans from Saigon to Paris. We decided to go to Paris to meet her. It was an unscheduled flight and all we knew was that it would arrive sometime in the next twenty-four hours. We sat in the airport nearly the entire day and night when finally the plane landed and all these children and babies straggled out. Bringing up the rear was a tiny Belgian nun we knew would be Sister Pascal. She must have recognized us, for she walked toward us carrying a little plastic basket. "Monsieur et Madame Previn," she said, "voici votre bébé." She handed us the baby and Mia burst into tears. I was looking at the tiniest two-month-old baby I had ever seen. Her papers were pinned to her blanket. We looked up and the nun had disappeared, as though she might have been afraid we'd change our minds.

Shortly after Lark's arrival Mia became pregnant. André was feeling paternal in ways he'd never felt before. Some of his happiest moments were those he spent roughhousing with the three-year-old twins and he loved to notice every ounce of weight little Lark put on and to watch her reach out from nightmarish infancy toward her new parents. André and Mia spent hours choosing names for their unborn child and agreed that if it were a boy they would name him Django, after the legendary gypsy jazz guitarist, Django Reinhardt. Perhaps fortunately for the child André was present at the birth and "even at one breath old this blond and angelic face came out and I knew he was no Django." Instead they named him

Fletcher. The following year they adopted two more girls, Summer, a Vietnamese, and Soon-Yi, a Korean, making a total of six children to fill The Haven.

His home, his family, and his orchestra were all in England, the place where he'd longed to live since first setting eyes on it. The orchestra was riding a crest of popularity and sounding better than ever. In André's words, "They all love playing and they all love being the LSO." Said Harold Lawrence in a television interview, "There is nothing to replace the esprit de corps that you have with an orchestra that is organic, that has a history and a tradition and a feeling of belonging. This is something that is irreplaceable and this is what makes the LSO what it is."

"To see Previn conduct the LSO," one critic wrote, "is to see a man in love."

In March 1975 it came as a stunning blow to the orchestra and to much of England's concert-going, television-watching, record-buying public to learn that André had accepted what he termed "a practically utopian offer" from the Pittsburgh Symphony Orchestra.

The LSO's chairman, Howard Snell, and others on the Governing Board decided it was high time to hand André his two-year notice.

XXV

Howard Snell was an extraordinarily gifted trumpeter, a man with a hard, brassy personality that matched his instrument. He had watched a great many conductors in his day and felt he knew a thing or two about conducting; in fact, he thought he might like to become a conductor when his lip gave out and his trumpeting days were over. Snell's ideal conductor was a brusque man with a no-nonsense attitude about music, gray-haired, stern, commanding; in short, a martinet. That was the sort of leader the LSO should and did not have, Snell thought. From the outset he had been vocally opposed to André Previn and over the years his opposition had remained firm, while support of André's cause ebbed and flowed.

The position of chairing the nine-member LSO Board had never been easy. Horn player Barry Tuckwell had resigned in exasperation, as had his successor, double-bassist Stuart Knussen. But Snell seemed to relish the job and, since taking over as chairman in 1972, he had steadily deepened his imprint on the Board and, consequently, on the orchestra. Gradually, a plan for ridding the LSO of what he considered its chief drawback, André Previn, fell into place.

The plan called for first getting rid of manager Harold Lawrence, who was a fellow American of Previn's and who had been the chief instrument of Previn's coming to the LSO in the first place. Since Snell and Lawrence almost never agreed on management matters and since Snell's opinion usually counted more than Lawrence's, it was not difficult to make life sufficiently miserable for the manager so that he would want out.

When Lawrence left, he was not immediately replaced. A majority on the Board wanted to rehire Ernest Fleischmann, the previous manager, who had led the LSO through some of its most difficult times. But Fleischmann, by then comfortably ensconced in Los Angeles, turned down the offer. That left Snell free to offer the job to his personal choice, John Boyden, a man then associated with the LSO's arch-rival, the London Philharmonic Orchestra.

In 1975 the *Times* of London called the LPO "the most successful runner in this race at present" and pointed to the fact that the Philharmonic had been the only one of the city's major orchestras to end the previous season out of the red, with a surplus of £15,000. Much of the credit for its healthy performance and growing international reputation was given to management.

Like the LSO, the LPO was self-governing. But unlike its rival, the Philharmonic was a harmonious, smooth-running operation, unbeset by the clash of personalities that regularly wracked the London Symphony. Unlike the LSO, it did not engage in running feuds with its managers and as a result for the past seventeen years it had been managed by only one man, Eric Bravington.

Under Bravington the LPO had built up a reputation for solid, traditional quality, concentrating on what he called "a European sound." There was no gimmickry about their concertizing; they never appeared in public without white ties and tails. The players respected their resident conductor, Bernard Haitink, and they took great care to choose only the cream of the guest-conductor crop, selecting those with the greatest international reputations. They went back to those conductors again and again, with the result that those men regularly brought recording contracts to the LPO.

In 1975 the scuffle for recording engagements had become

warfare among London's orchestras. More and more the big record companies were looking eastward, to the continent of Europe, where many new recording facilities were being built and where the musicians' scale was often lower than in Britain. But the London orchestras had come to rely on recording sessions for as much as fifty percent of their annual revenues. As André told an interviewer, "recordings are the life's blood of the English orchestra." André's own recordings with the LSO continued to outstrip in British sales those of any other conductor, even Karajan, and critics and conductors had begun to observe that the orchestra played better for André than it did for other conductors. Consequently those other conductors were starting to take their contracts elsewhere.

To make matters worse, the LSO had lost out to the LPO on a lucrative project by EMI Records called "Classics for Pleasure." Designed to present the "warhorses" of the orchestral repertoire as performed by one great orchestra at a price below that of the standard LP, "Classics for Pleasure" proved to be a goldmine for EMI as well as for the LPO, claiming a sixth of the entire classical record sales in Britain. By mid-1975 the LPO offices were hung with four silver records—each indicating sales of £75,000—for discs of the 1812 Overture, Strauss waltzes, and piano concertos by Tchaikovsky and Grieg. The brains behind the "Classics for Pleasure" series and the man who managed the project for EMI was John Boyden, Howard Snell's choice as manager of the LSO.

Boyden virtually named his own price. The Board realized it could not afford a long, destructive interregnum like the one they'd suffered between Fleischmann's departure and Lawrence's arrival, so they gave in to Boyden's demands. In addition to a three-year contract at £12,000 a year, he received the unprecedented title of Managing Director and, most important of all, a seat on the Board, something never before granted to a nonmember of the orchestra. Howard Snell was ready for his next move, bringing into the organization the sort of conductor who would show plainly the leadership the LSO needed and wanted. By this move he expected to embarrass André into leaving of his own accord or, failing that, to begin the process of phasing himself out. The man Snell chose to accomplish this was Eugen Jochum.

At seventy-three Jochum was a man of considerable accomplishments, though his was by no means a household name in the musical marketplaces of the world. He was a solid German conductor, devoted almost exclusively to two tasks, those of interpreting the repertoire from Mozart to Bruckner and "building" orchestras to achieve a full-bodied, Germanic sound. Almost single-handedly he had raised the Hamburg Orchestra out of the ashes of the Second World War and reconstructed it as a first-rate ensemble of musicians. John Boyden had gotten to know him through Jochum's guest conducting and recording work with the London Philharmonic.

To Boyden, Eugen Jochum had "a wealth of knowledge of the German classics," an area in which Boyden felt his new orchestra was markedly weak. He thought the LSO should turn away from the late-Romantic and post-Romantic music in which André Previn was most at home and turn instead to the bread-and-butter compositions of Beethoven and Brahms, the music that Eugen Jochum knew so well.

In the spring of 1975, not long after André announced his decision to add the Pittsburgh Symphony Orchestra to his list of responsibilities, Boyden brought Jochum in for a series of four Beethoven concerts with the LSO at Royal Festival Hall. The concerts went off quite well and the orchestra liked playing under Jochum. In between concerts Boyden and Snell negotiated a deal with the German conductor and his manager. In exchange for being named "conductor laureate" of the LSO, Jochum would conduct exclusively for the LSO in Britain, effectively pulling his rug out from under the LPO. It was all consummated without the consent or even the knowledge of André or the orchestra members.

"We're very pleased that we've got Jochum," John Boyden told a news conference. "It's going to make a lot of difference in the future." Jochum's reputation as a trainer, Boyden contended, was "just an additional asset. His prime asset is that he's going to be the next Great Man."

But there were also leaks to the press from the anti-Previn

faction on the Board, who now were in the majority there if not among the orchestra as a whole. "What the present situation is about," said one, "has nothing to do with musical or artistic matters. It has to do with public personalities." And another: "The Board just frankly don't feel that Previn is a great conductor. He just doesn't compare with a Jochum or a Karl Böhm."

It was assumed that André would bridle at such remarks and feel slighted that his opinion was not sought in the matter of choosing a "conductor laureate." Instead, he turned the tables on the Board by accepting Jochum's appointment gracefully, seeming almost to take credit for the whole thing. He looked forward to working with the esteemed Dr. Jochum, he declared, and anticipated that their talents and specialties would complement each other to the great benefit of the London Symphony Orchestra. If the Snell-Boyden plan was to rid the orchestra of Previn, then clearly a frontal assault would be necessary. They waited until André would be at his most vulnerable, in Salzburg.

If the invitation to attend the Salzburg Festival the first time had been, as the *Times* put it, a "signal honor," then to be invited back a second year had to multiply that honor a thousandfold. It meant that some highly critical audiences and directors had been impressed that the LSO truly was one of the great orchestras of the world and that the orchestra and its unusual conductor had more than novelty appeal to the international audiences.

André's concerts with the LSO at Salzburg were near the end of the festival, after the orchestra already had been conducted to great popular and critical acclaim by Karl Böhm, Leonard Bernstein, and Seiji Ozawa. However it was not until André picked up the baton that the LSO really let itself out and went into high gear. Edward Greenfield wrote in the *Guardian* that "he has the ability more than anyone else to rally the LSO into producing its finest form with the minimum of pain—something even his critics concede."

Indeed, all the critics at Salzburg agreed. Even André, usually his own most severe critic, observed that "it happened that

year that my concerts were the best, in terms of program, playing, and audience reception. I remember coming out of a concert flushed with success and a feeling of pride in the orchestra.
And I remember picking up the newspapers next morning to
read the notices and remarking on how great they all were.
Later on I dropped in on one of Lenny's rehearsals. That's
when Boyden came in and said he needed to talk to me."

André did not like John Boyden; their personalities clashed.
He admired Boyden's business acumen but thought of him as
"a salesman more than anything else, an astute maker of cheap
records." He knew well enough of Boyden's reservations about
André Previn and he knew those reservations were shared by
Howard Snell. Even though the Board members had sworn
themselves to secrecy concerning their deliberations about his
success or failure as their leader, André had his informants on
the Board and he was aware of the mounting tide of opposition he faced. However, he was confident that the Board
would take no drastic action without consulting the membership at large, and he still felt secure about his support within
the orchestra as a whole. Consequently, Boyden's remarks
caught him completely off guard, while he was still basking in
the morning-after glow of a triumphant evening.

We sat down off to the side somewhere and Boyden
proceeded to tell me that it was no reflection on my
abilities, but the Board felt it was time for a change.
At the end of two years, as stipulated in my contract,
I would no longer be principal conductor. I admit I
was stunned, but I'd been in England long enough to
know how to play things coolly. I simply said, "I see."
He told me he was sorry to give me "this paper with a
black spot on it," and he laughed a bit maniacally,
"but that's the way we want it. I hope it won't
change anything." I said, "Of course it's going to
change things, John. What are you talking about?"
Then an interesting thing happened. He asked me
to do him a favor. He said, "We're in Salzburg and I
wouldn't want it to get out. Don't talk about this to
anybody." I said, "Of course not. Why should I?"

And then he added, "I mean the orchestra. Don't talk about it with the musicians."

It suddenly dawned on me that the orchestra didn't know anything about this as yet and Boyden confirmed that they did not. I found this very strange, since the LSO is supposed to be a cooperative and since they were the ones who had hired me. It seemed only fair that they should be the ones to fire me.

André says that he acceded to John Boyden's demand for secrecy, telling only his manager. It is interesting to note, however, that among the critics in Salzburg that August was Edward Greenfield, a sometime confidant on matters pertaining to the orchestra's image. It was Greenfield's paper, the *Guardian*, that broke the story on August 25.

The headline on the top of the front page shouted: LSO TO END PREVIN CONTRACT. The article set the matter down in great detail, beginning, "The London Symphony Orchestra is expected to be told at its rehearsal today that André Previn is having his contract as the orchestra's principal conductor terminated in two years' time." The implication of a coup d'état was unmistakable. Reporters Christopher Ford and Tom Sutcliffe had done their research well—or else had it handed to them. André made himself unavailable for comment, although "a source close to him said that his warm feelings for the LSO remained unchanged." John Boyden, however, was very available, and very clear in his message:

"It was never intended for André Previn to be conductor for life. After all, he's only forty-seven now. [Actually he was only forty-six.] It would imply his staying at the orchestra for another forty years. He's been principal conductor for seven years already, which is longer than anybody—even Hans Richter—in the orchestra's history. Whatever transpires, he's principal conductor for the next two years."

According to the newspaper's sources, André would be offered the position of "chief guest conductor," in exchange for some sort of agreement to restrict his work with other London orchestras. "Our relations with Previn are good," said Boyden. "I'm sure he's happy." He went on to say that "perhaps there's no necessity for the orchestra to have a principal conductor."

Boyden confirmed to the *Guardian* that nothing had been discussed with the LSO rank-and-file and that he wanted to give them the full story before he blurted it to the press. He then proceeded to blurt it to the press:

"The negotiations have been completed over the end of his existing terms of contract. But I believe this is something the orchestra must be told first. I feel quite strongly about this. It's very much an internal matter." If it was such an internal matter, some orchestra members wondered, then why were they reading it in the morning paper before Boyden and Snell told them about it that afternoon?

André denies that he had anything to do with leaking the story to the *Guardian* and perhaps he did not. But it seems obvious that the leak came from someone who wanted André in, not from someone who wanted him out. It was as adroitly engineered as the hiring of a photographer to flood the market with photographs of André and Mia when she was pregnant and unmarried. What could not have been planned in advance was the fact that Boyden so completely fell for it as to tell the reporters everything they wanted to hear.

With the LSO back in London after its Salzburg triumphs, the rehearsal scheduled the afternoon of the twenty-fifth was not one of André's but that of an unfortunate guest conductor who must have felt a bit like Daniel in the lions' den after reading the morning *Guardian*. It should have been a happy, harmonious rehearsal, because it inaugurated the Henry Wood Rehearsal Hall in Southwark. After years of shuttle-rehearsing, the LSO finally had a home. André had not even seen the finished building, having been away from London most of the summer, and he told reporters gathered outside that he was there just to look over the new place.

He arrived with Jasper Parrott fifteen minutes before the start of the two-thirty rehearsal. He fended off inquiries about the *Guardian*'s story. "All I will say is that it's absolutely premature. I have no idea what Mr. Boyden's up to. I'm as anxious as anybody to get it straight." These remarks came as he left the hall, after spending thirty minutes cloistered with management personnel. Jasper Parrott stayed behind, overseeing the drafting of a statement to the press.

At four forty-five, while the orchestra was still in rehearsal and had not as yet been able to discuss the situation, a statement from John Boyden was read to the reporters and cameramen gathered outside the hall. Rather than face the reporters himself, Boyden sent his promotions manager, Wilson Strutte, who read the release in dry tones:

> The report which appeared in the *Guardian* today is totally incorrect. The open-ended contract between André Previn and the LSO exists as before and the orchestra looks forward to a long association with Mr. Previn.
>
> The appointment of Eugen Jochum, which was dwelt on at some length in the *Guardian* report, is an integral part of the plans for the future and André Previn wishes to state that he welcomes this association. Of course conversations are taking place continually in an effort to make the most of relations with André Previn. John Boyden deeply regrets the attempt by the *Guardian* correspondent to fabricate a story where none exists.

While the statement was being read, Jasper Parrott telephoned André, who returned and was let into the hall through a back entrance just as the rehearsal broke up. He spoke warmly to the orchestra members, reassuring them that their relation would continue as before, as far as he was concerned. This merited a round of applause from the orchestra. As he left, André refused to answer questions and effectively concealed his emotion, but as one reporter noted, "Mr. Parrott at any rate was looking happy with the outcome."

The *Guardian* and a few other papers kept up the publicity barrage for a few days. Edward Greenfield wrote a long article in condemnation of the Board's tactics. "André Previn, the man who has led the way in this country against the old idea of a conductor as a mandarin figure, was being told his image is wrong . . . it was surely like asking for a divorce when a marriage is going well on the grounds that it might go wrong later." The conservative *Times* simply buried the story, except for a full-page story by its "Insight" team in the Sunday edition of August 31.

The headline read: THE MAKING OF A ROSTRUM PUTSCH, and the article went to great lengths to detail the LSO's "bleak commercial future" and the "worried reassessment of their international image."

"It is now almost certain," the article boldly began, "that André Previn, principal conductor of the London Symphony Orchestra, will change his present relationship with them in two years' time . . . one of London's leading orchestras is now split into opposing camps in what one of its directors bluntly called a 'rather nasty business based on the building up of personalities.'"

Theorizing that the LSO-Previn dispute was merely a side skirmish in the battle between the LSO and the LPO over revenues, the *Times* article concluded that "Previn may be the first victim in what could now prove to be a very bloody war." The less conservative *Daily Mail* said that, no, this was merely the last battle in a seven-years' war that had begun with André's appointment in 1968. The LSO was simply fed up with being known as "Andy Previn's Band."

Whatever the larger implications of the imbroglio, André moved swiftly to consolidate his support, for he had no intention of leaving the LSO under fire. At a rehearsal the following week in Edinburgh he picked a moment when John Boyden was in the hall to stop the musicians and compliment them on their work. "You know, that really wasn't bad," he told them. "I wish a lot of people would stop trying to get the LSO to sound like a German orchestra. I've heard quite a few German orchestras in my travels that would do well if they tried to sound a bit like the LSO."

The following month, at a general meeting of the orchestra, a vote was called on whether or not to accept the Board's recommendation that André be given his two years' notice. There were only fourteen votes in favor of the resolution. At the same meeting Howard Snell announced he would resign as chairman of the Board at the end of the year and told the orchestra he regrettably would not be able to go with them on a tour of the Far East scheduled to begin the following week. For Snell, that turned out to be a happy decision.

Since long before the days of jet travel, symphony orchestras have enhanced their reputations at home by giving concerts abroad. Consequently, an orchestra manager, in addition to possessing keen business judgment, psychoanalytic powers, and a smooth veneer of imperturbability, must also be able to function as travel agent and tour guide. That certainly was no part of John Boyden's experience, for he never had had the opportunity of traveling with an orchestra on a tour which he himself had arranged. Instead, his downfall was brought about by a tour set up by no one in particular, in that twilight zone between Harold Lawrence's farewell to the LSO and John Boyden's hail.

The October 1975 tour of Japan and Korea was three weeks long, but to André it seemed interminable. "It was a purgatory. We went cross-country every day, zigzagging back and forth. The hotels were bad. Food was dreadful. The planes were awful. Conditions in general were fearful and morale was nonexistent."

As usual, there were reporters along on the tour and the journalistically objective accounts are no less horrifying than those of the conductor. "It was gruelling, uncomfortable, disorganized, and just plain tatty." There are descriptions of the musicians struggling to dress for a concert, almost before the public, in a ramshackle, unheated Seoul school-hall. There are tales of the players gagging down breakfasts of boiled rice and fish heads and of wanton attacks by hordes of Korean prostitutes. There is the story of the musicians unwinding at a birthday party in Kobe and spending one of the tour's two free days in "varying degrees of hilarity and drunkenness" to relieve the tensions of the trip. It was pointed out that John Boyden, a nondrinker, did not participate in the party.

The reporter who wrote that account was a petulantly attractive woman of thirty, Anna Motson. A graduate of Oxford and a free-lance journalist, Miss Motson solicited and was granted a commission from the *Sunday Times* to cover the tour. She hoped that the LSO would pick up her travel and expenses, but John Boyden flatly turned her down. Instead, she managed to talk the public relations department of Japan Airlines out of a ticket, economy class.

"She was very pretty and was paid a lot of attention on the tour by the musicians," André recalls. "She would come and talk to me whenever she could and, the LSO being the randy bunch they are, they assumed I was having a thing with her. Maybe it's too bad, but in point of fact I wasn't. Still, she was great fun to have along."

On the flight back to London, Motson wrote a personal check for the difference between economy and first class so that she could continue her interviews with André. She also had requested an interview with Boyden, but he begged off to get some sleep aboard the airplane. Instead, he agreed to speak with her during a one-hour stopover in Alaska, assuming that it was a part of her work for the *Sunday Times*. At the Anchorage airport, Anna Motson sat at a table with John Boyden, her tape recorder between them, and over bad coffee they talked about the LSO.

Motson began with what she thought was a fairly innocuous and rather obvious question concerning the hardships of the just-ended tour. Boyden's unexpected answer led her into questions which, she says, she otherwise never would have thought to ask. Back on the airplane, André saw her coming toward him carrying the tape recorder and wearing a curious expression on her face.

> She came over and sat next to me and said, "I have an interview on this tape which is the most unbelievable interview of my life." I asked her what it was

all about and for a moment she considered letting me
hear it but then said, "I think it would be very smart
if I didn't tell you anything about it. Forgive me, I
know we are friends, but I'm also a journalist. I can't
let you hear this."

When she got back to London, Miss Motson went first to
the *Times*, where she said she had something that was hot,
that it concerned the orchestra but did not fit into the proposed article on the tour for the Sunday magazine. The *Times*
turned her down and she quickly made a deal with the *Guardian*. On November 19, 1975, *Guardian* readers were treated to
a front-page story which was nothing more nor less than a tran-
scription of Anna Motson's tape-recorded interview with John
Boyden. It began with a rather astonishing statement by
Boyden that the musicians were just plain stupid to complain
about the rigors of the tour.

"You cannot expect to go to a foreign country and find that
things are the same as in England," he said. There had been
many complaints about the uncomfortable buses, for example,
which were based on ignorance and selfishness. "The seat is a
certain width because of the little Japanese bottom." Boyden
was sick of playing "Big Daddy" and sorting out all the
players' complaints. Far worse than any inconveniences of the
tour, he argued, was the "lack of maturity" evidenced by the
musicians' "drinking and staying up all night."

"There are more than a few people who are simply using the
LSO for their own purposes, for the money they get out of it,"
he went on. "They don't really care about the music. If you really believe that these people—who include the beer-swilling
crowd who showed up so badly on this tour—have *feelings*
about the music they play, then you're being very naïve."

What about André Previn? "Far too highly paid. I don't see
why just because a man is seen to be a box draw and his face is
seen on television, he should be paid a sum of money so completely out of proportion to that paid to the orchestral
players."

As to André's vaunted ability to pack a house, Boyden observed that the LSO would be much better off with a less expensive man who only sold seventy percent of the tickets. "And don't tell me that it's better for the morale of the orchestra to have a full house, because you are again ascribing feelings to these people which they just don't have. I tell you, as an orchestra it's far better to have the money."

The *Guardian* had done it again. The players were furious and this time they were not going to conceal their emotions from the press. "I am appalled," said Jack Steadman, a twenty-year veteran of the LSO violin section. Boyden was wrong about the orchestra's feelings, insisted tuba player John Fletcher, "Our morale is better when the house is full." Thomas Russell, a veteran of orchestra management with the LPO, told reporters that Boyden "shows a complete misunderstanding of the psychology of orchestral players." Violist Max Burwood fumed, "The man must be a maniac. What does he know of our orchestra? What does he know about musicians? He has only been with us for a few months." London impresario Victor Hochhauser agreed, saying, "Mr. Boyden's criticisms cheapen one of the world's great orchestras."

Boyden's answer was to write an angry letter, not to the *Guardian* but to the *Times*. Calling on the memory of his father, who had been an orchestra player himself, Boyden maintained that he had "absolutely no contempt" for the LSO musicians and that he had "the greatest possible interest" in their welfare. He charged that Anna Motson had interviewed him off the record, with the understanding that she was writing an article for the *Sunday Times*, not the *Guardian*, and that she had promised to show him the article before she handed it in. Boyden expressed his regret and resentment "that she has seen fit to use these off-the-cuff remarks in such an unhelpful way."

Motson fired back a letter to the *Times* in which she denied having agreed to show Boyden the article before publication and insisted that he had been very much aware that what he said was being recorded for use. "At no time did he request either directly or by implication that any of his remarks were off the record." She acknowledged that the purpose of the interview had been to wrap up her research for the *Times* article on the tour, but that "the astonishing answers he gave to what can clearly be seen to be routine questions deserved immediate publication."

Coincidentally, the flurry of publicity came just a week before the annual general meeting of the LSO. It was at this meeting that Howard Snell was to step down as chairman. His position and two others on the Board were to be vacated by rotation and other players elected to fill their seats. One who was nominated and expected to be elected was Anthony Camden, a virtuoso musician and a strong supporter of André. Before the general meeting it was arranged that both current and incoming Board members should listen to Anna Motson's tape.

André was asked not to attend the membership meeting, so he went to the theater that night with Mia and some friends. The meeting lasted ninety minutes, with John Boyden in attendance throughout since he had placed himself on the orchestra's Board. First the members voted once again on the Board's recommendation to end André's contract. This time there were only three members not on the Board who voted "aye." Next there was a vote on a motion to cancel John Boyden's contract. Boyden was allowed to speak in his own behalf, but the motion passed almost unanimously. Then came a motion from the floor to unseat the entire Board and elect a new one. That too met with very little opposition.

When it was over Howard Snell gamely gave the report to the conclave of press and orchestra staff who were waiting outside. "Mr. Boyden's contract as managing director has been terminated," he said, "effective immediately." In answer to questions, Snell had to admit that the remarks by Boyden, the man he'd brought in to help him get rid of Previn, were "lunatic." He said, "Everyone in the orchestra, including myself, was very shocked." Not long afterward Howard Snell resigned from the LSO to pursue his career as a conductor.

The rank aroma of the "Salzburg coup" and the "Anchorage attack" lingered over the LSO for some time, despite an agreement by the players, André, and other orchestra personnel not to discuss it among themselves or with outsiders. For one thing, John Boyden sued the orchestra for the remainder of his three years' salary, saying that he felt "sick" over the fear that "nobody will want me now." He lost the suit and had to pay court costs, but he went on to form a company called Enigma Records with which he eventually turned a handsome profit.

The *Daily Mail* published an article about the "intriguing friendship" between André and Anna Motson, implying but not stating directly that the two had shared more than a pair of airline seats during the tour. Both threatened the newspaper with a lawsuit unless it printed a front-page retraction, which it did.

The whole affair seemed to leave André in as secure a position as he'd ever held with the LSO and, curiously, seemed to have brought the members of the orchestra closer together. André recalls a conversation he had over tea one morning, several months later, with principal bassoon player Robert Bourton.

"You know all those things Boyden accused us of," Bourton said. "I'm quite sure some of us have been guilty of some of them. Sure I've gotten drunk and sure I've been late to rehearsals. I think I could have taken all that. But don't let anyone tell me I don't love music. What the hell do we go through this kind of life for if we don't love music?"

XXVI

It was a bitingly cold night in Pittsburgh and André coveted the long fur coat of the lady who was driving him to the after-concert party. She was an attractive woman in her forties, stylish, and, André guessed, probably richly dressed beneath that lovely coat. She was someone important on the orchestra Board, he knew, but he couldn't remember her name. She was trying to make conversation about the weather and the people who came in late for the concerts, while he couldn't get his mind off the concert he'd just conducted.

He'd been with the Pittsburgh Symphony just once before, in 1968, nearly ten years earlier, and early on in his career as a conductor. Small wonder they'd waited so long to invite him back. Now it was as if they had been playing together for years. The rapport had been instant, from the first moment of rehearsal, and the concert had been one of those rare events that transported him into a world beyond the confines of the podium and the stage. He was glad this would be a three-week visit instead of a typical one-week stand, because he looked forward to working with the Pittsburgh Symphony again.

André wondered about the future of this orchestra, with William Steinberg as ill as he seemed to be. He'd heard gossip from the players about the Board searching for a new music director, but after so many years of Klemperer, Reiner, and Steinberg, the task of filling that post would not be easy. There were rumors that James Levine of the Metropolitan Opera was

Accepting the ovation from the audience after his first concert as music director of the Pittsburgh Symphony Orchestra. *(Courtesy Guild Photographers)*

With his Hollywood friends, the composer-conductors John Williams (l.) and Miklós Rózsa (r.).

André at ease in his Pittsburgh apartment.

A toast from Pittsburgh Mayor Richard Caliguiri, prior to the European tour of the Pittsburgh Symphony Orchestra in 1978. *(Courtesy Ben Spiegel, official Pittsburgh Symphony photographer)*

With Ella Fitzgerald and Keter Betts, bass player, during the course of a "Previn and the Pittsburgh" television program. *(Courtesy Kenneth Love)*

With his old friend, jazz drummer Shelly Manne.

André Previn with his and Mia's six children, Christmas 1979. Left to right: Lark, Sascha, Summer, André, Fletcher, Matthew, Soon-Yi.

André and the twins.

André Previn with Matthew and Sascha, Summer 1980. *(Courtesy Suzie E. Maeder)*

the heir apparent. Whoever got the job, André hoped it would be someone with the energy to keep it sounding as good as it had sounded tonight.

The glamorous Board lady was still talking when they arrived at the party, well behind most of the guests. André could not keep from staring when she removed her fur coat and revealed a vast expanse of cleavage, tantalizingly exposed by a dress that was cut down to the navel. He felt there was trouble coming when she said, "Now let's you and I have a drink."

André smiled as unselfconsciously as he could and told the lady he would join her after he'd had a word with orchestra manager Seymour Rosen, whom he spotted in a corner of the room. Rosen recalls André's plaintive, "Look, Sy, I need help. I've been away from home about seven weeks now and during that time I've been talking with a lot of trombone players. Now those guys are wonderful company, of course, but nowhere near as appealing as that woman is trying to make herself. She's a member of your Board, so I don't want to offend her, but what I do not need at this time in my personal history is to be . . . well, I arrived with her but I'd rather not leave with her, if you get my meaning."

Rosen was amused and slightly touched by this demonstration of moral integrity from a man whose standards had been so publicly criticized. Rosen agreed to leave the party early and drive André back to his hotel. In the privacy of the car, Rosen decided on the spur of the moment to feel out André on the subject of the Pittsburgh Symphony and its search for a music director. The manager did his level best to couch the question in ambiguity.

"André," he said, "I am going to ask you a question which I have no right whatsoever to ask you at this moment. But if you can't give me an answer now I probably never will have the right and very likely I never will ask it at all."

"What the hell are you talking about, Sy?"

Finally Rosen took the blunt approach: "Would you consider being music director of the Pittsburgh Symphony?"

At that point Rosen had not discussed the possibility with the Board or with the orchestra. He had received "a lot of posi-

tive feedback" from the musicians after their rehearsals with André, however, and this was unusual.

Not only were the musicians excited about what he was doing now, but many of them had seen this man and played under him nearly ten years before and they were extremely impressed by the way he had grown. So was I. André had learned his trade and had become a first-class conductor. That much was apparent from the first rehearsal. The players were happy to be making music with him. Besides, we were getting a bit desperate to find a successor to Steinberg. I won't mention any names, but we'd been counting very heavily on having our choice of two conductors, both of whom had led us on for a considerable length of time and neither of whom was working out in negotiations with the orchestra. Suddenly the idea of having André Previn was like salvation. So I popped the question.

To André the offer came "out of left field." It seemed to him a sort of déjà-vu experience from that time in the past when, still in the delirium of having his first orchestra, he was offered his second. He'd had no real choice then but to jump at the offer and hope it wouldn't be too much for him. But now he was older, nearing fifty, and not at all certain he could take on the responsibility in Pittsburgh without slighting his commitment to the LSO, even providing the two schedules could be interfaced. His first reaction was to say, "Sy, I can't tell you how enormously flattered I am. But it so happens that I've far from finished what I want to accomplish with the LSO and I'm just not sure I can cope with the two orchestras at once. Now if you could continue along another couple of seasons under Steinberg, I'd be glad to come in and guest regularly and perhaps after that we could work something out."

But Rosen saw that he had one foot in the door and decided to press his case rather than accept the gesture. He went up to André's hotel room and the two men talked for three more

hours about the needs of the Pittsburgh Symphony, its strengths and weaknesses, about the relative flexibility of the Pittsburgh schedule and about living in the city of Pittsburgh. Finally an exhausted André pushed Rosen out the door, promising that he would telephone Ronald Wilford to discuss the matter with him, first thing in the morning.

Rosen left the hotel convinced that he had the conductor Pittsburgh needed. He was very much aware of Ron Wilford's passionate belief that André had to act quickly to reestablish himself, with his new credentials, in the United States. Wilford was at odds in this regard with Jasper Parrott, who favored a European strategy over an American one for bolstering André's international reputation. Rosen was inclined to believe that Wilford would do everything in his power to nail down a position for his client on this side of the Atlantic, where Wilford could have greater control over André's affairs. If the ball was in Wilford's court, then Rosen felt confident of eventually securing André's agreement. Now he had to convince the Board of Directors that André Previn was the conductor of their choice.

For more than eighteen months a Search Committee of the Board had been trying to solve the problem of a successor to the fading William Steinberg. The committee's failure to this point had prompted barbs in the press and a growing edginess on the part of the players as well as the Board. At the request of the entire Board, an Artistic Advisory Committee of musicians was formed to assist the directors in their search, but they had been turning into one blind alley after another.

Rosen took his case for Previn first to the players' Artistic Advisory Committee, for he knew that was the path of least resistance. For much of the previous two years Steinberg's health had been precarious and the musicians had played under a wide range of conductors, from wizened graybeards to wunderkinder and until Previn no one had come along who could get them to sound the way they knew they ought to sound. What's more, he achieved the desired results with virtually no tension at rehearsals. The players not only respected him but also enjoyed being with him. When the committee heard from Rosen that André might accept the job if it were offered, they held an instant and unanimous vote.

Armed with the Artistic Advisory Committee's support, Rosen approached the Search Committee that same afternoon. It happened that one committee member had been associated with the Houston Symphony at the time of André's tenure and, like so many who were not present at the closed-door meetings, this person was convinced that André had been drummed out of town as a result of his flaunted dalliance with Mia. It delighted Rosen to squelch the fear that Pittsburgh might be in for some such scandal by recounting André's successful bout with temptation at the post-concert party. To this Rosen added his personal conviction that part of André's interest in Pittsburgh was the chance it offered for further strengthening his family bonds. Mia was homesick for the United States, he'd been told, and she was escaping England more and more frequently to her private retreat on Martha's Vineyard. Furthermore, said Rosen, "although Previn's life in London seems idyllic, he is an American and I think he has a strong sense of wanting his children to know what his country is like." Waving fatherhood and the flag, Rosen got his proposal through the committee. There was no doubt that the recommendation would be approved by the entire Board of Directors.

Rosen and Ron Wilford quickly hammered out an agreement whereby André's initial commitment to Pittsburgh would be only half of the twenty-eight-week subscription season and Steinberg would remain on as "Music Director Emeritus," assisting in the orchestra's artistic management. That arrangement, along with a generous salary and the fact that he genuinely enjoyed working with the Pittsburgh musicians and saw a potential for accelerated growth under his leadership, made the offer seem "practically utopian" to André.

He had lived for seven years in London with the knowledge that he was working for the orchestra; the orchestra was not working for him. It had become a source of pride to know that his performance was being judged constantly and was being found acceptable by a hundred outstanding musicians. With two years' notice they could hand him his walking papers any time they felt he was falling below their standards. In Pittsburgh he would be faced with a group of non-musician private citizens, a Board of Directors, who could force an orchestra to accept a leader they might not want. He realized from his experience as a guest conductor with several orchestras that this could bring about an adversary relationship between a conductor and his players and that any hope of making good music together could be dashed before it ever had a chance.

Determined not to get off on the wrong foot with this orchestra, he demanded that the players themselves be given the right to confirm or deny his appointment. "I've gotten used to the English system," he said, "and it's going to be hard to become an American conductor again. I must know that, of all the people you've been shopping around for, I am right now the first choice of the musicians, that they genuinely *want* me." Rosen tried to argue him out of that position, saying it would put him on the wrong footing with the musicians, who were used to obeying orders and who might prove rebellious given a taste of self-determination. But André stood firm and Rosen agreed to put it to a vote as soon as André's three weeks with the orchestra were over.

The guest engagement ended with a concert in Charleston, West Virginia. There André was to play and conduct the Mozart Piano Concerto in C minor. But upon arriving at the theater he discovered that the rented piano had acquired a broken string in the course of being moved by truck in a snowstorm from an auditorium where it had been used for a rock concert the evening before.

With only two hours to spare before the concert, a tuner was called in and he managed to get most of the strings back to pitch, but there was no time to restring the E-flat in the middle octave. Since that note holds an important position in the C minor chord, it seemed a bit reckless for André to attempt the C Minor Concerto without it. But, as one member of the orchestra recalls, "somehow he managed to play around that missing note so that the audience had no idea that anything was wrong. If there was any doubt in anybody's mind, the way he handled that situation removed it entirely."

The following week the vote was held and recorded as unanimous in favor of appointing André. The only one left to be consulted, though he had no vote, was William Steinberg, the man who had led the Pittsburgh Symphony Orchestra for twenty-three years. Rosen called on him at home, where he was laid up with shingles, and Steinberg learned for the first time that his successor was to be André Previn.

According to Rosen, the old man clapped his hands on the mattress with an air of finality and said, "It's done. Who was the genius who managed to bring us this wonderful talent?" Rosen acknowledged that he'd played a role in bringing it about and Steinberg simply smiled and said, "Good."

Throughout the negotiations in February, not a word was leaked to the press, so that in March, when the appointment was announced simultaneously on both sides of the ocean, the people of Pittsburgh were just as surprised as were the musicians of the LSO. The news caused a flood of advance ticket requests for André's first season, that of 1976–77. Subscriptions for the 1975–76 season in Heinz Hall were already sold out, as had been each season since the glamorous hall, a former movie palace, opened in 1971. Now there was talk of a "glamorous" conductor to match the hall and the conversation at cocktail parties revolved around the image of André Previn and how he soon would turn the "big five" American orchestras into the Big Six.

André's own plans in this regard were apparent from the start. On June 25 he made his first visit to Pittsburgh after the announcement and he told reporters at a news conference that although it was now difficult to call the Pittsburgh one of the world's great orchestras, this was only by reason of insularity, not of ability. Given a few years of the right exposure, he said, their status on the international scene would be very different. "I have great ambitions for this orchestra," he said, "and for myself in conjunction with it."

The orchestra he took over in 1976, the year of America's Bicentennial, had a history which stretched back almost to colonial times, to the industrialization of Pittsburgh in the early 1800s. The steel mill town was a haven for Central Europeans, particularly for the Germans and Poles who brought to the United States their habit of enjoying good music. Organized music ensembles began performing regularly in Pittsburgh as early as 1807 and a century later they had coagulated into a genuine orchestra, the forerunner of the symphony. But Pittsburgh had other things in mind at the time and the concert hall was closed down until the orchestra reassembled in 1926. That became the official starting point of the Pittsburgh Symphony Orchestra and so it was that André's first season coincided with the orchestra's Fiftieth Anniversary celebration.

The orchestra had long been evangelistic in its approach to music, quite the contrary to what André had experienced with his earlier American orchestra. In 1936, under Otto Klemperer, the Pittsburgh had taken early advantage of the opportunities provided by what was then not the media but only the medium, giving nationally broadcast radio concerts. Klemperer's reign as music director gave way to that of Fritz Reiner and when Reiner left for Chicago, the post was left vacant for several seasons until, in 1952, William Steinberg settled in Pittsburgh. By 1975 Dr. Steinberg had become as solid a symbol of the city's culture as was steel of the city's economy, so that his was bound to be a hard act for anyone to follow. It was no doubt a relief to André that Steinberg would not be removed from the music scene by his own arrival but would remain highly visible as Music Director Emeritus, in which capacity he was to serve until his death in May 1978.

Steinberg's long tenure had been one of economic prosperity for the orchestra. As the custodian of Pittsburgh's best performing hall it garnered substantial rental revenue from the resident dance and opera companies and from the bookings of concert and recital series. As the town's only large-scale assemblage of professional musicians, the orchestra also was in demand most of the year for non-orchestra functions. In addition to the twenty-eight-week season at Heinz Hall, there was a heavy touring commitment to the heavily populated industrial communities surrounding Pittsburgh and in the Allegheny Region. Other income came from highly successful community fund-raising drives as well as interest from a substantial endowment fund which provided more than twenty percent of the annual budget.

Ronald Wilford viewed Pittsburgh as "the opposite of Houston, with a Board of Directors interested in having a broad base of support that will properly finance their orchestra. In Pittsburgh the people are genuinely interested in having a good orchestra. They've renovated a fabulous old hall and the city is one of the most prosperous in the country. I think André can make that orchestra into one of the greatest orchestras of the world."

Rarely praised for sylvan beauty, Pittsburgh and its immediate environs seemed hardly the place for a man so in tune with the bosky pleasures of the English country life. Yet André was determined to establish permanency in Pittsburgh so he set about looking for a house, only to discover that "the ones I can afford are too ugly. The ones I like are for the millionaires." So he took an apartment instead, which he steadfastly referred to as a flat, near downtown and about ten minutes away from Heinz Hall. Once again he resigned himself to the life of a transoceanic commuter.

The Pittsburgh strategy, as Sy Rosen had surmised, was as warmly welcomed by Ronald Wilford as it was coolly received by Jasper Parrott. From his vantage point in New York, Wilford saw what Parrott could never appreciate, that while André might be acclaimed as a monumental conductor in England, he still retained his Hollywood playboy image in the United States. Previn the Great Conductor still had no calling card on Wilford's side of the Atlantic. He had no trouble booking him for guest engagements with managers who were acquainted with the profession on an international scale, but the audiences still came to hear him out of curiosity and Wilford knew that could not last forever. By this time, even disregarding his long list of accomplishments with the London Symphony, André had successfully conducted most of the planet's major orchestras, including those of Amsterdam, Berlin, Cleveland, Copenhagen, Los Angeles, New York, Paris, Philadelphia,

Prague, and Rome. Yet, after André's well-received appearance with the Chicago Symphony only a few weeks before his invitation to Pittsburgh, one critic had tossed off the concert as "exactly what one would expect from the winner of four Academy Awards." And this had been after a reading of Vaughan Williams' Fifth Symphony, a work dear to André's heart, which brought solid applause and cheers from a fairly knowledgeable audience.

It was against this background that Wilford read a New York *Times* article which confirmed his worst fears as well as his certainty that the Pittsburgh strategy was the correct one for this stage of André's career. CAN PREVIN SUCCEED DESPITE SUCCESS? the article's headline asked. The writer detailed an incident in which he had gone to the classical counter of a Manhattan record store seeking a copy of André's latest release, only to be told by a haughty salesperson, "André Previn? Pop counter's to your left."

"On this side of the Atlantic," the article continued, "Previn's pop image still prevails, an image he hopes his appointment as music director of the Pittsburgh Symphony, effective this September, will help correct."

XXVII

Throughout his career, André's image has always posed a far greater problem than any musical shortcoming. Schuyler Chapin, among others, sees that as a direct result of André's failure to bring all his sundry interests together under one recognizable roof, preferring to dash off in pursuit of whatever quest enthralls him for the moment. "André Previn never stops," Chapin muses. "I wish he would, to consolidate his talents."

He is, in the vernacular of the seventies, a potentially great man who does not quite have his act together. Yet, looked at the other way around, perhaps it is simply because he is a man of so many parts that it is difficult for an observer to concentrate on any one of his achievements without losing sight of the whole man. His apparent variegation may stem from his ability to comprehend music in all its aspects, unlike most of us who limit our enjoyments for the sake of better savoring them.

Even Ron Wilford, who's been perhaps as close as anyone to André through the years of his classical recognition, has trouble defining his client. "I think he's probably had a very hard time bringing together the many facets of his life. One thinks of him as an American, but he's not; he's a citizen of the world. He's a German-Jewish-French-Hollywood-American-Classical-Jazz-Pianist-Pop-film orchestrator-composer-conductor. Somehow it's very hard to bring all that together in one person. When you think of all the careers he's had, that he's concurrently *having*, well, I don't know of anybody who's ever done that. What does that make him?"

It makes him, at least superficially, a man whose medium is truly his message. Although in private he will use his musical experiences as a breeding pond for universally applicable ideas, in public he restricts his communications to matters of music, almost as though he were a musical missionary in the modern age, using the mass media in precisely the same way that electronic-age religious groups do with their televised proselytizing. In Pittsburgh, indeed in the United States, he found vast multitudes awaiting his message, that great music is greatly approachable and easily enjoyed.

Michael Kaye, successor to John Boyden as manager of the LSO, speaks for the entire serious music profession when he says, "André's television work has made us appealing to a lot of people who might otherwise have looked on us as a lot of boiled shirts scraping and puffing away for our own amusement. That TV camera is like a microscope and what comes across on television is what André is—a witty, humorous, relaxed, nice man. By being our representative he's made us all seem like human beings."

With the help of Ronald Wilford, André launched his "American outreach" from the moment he made the decision to accept the Pittsburgh podium. He knew that television had to be a part of bringing him and the orchestra to the attention of the American public and he saw that the only logical approach to that end would be through the Public Broadcasting Service. By a fortuitous circumstance, he was guest conductor of the New York Philharmonic when PBS inaugurated the television series "Live from Lincoln Center" in January 1976.

In what was considered a programming coup, PBS had two "folk heroes" of the classical music world, André and Van Cliburn, for that concert. Artistically, the concert had its high and low moments, but André's relaxed, professional manner of dealing with the television people—after doing it in England for years—opened a lot of doors at PBS.

In Pittsburgh, André's alliance with the orchestra seemed of such import that a commercial television station, KDKA, went to work on a documentary about the orchestra's first fifty years and arranged to broadcast the first concert of the season from Heinz Hall, complete with six cameras and an intermission interview with André. From that first concert together, Previn and the Pittsburgh were recognized as a "media event."

Since the sound of their names together also had a good ring, it was only logical that the city's PBS affiliate, WQED, should use it as the title of its proposed series of taped music-talk programs, to be aired nationally over the network. With an underwriting grant from the Alcoa Foundation, PBS jumped on the idea and it was agreed that the series would begin taping for airing in the spring of 1977. Over the next three years "Previn and the Pittsburgh" would become the most highly rated music program on public television in America—which is to say the highest rated television program dealing with serious music anywhere in the United States. Not since the days of Toscanini and the NBC Symphony Orchestra had a music program so captured the American imagination.

The conceit of "Previn and the Pittsburgh" was that André would simply engage a fellow musician, usually an old friend, in witty and lively conversation. Out of the conversation would grow a need for music. Of course all this had to be carefully structured within the confines of a sixty-minute program so that only seven to ten minutes would be occupied by talk and the bulk occupied by music.

PBS producer Stephen Dick admits he was concerned at first that "we were going to get a wonderful series of TV-style musical analyses of some favorite works" in the style of Leonard Bernstein's lecture-concerts of the early sixties. As Dick points out, most conductors are limited in their range of experience to the music which fills their lives and that is all they can talk about. Furthermore, they frequently have such strong convictions that their attempts at making conversation do turn into lectures. No conductor ever managed to pull that format off with the aplomb and charm of Leonard Bernstein.

"Previn saved us," says Stephen Dick, by declaring "No, I'm not Lenny." André's approach to talk was not talk about music but "talk pure and simple . . . stories, gossip, gripes—conversation the way it once was. The results have been little short of astounding."

André dropped his resistance to being associated with jazz and Hollywood because he recognized that those associations were almost all he had by way of allure to an American audience. From Hollywood he invited his old songwriting pals Betty Comden and Adolph Green and—reeling with the success of his scores to *Star Wars, Jaws,* and *Close Encounters of the Third Kind*—John Williams, who was joined by Miklós Rózsa. For the "Movie Music" show André invited an audience of movie enthusiasts to the taping.

Viewers around the country were treated to the composers' reminiscences of their days together in Hollywood when, as André remarked, there were a lot of their confreres who "couldn't find middle C with a magnet." Betty Comden admitted that Adolph Green was getting better at arriving for work on time and Green demonstrated his musical memory by singing the second movement of Beethoven's Second Symphony, mimicking the entire orchestra as he went along.

From his jazz period, André recalled the incomparable Ella Fitzgerald and got her to unwind as she seldom does in public. He introduced her by saying, "If you ask any jazz musician in the world, 'Who's your favorite singer?' the only way that discussion can be prolonged for even another ten seconds is if the answer is, 'You mean, other than Ella?'" Ella confessed that she started out in show business wanting to be a dancer and then, in a moment that was completely unrehearsed, she complied with André's request that she compose a song off the top of her head while he accompanied her on the piano.

Other than Art Tatum, the jazz pianist André most admires is Oscar Peterson, so it was only natural he'd want to do a show with Peterson and it was only natural that they'd wind up talking about Tatum. Sitting at the piano bench with André on a stool nearby, Peterson recounted the story of how he once followed Tatum's gig at a small jazz club. The piano was missing about seven notes and Tatum hadn't complained about that for the length of his engagement. But on the last night he spoke up to the manager. "Look," he said, "this piano's in pretty bad shape and you've got this young man Peterson coming in next week. You really ought to fix it up for him." "What are you talking about," the club manager snapped, "I just had that piano painted last week." That prompted André to confess that for wear and tear on a piano, the musician he'd been most loathe to follow was Dave Brubeck. "Yeah," acknowledged Peterson, "Dave does get excited."

There were, of course, more "serious" musicians who appeared on the program—although sometimes the conversation with them was just as light. Sir William Walton, in a program devoted to his *Belshazzar's Feast*, drew laughter when he admitted that he could not play a single instrument, despite having written some of the century's finest concertos for viola, cello, and violin. Pinchas Zukerman told the audience that he decided to grow his beard in a fit of jealousy. His friends kept admiring how wonderfully his pregnant wife was growing and "I wanted to grow something too."

"Previn and the Pittsburgh" was a resounding triumph for André in 1977. Perhaps on a par, though less widely recognized, was his success in luring a major record company to Heinz Hall to put the Pittsburgh Symphony back on the world's turntables, from which it had been absent in the form of new releases for many years. In addition to the bait of the first pairing on disc of Previn and the Pittsburgh, the Heinz Hall recordings titillated audiophiles with the first quadraphonic releases of the Sibelius Second Symphony and, on the second disc, the ever-popular *Zigeunerweisen* of Pablo de Sarasate and the infrequently performed First Violin Concerto of the nineteenth-century composer Karl Goldmark. The soloist in the Sarasate and Goldmark scores was violinist Itzhak Perlman.

The recordings received a great deal of critical attention, most of it favorable, with such accolades as "plush, smooth, and disciplined" and "performed with dramatic sensitivity." They were released on the Angel label in the United States, in Great Britain, on EMI's HMV label.

André's security and success with EMI is perhaps second

only to that of Herbert von Karajan. Since his recordings of Gershwin and Ravi Shankar for EMI in 1971, André has kept up the pace he established with his first recordings with the London Symphony Orchestra for RCA six years earlier, making an average of one LP a month. That means that in the sixteen years from 1965 to 1980, André has recorded nearly two hundred LPs. In the cottage behind the main house in Surrey he keeps a copy of each of those records, but he almost never listens to them.

> I don't keep scrapbooks of reviews and articles and I
> don't play my records. Occasionally, when I'm going
> to tackle a piece I haven't done in ten years, I might
> take out my record to see what my musical thoughts
> were back then, to see whether I've changed my
> ideas. I have trouble when I listen to a recorded per-
> formance in the car telling whether it's one of mine.
> It's a lot easier to tell when something is not mine
> than when it is, by certain exaggerations, certain
> rubati I'd never make or accents I don't want. But I'll
> never just go home and put on one of my own rec-
> ords. Once I leave the studio, that's it.

In fact, André's abdication of his performance begins even before he leaves the studio, at the moment he closes the score. On most occasions he prefers to leave the engineering of a recording to the engineers. More often than not he will simply walk out when the session's done, leaving the producer to decide which takes were the best and which should be reproduced on the record. Some of his colleagues consider this poor judgment on André's part. Vladimir Ashkenazy points out that "producers are a funny lot. They are likely to choose a take which is, for some stupid reason, more convenient for them over one which is more musically satisfying. André does the session, goes home and leaves it in their hands. I think he should choose."

André seems to feel that his choices are all made before the music is played. He has chosen the repertoire and, equally important, he has chosen the right orchestra to perform that repertoire. As his own international stature has grown, he has been able to select orchestras more freely with regard to their specific styles and instincts befitting the music he intended to record.

> Finally I am able to say which is the correct repertoire to record with which orchestra. To do a complete Richard Strauss cycle with the Vienna Philharmonic makes sense to me, as does a complete Shostakovich cycle with the LSO and the Chicago Symphony; and since Chicago has never recorded a complete *Daphnis and Chloe,* that makes sense. Can you think of a more apt place than Dresden in which to record the Brahms *Requiem?* Haydn, Mahler, and Brahms are particularly good for Pittsburgh and everything's good for the LSO, except possibly Mozart and Haydn. Especially Mozart.
>
> Out of the several orchestras that have approached me to do records, the only one I've turned down has been Philadelphia. Now, no conductor who ever picked up a stick would turn down Philadelphia, but I had to. I said no because there are so few companies willing to record in America and so few American records that EMI can afford to make. I asked Peter Andry point-blank whether, if I made records for them in Philadelphia, they would be less likely to make records in Pittsburgh. They said yes, so I said no. The orchestras in Philadelphia and Pittsburgh are in the same state, competing for the same state subsidies. We go after a lot of the same money. That would be the worst double-cross I could pull.

In addition to André's continuing association with EMI, the Pittsburgh Symphony Orchestra has signed a contract to record with André for Philips, so that once again Pittsburgh is established as a major orchestra in the eyes of the recording world. André remains loyal to EMI, as well he should, considering the freedom the company has given him over the years in terms of building his recorded repertoire.

The company's repertoire demands have been minimal since the early days of launching the EMI-Previn partnership with works such as the *Sitar Concerto* and the *Rhapsody in Blue*. There have been the occasional *1812 Overture* and *Bolero*, to ensure good sales years, but for the most part the selection of repertoire has been left to André. "They don't let me do whatever I want to," he is quick to point out. "The only one who has carte blanche at EMI is Karajan."

On the other hand, Karajan would not be likely to talk the company into a recording of Messiaen's *Turangalila* or, for that matter, of Poulenc's *Concert champêtre*. EMI certainly has not been "hidebound about typecasting" André. When he began to read that Rachmaninoff, Prokofiev, and Shostakovich were his "little corner of the repertoire," he announced that he'd like to record Haydn's *Paris* Symphonies and there was no opposition. Troubled by implications that he could not conduct opera, André sold EMI on a cycle of Benjamin Britten, beginning with *The Turn of the Screw*.

Indeed, André's approaches to opera have been halting. When he was managing the Metropolitan Opera in New York, Schuyler Chapin tried to arrange a debut for André but found him "suspicious of opera," something Chapin found "puzzling in someone of such eclectic taste." There was the RCA recording of Mozart's *The Impresario*, which may have been predestined not to sell. There was also the revival of William Walton's opera *Troilus and Cressida*, which was to have marked André's operatic conducting debut at London's Covent Garden in 1977. But André canceled that engagement because of illness. Dame Janet Baker, one of the principals of that Covent Garden production, attributes André's cancellation to overwork.

> André is a man who requires very little sleep; he pushes his work load right to the top of his limitations. Imagine, with all the facets of his life, imagine the amount of music he stores in his head at one time. Well, with the *Troilus* he'd just gone over the top. I felt for that man so deeply. We were all

depending on him so desperately. Nobody knew that more than he did. He knew what he was putting his friends through.

His Covent Garden debut went down the drain, but André had committed himself already to conducting opera in Cologne and Copenhagen, so he resolved that he would limit his opera conducting to works he genuinely admired. *Wozzeck, Fidelio, Boris Godounov, Katerina Ismailova, Dialogues of the Carmelites,* operas by Mozart, Richard Strauss, Johann Strauss, and Puccini hold interest for him "as a theater-minded person," but much of the standard operatic repertoire leaves him cold.

> When it's grand opera in the purest and worst of the nineteenth-century tradition, I always find a lot of it slightly ludicrous. Some of the libretti are beyond me. I mean, even if the music is a work of genius, who ever understands *Il Trovatore?* That's the point with me, though it's not the point at all for someone who adores operatic singing per se. I would have to involve myself so deeply in Verdi to understand it to the degree that I could get over the things I dislike, and I'd never have time for the things I really want to do. I will openly admit that that's my shortcoming, but I'm stuck with it. I'll probably never be asked to conduct *Rigoletto* in Milan.

To Schuyler Chapin, the lack of interest in "operatic singing per se" seems a contradiction in a man who otherwise takes such delight in working with singers. "He is a fabulous accompanist," says Chapin, "not in an oom-pah-pah sense, but in a participatory sense. He is a partner to the singer and together they make music."

André's success as an accompanist stems from his jazz years when, as Doug Ramsey observed, he "often played better on other people's records than on his own." Another critic in another genre, the New York *Times*'s Harold C. Schonberg, paid close attention to André Previn the accompanist in his review of a 1980 concert by the Pittsburgh Symphony at Avery Fisher Hall. The soloist in Prokofiev's Third Piano Concerto was the Cuban-born virtuoso Horacio Gutiérrez.

Schonberg found it "a pleasure to observe the close relationship between piano and podium. Mr. Previn, who himself is a good enough pianist to handle the Prokofiev Third, knew every note of the score, and in the tricky moments he maintained close physical as well as musical liaison with the pianist, all but leaning over the keyboard to make sure that entrances would be right on the button."

Even André, sparing as he is in self-serving remarks, is forced to admit that "I am a good accompanist. It's one of the few blanket statements I'll make about my career." And confirmation of that comes from virtually every corner of the musical arena.

Janet Baker has been accompanied by André both as a conductor and a pianist and remembers the first vocal-piano recital they did together, in Los Angeles, as one of the most exciting moments in her career. "To have the Lieder repertoire played with that kind of security is indescribable," she says. "It's only happened for me with one other keyboard master, Daniel Barenboim. It's the sort of extraordinary security a professional accompanist can never achieve."

> When I was going to do something with a phrase, he was right there doing it with me. Instead of having a mood change a fraction behind, we felt the same thing together. When two people are doing that without talking about it, that's the height of music-making. You can't plan it. We all must obey the music, but this comes out of the moment. By the grace of the Almighty or the audience or the temperature— something happens and one remembers it all one's life. We'd worked hard, but this was unexpected. It was thrilling.

For the pianist Vladimir Ashkenazy, the pleasure of performing under André's baton is that "we communicate so easily. We don't need to talk about what we are doing because we understand each other without words." Another pianist, Alicia de Larrocha, had high praise for André following a series of all five Beethoven Piano Concertos with Previn and the Pittsburgh Symphony, of which *Stereo Review* wrote "there was an almost palpable sense of communication between conductor and soloist."

Said Miss de Larrocha, a veteran of fifty years of concertizing, "He could always see the direction I was taking and anticipate what I was going to do. For that you must be more than just a good conductor. There are lots of good conductors, but this kind of rapport happens seldom even with great conductors."

If there has been any criticism of André's accomplishments as an accompanying conductor, it is that he sometimes goes too far in acceding to the wishes of the soloist so that the composition suffers. Harold Lawrence observes that André is "extremely sensitive and perceptive as an accompanist and if there is anything to criticize it is that he is maybe too deferential. The friendship he feels for certain musicians, such as Ashkenazy and de Larrocha and Kyung-Wha Chung, can be carried to the extreme at which the orchestra loses its bite. The conductor becomes no longer a partner but a servant, a handmaiden of the soloist."

André counters that "an Isaac Stern has the right to demand certain bowings and slightly unorthodox variations. The first time I do a concerto with a soloist I mark in my score what that soloist wants with his initials next to it. The next time we do it together I have the orchestra pre-rehearsed in every one of those variations so that when he comes to rehearse I know every time he's expecting to have to make a correction. And I enjoy the expression on his face when he discovers it's already been made."

There are some conductors who put far less effort into preparing a concerto, realizing full well that the audience is going to be paying its closest attention to and reserving its greatest applause for the soloist. But André maintains, "I treat a Mozart concerto accompaniment the same way I treat a Mozart symphony. If someone could prove to me that composers took the composing of concerti any less seriously than they took the composing of symphonies, maybe I'd change my mind."

As an accompanist of concerti, André is taken very seriously indeed by Seymour Rosen, who maintains that André's only peer in that regard is the Philadelphia Orchestra's laureate conductor, Eugene Ormandy. "They come from the same background, both having been commercial musicians," says Rosen. "They both go out there and do the job. They can react quickly, like cats, to what a soloist is doing. I've worked as a manager with both of them and they're the greatest."

André's own excellence as a pianist is praised by Vladimir Ashkenazy, who describes him as "a natural pianist with such good hands." The naturalness of his playing is an essential ingredient, Ashkenazy believes, since his main business of conducting doesn't allow him a great deal of time to practice the piano. This problem is shared to some extent by pianist-conductor Daniel Barenboim, although Barenboim divides his time a bit more equally between the two professions. Barenboim tells the story of hearing the beginning of a Mozart Concerto on his car radio just minutes before he arrived for a rehearsal and of being so impressed by the pianist he had to sit in his car until the concerto ended, twenty minutes later, just to find out who it was. He knew the pianist was someone very good, perhaps Rudolf Serkin or Alfred Brendel. But as the piece went on he ruled each one out. For a moment he thought it might even be his own recording, but he heard a phrase that was distinctly not his. At last the Concerto ended and he heard that it was André Previn at the piano with Sir Adrian Boult conducting. Barenboim confesses that he was surprised because, like most people, he tends to think of André as a conductor first.

A truism seems to be that whatever André Previn does in music, he does well. Even his early film scores, certainly his later ones, even his jazz piano and arranging were a cut or two above the standards in those fields. The same can be said of his compositions in the classical genre, although André tends to slough them off as busman's holiday stuff. His work is thought of very highly by the musicians who perform it, as well as by composer-conductor John Williams.

"André really puts himself down as a composer," says Williams, "but of his generation I think he is one of the most able and apt. If he'd made a different decision along the way, he might be one of today's very important composers. Who's to say? It's all chicken-and-eggy. André's choice for conducting doesn't diminish his aptitude for composing."

Some outside stimulus is usually required to stir André's composing muse. It could be the special request of a friend or an occasion which demands special music. The lively fanfare that introduces "Previn and the Pittsburgh" is from his own pen. When Ashkenazy got André's commitment to a piano concerto, they set a deadline for completion by Christmas, 1980, and Jasper Parrott immediately began offering it for Ashkenazy's 1981 concerts and arranged a recording to boot— all to seal André's commitment to finishing the piece.

"Why don't you wait until you see it before you go promising to play it around the world?" André asked. "You might not like it, Vova." But Ashkenazy resorted to flattery: "I've heard enough of your music to know it will sound terrific. Anyway, if it doesn't sound as terrific with the piano and with the orchestra as you and I hope, it still will be worth playing."

André decided that the perfect infant gift to the offspring of Itzhak and Toby Perlman would be a violin serenade. Unfortunately, he had to begin writing before the baby was born and didn't know whether to compose a "masculine" serenade for Noah Perlman or a "feminine" serenade for Naava Perlman— the same sort of agonizing many of us go through over buying pink or blue baby blankets and rattles. Rather than compose a yellow, all-purpose serenade, André wrote two serenades, one "to Noah," the other "to Naava." When Noah was born, he presented both serenades to Itzhak and said, "Now you owe me another baby."

There was no pressure of any kind, however, involved in André's embarking on the course which led to *Every Good Boy Deserves Favour*. The title is from the acronym which reminds British music students of the notes which fall on the lines of the treble clef—E, G, B, D, and F. In the United States it is more commonly "Every Good Boy Deserves Fun." The title evolved much later, but the notion sprang into being in 1974 when André went to his favorite playwright, Tom Stoppard (*Rosencrantz and Guildenstern Are Dead*), to discuss the possibility of their collaborating on a play with music that would involve a full-size symphony orchestra on stage.

"Invitations don't come much rarer than that," said Stoppard and he accepted the challenge. Drawing on his only musical experience, that of triangle player in a kindergarten band, Stoppard developed a scenario. The main character became a lunatic triangle player who thought he was a millionaire owner of an orchestra. That conceit labored in the creative quagmire for the better part of two years, until Stoppard chanced to meet a Soviet exile who had been through the psychological mill of Russia's prison-hospital system. Suddenly the triangle player was a Russian, sharing a cell with a political prisoner, and Stoppard had his play.

With the addition of music, the Stoppard-Previn *EGBDF* became a London hit in 1977. Despite enormous production demands, notably a performing symphony orchestra, the play went on the road, to the Kennedy Center in Washington, D.C., to the Metropolitan Opera House in New York, and to Heinz Hall in Pittsburgh. A French-language version played to packed houses in Paris and the work met with similar success in Israel, Scandinavia, Switzerland, and Vienna.

The success gave rise to plans for a Previn-Stoppard opera, but that project has remained stalled for want of an agreeable subject. ("Tom was working on a play about Hemingway and I suggested he turn that into a libretto," quips André, "but it just wouldn't work, I suppose.") Nevertheless, Jasper Parrott has encouraged André to expand his efforts as a composer.

> André is one of the most widely gifted people in the arts. He's extraordinarily informed about artistic matters. I think it's terrifically important that these other aspects of his creative makeup should have scope. *EGBDF* and its success internationally, despite its being incredibly hard to put on, will encourage André

to be less diffident about his creative gifts. I'm certain
he has a number of important works in him that
must be allowed to come out. Theatrically he has
ideas which are fascinating and we see very few successful theatrical works nowadays. I see signs that he
is going to let himself function in this field.

Perhaps so, but André has never made any bones about the
fact that he does not see himself as a capital-C composer. To
support this thesis he argues three fairly unassailable points:
that he most often demands a *reason* for writing a piece of
music; that he cannot work without a deadline, even an
artificially created one; and that he never strives for immor-
tality with his compositions. He goes so far as to declare himself undeserving of the respect shown his compositions, since
most of it derives principally from his status as a conductor
and the contacts thus afforded him.

A real composer is one who can't help it, one who is
driven to put his insides on paper, who doesn't care
whether his music is performed during his lifetime,
but feels certain it will be performed after he's gone.
I'm simply a man who enjoys writing music. Most of
what I write sounds pretty good, but I have no
delusions about its being played after I die; I just
want it played next week.

Let's say there's a gifted composer slaving in a gar-
ret somewhere and we don't know about him because
his music is not submitted. That fellow's quite possibly a great genius, unlike myself, but *he* doesn't know
the people who want the right pieces written. I'm
guiltily aware of my unbelievably luxurious position
in having Perlman come to me to ask for encore
pieces or Ashkenazy wanting a piano concerto or
Janet Baker saying, "André, do be a love and write
me some songs." There are dozens of infinitely more
worthy composers who would give their eye-teeth for
that kind of chance and that kind of ultimate exposure, but they don't have the opportunity. At the

same time, it would be a terrible silliness of me to say, well, I don't deserve it so I'd better not write it.

The brass tacks of it all are that André composes for the same reason he conducts. He is "crazy about music, just a big fan." One of those rare individuals who's been able to make a life out of what for the rest of us would be an obsessive hobby, André can talk about music for hours without evincing the slightest trace of boredom. There is always a crescendo of excitement in his voice when he talks about music.

I'm really lucky to be so crazy about music, so enamored by the sound of it. If I hear a piece that I love but haven't heard in a while, I love the piece still and I love the privilege of hearing it. I may get angry, on a secondary level, at a performer for mistreating the music, but I'm still happy to have been there to hear the notes come out. I feel sorry for critics who get dulled down to the point where they're nothing more than reacting machines no longer pleased to hear Brahms Four. They've got to the point where the music itself no longer speaks to them, only the interpretation. I'm still childish enough in my musical attitudes that I'd love to hear the Brahms Fourth Symphony played by the Used Car Dealers Orchestra of Akron, Ohio. I wouldn't expect to hear it played to perfection, but I'd still love to hear it.

My profession is the best profession in the world because it is nearly impossible to be bored in it. If I ever got bored backstage in advance of doing a great piece of music, I'd hang it up. Artur Schnabel once said, "Great music is any music which is always better than any performance of it." That means in very practical terms that you can run at that great piece of music all your life and never hope to catch up. You only can get a little closer each time you perform it. So every time you do the Brahms Four or the Beethoven Five or the Mozart G Minor—to name but three overplayed pieces—it really is a premiere, every time, a renewal not only of your knowledge of the piece but of your faith in music.

Because it's so impossible to get bored with music, you don't grow prematurely old in your job, because it's the boredom that makes for such disillusionment in so many people my age, the endless repetition of their work without the glimmer of hope of finding something new each day. Take the Certified Public Accountant who gets a new account; I can't believe that new set of figures he works on thrills him simply because they are different from yesterday's figures or that he discovers new meanings behind the decimal points.

But with a first-rate piece of music, there are so many things that go into it that, even though you may be bored with the physical aspect of slogging through it, still the thrill of that music can be renewed nightly, with every hearing and every playing. It's impossible to get bored.

All in all, I'm just a big fan. When I spend a day without music, without performing, playing, hearing, or thinking about music, I consider that a wasted day. When I get a day off I can be extremely happy to lock up my baton case, but that doesn't mean the day will go by without music. Either I'll sit and read through scores or play records or maybe just relax and think about a piece, but I'm never shut off from music. That would be like burning off an irretrievable day.

On such "leisure days" there are certain pieces to which André has listened over and over but which so far he has been unwilling to perform because, he says, he is "in awe" of them. Two such are Bach's *St. John* and *St. Matthew Passions;* the *Missa Solemnis* was another, until he found the courage to approach it. However, he does not accept the notion that there are works from which any conductor should shy away until he has reached a certain maturity, a philosophy espoused by Carlo

Maria Giulini among others. He says he can "understand that intellectually, but not emotionally. If there's a piece I love a great deal I don't have the strength to withstand doing it. In a way I envy Giulini's patience, though it's a little priest-like, but I can't emulate it."

For much of his career André has been dogged by labels, the most recent being "late-Romantic specialist." In the beginning there was a degree of truth to that since, as John Green observes, André did launch a conducting career, "with a lamentably limited repertoire. Walton, Vaughan Williams, and Rachmaninoff—that's what he recorded and that's usually what he played." However, Green goes on to say that "in a comparatively short time and fairly late in life he developed a full-scale symphonic repertoire: Classic, pre-Classic, Transitional, Romantic, post-Romantic, French Impressionist, Contemporary. That's phenomenal."

The common thread through all this repertoire is one of enjoyment. André simply will not play a piece—outside of the occasional "duty piece"—unless it pleases him greatly. Even taking into consideration his dislike for full-scale opera, it is surprising to note that operatic overtures, intermezzos, and the like are seldom found in a Previn program. Wagner is missing nearly entirely, as is another post-Romantic German, Anton Bruckner. Some critics consider those to be inexcusable repertoire gaps; "blind spots," John Boyden called them.

"There is a lot of great music which does not appeal to me," André admits. "I can see the towering genius in it but I don't want to do it." He reasons that one musical life is simply too short to comprehend fully the vast panorama of music and that it is "truer to one's self to interpret only the music which means a great deal to you."

Clinging to the premise that beauty resides in the ear of the listener, André dismisses the entire rock music industry, despite its vogue among many of his peers. The appeal of rock, he argues, is "tribal, not musical. I'm put off by the musical illiteracy and the lack of grammar. I know it's the only kind of music that is popular all around the world, but I've just decided to be like one of those ninety-year-old colonels who sit around in English clubs: the rest of the world is full of shit and I'm *right*."

One summer as he was spending some time with Mia and the children at her home on Martha's Vineyard, off the coast of Massachusetts, André unveiled his sentiments about rock to their neighbors, rock stars James Taylor and Carly Simon. The Taylors ("as dear two people as I've ever met") decided they would give him a private, week-long seminar in the mysteries of rock and its development post-Beatles. André maintains he did his level best to purge his mind of all negative predisposition. He posed questions, asked to hear things several times over, observed nuances in the music, and even struggled to understand the lyrics. Then, after several hours of the first evening, he fell apart, rolling with laughter on their living-room carpet. "I can't help it," he groaned, "because you've helped convince me I've been right all along. This really *is* the biggest load of crap I've ever heard."

> It is undeniable that I once had a great interest in the pop culture, but that interest was on two important levels. First, there was Broadway music at its best: Kern, Gershwin, Arlen, with their extremely sophisticated writing. Then there was the jazz of my day, also extremely sophisticated, played by virtuosos who knew their instruments inside and out.
>
> Today's pop culture, this doggedly determined adulation of the primitive, goes against my grain. There are singing idols who boast openly that they can't sing, players who destroy their instruments on stage. That bothers me as a musician. I've spent my life practicing and studying music and then I see people who identify themselves as "musicians" on their passports when they don't know how to read a note of music. That offends me. On a very primal level it offends me.

Not such a far cry from his ragings about rock are André's feelings about avant-garde music, although he couches those feelings in more carefully chosen phrases. Since he is classed by many as a champion of contemporary music, this "blind spot" is not so readily apparent, even though André is the first to acknowledge its existence. To qualify as contemporary rather than avant-garde, a work must sit squarely in the mainstream of "classical" music development, must employ the same musical "language" as classical music and, in personal terms, must have something to say to André. Anything else is labeled avant-garde and is shunted to a side trestle.

André's theory is that there are plenty of capable conductors around who enjoy and understand that sort of music and who therefore can give it proper interpretation. "I have no business conducting a new piece by Boulez," he says, "because I don't know what he's after. I don't understand the *responsibility* of the piece." He says that each time he's made the mistake of playing such a work he's managed to get the right notes at the right time but has felt "no consummate involvement in the music beyond the fact that I'm pleased we've actually managed to execute it correctly. So I'll leave it to others who perhaps find Schubert a lot of boring history. A musical life is so short."

André's readiness to exclude from his portfolio the output of certain composers is excused, perhaps, by the fact that when a composer's work does "speak" to him he will do everything in his power to see that his message is conveyed to the rest of the world. Thus almost single-handedly he aroused the interest of the musical world in the Rachmaninoff Second Symphony (in the unedited version which he brought back from Leningrad) and made it a staple of the British musical diet. On the other side of the ocean he awoke many Americans to the multiple delights of William Walton. And over many years his has been one of the loudest of Western voices proclaiming the greatness of Dmitri Shostakovich.

In a place of honor on the bookshelves that line the walls of his thatched cottage at The Haven, among the works of Huxley, Proust, Austen, Woolf, Galsworthy, Wilde, and Maugham, sits the memoirs of Shostakovich, *Testimony*, smuggled out of the Soviet Union and published in 1979. Branded as a forgery by the Soviet Government and dismissed as apocryphal by some Western experts, the book boasts a "blurb" of support from André Previn. He says that the authenticity of *Testimony* is apparent from his own research and from that of his musical friends inside the U.S.S.R. He calls it a "book filled with quiet heroism. The fact that this man turned out some of the twentieth century's greatest symphonies and quartets under those circumstances is beyond belief."

Out of sheer admiration for Shostakovich and his music, André organized an enormous Shostakovich Festival scheduled for 1983 in London. While all of the composer's output is beyond the scope of the festival, the project still is so vast that he has had to enlist the aid of several other conductors to bring it all together. He continues pursuing a personal goal, that of recording all fifteen Shostakovich symphonies, and by 1980 he had finished more than half, Nos. 1, 4, 5, 6, 8, 9, 10, and 13.

> I'm sorry I'm not a string player because I would love to be part of those late Shostakovich quartets, from the Eighth on. They are unbelievable, like reading someone's diary in bars of music, like eavesdropping. They're almost too personal.
>
> And the symphonies! The output of those fifteen symphonies by one man, as far as I am concerned, constitutes the major output of the symphony in its classical form in the twentieth century. Sibelius' are immortal, but I can't think of them as music of this century. Even adding Prokofiev's I would say Shostakovich beats them all. As a force, as a power, those fifteen symphonies are inimitable. In addition, you can hear any four bars of any one of those symphonies and know beyond a doubt they cannot have been written by anyone other than Dmitri Shostakovich. That is some accomplishment.

But even toward less towering figures than Shostakovich or even Walton and Vaughan Williams, André has shown tremendous enthusiasm and given gratefully acknowledged support. Just before becoming conductor of the Boston Pops, John Williams confided that André had long been after him to quit the film business and "get on with serious composing." Practically from the day of their first meeting, said Williams, "it's been that kind of encouragement from him. He's played anything I've ever written, the minute the ink was dry on the paper, and sometimes even before it was dry. He's given me a belief in myself that otherwise maybe would not have been there."

Similarly in the 1960s André espoused the cause of a young British composer, Oliver Knussen. After being shown a Knussen symphony, he decided to program it on one of his concerts with the LSO. He discovered only later that Ollie Knussen, son of the LSO's then-principal bass player Stuart Knussen, was all of thirteen years old. He took the symphony back to Houston and played it there to high critical praise, withholding the truth about Ollie's age from the Board and from the press until *after* the concert. In the intervening years he has remained close to Knussen, advising him, performing his music periodically and arguing with him when his musical bent "slips into craziness."

André finds it amusing that after so many years as "the kid," his hair is finally turning gray and he can now play a more avuncular role with respect to younger colleagues. Less-experienced musicians find him generally understanding, empathetic, and helpful. "It has been my remarkable luck," he says, "to have been able to give a lot of very good people their debuts." Those people have, for the most part, been soloists rather than conductors. For neophyte conductors he can offer little other than sympathy.

> It used to be that a young conductor could always manage to make a few records, if he was good, at least in Europe. Then, after a few years of hard work, he'd have a name for himself. The records would feed engagements, which would feed more records, which would feed more engagements, and so on. But now, with the lamentable cutback in recording, the major

companies and even the minor ones have to restrict their output, for the sake of economics, to the most salable names. It's become almost impossible for a music director to say, "Here's that new conductor I've been hearing so much about. Sounds pretty good. Let's give him a shot." There are names that have been given to me as hopefuls and I am told that they're good but I simply don't know that for myself. I haven't heard them and there's nothing I can listen to. It's going to be damned hard for the next generation of conductors to get going.

Without a sample case of recordings there is little the young conductor can do but maneuver artistically and/or politically to get his own orchestra, a method André despises, never having had to resort to such tactics himself. The classic illustration is the advice given by Leopold Stokowski to a fledgling conductor on securing an orchestra of her own:

> First, you mustn't set your sights too high. For your first orchestra don't go after Boston or Philadelphia. Instead, you must figure out quite systematically which city has an orchestra with a small-enough season that you can handle it, yet a large-enough season that you'll be able to learn a few pieces. The players should have enough proficiency to play the works you want to conduct but they must not be so good as to make you afraid to stand up in front of them.
>
> When you have identified such an orchestra, then you must find out who its conductor is and see if you can arrange to have him fired.

Such is the reality of the music profession in the late twentieth century. It is a reality André faces each time he is presented with a talented child by parents who live in constant dread of the child's not becoming an international success. He professes a strong belief that children who are forced into the music profession by manipulating parents and teachers not only are done irreparable personal harm but represent a trend "harmful to the whole aesthetic of music."

I tell the parents of a gifted child, "Look, if he learns to play well, won't that be your gift to him of a lifetime of pleasure? He doesn't have to become Rudolf Serkin or Yehudi Menuhin, does he?" To which, of course, the parents will answer, "Oh yes he does." Or else they will accuse me of elitism.

Why is it so different for a kid who likes music as compared with one who likes to draw or to read? Their parents don't push them to become Van Goghs or Hemingways. I find it very sad that musical talent brings out the worst in so many parents. It could spoil music forever for their children. Even worse, it could swell the ranks of third-rate, penniless professionals.

On one of his motor trips through the English countryside (usually taken with cassette player turned up loud, hands conducting the steering wheel and car dancing along the road) André stopped for a meal and a rest stop at an inn where he was instantly recognized by the keeper. Instead of seating the famous conductor of the LSO at an ordinary table, the innkeeper ushered André into a private back room, which just happened to contain a large piano. The innkeeper's gangly son was dragged in by his serving apron, introduced, and deposited on the piano bench with orders to "Show Mr. Previn how good you can play."

The boy's technique was practiced but he showed a total lack of feeling for and commitment to the music. Coming to a rapid boil, André had no idea how he could extricate himself from this situation without causing embarrassment for all concerned or prolonging the ruination of a young man's life by lying about his talent. When the father at last left the room to start André's order, André stopped the boy and asked him why he wanted to play professionally.

"I don't, sir. It's my old man," the boy answered. He then

proceeded to pour out his anguish, pleading for André's help in convincing his father that in fact he was not cut out to be a musician. He was not nor had he ever been interested in music but could say nothing to bring the endless cycle of lessons and practice to a halt. Perhaps a word from Mr. Previn would change his heart.

When the innkeeper returned, André began with praise for the boy's obvious studiousness and the man's admirable discipline and thoroughness. But he felt he would be unfair to so gracious a host if he failed to point out the apparent lack of musicality and genuine love of music which would be necessary for the boy to embark on a professional career.

"Just like all the rest of 'em, aren't you?" the man blurted out. "None of you high-an'-mighty people can stand the thought of youngsters taking over your bloody jobs."

That was too much for André, who rose from his chair shouting that the man must be a goddamned fool not to see that his son didn't want to be a musician and would be a hell of a lot better off if his father would spend his money putting the boy through dental school. He drove off without any supper, too upset even to turn on the tape deck.

> If someone learns to play well enough to give himself, his family, and his friends pleasure and endless hours of sanguine relaxation, that certainly must be worth the many years of music study. He doesn't have to join an orchestra or go on an international tour, he doesn't even have to play in public to make it all worth while.
>
> Before the advent of the phonograph, the radio, and the television people *had* to make their own music. They sang together around the family piano and they played solo or four-hand. No matter how easy or difficult the music might have been, it was terribly valuable to the people involved.
>
> If you learn to sight-read a Mozart sonata—no matter how well or how poorly—you'll learn more about Mozart and his music than you could get in six

months at a conservatory. If you realize that you
don't play it as well as it might be played, then you'll
want to hear someone who *can* play it well. You'll become a concert-goer or a record-buyer. I also think
that if more people learned to play on an amateur
level—not as hacks but as genuine lovers of music—a
whole new market for composers would open up, the
kind of market there used to be, because suddenly
there would be this great need for music that could
be played in the home.

Music is played in André's home. Each of the children has
developed some degree of excellence on an instrument or two,
though so far none has played with any detectable degree of
genius. With the help of cassette recorders scattered about
The Haven, all at child-level, they are able to hear what they
sound like as well as to play the music of professionals and
develop their individual likes and dislikes.

At bedtime one is likely to encounter a serious discussion between the twins, Matthew and Sascha, concerning what the
last music of the evening should be. Matthew is waving a
Haydn tape as Sascha punches up something by Handel on
their bedside recorder. With authority, Matthew grabs the recorder and switches tapes, declaring that "your old Handel is
nice enough if you want to lie still and fall asleep, but this
Haydn will be great for jumping to."

Thus is the old theory that children require "program"
music shot full of holes and André's contempt for Mrs.
Moore's Music Appreciation class proved valid. Though he
sheepishly admits to "breaking in" his own children with *Peter
and the Wolf* and other programmatic fare, André's hackles
are still raised at the mention of "music appreciation." He has
developed his own pedagogical theory, that music and music
notation should be taught in lower grades, just as the rudi-
ments and simplest expressions of foreign languages are taught.
"Music as a Second Language" courses, he believes, "would
unlock an amazing door for children. Why is that impractical?"

That sort of foot-wetting in music, he declares, would give

children motivation to learn more, the first step in his goal of reintroducing "live" music in the home. It would put young people on the path of knowledgeable listening, as opposed to "letting music run over you like a warm bath so that it does nothing more than make you feel good. Oh sure, there are times for that kind of listening—I do it myself now and then —but if you can come to know just a little something of how music is put together you will solve so many mysteries. Listening to music is a talent, like playing music, and that talent can be developed. That's Aaron Copland's theory and I believe it too."

XXVIII

Over the course of his career André has had two glaring instances of confrontation with an orchestra or its Board: the falling-out with Houston in 1967 and the LSO blowup in 1975. In both instances, whatever bad blood there was did not come between André and the orchestra as a body; rather, it was between André and the Governing Board—the Houston Board of Directors and the LSO Orchestra Committee. And in both cases the arguments against him dealt very little with his abilities as a conductor and very much with his skill as music director. But by the time André arrived in Pittsburgh he'd come to the conclusion that, after all, there was not so much difference in kind as in degree between the two jobs.

The responsibilities of conducting, he believes, are analogous to a triangle, which will ring wherever you strike it but which yields a slightly different sound from each corner or side. The three responsibilities of conducting are to the composer, to the orchestra, and to the audience. Those of a music director are precisely the same, but with slightly different emphasis among the three. The responsibilities to the composer and his music are fairly obvious, but the others bear scrutiny.

Insofar as the audience is concerned, André maintains, it is not so important that a piece of music, chosen by a conductor, should please an audience, so long as it is heard by the audience in the manner prescribed by the composer, implying a proper job of conducting as well as proper orchestra-training by the music director. More basically, it is a music director's responsibility, through his skillful programming of an entire season and his sheer capacity to draw people to the hall, to provide an audience for the performance. "A music director has to make sure an audience is in the hall to hear a piece they might not like." He would argue that "crusaders who exclude the audience from consideration and turn the making of music into an exalted priesthood" are bad conductors and worse music directors.

Since sold-out seasons *do* make for happier orchestras, notwithstanding John Boyden's suggestion to the contrary, there is an even greater reason for consideration of the audience, its wants and needs. "An orchestra should be as happy making music as the terribly difficult circumstances allow," André insists. To this end the music director should strive to build "a taken-for-granted pride in being in that orchestra," something in which the guest conductor can concur but not greatly assist. The members of the orchestra must "continually play better and they have to get along among themselves, with the music director and with the rest of management," or the music director is not doing his job.

This, he believes strongly, is the touchstone of a music director, his ability to perform with and not against the orchestra as a body. "The music director and the orchestra cannot be on opposite ends of a court trying to serve past each other. They have to have the same goals in mind, they have to be after the same things." And that, in a nutshell, is André's summation of what a music director does.

When an orchestra is confronted with a new music director, whether elected or appointed, there is a certain amount of suspicion in the minds of the players, along with hope. They cannot help but ask, is he with us or against us? And, when the orchestra is anything but a self-governing one, is he on our side or the Board's?

Indeed, there are those who would argue that, outside of London, André's triangle of responsibility for the music director should be expanded by a fourth side: responsibility to his Board of Directors. It is something of a paradox in his career that while he sees clearly and performs quite well the task of wooing and winning Boards of Directors, he seems to lose interest in them once the marriage is consummated. Certainly it was that way in Houston and, at least according to Seymour Rosen, it was also that way in Pittsburgh.

In the two years that Rosen managed the Pittsburgh Symphony Orchestra with André at the helm he never was satisfied that André understood, much less fulfilled, his responsibility as music director to the Board. Rosen believes that André is already one of America's greatest conductors but that he will never be a great music director unless and until he places his duties to the Board on a par with his duties to the orchestra.

"When we first discussed the job in Pittsburgh," says Rosen, "he told me his view of the music director's role. He was there to make music and to help the orchestra make music better. That's very constructive but that's not all there is to it. He never understood the role a music director has to play in the community or the support he has to give his manager and his staff with the Board of Directors."

Rosen illustrates his contention with the story of André's refusal to go before the Pittsburgh Board and argue his case for a proposed tour of Europe in 1978. The tour was all André's idea and preliminary estimates indicated that it would cost in the neighborhood of $350,000. Instead of stating his case personally before the Board, André left it up to Rosen and his subordinates, very nearly losing the tour and potentially damaging his own reputation. "How is the manager, who's supposed to work for sound fiscal management, supposed to tell the Board to go out and raise $350,000, or let us operate in the red?" Rosen wondered. "For what? For the city's prestige? For André's prestige?"

It is in the financial arena that André encountered the greatest and most critical difference between the self-governing orchestra he'd grown accustomed to and the Board-governed orchestra in Pittsburgh. The difference there is as between night and day, and his realization of that fact seems to have grown in subsequent years, since he is far less willing to leave the responsibility of anything so momentous as a tour to the persuasive powers of his manager. His respect for Boards of Directors has grown.

A Board of Directors is appointed and consists partly of management and mostly of interested figures in the community who contribute heavily toward the orchestra's upkeep. Theirs is quite a different point of view from that of the orchestra governed by its own members. They each expect something in return from their conductor, but surely the end has to be different.

In any English orchestra the conductor is an employee of the orchestra and therefore he is constantly reminded that he works for them. All of us who have orchestras in London know that there must come a cut-off point in our authority, even over musical matters. Certainly we have nothing to say about tours or holidays or time off or choice of cities. A Board in England, made up of players, is very much concerned with the Government and its arts subsidies. What will it do for us in return for a certain number of British works played? How can we get a grant to go on a tour? Is it worth our while to play elsewhere in the city and what additional backing will that give us? How can we best represent the orchestra as well as the country on tour, from the governmental point of view, because we have to rely on the Government?

If you take all those considerations away, as we have in America, and surround yourself instead with people whose aim might be the collection of money for the orchestra—only all the money's got to be private—then suddenly the circle of people who are involved with the orchestra is quite different. Whereas in England there are very few non-players involved with the orchestra, an American industrialist can become very much involved if he gives the orchestra a certain amount of money. And for that money which he can't supply he will call on his friends who are chairmen of some other Boards. Sud-

denly there's this endless daisy chain of money people, some of them sincerely interested in music, some
sincerely interested in the tax write-off, and some simply interested in maintaining their status in the community. Yet all of those people, regardless of their interest in music, have to be treated very, very carefully
by the orchestra management and especially by the
music director. It's a different game than the one I'd
grown accustomed to in England.

As to which system I prefer, I really don't consider
any one better than the other. It's just as foolhardy to
think that any Government today is going to be able
to subsidize all the arts worthy of being subsidized in
its country as to expect private finance to be able to
carry the whole cart alone. I suspect that the ideal,
which is yet to be arrived at, would be a healthy combination of the two systems.

In addition to his awakening to the reality of Board politics,
there were several more culture shocks for André in learning to
be a music director in the United States, particularly in regard
to the many ways in which a non-self-governing American orchestra could manage to govern itself. He'd grown accustomed
to the need for talking everything over with the players of the
LSO and, though he made jokes about "taking all day to decide what color ties we're going to wear," he did develop
powers of persuasion which usually got the job done that he
wanted done. In Pittsburgh he encountered anew, for he'd met
it before in Houston, the American Federation of Musicians
and began to understand, from a union's point of view, the
usefulness of committees.

The good symphony orchestra has become so international and so reliant on money and unions and committees and contracts that every orchestra has its
problems, and those problems tend to be in the same
general areas. I suppose there are even more committees in America than there are in England. In Pittsburgh once I made a little joke in the middle of a re-

hearsal about our music stands, which were old and tended to slip and make clunks during performances. I asked whether that matter belonged to an existing committee or would we have to form a slipping-music-stands-and-getting-new-ones committee. There was dead silence. They did not see the humor in my remark. But it just seems to me that if you order a ham sandwich you have to go through the Ham Sandwich Committee, and if you want it with cheese, well that's a different committee. They usually find a solution to the problem and make it all work; it's just that sometimes the solution is arrived at rather the hard way.

André always has been known for his sympathy toward musicians and their struggle for survival. Once, when asked whether London musicians had it tougher than orchestra players in other European countries he answered, "No need to stop at Europe. If there's a North Pole Orchestra, those people have it better than the ones in London." His championing of musicians' causes has brought criticism from fellow conductors and from his own management. While he has mixed feelings about the musicians' union, he recognizes the need for its existence. "In the old days a conductor could say, 'I don't like your tie. Get out.' Of course that's monstrous and of course what we have now is infinitely better, but with the union I find it damned near impossible to replace anybody no matter how much he or she might be hurting the orchestra. It takes an Act of Congress and then of God to give somebody notice in America."

His first brush against union protectionism came in Houston, when he tried to clean house in the rear of the violin section. There was one woman in particular who was holding back the section, and indeed the entire orchestra. André went to the Orchestra Committee to say that he wanted to replace the woman, only to be told that this would be a terrible thing to do because she had been with the orchestra so long. He managed to talk the committee into giving her a proficiency examination, much like an audition for a new player.

With André and the Committee members looking on, the woman sat down and in complete calm went through a few of the same pieces she had been playing with the orchestra for years, the opening of the Strauss *Don Juan,* the Mozart G Minor Symphony, and other standards of the repertoire. After twenty minutes André stopped her and, after she had left the stage, he turned to the Committee members and said, "I don't suppose I have to talk about it, do I?"

There was no argument that the playing had been bad. Hardly a single bar had been played decently and there was even general agreement that this sort of playing would eventually drag the orchestra down, but the best André could do was to get the Committee members to go off for a private vote. They came back with a majority decision: the woman stayed.

It was a blessed relief for André to find in London that with the players thinking of themselves as management rather than as labor, professional pride teamed with pounds-and-pence pragmatism to weed out the poorer players, usually before they became a problem for the conductor. "When somebody's lip goes or his fingers get rheumatic or he's a drunk or he's always late or he can't get along with the conductor or he's got a horrible instrument, his friends in the orchestra will have a little talk with him. If that doesn't work, he's finished. The orchestra meets and votes and that's it. He can't say that sonofabitch of a conductor or that dirty bastard of a manager has it in for me. He's been told by twenty fellow musicians, 'Look, old man, it isn't good enough anymore.' Who's he going to hate?"

But a music director who's been protected by that system suddenly runs up against a very different situation in the United States, as in most other parts of the world. He now is faced with having to drop the axe himself. He discovers that the people who most need replacing are the ones in the back rows, players who've been around a long time, who've never made waves but who've made a lot of friends. They've never been called upon to play solo and perhaps their faults have lain hidden; they've grown rusty and they've grown old. They are, perhaps, two violists in the back row whose presence is hardly noticed; but a good music director knows that replacing them with two strong players will add tremendously to the strength and versatility of his ten-player section.

This was the situation André faced in his first season at Pittsburgh. His experience in Houston had taught him that he could not count on the support of the Orchestra Committee, yet he knew he would have to fire some people or resign, for without the personnel improvements the orchestra could not progress. The players he needed to fire were, for the most part, at the end of their playing careers, so there was no hope of their finding positions in less prestigious orchestras; he would be dooming them to finish out their days in classrooms or as neighborhood music teachers, a bitter prospect he knew from his father's experience. He swallowed the pill and approached the Orchestra Committee with his list, telling them that "These are the people who will have to go. Otherwise they'll be a rot that grows and grows." Predictably, the Committee members shook their heads and talked of all the years these fine players had put in.

> I then said to them one of those things a music direc-
> tor hates more than all else. I told them to go off and
> discuss it among themselves. If they came back to me
> and said they had a good orchestra—which they did
> —and that it was as good as they wanted it to be,
> then I would not bring up the subject of firing again,
> now or in the future. On the other hand, I said, if
> they decided they'd like to have a renewed lease on
> musical life, make more records, tour more, be more
> prestigious, get better and make a stab at becoming
> an undisputed member of the top five or six Ameri-
> can orchestras, then they should agree with me that
> this sort of unpleasant thing would be necessary now
> and probably again in the future. After a long time
> they came back and said they thought the orchestra
> ought to improve and I said, fine, let's go.

There actually were relatively few firings. He found that he could offer some of the older players early retirement that season or the next and he managed to switch some others around within the section. His only real problem came with a younger musician who was an excellent technician but who had great trouble counting complex rhythms and who therefore destroyed any attempt at achieving a solid ensemble sound. "We had to do something," André knew, "or we could eliminate the entire twentieth century. This person couldn't come in right on anything past Dvořák."

When he finally handed the player his walking papers the man demanded reasons for his dismissal. He maintained no one had accused him in the past of being unable to handle modern music. "I took a deep breath and I thought I was going to faint because I hated so thoroughly what I was about to do, but I said, 'Look here, if you won't buy it any other way, I'll make life easy for you. I don't like the way you play. How's that?' Well, now he understood and he walked off happy because he was in a rage. He could go to an audition somewhere and say, 'That prick Previn didn't want me, that's all.'"

After three seasons in Pittsburgh, André had achieved the "sound" he wanted from the orchestra—which basically meant that it had no identifiable sound but was able to change its colors like a chameleon, dashing from one kind of music to another without clashing horribly with any composer's intent. To achieve this he had to rid the orchestra of many of the habits it had developed under three successive German-trained conductors.

Victoria Bond, a young associate conductor who came to the orchestra in 1978 on an Exxon/Arts Endowment fellowship grant, believes that André has worked wonders in "really changing the Pittsburgh sound from something Germanic and thick." Bond, who sat in the hall during André's rehearsals taking notes on balance, finds him a "fanatic" in that respect. "He hears extremely well. He's very conscious of tone and balance and he strives for lean orchestral textures."

André's tenets in this regard differ from many of his contemporaries'. Whereas much has been written, and most of it with glowing pride, about "the Philadelphia sound" or "the Berlin sound," he wants no part of creating a "Pittsburgh sound" or "London Symphony sound." He has no ambition for either of his orchestras to be instantly recognizable on recordings, whether playing Haydn or Ravel, nor does he hope to achieve the sort of stylistic recognition of a Stokowski or an Ormandy, though he admits such a style can be sensational and unmistakable. Instead, he points with pride to the claim by Jack Brymer, the former principal clarinetist of the LSO, who wrote in his book *From Where I Sit* that he could always tell a recording the orchestra had made with André Previn by the fact that the note values and the rhythms were clearer than with any other conductor.

> It would never occur to me to have the ambition to inflict my "sound" on an orchestra. It is very dangerous to put the peculiarities of one's own musical taste above the wishes of the composer; it's that simple. It's inevitable that one's own personality creeps into the sound, but you have to remind yourself that you're not in the same league as the composer and if you don't represent the composer you're not only doing him and the audience and the orchestra a disservice, you're in the wrong job.

André's deference to the composer may be due in part to the fact that he is a composer himself. Just as he understands the demands on a piano soloist as a pianist, so can he comprehend the great number of stimuli that can go into the writing of a piece of music and influence the medium as well as the intended message of the composer. Consequently he believes that studying a score requires the study of much more than the score. He discovers as much as he can about the composer, his life as well as his other works. He reads about the period and the place in which he worked. He wants to know the musical habits of the time and the demands of politics and patronage which may have been imposed on the work. Only then does he bring that knowledge to bear on deciding what the composer wanted to hear in his piece of music.

In the case of eighteenth-century music, this requires a knowledge of contemporary orchestration and instrumentation. Although he enjoys hearing pieces played on instruments of the period, he does not conduct that way because "I can't believe that if Mozart would have had a modern clarinet he wouldn't have used it. At the same time, to do Mozart or Haydn with eighteen strings is insanity because that's forcing a sound onto a piece that Mozart could not possibly have imagined. More facility, better instruments, better playing, sure. But not a different sound."

In the case of a new piece of music, discovering the composer's intent is not so difficult; the composer himself may be at rehearsals to answer questions. But "there are so many things that can go wrong, such as entrances and attacking notes evenly, especially if it's a typically complicated new piece with typically limited rehearsal time." But old or new, there is more to getting an orchestra to play a piece properly than getting the notes right.

> Balance, in a lot of music, is not marked precisely. Some composers, like Mahler and Berlioz, were very good about their markings while others, Brahms for instance, just give the same dynamics to the whole orchestra. Obviously if a section is just marked "forte," a forte in the trombones is going to drown out a forte in the flutes. The conductor has to look at a piece and decide how he's going to balance the sound to get the effect the composer wanted, not the effect *he* wants. Of course there are some pieces where the *effect* is everything and the composer just wants the conductor to get it any way he can. Anything's fair game in *Pines of Rome* because surely what was in Respighi's mind was to overpower an audience.

The one group of people whom André strives never to overpower is the orchestra. The antithesis of the "martinet" conductor, André manipulates his players through carefully planned applications of honey rather than vinegar. Yet when Stephen Sondheim asked whether in fact he *ever* lost his temper at rehearsal, André had to admit that on occasion he has been known to throw a tantrum, "one of those storybook tantrums where you scream bloody murder and stomp off the stage." Invariably, however, such rage-venting occurs only when something has gone wrong on the periphery of the music-making, when the music hasn't been sent down or the chairs haven't been properly laid out or when no one can locate a battery for a headset so that the television floor director can communicate with the director in the control booth. It is almost unheard-of for him to lose his temper at a musician.

> I think musicians work very hard to make the music come out right and I get mad with the sloppy lack of coordination in the non-musical aspects of our profession. I would like the people whose involvement does not actually include the making of music to work one third as hard as the rest of us do; one half would be too much to expect and one third as hard isn't enough. So I get mad at the copyist who can't get the parts finished on time and I get mad at the bus driver who doesn't show up to take us back to our hotel until eleven when he's been ordered for ten-thirty. But I don't get mad at musicians for making mistakes or for being late if the traffic is unavoidable. It's so hard to make music under the best of circumstances, why make it harder by riding the musicians?

When he sees a young conductor making what he considers the basic mistake of mistreating an orchestra, André will assume his "avuncular role" and try to get him to change his ways. However, the tradition of conductors browbeating orchestras into submission can be a hard one to break.

In London once he treated a widely respected young colleague to lunch just to talk him out of his habit of referring to the players as "flute," "trumpet," and so on instead of by their names, which the conductor knew well enough. After listening to André's argument the colleague informed him that he was dead wrong. "Conducting is an authoritarian profession," he said. "If you start thinking of your orchestra as a bunch of individuals your authority suffers and so does the performance. You cannot afford to think of them as anything other than your instrument."

There are few clichés which set André's scalp to bristling as that one does. He once told an interviewer, "I think the one important thing to remember when you rehearse an orchestra is that an orchestra is not a nameless, faceless large instrument. It is comprised of a hundred or so *individuals*, all of whom probably have played more music than you ever will and all of whom have private and personal opinions and problems. A conductor cannot treat them as his personal instrument."

Of course it is true that while some instruments are put together with a great deal of tender loving care and while some violinists would swear that their Stradivari or Guarneri is a living personality, no instrument is more than a carefully made object of brass, wood, or gut. An orchestra, on the other hand, appears to André as a complex colony of life, a "mini-civilization" he calls it. "They are a group of talented, experienced individuals who have got together by common consent to make music not under you but with you. Treat them the way a pianist treats his piano and you'll defeat yourself."

Victoria Bond credits André with changing her attitude about the musicians and, as a direct result, with changing her own rehearsal technique "drastically and in a very short time." She says that André does not so much want to be friends with his players as to know them individually. He once quoted to her some good advice from Stokowski: "You can make a mistake and certain people in the orchestra will forgive you because they love you and are rooting for you no matter what you do. There are others who will always hate you, even if you send them Christmas cards and ask about the health of their wives and families. And there are others, the majority, who are undecided about you; those are the ones you have to work on."

André's technique for "working on" the musicians is to keep things light at rehearsals. He might start off by cracking a joke and then saying, "Okay, let's give this symphony a whirl." A horn player is unclear about a particular note and André will toss off the answer, "Oh, I suppose an F natural would do nicely there." Disappointed at a weak attack by the triangle player he quips, "Did someone lose a cuff link?" And correcting a *tutti* in a particularly thorny modern piece he looks at

the first trombonist and says, "Carl, suppose you try sneezing on that A-flat."

If it is a new work, one which needs a good deal of correcting, André will not stop at every wrong note, fearing he might "throw them into a kind of catatonic state." Instead, he lets them play for a long stretch, until a logical stopping point is reached, and he goes back and makes corrections, all of which he has managed to retain in his head. "I find that the second time around they will correct themselves to an astonishing degree."

For a conductor who puts such stock in rehearsing, André is extremely easygoing when it comes to making rehearsal demands on the orchestra. He does everything in his power to keep from going overtime—less out of fear of spending money than out of concern for the players' well-being, having spent so many years with the LSO musicians, whose schedules are often figured to the minute so that they can dash from one place to another. If he has performed a piece several times with the orchestra, there may be no full rehearsal of that work before a concert. Rather, André will have done his homework and made a list of critical points in the score of which the orchestra is then reminded, either verbally or by playing through those phrases. Unlike Georg Solti, who believes in whipping a piece into perfect form on the morning before a concert, André fears that overworking a piece will result in the orchestra's becoming bored with it so that in performance it will be treated perfunctorily.

The lesson was driven home in his first season with the LSO, when André watched another conductor put the LSO through the *New World Symphony* twice in the span of a two-hour rehearsal, despite the urging of the concertmaster to "just tell us what you want and we'll give it to you that way tonight." As it turned out, the man got what he wanted the second time through in rehearsal, but by that evening the players were bored to tears with the music and the performance was, in André's estimation, "absolutely hateful."

The next day he decided to take a chance. He had a rehearsal for that evening's performance of Rimsky-Korsakov's

Scheherazade, "a piece with a lot of dangerous corners in it."
He determined that the orchestra had not played it for anyone
else since the last time he'd conducted them in it, then he
checked the string parts to make certain his markings were
still there, and they were. "Well," he told the musicians, "Let's
have a day off."

"We had no rehearsal and they played me a performance
that night which was absolutely wonderful. It wasn't perfect,
mind you, not the sort I'd want preserved on records, but it
was spontaneous and accurate and wonderful. I think it's important to have that kind of overt demonstration of faith in an
orchestra once in a while. They'll respond with faith in you."

Occasionally André will use another trick of "faith" just to
force the musicians to listen to what they and their co-players
are doing. In the middle of a performance he will stop conducting "just for eight bars or so" if he feels the musicians are
not quite together. "That throws the orchestra forcibly into listening to each other play and everything gets straightened out
without any benign help from you. When you're just starting
out as a conductor you think that if you don't wave your magic
wand everything will fall apart, whereas very often you can be
a big help by not doing anything. That's a hard lesson to
learn."

André's seemingly relaxed methods can be deceiving, particularly when it comes to the matter of beginning a musical
sound at precisely the right moment in time. "Clarity of
rhythm" he calls it and one of his first steps toward achieving
it in Pittsburgh was to break the orchestra's habit—time-
honored in Europe—of attacking a note a split second behind
the conductor's beat.

> Every conductor has his own tiny corner of maniacal
> concern and attention. Some people occupy them-
> selves endlessly with string phrasing, others with
> structure. I am very severe with myself and with or-
> chestras when it comes to clarity of rhythm. I'm talk-
> ing about pulse and rhythms within the bar line. I
> don't mean just in the obvious places, like *The Rite
> of Spring,* but also in music that doesn't seem to have

a rhythm problem, say, *Afternoon of a Faun*. I want
to hear, at least subconsciously, where the pulse is at
all times. If I ever harangue an orchestra or approach
overrehearsing, it is because I want the clarity of the
pulse of the music apparent not just to me but to
them. All the time.

I'm sure every conductor in the world would say,
"Well, naturally." But it isn't natural at all because
these things go to pieces, especially with repeated performances. Also, I've found there's a great deal to be
gained by making the orchestra aware that the rhythmic pulse has a lot to do with the structure and the
curve of a piece, not just within the bar line but over
the course of the entire piece.

If there is a phrase which is rhythmically stated one
way, then is repeated differently, ever so slightly
differently—even if it's unheard, in the middle of a
blazing *tutti* and played only by the oboe and English
horn—if everybody becomes aware of it then you get
a more committed, careful, and watchful kind of playing. Once that becomes second nature, the playing of
even familiar pieces stops being mechanical.

The lesson was learned early on. Pierre Monteux drilled into
André the notion that even French Impressionism, so often
subjected to mushy, indistinct treatment by an orchestra, is in
its design some of the world's most meticulously structured
music. His study of English music, not unlike French Impressionism in many ways, led him to look for hidden rhythms
behind every gently flowing brook and heather-scented breeze.
"Even in the slow movement of the Fifth Symphony of
Vaughan Williams, which seems little more than a series of
beautiful, lovely wanderings, if you pay absolute attention to
the value of every note you find that there is much more there
than a hovering cloud."

This sort of attention to "rhythmic clarity" has had a notice-
able and benign effect on André's conducting style. Not only
the orchestra but the audience as well understands what,
through the movements of his hands, fingers, arms, and baton,

he is communicating to the orchestra. The result is that what critic Gillian Widdicombe could once dismiss as "a kind of paddle" is described a decade later by Harold C. Schonberg as "a clear beat and steady rhythm." Janet Baker, precise as she is generous in her praise of André, says, "He has this fantastic sort of loose wrist motion and in it you can see a crystal-clear, geometric security."

For André's own security on the night of a concert he must arrive at the hall in plenty of time, at least a half hour before starting time. For one thing, he lives in fear of either absent-mindedly taking a wrong turn or else getting stuck in a traffic jam. ("That could be termed a plea for lovable eccentricity, but it isn't. I do it all alone, so I'm not impressing anybody.") Moreover, he feels it important to give the subconscious atmosphere of the music and the hall time to make itself felt. "I like being in the place of music-making before the music starts," he says. "I know there must be a difference between belting through the stage door and giving the downbeat and being within those walls for a half hour and letting the atmosphere take over."

Once inside he has a cup of coffee and wanders through the corridor listening to and laughing at all the customary musicians' jokes. He asks a question or two of management personnel concerning the next day's rehearsal. Fifteen minutes before concert time he goes into his dressing room and changes into full dress. The soloist comes in for a last-minute conference and an exchange of good lucks. The soloist also has been in the hall early "to try the piano." André has tried his orchestra and is satisfied they will do the job as expected. There is a knock on the dressing room door and a voice calls out, "Five minutes, maestro."

At five minutes before the concert, André draws a curtain around the outside world. A guest in his dressing room will find him unresponsive to questions or giving answers that make no sense. He is now *in* the music and nothing else matters.

On most evenings this has nothing to do with nerves, for he

has given up being nervous long ago, except for very special occasions when he is conducting the Beethoven Ninth or the Brahms *Requiem*. Otherwise, there is just a trace of that fear he missed so many years ago in Hollywood. His only sleepless nights now are *after* concerts, when he conducts the work over and over in his head, catching little mistakes each time. But he has nothing but pity for those colleagues who go into cold sweats every time they walk out on stage. "You'll drop dead after one season," he says, "unless you begin to realize that every performance can't be a calling to the priesthood."

Indeed, the only thing that actually makes him nervous now is poor preparation, through inadequate rehearsal or last-minute program changes. Then "I get nervous for the piece, not for myself. I hate that someone, either alive or long dead, should have put so much blood, sweat and tears into that piece and I might be about to shortchange the composer and the audience."

Inevitably, there are mistakes in the performance, for that is the nature of live music. André may be one moment "as calm as Karl Böhm conducting the *Jupiter*," and then as the need arises he will feel a rush of adrenalin and a rise in temperature. His face gets red with concentration and his clothes dampen with perspiration. A half measure after the mistake is corrected, physical calm returns and after the concert he is likely to be laughing about it all.

Interestingly, a quite opposite physiological change occurs when he performs as piano soloist with an orchestra. Then, even without mistakes, he may feel an icy fear grip his hands and his fingers will numb and begin to slip from the keys. This may be due to his inability to keep up the practice of his piano-playing, or it may be due simply to the fact that a soloist traditionally plays without the music in front of him.

Arturo Toscanini made scoreless conducting fashionable and he has had numerous disciples in that school, today's most notable one being perhaps Zubin Mehta, who considers "eye contact" with the musicians of paramount importance and a score a great hindrance. "Those of us who tend to use scores," says André, "such as Colin Davis, Georg Solti, and myself, don't

actually *look* at the score very often. As for me, even when I
do conduct from memory I like having the desk there. I like to
be able to reach out and touch it. Isaac Stern once told me
that it restricts my movement, but I *like* having that piece of
wood there. Without it I get a curious limbo feeling, like I'm
going to pitch over into the violas."

Having once heard a concert in which a conductor's reliance
on memory rendered him unable to rescue a soloist from a
memory lapse, André is hard on conductors who spurn the
score. The concert in question involved pianist André Watts, a
distinguished soloist who nevertheless managed to lose his way
in the first movement of the Brahms D Minor Concerto. The
distinguished conductor could not seem to give the right cue
to help Watts on his way and the result was a sort of swim-
ming-around by the orchestra for forty-five seconds, which
seemed like an eternity.

> I have unbounded respect for this man, but his habit
> of accompanying from memory—and I'd say this to
> his face because we're colleagues—I think it's a con-
> ceit. Who cares whether he knows the piece? It
> doesn't matter with respect to "immersion in the per-
> formance." You're gambling here with some poor
> bastard's solo. I saw the same thing happen with
> Rubinstein and Rubinstein instantly mimed to the
> audience: "This is not my fault, ladies and gentle-
> men." Which of course was ruthless of him. Still, I
> can't see why people accompany from memory be-
> cause anything can happen. I mean, my God, if
> André Watts can make a slip in Brahms One it can
> happen to anybody.

It can be argued that the benefits outweigh the perils of
scoreless conducting, but it is a sure thing that André will
not hear a great deal of criticism from the press on that score.
If he were taken to task for "lack of immersion," chances are
he wouldn't even read it for it is rare that André scans a newspaper for a review of the previous night's perfomance. He will

look for reviews in "important" places where he performs infrequently, such as New York, Paris, Berlin, and Vienna, but he maintains he has never read a review of one of his concerts in Pittsburgh, "even though both critics are friends of mine." What really stopped him from reading the critics was a conversation he had with Alan Jay Lerner.

"When I write a play," said Lerner, "I get reviewed maybe once every two years and then my life depends on it. But you do how many concerts a year, 125? And when you figure an average of three reviews a concert, that's 375 reviews every year. You can't even read 375 reviews and you sure in hell can't believe them, one way or another."

Instead, André depends on his own judgment, and his instincts about a performance. "I know when a performance has been good or bad," he says. "Sometimes I come away very pleased, sometimes I come away suicidal. But eighty percent of the time I come away dissatisfied with parts of the concert and knowing that all-in-all much of it was pretty good. Anyway, by now I'm secure enough to know that I'm going to be working next year no matter what any critic says."

If André errs, it is not on the side of overestimating his own value. A quote that had very deep impact on him as a child came to him from Thomas Mann, relayed by his father. The two had attended a pompous lecture together and at the conclusion Mann told Jack Previn, "That man was not big enough to make himself small." The meaning sank in and was recalled several years later when Monteux chided him for falling into the sin of pride by his blatant imitation of Leonard Bernstein. On the podium, André has ascetically discarded the excesses of youth and cultivated a self-effacing style that is the very opposite of flamboyance. Now the critics he doesn't read have, in large measure, declared that a flaw. The argument goes that his lack of "body language" in conducting fails to involve the audience (and sometimes the orchestra) fully enough in the dynamics of the music and indicates a degree of actual disdain for that audience. None of this might be worth mentioning except for the fact that similar concerns are expressed by some of

André's friends and admirers, notably Schuyler Chapin and Harold Lawrence.

Lawrence, who first championed André's cause in the LSO, says that his "tendency to understate," one of the things that so attracted the British audiences to his podium style, now may inhibit André's interpretations of some works on the grand scale. Chapin, whose foresight helped launch André's classical recording career, sees it as André's desire not to "trespass on an audience's emotions," and compares him to Jascha Heifetz in this studied coolness and concentration which seems to dismiss those emotions as irrelevant.

In terms of doing justice to the music, Lawrence maintains that André's reputation was saved in the early days by the fact that he conducted so many pieces which, in the hands of less-reserved young conductors, sound effusive and overblown. The Rachmaninoff Second Symphony is his perfect example since, "while Rachmaninoff's music was weeping and wallowing, André's conducting was saying, 'Now hold on to it, don't let yourself start crying.' His dropping curve was matched by the rising curve of the music and a perfect balance was struck."

By contrast, in works which are emotional only in the most profound ways, André's reserve refuses to cut open the heart of the music and set the audience's hearts to throbbing in sympathy. "André is afraid of the big gesture," Lawrence believes. "He is afraid to *seem* flamboyant."

When André does let go of his own reins in a performance, contends Schuyler Chapin, "it's hair-raising exciting." This "letting go" is more likely to happen in the accompaniment to a concerto, when André—simply because he is so self-deprecating—lets himself be swept along by the emotional tide of a soloist. After a concert with André Watts playing the Saint-Saëns Second Concerto a critic wrote, "Watts's fire seemed to ignite Previn." And to those who were there the effect was astonishing.

Lawrence craves to see André "grit his teeth and lunge into the music with his heart and soul. I think he understands what needs to be done but he doesn't always have that inner compulsion to get under the skin of a work. He shies away from it." To Chapin, the remarkable thing is that André has gotten so far *without* that compulsion.

"Everything is open but the last door," Chapin says. "He's got to reach inside himself and open it. If he could only do that it would catapult him into the public's bosom, and that's where he belongs. The machinery for doing that is already there, and it would make the difference between his achieving fame and his going down in history as one of the great conductors of our century."

André's reaction to this sort of suggestion is a smiling nonchalance, which he credits to "encroaching age or thirteen years of living in England." He says that far from being a restraining influence, Monteux's early advice actually set him free to be himself. Moreover, he cannot detect any audible difference in the orchestra based on the grandness of his gesture. "I have found out," he says, "that by leaping six feet into the air you do not get them to play the sforzando any louder." Nor does he feel that audiences respond to such blatant attacks on their emotions.

> If the equation were: do that and the audience goes crazy, I might give it a try. But it is far from being an unfailing device. It is possible to go through all kinds of gymnastics on the podium and be left with the complete apathy of the audience. Also, it is possible to be absolutely quiet, like Reiner or Monteux, and make the audience totally thrilled with the music. Therefore, I might as well do what comes naturally.
>
> Lenny, who is now over sixty years old, still conducts like a twenty-year-old. That is his nature. He is expressing through his body a certain musical personality and to hell with what it does or doesn't do to an audience: it elicits good performances from an orchestra. It's sincere with Lenny; I imitate it and it becomes fraudulent. You have to behave totally normally on the podium and that takes years to learn.

As a member of the audience, Chapin disagrees. "You begin to expect that kind of communication from the podium after you've had it from Bernstein and from Mehta and even from Karajan, with his humble act. All of them are showmen, besides being great conductors, and André is not. He treats an audience rather cavalierly. He comes out and bows and that's it."

Clearly there is room for disagreement, and Dame Janet Baker disagrees. She sees André, along with Zubin Mehta and a handful of others, as members of a breed of "super-conductors" who write their own rules and must be allowed to live by them. "Zubin is the embodiment of the conductor of 'body-poetry,'" she says, "where every time a moment builds in the music you can see it build up in the body of the conductor. André's body poetry is of a different kind and maybe this is what people miss in him. But I can see it. I can see him now, with his head down, sort of keyed into the earth. But, my God, it's *there*. André's himself, and he gets on with the job. What more could anyone wish for, professionally or personally?"

XXX

One night after a concert with the New York Philharmonic, André welcomed into his dressing room a woman who had been in the concert management business for many years. The woman looked around at the dressing room, empty except for a change of clothes, a suitcase, and a few scores, and she said, "My God, André, there's nobody here with you? I must have been in this dressing room a thousand times after Lenny's concerts and it was always filled with people laughing and congratulating, flowers and champagne everywhere. You just finish the concert, have a bite to eat, and it's all over." André had no idea what the woman was talking about. This was the way it always had been with him, from his earliest concerts in Los Angeles, when more often than not even his family had been too busy to attend.

Jasper Parrott observes that "for somebody who's always been in the news, so visible, André is actually one of the most private, most unpretentious people I know. I argue with him a lot about this, suggest that he concern himself more with prestige, but he refuses to have anything to do with it."

His scornfulness of the trappings of success is most visible in his choice of personal transportation. Ever since his first California convertible André has realized that he cares very little for cars and expects nothing of them but that they have "four wheels and a cassette deck." In England his battered Volvo is a running (usually) joke at Festival Hall and in Pittsburgh he keeps an old brown Chevrolet which is so nondescript he has to leave a snowbrush on the front seat at all times to make sure he can find the car in a crowded parking lot. He takes no pleasure in his cars, yet uses them as a means of escape, turning the cassette volume up as loud as the tiny speakers will bear. Oft-taken trips are catalogued in terms of the elapsed musical time from point to point. "I think of my friends' homes in terms of repertoire. So-and-so lives Brahms One away, or that's a long drive, the Berlioz *Requiem*." Actually, the repertoire is more often chamber music.

In Pittsburgh, his "home away from home," André lives in an apartment complex atop Mount Washington. With no family around he lives a rather spartan existence, going to dinner, the movies, and the galleries with friends associated with the orchestra. "Or we'll just sit around having drinks or maybe play a little chamber music. It's not home but it's a place filled with people about whom I care, so it's not so bad."

Sid Kaplan, the orchestra manager in Pittsburgh, once caught André between rehearsals carrying a double armload of dirty clothes into a laundromat. "You mean you do this stuff yourself?" Kaplan asked, and André replied, "You mean Karajan *doesn't?*"

> The ideal would be to have someone to do all those chores and leave me to worry only about conducting. But I won't surround myself with paid help and the idea of an entourage repels me. I sometimes think of having a personal manager or personal secretary, but I really don't want anybody around all the time, not someone I'm paying to be around.

Nevertheless, André does not see himself in his peripatetic profession as a lonely man, nor does his friend Adolph Green: "In many ways André is self-sufficient. He adjusts easily either to being with someone or to being alone. Anyone who discovers him is crazy about him. I wouldn't call him a lonely figure."

Yet André himself is forced to admit that the glamour of travel and meeting new people, seeing new places, can rather quickly become old hat. "There is always the hateful, wrenching, and lonely business of preparing to leave the people you love and the home you love," he says. "I have learned that when I check in at the airport desk I enter a sort of limbo and I don't come out of it until I get back home. Meanwhile, I go on doing my work."

For all its rigors, life on the road can produce some of music's most hilarious moments. Just getting to one's destination can be ludicrous enough: dashing out of Heinz Hall after a Brahms *Requiem*, no less, into a waiting, ticking taxi; ripping off the sweat-soaked tie-and-tails and throwing them into a duffel bag as the change is made into sweater and jeans, with the cabbie staring into his rear-view mirror in disbelief; stuffing a handful of bills into the driver's hand and hearing, "Want I should circle the terminal so you can zip up your fly?", making the last call for passengers on a flight that will eventually land in Vienna, with barely enough time to arrive for the start of rehearsal.

The "convenience" of modern-day travel has its inconveniences, as André and the LSO discovered upon their arrival in Columbus, Ohio, on one of their first American tours. The vacuum lock on the plane's cargo hatch refused to open and the orchestra refused to budge until its instruments were removed safely from the plane. For six hours they sat in the airport before the gear was finally unloaded. By that time it was too late to check into their hotel rooms, so they went directly to the auditorium and changed there into their concert attire.

Suffering badly from "jet-lag," some of the players began nodding off in their chairs during the pre-performance tune-up, so that when André strode on stage they were none too ready to begin. Unluckily, the opening piece was Beethoven's Fifth Symphony, with its notoriously difficult entrance, and André knew the evening was lost as soon as he gave the infamous downbeat. "I later on gave a large prize to the single second violinist who came in correctly. Things snowballed downhill from there. I simply can't think of an orchestra bad enough to compare it to. We sounded like the rankest bunch of amateurs ever assembled."

At intermission very few words were exchanged, only glares and hangdog expressions. Until one of the assistant managers ran breathlessly backstage with word that nearly the entire Cleveland Orchestra was in attendance to hear England's prize players. André helped spread the word, hoping the LSO would be too embarrassed to continue in the vein of the first half. Sure enough, "the LSO, being the extraordinary animal that it is, rescued our reputation with a phenomenal second half. Somehow the hysteria of the evening took over and we played *The Rite of Spring* like demons. It was wonderful."

Then there was the time André first mounted the podium of the Academy of Music in Philadelphia, starchly erect in his white tie and tails, and then fell down on the other side. The audience tittered, the Philadelphia Orchestra roared. "They adored it. The conductor was an idiot and he had their generous help from then on," André recalled in a Dick Cavett interview.

A less-acclaimed descent was made in 1974 by the horn virtuoso Barry Tuckwell. In Bonn, Tuckwell had joined the LSO and tenor Robert Tear in a performance of Benjamin Britten's *Serenade*, at the end of which the French horn is supposed to leave the stage for an unaccompanied moment in which the horn grows fainter and fainter. The effect proved difficult to achieve in the small, heavily draped theater until Tuckwell opened a door to a freight elevator and played from there. "Wonderful, Barry," André called. "The sound's just whacking out. That's fantastic. Do it that way this evening."

But the effect at performance was even better than it had been at rehearsal. It was "the most phenomenal *diminuendo* I'd ever heard," says André. "I was stunned by the sound." It was followed by a tumultuous ovation. André stepped down and shook Tear's hand, then gestured to the wings for Tuckwell. He did not appear. André took a bow, Tear took a bow, the entire orchestra took a bow, but still there was no sign of the horn player. Suddenly he ran full tilt onto the stage, all out of breath, just in time for the final bow.

"What the devil happened?" André asked as they walked off together.

"I've been trying to find my way up from the basement," Tuckwell panted. "Somebody rang for the bloody elevator just as I was starting the *diminuendo*. I hope you could hear it."

Audibility was a much greater problem for the LSO's percussion section at the Flanders Festival in Brussels. This time there was a missed flight connection and the orchestra had to take the stage of the glittering Palais des Beaux Arts in street clothes. Again there was the question of where to play an offstage instrument, the chimes in Berlioz's *Symphonie Fantastique*. The principal percussionist located a door which, when propped open, gave him sufficient visibility to the podium and should have allowed him to give the proper otherworldly effect in the Dies Irae section. At last the chilling moment came and André gestured to the chimes. "The first two notes were the sound of a pewter cuff link tapping against a bannister." The percussionist realized instantly what had gone wrong: the chimes had been stuffed with cotton wadding to protect them on the flight and in the rush to the theater no one had remembered to unstuff them. He reared back and struck the third note with all his might, only to find that that chime happened to be the one into which someone had *forgotten* to put the wadding. The effect was jarring, and it sent the other players into a paroxysm. The result was not quite what Berlioz had in mind.

Sometimes the horror tales of touring come from a piece having been played too often on the road, as opposed to suffering from too little warm-up time. One occasion graven on André's memory is the time he took the LSO on the road with Radu Lupu in preparation for a Festival Hall concert and then a recording of the Grieg Piano Concerto. By the time they arrived in London they'd played the piece so many times it was second nature. Almost second nature.

Things were going swimmingly. "Every nuance was down to a fine art. I was completely used to every one of Radu's rubatos. I was enjoying it so much I decided, what the heck, no need for me to turn those last few pages." The concerto concludes with three great fortissimo chords, which always have a cheerleading effect on the audience. To play them precisely together requires great concentration and a sharing of rhythm between the conductor and the pianist. "I looked at Radu and he looked at me and we went *BANG!* Perfectly together. There was a pause and then another *BANG!* Then, for some reason, I dropped my hands, forgetting the final chord and expecting the applause. The end result was that Radu and about four second violins started in, then applied the brakes, playing a pianissimo *plink* to end the concerto. Radu looked at me and burst into laughter, first at what had happened and then at the look on my face. We walked off screaming with laughter. If that had happened to me at the beginning of my career, I'd be a dentist now somewhere in North Dakota."

André considers that one the worst faux pas of his career, but there was another time when his memory came to the rescue, just as it had failed him in the Grieg. He developed the habit of having his most-used scores permanently bound ("not in hand-tooled leather, just sturdy blue cardboard") to keep them from being crushed in suitcases or returned by mistake to publishers along with rented orchestra parts. He now has several hundred such scores, all bound alike. So it was that he discovered, as he opened his score to conduct Martha Argerich in Prokofiev's Second Piano Concerto, that the librarian had brought him the Brahms *Variations on a Theme by Haydn.*

Rather than cause a disturbance, he decided to conduct from memory, but he thought he'd better turn pages now and then to keep the orchestra and pianist from getting the jitters. It worked fine, except that he ran out of pages before he got to the end of the music and except for the musical jokes that kept cropping up as he heard Prokofiev's music rising out of Brahms's notes. "I was close to hysteria by the end and as we walked off Martha said, 'I've worked with you a great deal and never seen you in such a state of disarray.'"

One of the joys of touring with the LSO was the orchestra's insistence whenever possible on trying out each new hall before a concert, playing something loud and something soft, just to get a feel for the acoustics. Even when they were tired, the players would want a rehearsal before a concert. It came as something of a shock, then, for André to realize that the rules of their union rarely allowed the Pittsburgh Symphony to rehearse on tour, even if the musicians were paid extra for it. In advance of his first major tour with the orchestra, André pleaded the case for out-of-town rehearsals with the union in "a letter that made Patrick Henry read like a bum."

> I pointed out that if a painter has an exhibition in a city he hasn't been in, he goes and hangs the pictures himself so he knows what kind of light there is, the color of the ceiling, how far apart to hang them. Don't you want to know what you sound like?
>
> I tried to say that if we are a good-enough orchestra to tour and we go to a major city and we play major programs without knowing what the hall is like, we are liable to get indifferent to poor reviews and a poor reception elsewhere. The people at home hear about it, the community is disappointed, the money stops coming in, the record company isn't interested, the television stops. Going on tour means we are too good to stay within our city limits. If we don't play our best, then we are wasting everybody's money and good will, and our own time and studying.

The tour in question was the "$350,000 tour," the merits of which Sy Rosen had to pitch to the Pittsburgh Board. The money was raised, principally from private and industrial gifts, and the tour begun on May 21, 1978. It was to be the Pittsburgh Symphony's first trip to Europe in fourteen years, playing eleven cities in five countries—Austria, Germany, Norway, Sweden, and England—in twenty days to more than thirty thousand people. For André, who had just signed a new three-year contract in Pittsburgh, the greatest achievement of the tour was the rehearsal before the orchestra's first performance at the Musikverein in Vienna. But for the musicians, the tour was much more than that, beginning with the six standing ovations they received in Vienna, and continuing through round after round of concerts and parties and bus trips and hotel rooms. Somehow the strain never showed and just as the first Russian tour had cemented his relationship with the LSO, so did this European tour confirm André's relationship with the Pittsburgh.

"The orchestra grew and grew on that tour," says Sy Rosen. "André and the orchestra were growing and learning together, especially in their understanding and playing of the Mahler Fourth Symphony. His rehearsals along the way were carefully planned and the orchestra knew that he was really using that time, not just going through the motions. It all came together in Berlin. Everybody agreed that that was one week the Berlin Philharmonic didn't have to be there and the city still had itself a great orchestra."

The critics at each stop along the way had nothing but praise for Previn and the Pittsburgh. "André Previn is a musical ringmaster," the Vienna *Kurier* proclaimed. "The music all gushed forth like a stream." "Everything was melted into smooth clarity and sounded light and golden," wrote the Linz critic. In Munich, the audience was surprised to find "Viennese charm from Pittsburgh, a symphony orchestra based on the highest European traditions," and at the conclusion of the Mahler they rose in a spontaneous, stomping cheer. Later, that performance was voted the concert of the year in Munich. Bonn's *Die Welt* hailed the Pittsburgh's "glorious comeback under Previn," and declared the orchestra the rival of New York, Cleveland, and Boston. "André Previn has kindled much confidence in the Pittsburgh future."

That view was sustained in Berlin, the city of André's birth, where there were so many unpleasant memories. The stark Philharmonie, known as "Karajan's Circus," was jammed with standing-room patrons who'd read of the orchestra's earlier stops and, at the conclusion of the first movement of the Mahler, there was an unexpected interruption of applause. After the finale (which included the Spanish soprano Jill Gómez as soloist) many of the normally staid Berliners rushed from all sides to the in-the-round stage and besieged the musicians with cheers and embraces. It was that kind of evening.

The next morning's *Morgenpost* proclaimed that "the great success was due to André Previn" and that under his direction the Pittsburgh Symphony had to be classed as "one of the most renowned orchestras on the American continent." *Der Tagespiegel*, not to be outdone, declared the Pittsburgh "one of America's six top orchestras." At least abroad, the Big Five had become the Big Six.

The phenomenal tour concluded June 9 with a concert in another of André's "home towns," London. Royal Festival Hall, where he had so long led the London Symphony Orchestra, was filled as much out of curiosity to hear "Andy Previn's other band" as out of love of music. But those who were there for the music were not disappointed, nor was the irony of all the "European-sound" plaudits of Austria and Germany lost on the London critics, who recalled that André was very nearly tossed out of the LSO in favor of someone who could give them a "more European sound."

In no uncertain terms, the *Guardian* credited the Pittsburgh Symphony with producing "quite the most beautiful sound that any trans-Atlantic band has produced at the Festival Hall in years. The magician who worked this miracle (at the end of a tour) was our own André Previn."

After ten years with the London Symphony Orchestra, no matter what his accomplishments in Pittsburgh, the English did feel a certain proprietary kinship toward André. He was at home on their television sets, on the Festival Hall podium, in the village pub at Dorkney, downing a pint of bitters or sipping his four-o'clock tea with lemon. Pittsburgh might be his "home-away-from-home," Berlin might be his birthplace, and Los Angeles the city of his youth, but London and Surrey were the places where he truly belonged.

Walking through the woods behind The Haven, with the first brisk breath of autumn in the air and the first crisping leaves underfoot, André dodges a rusting tricycle and begins to reminisce about his years with the LSO.

In 1978, the LSO librarian, Henry Greenwood—a re-markable human being—came to me between re-hearsal sessions one day and said, "I've been putting together a repertoire list of you and the orchestra and it occurs to me that probably neither you nor anyone else has a conception of all the music you've been through together in the last ten years. I can't remember anyone conducting this much diverse music in the span of a decade." He showed me the list and it was staggering. Of course, what neither Henry nor anyone else knew about that list was that much of what I did with the LSO I was doing for the first time.

There was a period of a couple of years, early on, in which the schedule got so crazy that if the orchestra had expressed dissatisfaction with my work I privately would have agreed and I'd have had to leave. I was learning too much at too short notice. It simply was too much to do.

I saw myself in Seiji Ozawa, one summer when we both were at Ravinia. I heard him rehearse the Chicago Symphony in what I knew was his premiere of Schoenberg's *Verklärte Nacht*. I saw him that afternoon not knowing the piece at all, secluding himself in his room to study, then conducting it that evening as though he'd been playing it all his life. He collapsed backstage in a giggling heap and told me he'd never been so terrified of anything. I could empathize because I was doing it too. It was a dangerous sort of life.

And yet it fit the life-style of the LSO, with its kind of thoroughbred-racehorse population. It's such a volatile orchestra, full of nervous energy, playing with a quicksilver brilliance, on the edge of the cliff in Berlioz or Tchaikovsky. Working with that orchestra then was very dangerous and very enjoyable.

For his manager, Jasper Parrott, too little has been said "about the tremendous difficulty of what André did. When you are so visible, so easy a target, and you stand up before a great orchestra in an unbelievably wide range of repertoire, when you go on tour with them and are seen as their figurehead, the strains are remarkably acute. His classical recording career, which only effectively began in 1969, covers an incredible range. I doubt any other conductor, except Ormandy and Karajan, has recorded so much."

By 1978 André had been with the LSO three years longer than any other principal conductor, a truly remarkable achievement considering the volatile nature of the LSO within the already explosive musical atmosphere of London. According to his own statement on BBC Radio in 1967, conducting the LSO was André's idea of Valhalla and, as Michael Oliver wrote in a *Gramophone* article commemorating André's Tenth Anniversary with the orchestra, "If happiness is ambition fulfilled, then André Previn must indeed be happy, and he shows every sign of it."

In his program notes for the Tenth Anniversary concert, Edward Greenfield opined that André had achieved "household name" status in England on a scale unknown since the days of Melba and Caruso. As milestones of the ten-year association Greenfield cited the tour of Russia, the "resurrection" of the Rachmaninoff Second Symphony in its uncut version, the putting-down of the anti-Previn revolution, the association with the music of Elgar, Walton, Vaughan Williams, and Britten, and the Tenth Anniversary recording of Messiaen's monumental *Turangalila* Symphony.

In the decade of the seventies, Greenfield wrote, André had established "an attitude to music and music-making which depends not on convention but on immediate response," an attitude which very likely would have a permanent effect on England's music and one for which "he deserves our deepest thanks." Janet Baker went Greenfield one better and declared that André should be knighted. But the Queen apparently was not listening and bestowed the honor instead on Bernard Haitink, conductor of the London Philharmonic.

The LSO's post-revolution manager, Michael Kaye, talked about how well and in how many ways André's character suited that of the LSO. The uniqueness of André's American jazz background, said Kaye, and the excitement this generated in London was a perfect match for the "adventurousness" of the London Symphony Orchestra. And when the LSO gave a Tenth Anniversary Banquet for him, everyone was there, about four hundred strong, from the top levels of government on down. In a way it was his farewell supper, for the announcement already had been made: André was resigning his position as principal conductor of the LSO at the end of the next season. He would be named conductor emeritus.

"Eleven years as principal conductor is a *very* long time, particularly by London standards," argues Michael Kaye. "André's career is developing in places overseas. To be tied to one orchestra over too long a period in his artistic life becomes more a restriction than a help. I think André's period with the orchestra has worked well and has produced some very interesting results. It certainly has produced a great volume of recordings and many people have bought them because of André, more so than they might have had he been a conductor of a less clearly defined musical personality. I think all of that must be for the good of music. Everyone felt that the relationship, no matter how good, could not go on forever in the London scene, because we simply don't have the stability that New York or Philadelphia or Boston have."

And André's personal manager, Jasper Parrott, was in perfect agreement:

> We will now be able to economize on his time, achieve what is necessary without making untoward demands on his time. We can integrate his international activities in the best way so that he's not burning himself out learning new programs every day. It was necessary for him to cease his responsibilities to a London orchestra to achieve that. An orchestra in London can't afford free days. When a principal conductor here says no, he may be saying no to the income of a hundred people. There is a need here to build up an extraordinarily complex structure of work to provide the orchestra with full and lucrative employment and the onus of risk in that situation falls on the conductor: if he's worked to death, the orchestra will go on.

He's done the principal conductor bit in London and he doesn't ever have to do it again. His position in England will be a much more serene, regular contribution. He's undoubtedly one of the most loved figures here and in the future when he comes to conduct here it will be a great event. And so it should be.

True, André's concerts with the LSO will continue on a regular basis at Festival Hall, but gone will be the hectic trips by bus through the English countryside; gone, at least for the foreseeable future, will be the continuing presence of André Previn and his music via television in every British home. As Dame Janet Baker observed: "He got through to ordinary people in a way that nobody else does. In this minority world of ours, this little world of music, we want as many ordinary people as possible to join us and think that here is something they can get into. In every part of our country, it has been the ordinary people who've flocked to André's concerts. It's those people who are going to miss him terribly."

The 1978–79 season rolled by with an inevitable series of "lasts" that rivaled Beverly Sills's leave-taking of the stage. In April he left London for Vienna and a series of concerts with the Vienna Philharmonic, only to be met by a planeload of his friends from London, who'd come to help him celebrate his fiftieth birthday. André recalls the rehearsal on his birthday as being "a huge chord in G. People made speeches and there were lots of flowers and champagne and a cake. That night there was a huge party for me given by the Governing Board of the Philharmonic. It was very nice because it was all so unexpected."

There were more celebrations in London as the LSO season ground to a close. His next-to-last concert as principal conductor turned out to be the Seventy-fifth Anniversary celebration of the orchestra, and the orchestra turned that into *their* farewell to André, with a private dinner party and speeches all around. André remembered something funny to say about every member of the orchestra, just as he had remembered all their names at the first rehearsal. He declared he was happy

he'd be returning as conductor emeritus in the fall, even though he wasn't sure what a conductor emeritus was supposed to do. "I heard you first offered it to Karl Böhm, then found out he wasn't old enough to accept."

The next days saw the making of their 129th and 130th recordings together, including EMI's first venture into digital recording, a performance of Debussy's *Images pour Orchestre*. The other pieces recorded were Elgar's *Enigma* Variations and Shostakovich's Symphony No. 13.

André found the digital process fascinating, with "a great leap forward in dynamic extremes. At last I could indulge myself in *ppppp*'s and not have someone tell me it's too soft for a record. I actually listened to the results and found the sound very impressive."

The final concert was to have included André's "signature piece," the Rachmaninoff Second Symphony, but because of a scheduling mix-up earlier in the season that concert had to be moved up and a program of the just-recorded *Images* and Shostakovich Thirteen put in its place. The concert was musically outstanding but the program rather moody and morose and the critics had a field day analyzing what they assumed to be André's strange choice of repertoire for his swan song. Queen Elizabeth was invited to the concert but she did not come, sending in her place Prince Charles, who is a cellist.

Since André would be back the following season and since he would continue to make his home in Surrey, the leave-taking was not exactly tearful. In fact, he was positively jubilant, as he anticipated doing something he'd been wanting to do for twenty years: take a vacation. With the help of Jasper Parrott, Ron Wilford, and an agreeable Pittsburgh Board, he had succeeded in scheduling a six-month sabbatical, filled with nothing at all. He was looking forward to it like nothing in his life, looking forward to days with the kids and evenings with Mia, to traveling without the pressure of a concert tour and to staying home with absolutely no pressure at all.

> Solti said he took a year off at age sixty and it added ten years to his life. I've been looking forward to this

time of no performing for three years now. It's taken
me that long to plan an unplanned six months. I look
forward to not knowing what I'll do with it. I'm not
planning to go anywhere or do anything—outside of
an opera I'm working on for Stoppard and another
piece for Ashkenazy. I'm not planning to go anywhere, but I might. I've never had an unplanned existence in my entire adult life. I'm overworked and
tired and I need not give a serious thought to anything.

Unhappily, it did not come off quite as André had envisioned it. Instead, he found himself fretting out the sabbatical
in the worrisomeness of a third broken marriage. From the
South Pacific island of Bora-Bora, where she was making a
film, *Hurricane*, and reportedly romantically involved with a
Swedish cameraman, Mia wrote asking for a divorce.

XXX

Before and during the early years of their marriage, Mia did her best to let the role of André's mate suffice for her. She succeeded in putting her film career aside, as André had requested. Adolph Green observed that "Mia was tremendously proud of him and at least at times appreciated what he did." But André knew that her interest in music was "passive, not active," and as their marriage continued her presence by his side at concerts and parties grew less and less frequent.

She missed the frenetic pace of film life and at first tried to make do with occasional appearances in English plays. Then she hoped to enlarge her life by enlarging her family and soon there were the six children to care for, three of their own and three adopted. Perhaps she also hoped André's paternal instincts thus aroused would keep him longer at home, but professional demands were unyielding.

Sometimes Mia would greet him upon his return from a long trip with a demand that he now spend a protracted time with her and the children. André would give in and instruct his managers to cancel engagements, but that was too dangerous a practice to keep up for long. He tried cutting down on short engagements, accepting only longer stays of three to four weeks with an orchestra, but when he came home anticipating spending more time with the family, he would find that in his protracted absence routines had been established which did not involve him.

Mia finally put her foot down and returned to the business of film acting. Now it was she who would be away for longer stretches, on location for as long as six months. Usually she would take all or at least some of the children with her, serving to increase André's feeling of alienation from his family. Occasionally Matthew would be allowed to travel and stay with André, his twin brother Sascha being too attached to Mia to stay away from her for very long and not really caring that much for concerts and rehearsals anyway. "For a while," says André, "it worked." In the end, it was probably England that ruined the marriage.

> Having been chased all around the world by events in my childhood and then by my own career, it was necessary for me to zero in on a place that really spoke to me. I love England and it is necessary for me to be there. I think the European part of my childhood has prevented me from feeling the same sort of nostalgic ties with America that Mia has. I think she felt vaguely alien in England, whereas I felt I had at last come home.
>
> She loved the house. I think she still loves the house. I think that if the house and grounds could have been transported over the ocean and set down in America she'd have been infinitely happier. But she didn't enjoy living in England. Over the period of many years she grew restless there. She was a film actress and the British film industry was damn near dead. There was nothing for her to do. She grew weary of living in an English village and once the film career was resuscitated she simply decided that she could no longer tread water with her life.

André's managers on both sides of the ocean watched the marriage disintegrate, deeply concerned about what effect it might have on their client and friend. Of the two, Jasper Parrott in London was closer to the situation:

> That marriage was sort of an insoluble conundrum, two people with such strong personalities. It was

doomed. They couldn't both function in the same place. She never really understood the demands of a concert career. Many successful conductors have wives who sort of bundle around with them constantly and who provide the sort of cosseting they all need. André wasn't looking for that. The sadness of the marriage is that it was a sort of logical impasse: André would not have been happy, could not have functioned, living on her terms and she, apparently, could not function living on his terms.

Wilford puts it more succinctly. "I could never figure them out," he says. "I would sit there and listen to these two people tell me how much they loved each other and think, they're writing a script."

André and Mia have decided on joint custody for their children, the twins spending most of the year with André, the younger four with Mia in the States. Matthew and Sascha are close to their father and they would prefer to live in England, in the house they have known all their lives, going to school in Surrey, at a prep school in Godstone. Through the children, André feels an abiding kinship with Mia which he hopes will not diminish. There has been very little friction so far about which children spend how much time with which parent and when Mia took on a Broadway play she sent Lark and Fletcher back to The Haven.

"All that matters is that the children can count on having two parents who need them and love them and look after them and in whose lives they are a stable necessity. How that is divided into weeks and months and places on the globe is not terribly important." But André's face takes on a worried look as he says, "That is the ideal wished for the kids. There are problems of enforcing the ideal which scare me. But other than that, I'm on my way back to happy."

André tries very hard not to think of the alternatives, tries to forget what happened to one of the children of his first broken marriage. Claudia, the firstborn, was old enough to adjust.

When André and Betty Bennett parted, Claudia kept fond memories of her father by virtue of his coming to see her on weekends, taking her to amusement parks and art exhibits, showing her off to his friends. With one of those friends, Dory Langdon, Claudia developed an almost-sisterly relationship which continues to this day—long after André and Dory married and Betty settled into a happy, comfortable marriage to jazz guitarist Mundell Lowe. For Claudia's real sister, things went quite differently.

Alicia Carol Previn was nearly two years younger than her sister, too young for weekends out with Dad, or "Papa" as he preferred to be called, in imitation of his father. In fact, she was not yet born when her own mother and father separated. As a child, she knew André only as the man who would come occasionally to take her sister away and bring her back. She grew up as an outgoing, tomboyish girl who rode horses and arm-wrestled with the neighbor boys, not at all like her bookish, artistic sister, Claudia.

At the age of sixteen Alicia was introduced to a health food restaurant operated by a small religious cult, or "family," as they preferred to be called. The family conducted classes on their religion in the evening. Alicia began attending these classes, fascinated by the group's teachings on "nature" and "wisdom" and "the ancient teachings" and "the common denominator in all religions." It did not take long for interest to turn into obsession and soon she was working as a waitress at the restaurant, a full-fledged member of the family and a true daughter of its leader, who was known variously as "Father Jim," "Father Yod," and "Yahowha." His actual name was Jim Baker.

Baker looked like Michelangelo's version of God, with flowing white hair and a tall, commanding presence. He was reputed to have served time in prison for manslaughter, but none of his children believed this. His influence over his followers was benign in that he did not believe in drugs or drink; however, he insisted on being both father and husband to each of his "daughters," some of whom were no older than thirteen, and for the sake of his own family cohesiveness he demanded that all true believers renounce their "earth parents."

"My attraction to Father Jim was not due to the lack of a father in my life," Alicia insists. "First off, I fell in love with him, as every thing, every part of me was vibrating. I was totally fulfilled. But I don't believe there are different kinds of love you feel for your father or your husband. It's all one thing."

Betty immediately blamed André for Alicia's departure; "the overwhelming lack of a father," is how she put it. "It was an unbearable time for me and any residual bitterness I may feel about André has to do with our children and the abdication of all responsibility other than financial." Betty summoned André from England and together they tried to pry their daughter away from the cult. But "Lovely," as she had become known, threw up a wall wherever her "earth parents" were concerned. It was not until Jim Baker died in the crash of a hang glider and the "family" broke up that she began to drift away and back to Betty.

Alicia (or "Lovely," as she prefers) is multitalented. She plays violin, sings, paints, writes, and illustrates. When André was in New York in 1979 she flew there from Los Angeles hoping to win his support and assistance in getting some of her songs produced and recorded. Seeing her for the first time in five years, André was distantly polite. He explained to her that he knew nothing about current popular music and so would be of no help to her in arranging or producing her songs. Lovely seemed to accept that. "Maybe I'll buy him a couple of records," she said, "to show him what they're doing now with full orchestras and real choruses. It's disco, but it's real music."

André sighs wearily at all this. "Every time I talk to her she's written a book or illustrated a book or decided that instead she'll be a singer or a painter or a dancer or an actress or go fly a zeppelin. In the pop music field there are more charlatans than anywhere else. They tell her, 'Sure, baby, we'll make a record for you,' and she instantly goes out and buys the wardrobe for it. She wears tons of makeup and dresses like a misguided Sadie Thompson when in actual fact she's a dear,

sweet, funny girl. I'm convinced she'll come out of it eventually, but it will probably take a number of years."

Unlike Lovely, Claudia, who bears a striking physical resemblance to her Papa, testifies that André has been very support-
ive of her efforts to develop her talents. When she decided to
go to art school, he sent her to a friend of his, the art director
of Capitol Records, who advised her to try the Pasadena Art
Center rather than New York. "He wants me to try out my
wings," says Claudia. "He's very concerned about what I'm
going to do with my life and he's discussed it at length with
me. Sometimes I'm sure he'd like to give me a loving kick in
the pants."

It is important for Claudia to get to know her father, because she feels that he is so much a part of her. She is surprised
to find that so many of her mannerisms are unconscious imitations of his and yet there are so many things about him she
cannot understand. "Papa is a complicated man," she says.

John Williams has a theory about his friend André Previn.
Reduced to its simplest form it goes, if he'll just let himself
relax and grow old, he'll discover he's also become great. "The
art of quietude," Williams says, is what André needs to
develop. In a way, that was just what he was after in his sabbatical, which turned into six months of restless inner turmoil
after which he leaped into work like a man on fire into a
stream.

If Williams' theory is correct, then all André needs is to
slow down the pace of his life a bit, "thought processes, deci-
sions, schedules, the lot. Just put the brakes on a bit. Conducting is an old man's art and greatness will come to him. He's
better equipped than ninety percent of the great ones. He's
great already, but he just doesn't give the *impression* of being
great."

But André has never set great store by impressions, nor has
he been one to sit still for very long. Even music is something
to be "chased after," pursued like a vanishing dream that can
never be caught. And when he speaks of the future, impatience
sets an edge on his voice.

I suppose it's okay for a nineteen-year-old to think, in the privacy of his own room, "Someday I'm going to be the music director of the New York Philharmonic." Even though it only happens in novels. I suppose I could say I'd like to be the music director of orchestra X, but it's best to keep your ambitions not that specific or geographical. Ambition should be something pursued and never caught up with, so that you just go on seeing how long you can do whatever it is you do without making a fool of yourself.

When you think of how much music there is and how much of it is wonderful and how impossible it is to play it all in a lifetime, I know my ambition is to just keep going. There is so much music I want to be involved with. Also, I'd like my kids to grow up and be happy, doing what they enjoy doing. I'd like them not to be disturbed by the forces lurking in every corner waiting to pounce on every one of us. I'd like to be around to help them when they need help.

Those ambitions are deceptively simple-sounding, for they are spoken by a man whose father set his son on a path he believed would be impassable, warning him always of imminent failure and finally dying before the son could redeem himself in his father's eyes. To be around to help his children when they need help may be, after all, the loftiest goal possible for a man whose three marriages have failed. But any goal of André's must be expressed in musical terms, for those are the only terms he holds valid, the terms his father left him.

"I loved my father a lot," he says. "I'm sorry that what I do now, whether with excellence or ineptitude, he's not around to see. Because what I'm doing now is exactly what he *wanted* me to do and I didn't do it until after he was dead."

So André Previn continues chasing the music, music his father warned him he'd never be able to catch.

Epilogue

In the years since André relinquished the reins of the London Symphony Orchestra, he has forged close ties with a number of other orchestras on both sides of the Atlantic. In London itself, along with his regular stints as guest conductor of the LSO, he now conducts the other orchestras in that city as well. With the London Philharmonic he has recorded the Berlioz *Requiem*, and with the Royal Philharmonic he has concertized and toured to great acclaim. In Berlin he is welcomed by both the Berlin Philharmonic and the Berlin Radio orchestras. With the Vienna Philharmonic he has embarked upon an ambitious recording project that will encompass the complete orchestral works of Richard Strauss.

In the United States his non-Pittsburgh activities are principally with three orchestras: the New York Philharmonic, the Chicago Symphony, and the Boston Symphony. With the latter his work is mostly at Tanglewood, during the summer concerts of the Berkshire Festival, so that he can also work with the student conductors and the student orchestra of the Berkshire Music Center. Following one series of Tanglewood concerts with the Boston Symphony, critic Richard Dyer's review in the Boston *Globe* was headlined: PREVIN, BSO A GREAT TEAM.

His personal recording contract with EMI Music was renewed during the summer of 1980 for a period of three years. In addition, in the fall of 1980 a separate recording contract began with Philips Records that will ensure the continued availability of new recordings by Previn with the Pittsburgh Symphony Orchestra.

He has been the subject of a *New Yorker* Profile, cover stories in *Ovation* and *Stereo Review*, and extensive articles in other publications and media. Were he alive, even Jack Previn might admit that at last some of his dreams for his son have become reality.

Index